D1248436

99 DAYS

VERTIGO CRIME

WRITER
MATTEO CASALI

ART
KRISTIAN DONALDSON

LETTERS
CLEM ROBINS

99 DAYS

Will Dennis Editor
Ian Sattler Director Editorial, Special Projects and Archival Editions
Robbin Brosterman Design Director – Books

Karen Berger Senior VP – Executive Editor, Vertigo
Bob Harras VP – Editor in Chief

Diane Nelson President
Dan DiDio and Jim Lee Co-Publishers
Geoff Johns Chief Creative Officer
John Rood Executive VP – Sales, Marketing and Business Development
Amy Genkins Senior VP – Business?and Legal Affairs
Nairi Gardiner Senior VP – Finance
Jeff Boison VP – Publishing Operations
Mark Chiarello VP – Art Direction and Design
John Cunningham VP – Marketing
Terri Cunningham VP – Talent Relations and Services
Alison Gill Senior VP – Manufacturing and Operations
David Hyde VP – Publicity
Hank Kanalz Senior VP – Digital
Jay Kogan VP – Business and Legal Affairs, Publishing
Jack Mahan VP – Business Affairs, Talent
Nick Napolitano VP – Manufacturing Administration
Ron Perazza VP – Online
Sue Pohja VP – Book Sales
Courtney Simmons Senior VP – Publicity
Bob Wayne Senior VP – Sales

99 DAYS
VERTIGO CRIME

Published by DC Comics, 1700 Broadway, New York, NY 10019. Printed in USA. First Printing.
DC Comics, a Warner Bros. Entertainment Company.

HC ISBN: 978-1-4012-3089-0 SC ISBN: 978-1-4012-1533-0

SUSTAINABLE FORESTRY INITIATIVE
Certified Chain of Custody
80% Certified Fiber Sourcing and 40% Post-Consumer Recycled
www.sfiprogram.org

SGS-SFI/COC-US10/81072
This label applies to the text stock.

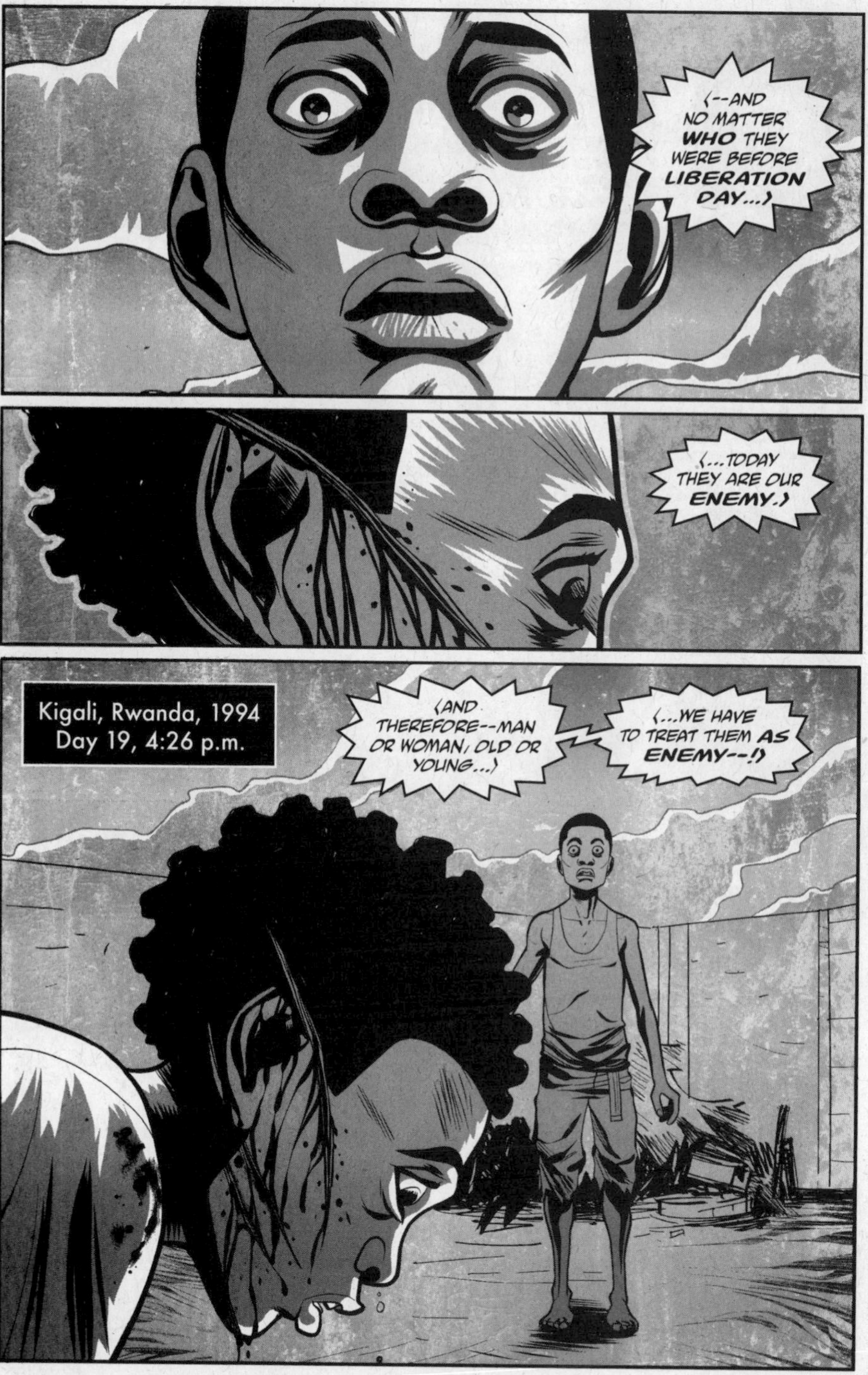
⟨--AND NO MATTER **WHO** THEY WERE BEFORE **LIBERATION DAY**...⟩
⟨...TODAY THEY ARE OUR **ENEMY**.⟩
Kigali, Rwanda, 1994
Day 19, 4:26 p.m.
⟨AND THEREFORE--MAN OR WOMAN, OLD OR YOUNG...⟩
⟨...WE HAVE TO TREAT THEM **AS ENEMY**--!⟩

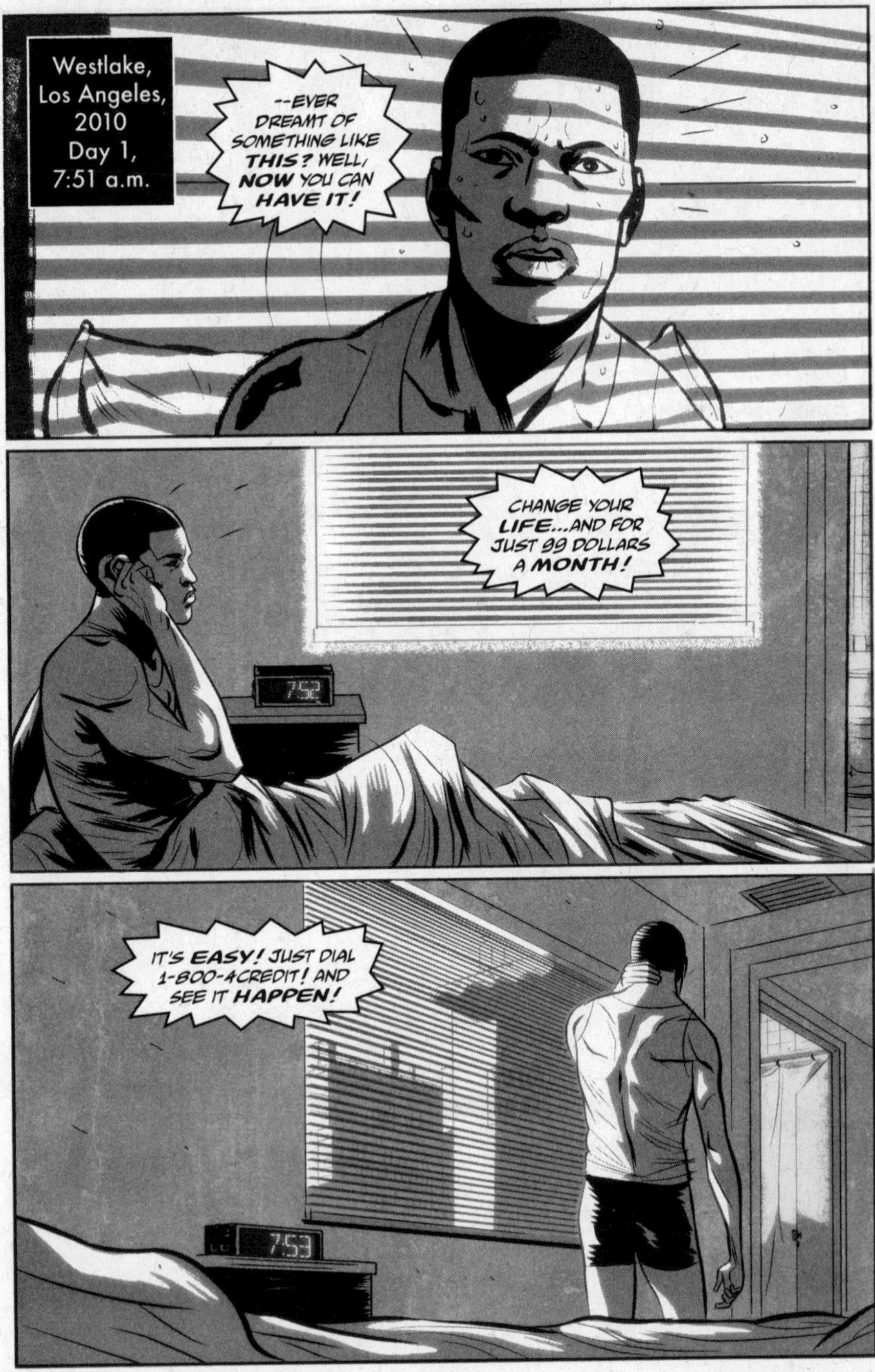
Westlake, Los Angeles, 2010 Day 1, 7:51 a.m.
--EVER DREAMT OF SOMETHING LIKE THIS? WELL, NOW YOU CAN HAVE IT!
CHANGE YOUR LIFE...AND FOR JUST 99 DOLLARS A MONTH!
7:52
IT'S EASY! JUST DIAL 1-800-4CREDIT! AND SEE IT HAPPEN!
7:53

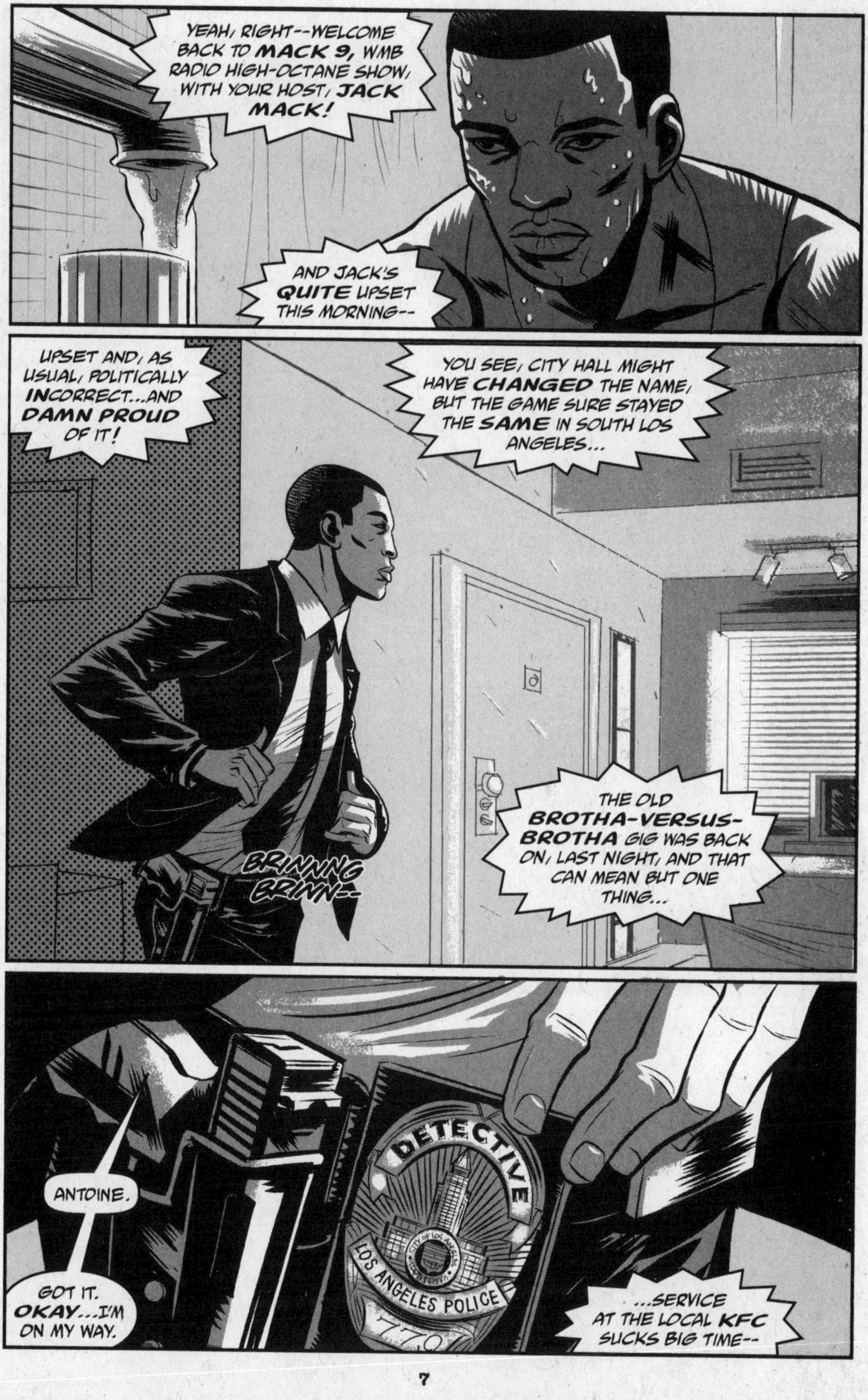
YEAH, RIGHT--WELCOME BACK TO MACK 9, WMB RADIO HIGH-OCTANE SHOW, WITH YOUR HOST, JACK MACK!
AND JACK'S QUITE UPSET THIS MORNING--
UPSET AND, AS USUAL, POLITICALLY INCORRECT...AND DAMN PROUD OF IT!
YOU SEE, CITY HALL MIGHT HAVE CHANGED THE NAME, BUT THE GAME SURE STAYED THE SAME IN SOUTH LOS ANGELES...
BRINNNG BRINN--
THE OLD BROTHA-VERSUS-BROTHA GIG WAS BACK ON, LAST NIGHT, AND THAT CAN MEAN BUT ONE THING...
ANTOINE.
DETECTIVE
LOS ANGELES POLICE
GOT IT. OKAY...I'M ON MY WAY.
...SERVICE AT THE LOCAL KFC SUCKS BIG TIME--

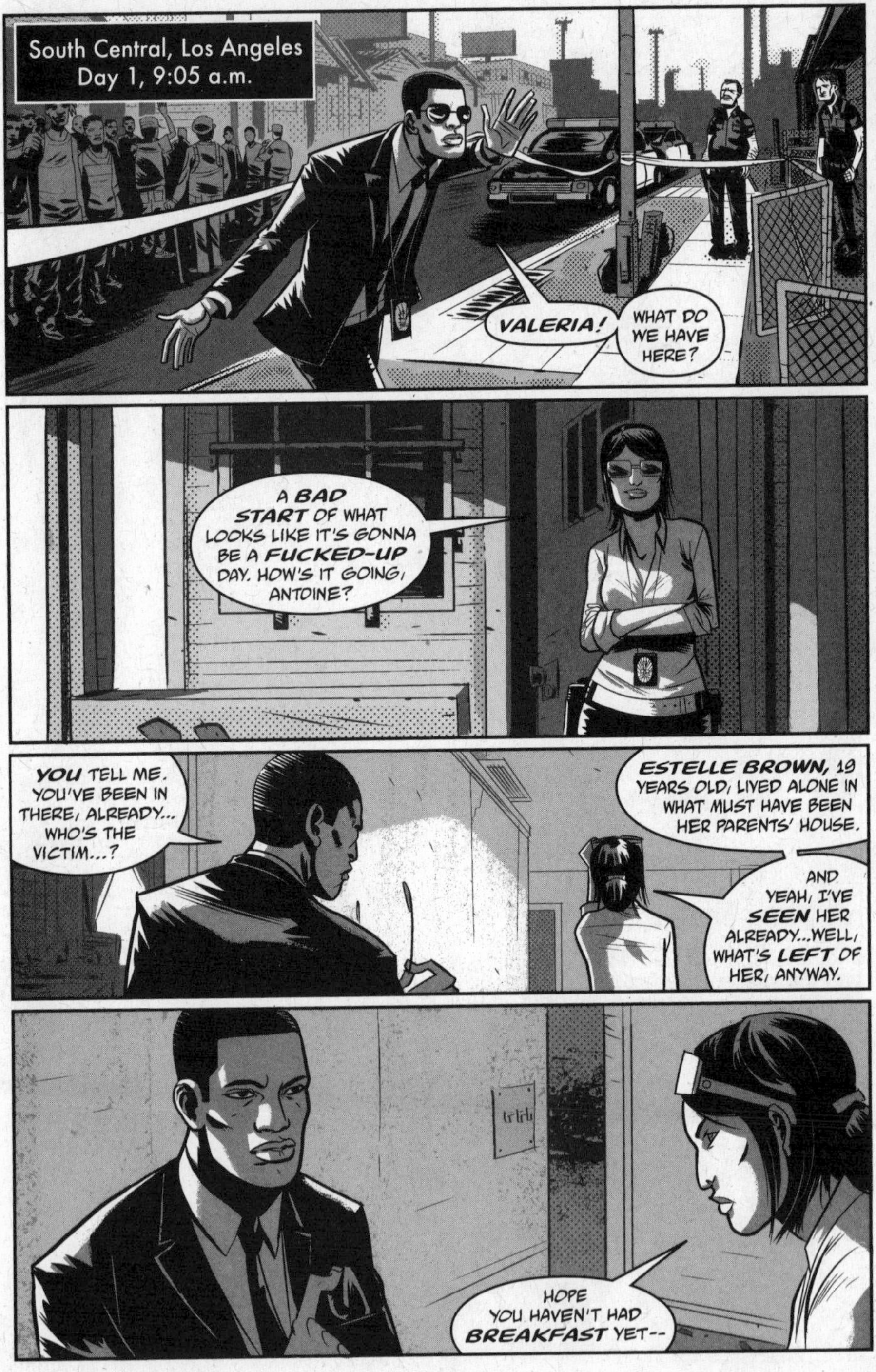

South Central, Los Angeles
Day 1, 9:05 a.m.
VALERIA!
WHAT DO WE HAVE HERE?
A BAD START OF WHAT LOOKS LIKE IT'S GONNA BE A FUCKED-UP DAY. HOW'S IT GOING, ANTOINE?
YOU TELL ME. YOU'VE BEEN IN THERE, ALREADY... WHO'S THE VICTIM...?
ESTELLE BROWN, 19 YEARS OLD, LIVED ALONE IN WHAT MUST HAVE BEEN HER PARENTS' HOUSE.
AND YEAH, I'VE SEEN HER ALREADY...WELL, WHAT'S LEFT OF HER, ANYWAY.
HOPE YOU HAVEN'T HAD BREAKFAST YET--

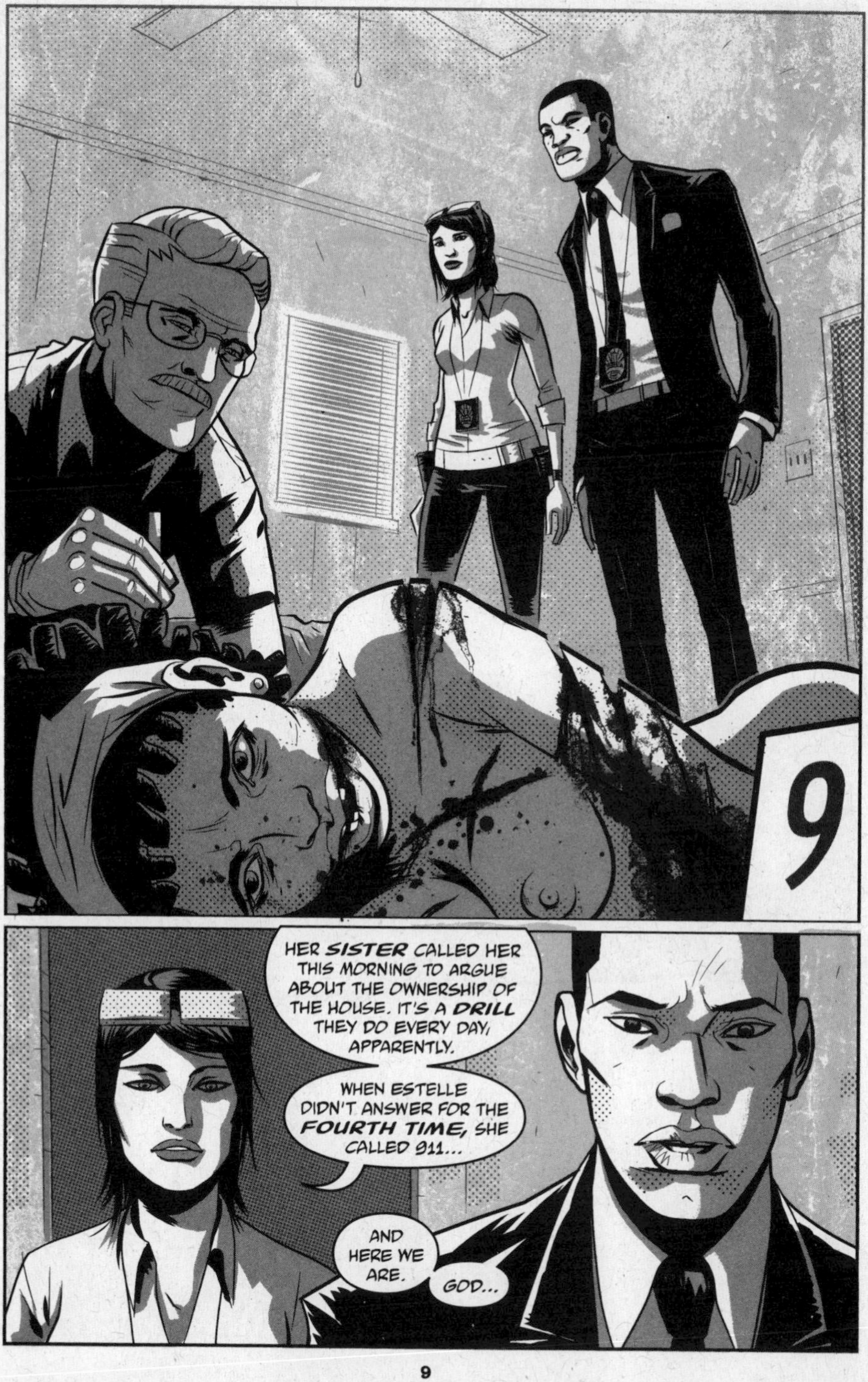
9
HER SISTER CALLED HER THIS MORNING TO ARGUE ABOUT THE OWNERSHIP OF THE HOUSE. IT'S A DRILL THEY DO EVERY DAY, APPARENTLY.
WHEN ESTELLE DIDN'T ANSWER FOR THE FOURTH TIME, SHE CALLED 911...
AND HERE WE ARE.
GOD...

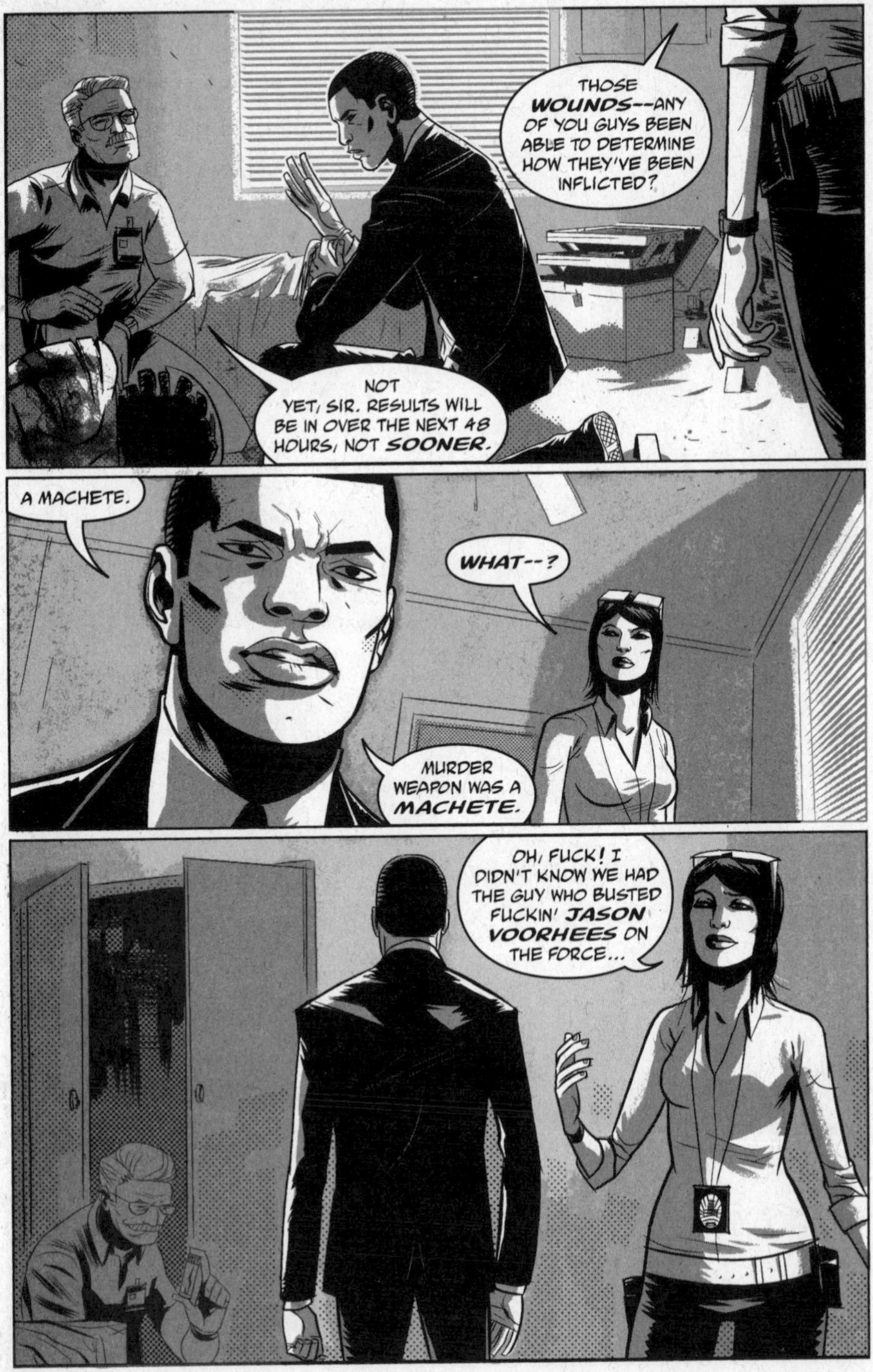
THOSE WOUNDS--ANY OF YOU GUYS BEEN ABLE TO DETERMINE HOW THEY'VE BEEN INFLICTED?
NOT YET, SIR. RESULTS WILL BE IN OVER THE NEXT 48 HOURS, NOT SOONER.
A MACHETE.
WHAT--?
MURDER WEAPON WAS A MACHETE.
OH, FUCK! I DIDN'T KNOW WE HAD THE GUY WHO BUSTED FUCKIN' JASON VOORHEES ON THE FORCE...

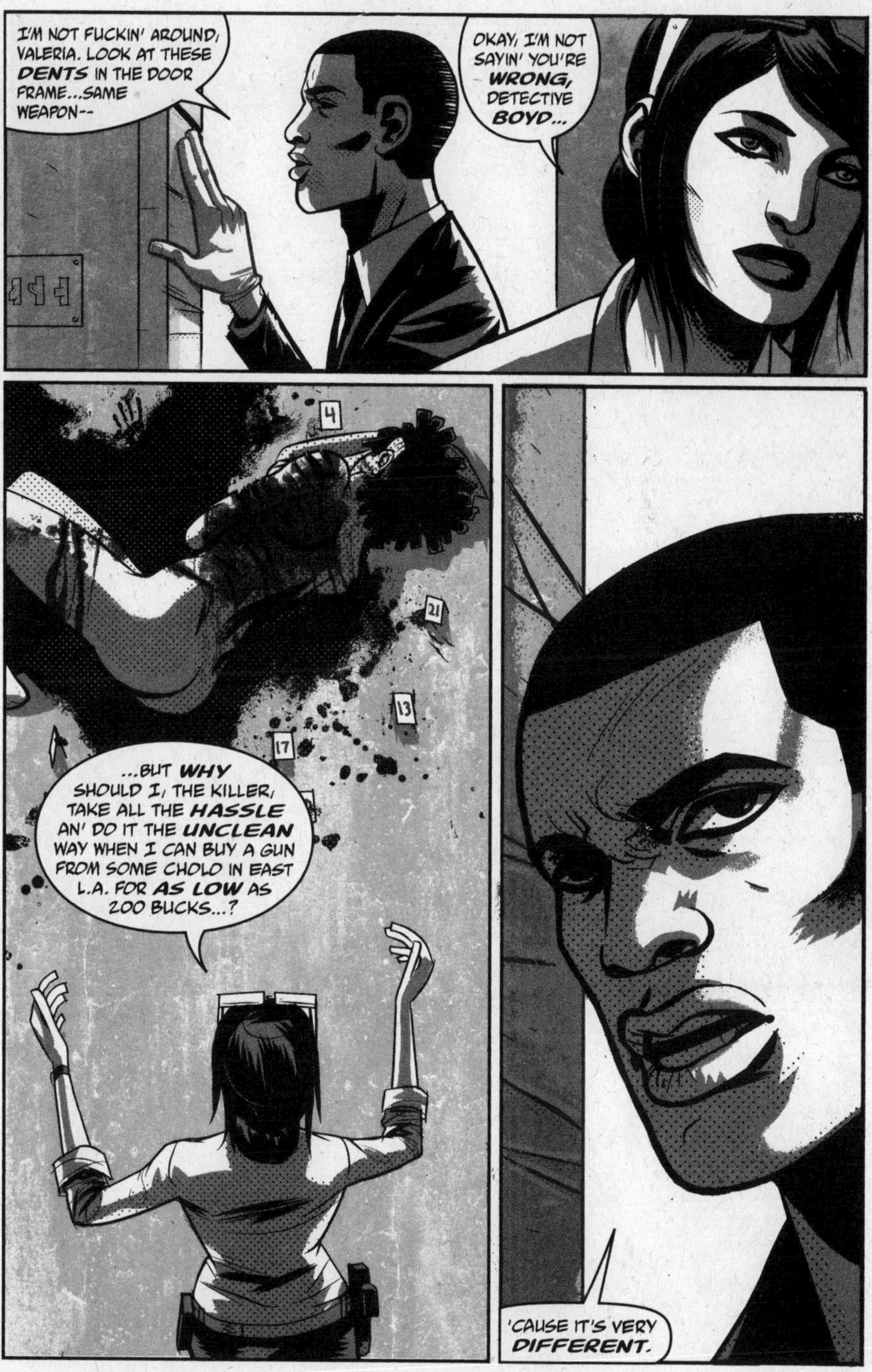
I'M NOT FUCKIN' AROUND, VALERIA. LOOK AT THESE DENTS IN THE DOOR FRAME...SAME WEAPON--
OKAY, I'M NOT SAYIN' YOU'RE WRONG, DETECTIVE BOYD...
4
21
13
17
...BUT WHY SHOULD I, THE KILLER, TAKE ALL THE HASSLE AN' DO IT THE UNCLEAN WAY WHEN I CAN BUY A GUN FROM SOME CHOLO IN EAST L.A. FOR AS LOW AS 200 BUCKS...?
'CAUSE IT'S VERY DIFFERENT.

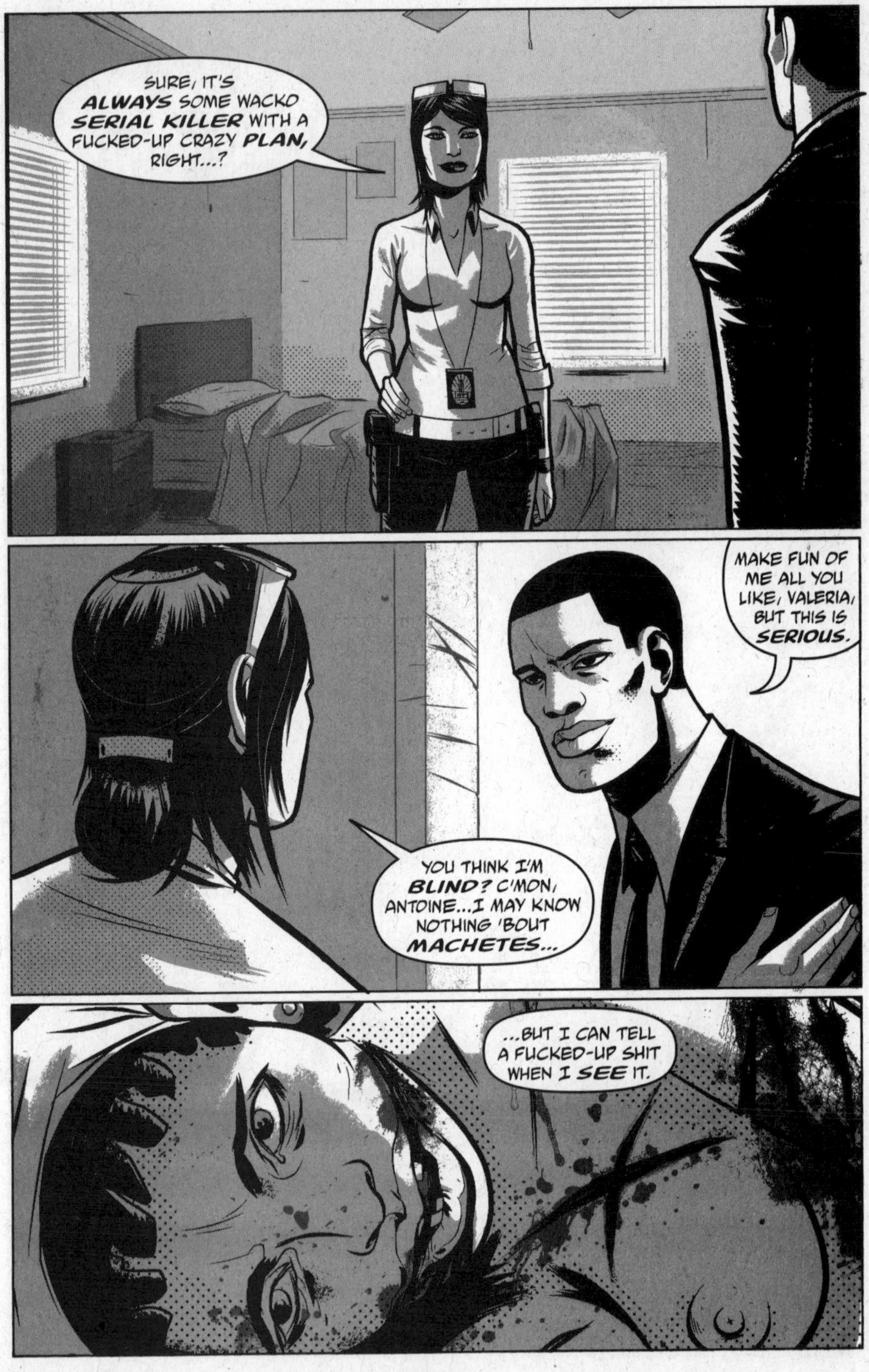
SURE, IT'S ALWAYS SOME WACKO SERIAL KILLER WITH A FUCKED-UP CRAZY PLAN, RIGHT...?
MAKE FUN OF ME ALL YOU LIKE, VALERIA, BUT THIS IS SERIOUS.
YOU THINK I'M BLIND? C'MON, ANTOINE...I MAY KNOW NOTHING 'BOUT MACHETES...
...BUT I CAN TELL A FUCKED-UP SHIT WHEN I SEE IT.

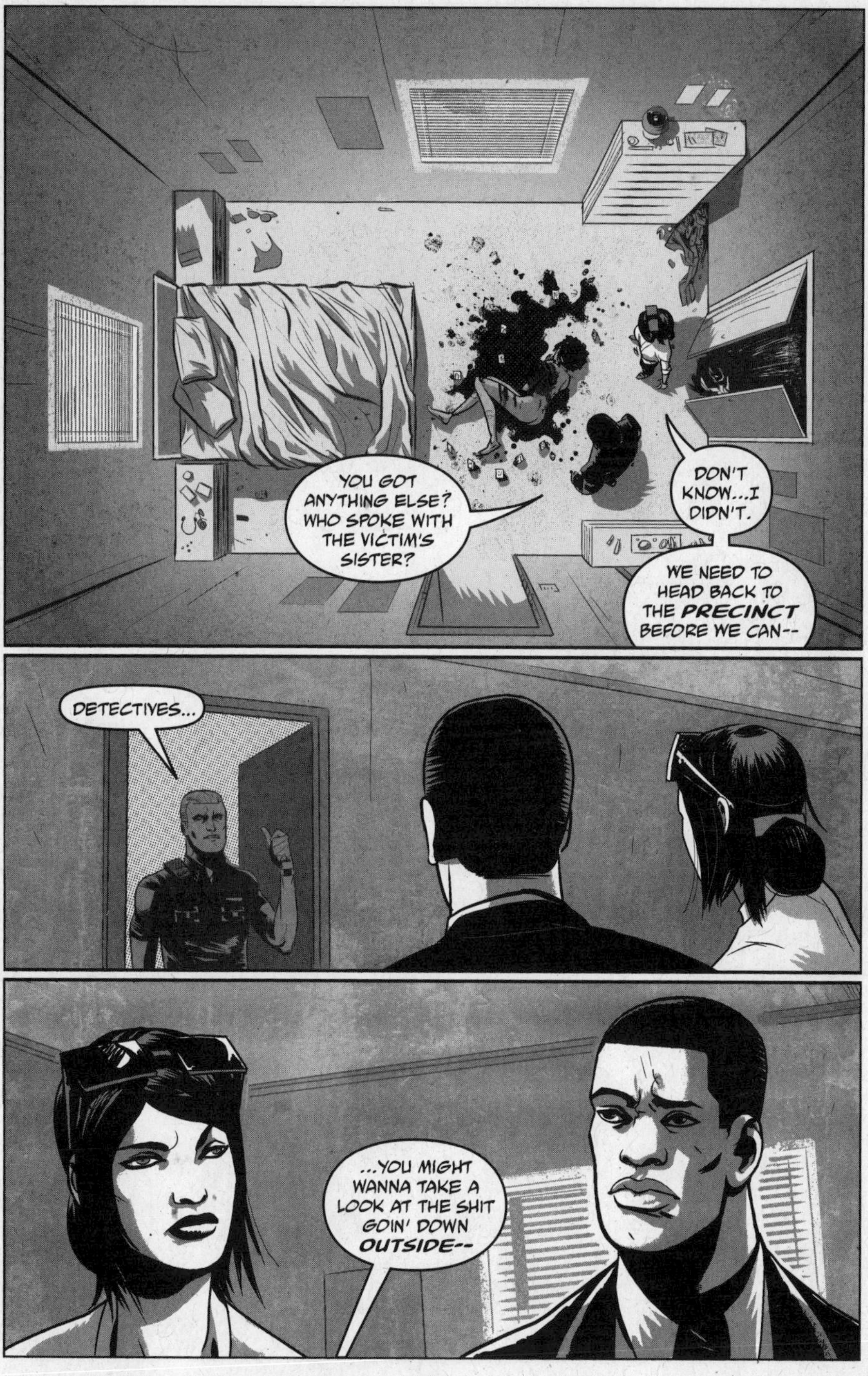
YOU GOT ANYTHING ELSE? WHO SPOKE WITH THE VICTIM'S SISTER?
DON'T KNOW...I DIDN'T.
WE NEED TO HEAD BACK TO THE PRECINCT BEFORE WE CAN--
DETECTIVES...
...YOU MIGHT WANNA TAKE A LOOK AT THE SHIT GOIN' DOWN OUTSIDE--

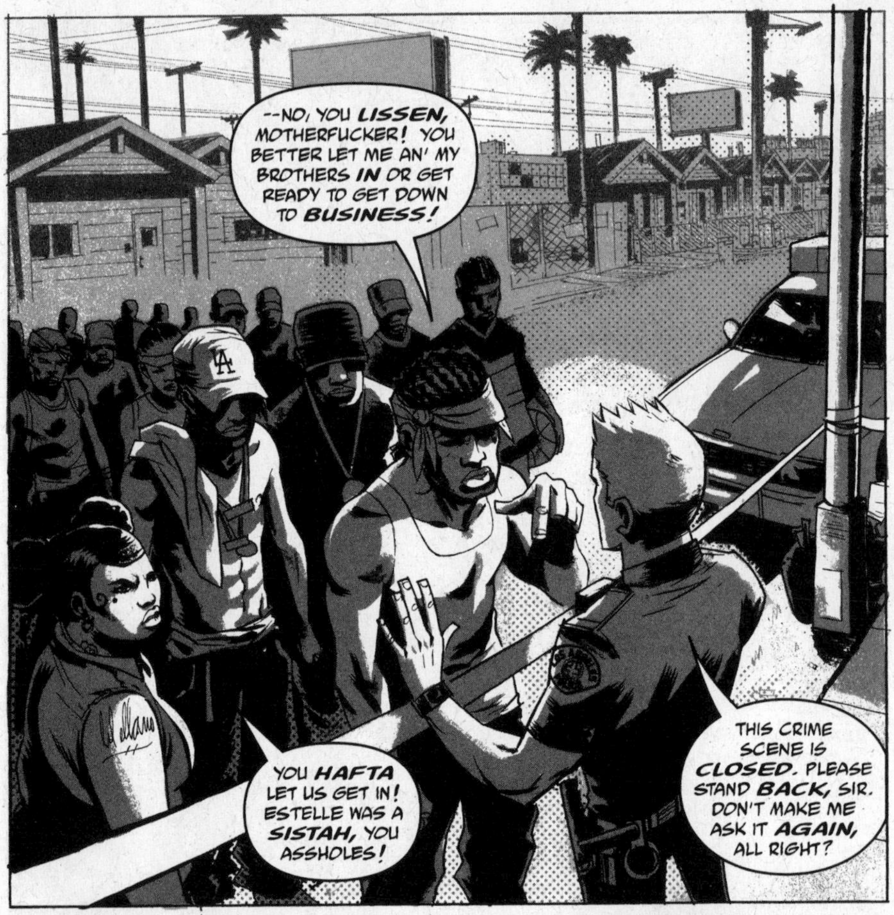
--NO, YOU LISSEN, MOTHERFUCKER! YOU BETTER LET ME AN' MY BROTHERS IN OR GET READY TO GET DOWN TO BUSINESS!
THIS CRIME SCENE IS CLOSED. PLEASE STAND BACK, SIR. DON'T MAKE ME ASK IT AGAIN, ALL RIGHT?
YOU HAFTA LET US GET IN! ESTELLE WAS A SISTAH, YOU ASSHOLES!

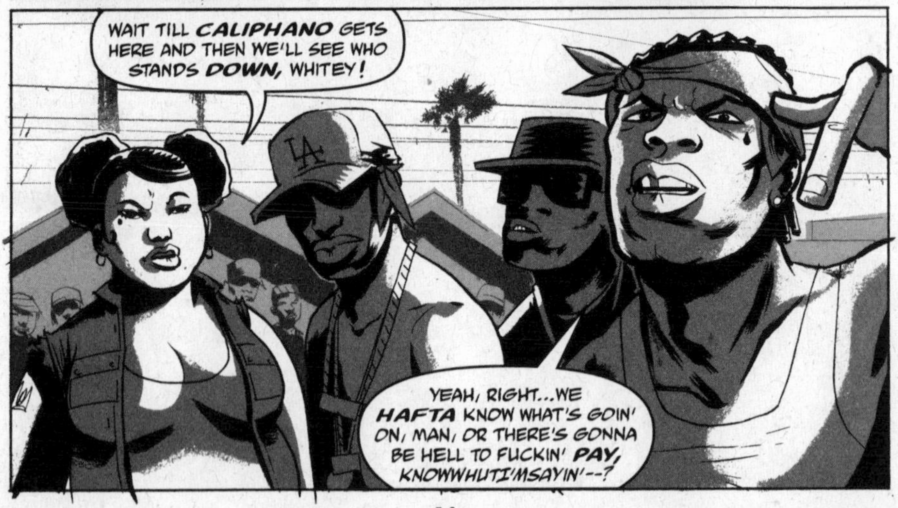
WAIT TILL CALIPHANO GETS HERE AND THEN WE'LL SEE WHO STANDS DOWN, WHITEY!
YEAH, RIGHT...WE HAFTA KNOW WHAT'S GOIN' ON, MAN, OR THERE'S GONNA BE HELL TO FUCKIN' PAY, KNOWWHUTI'MSAYIN'--?

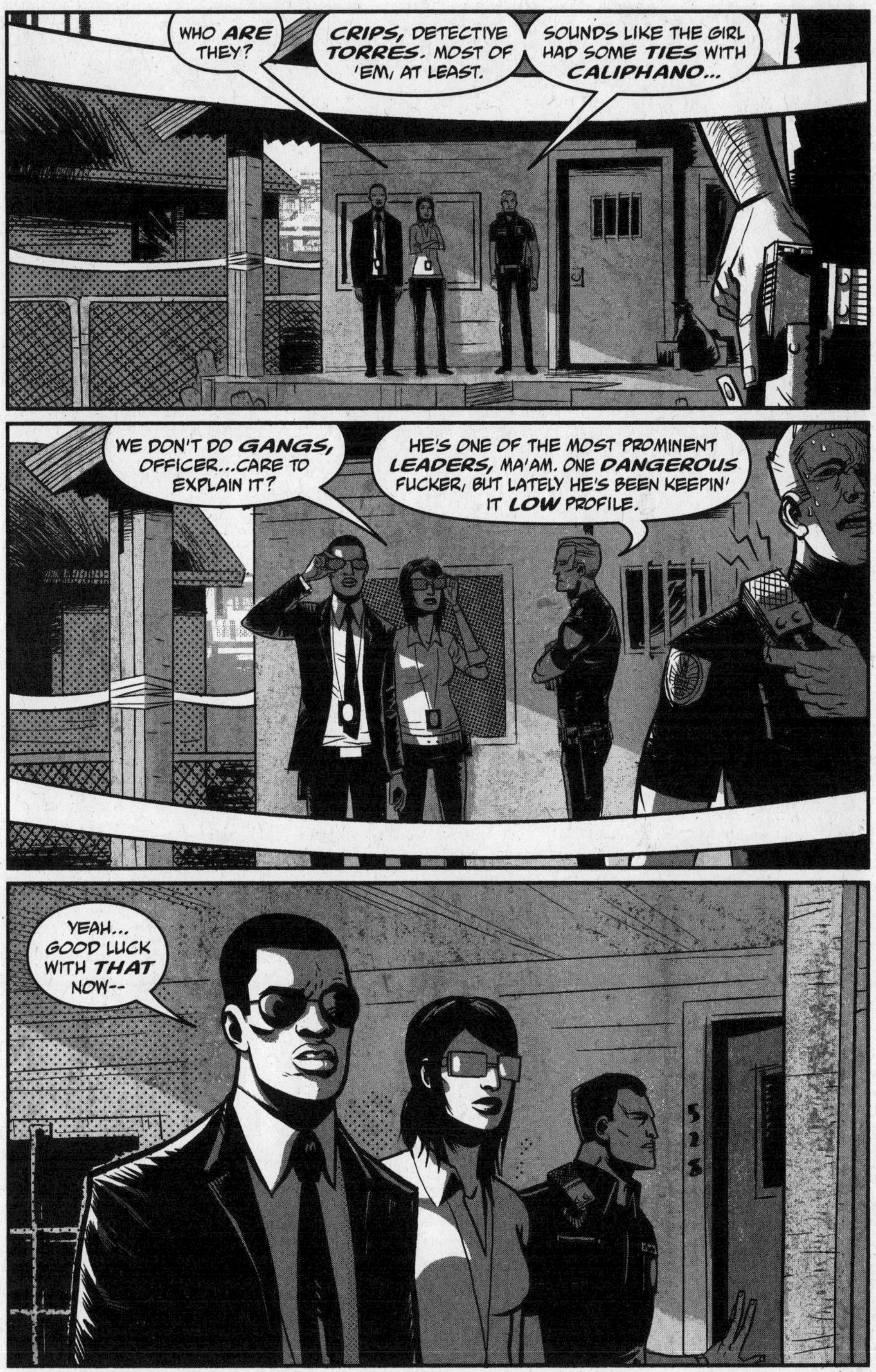
WHO ARE THEY?
CRIPS, DETECTIVE TORRES. MOST OF 'EM, AT LEAST.
SOUNDS LIKE THE GIRL HAD SOME TIES WITH CALIPHANO...
WE DON'T DO GANGS, OFFICER...CARE TO EXPLAIN IT?
HE'S ONE OF THE MOST PROMINENT LEADERS, MA'AM. ONE DANGEROUS FUCKER, BUT LATELY HE'S BEEN KEEPIN' IT LOW PROFILE.
YEAH... GOOD LUCK WITH THAT NOW--
528

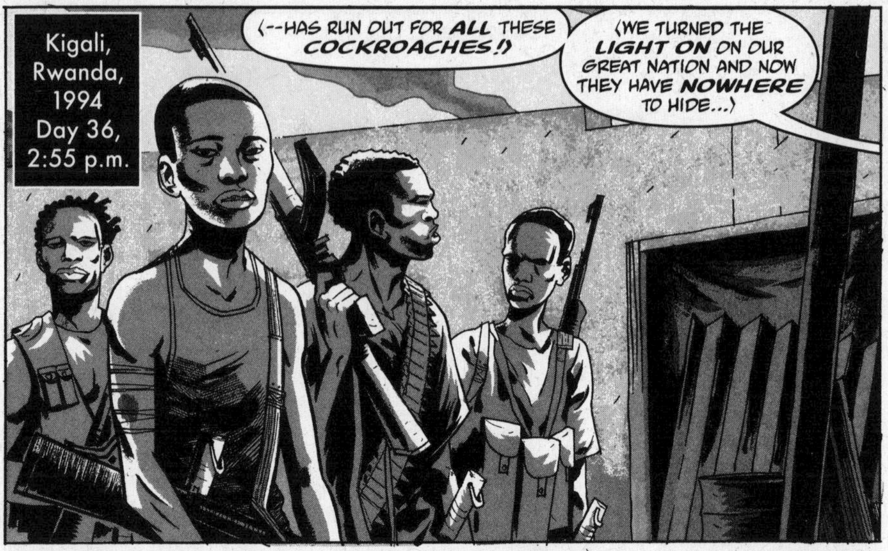
Kigali, Rwanda, 1994 Day 36, 2:55 p.m.
‹--HAS RUN OUT FOR ALL THESE COCKROACHES!›
‹WE TURNED THE LIGHT ON ON OUR GREAT NATION AND NOW THEY HAVE NOWHERE TO HIDE...›

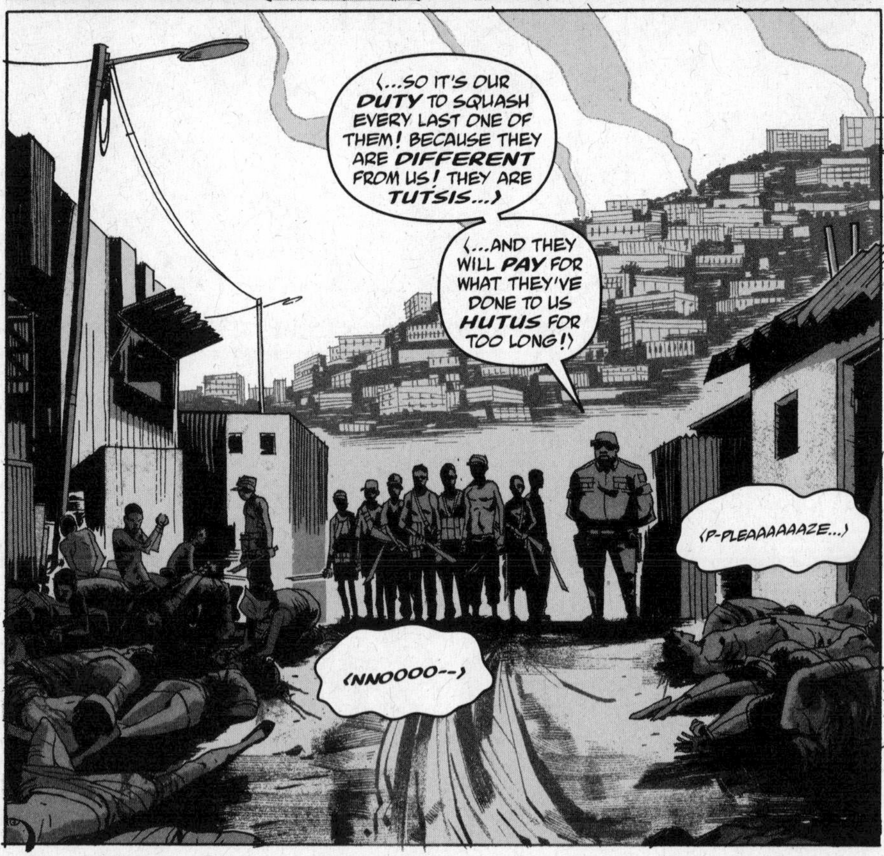
‹...SO IT'S OUR DUTY TO SQUASH EVERY LAST ONE OF THEM! BECAUSE THEY ARE DIFFERENT FROM US! THEY ARE TUTSIS...›
‹...AND THEY WILL PAY FOR WHAT THEY'VE DONE TO US HUTUS FOR TOO LONG!›
‹P-PLEAAAAAAZE...›
‹NNOOOO--›

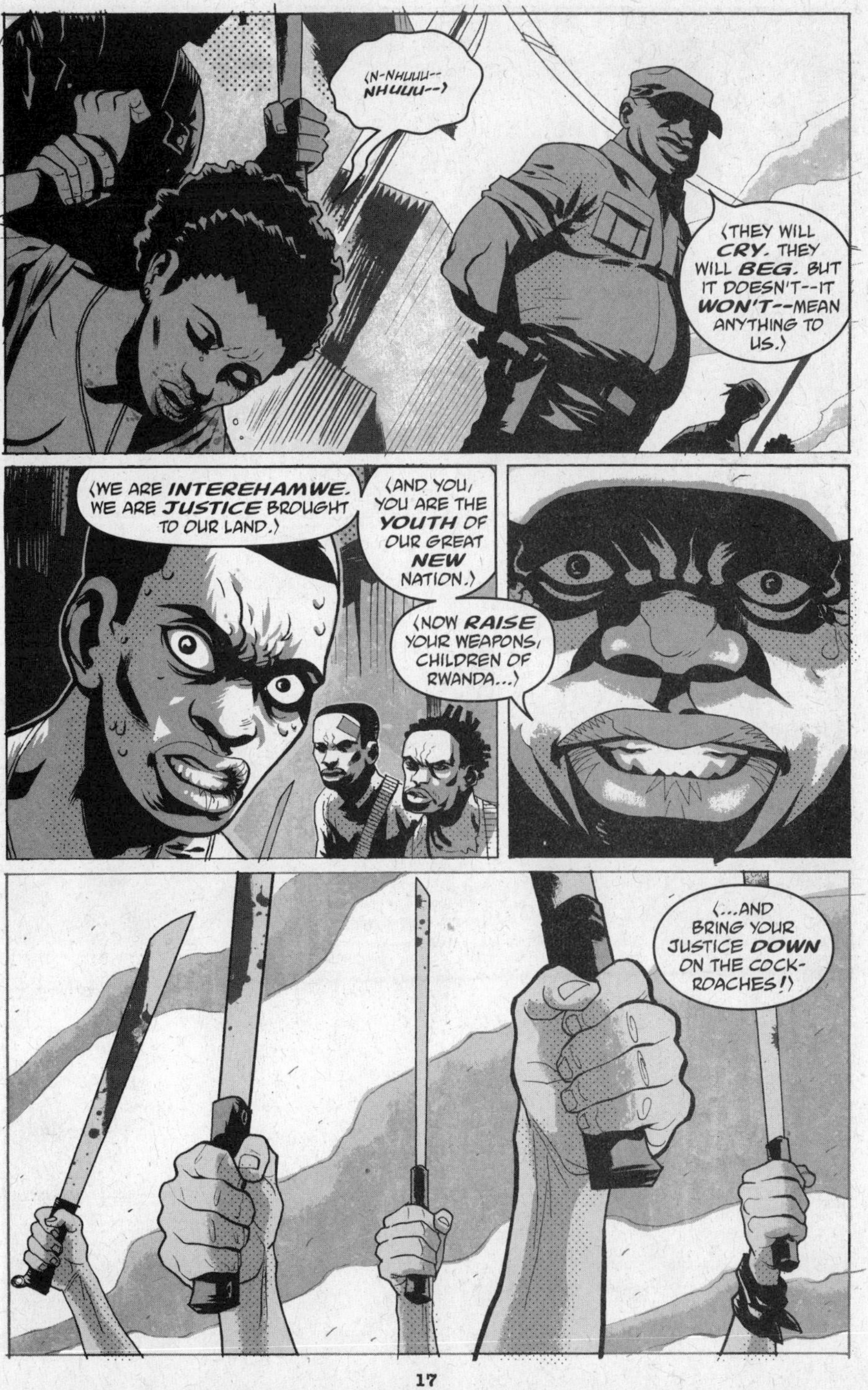
⟨N-NHUUU--
NHUUU--⟩
⟨THEY WILL CRY. THEY WILL BEG. BUT IT DOESN'T--IT WON'T--MEAN ANYTHING TO US.⟩
⟨WE ARE INTEREHAMWE. WE ARE JUSTICE BROUGHT TO OUR LAND.⟩
⟨AND YOU, YOU ARE THE YOUTH OF OUR GREAT NEW NATION.⟩
⟨NOW RAISE YOUR WEAPONS, CHILDREN OF RWANDA...⟩
⟨...AND BRING YOUR JUSTICE DOWN ON THE COCK-ROACHES!⟩

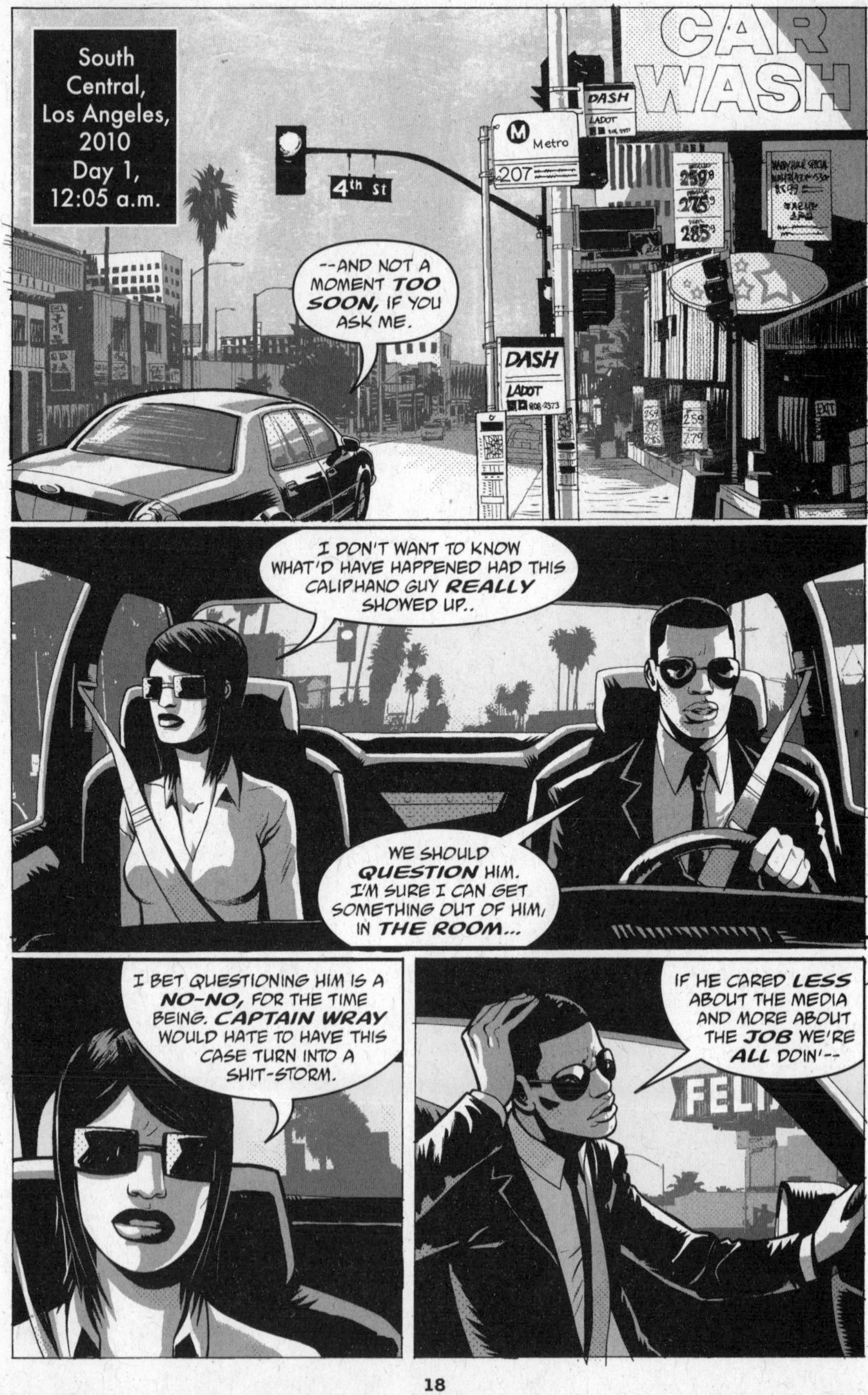
South Central, Los Angeles, 2010 Day 1, 12:05 a.m.
--AND NOT A MOMENT TOO SOON, IF YOU ASK ME.
I DON'T WANT TO KNOW WHAT'D HAVE HAPPENED HAD THIS CALIPHANO GUY REALLY SHOWED UP..
WE SHOULD QUESTION HIM. I'M SURE I CAN GET SOMETHING OUT OF HIM, IN THE ROOM...
I BET QUESTIONING HIM IS A NO-NO, FOR THE TIME BEING. CAPTAIN WRAY WOULD HATE TO HAVE THIS CASE TURN INTO A SHIT-STORM.
IF HE CARED LESS ABOUT THE MEDIA AND MORE ABOUT THE JOB WE'RE ALL DOIN'--

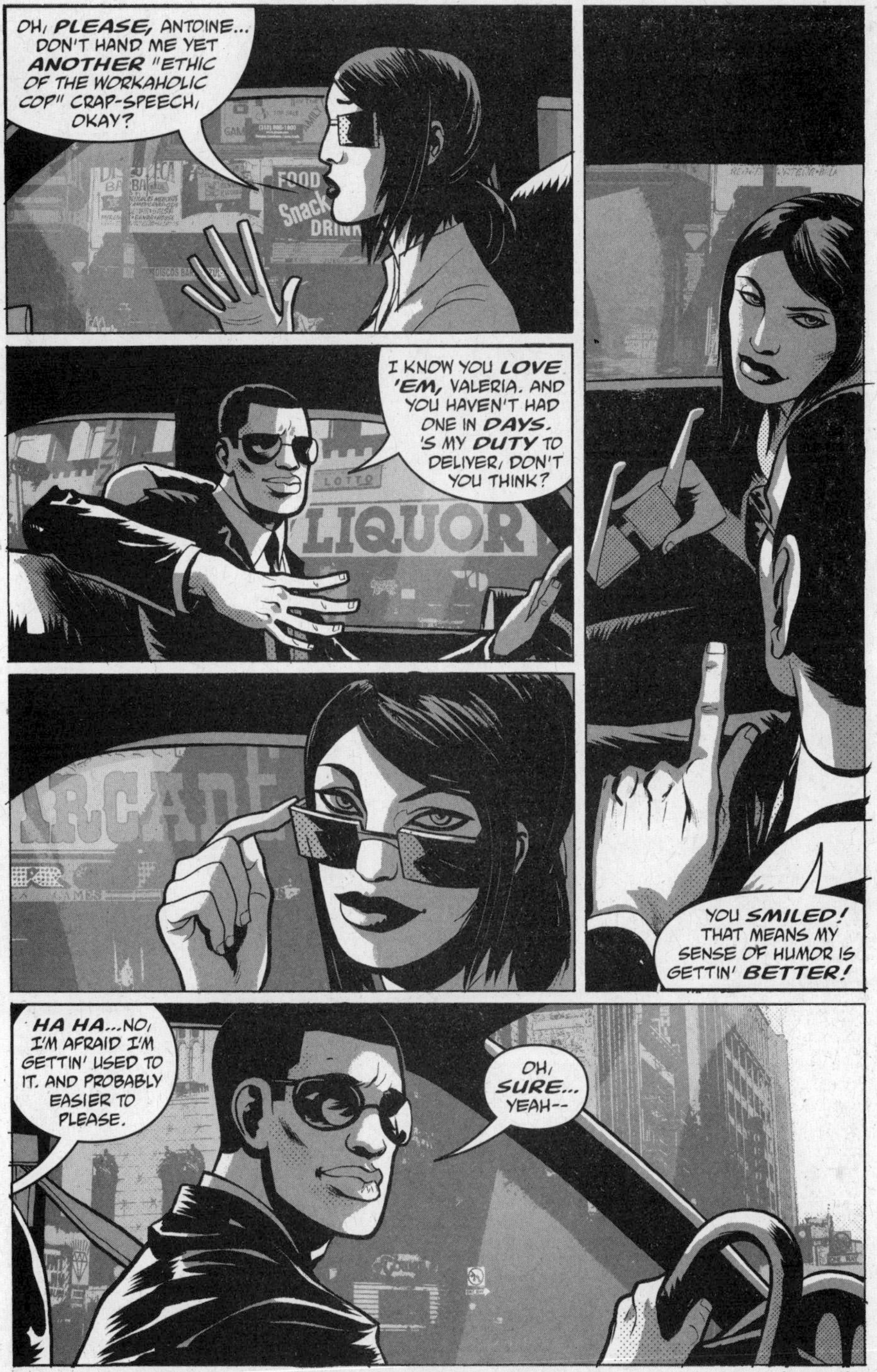
OH, PLEASE, ANTOINE... DON'T HAND ME YET ANOTHER "ETHIC OF THE WORKAHOLIC COP" CRAP-SPEECH, OKAY?
I KNOW YOU LOVE 'EM, VALERIA. AND YOU HAVEN'T HAD ONE IN DAYS. 'S MY DUTY TO DELIVER, DON'T YOU THINK?
LOTTO
LIQUOR
ARCADE
YOU SMILED! THAT MEANS MY SENSE OF HUMOR IS GETTIN' BETTER!
HA HA...NO, I'M AFRAID I'M GETTIN' USED TO IT. AND PROBABLY EASIER TO PLEASE.
OH, SURE... YEAH--

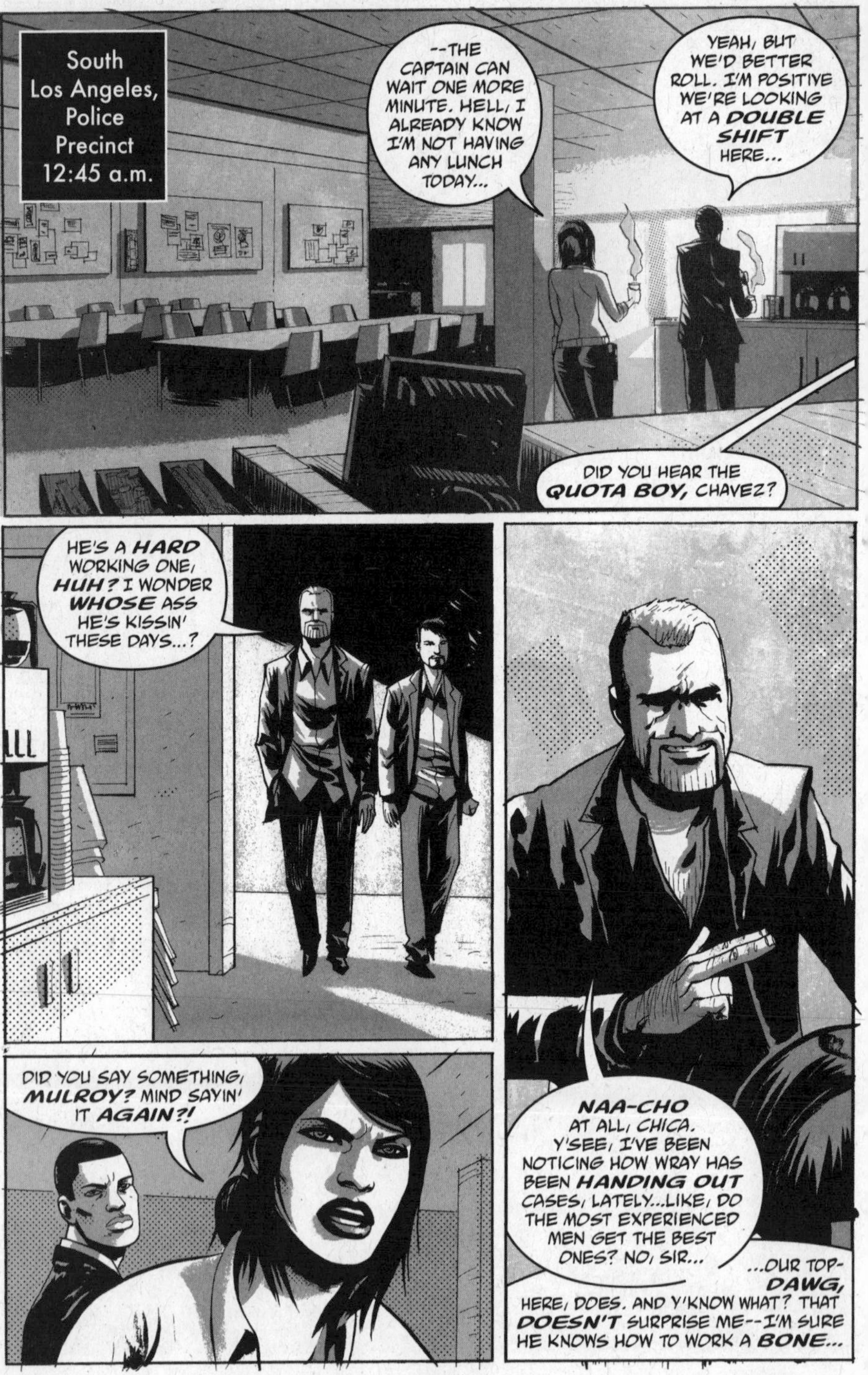
South Los Angeles, Police Precinct 12:45 a.m.
--THE CAPTAIN CAN WAIT ONE MORE MINUTE. HELL, I ALREADY KNOW I'M NOT HAVING ANY LUNCH TODAY...
YEAH, BUT WE'D BETTER ROLL. I'M POSITIVE WE'RE LOOKING AT A DOUBLE SHIFT HERE...
DID YOU HEAR THE QUOTA BOY, CHAVEZ?
HE'S A HARD WORKING ONE, HUH? I WONDER WHOSE ASS HE'S KISSIN' THESE DAYS...?
DID YOU SAY SOMETHING, MULROY? MIND SAYIN' IT AGAIN?!
NAA-CHO AT ALL, CHICA. Y'SEE, I'VE BEEN NOTICING HOW WRAY HAS BEEN HANDING OUT CASES, LATELY...LIKE, DO THE MOST EXPERIENCED MEN GET THE BEST ONES? NO, SIR...
...OUR TOP-DAWG, HERE, DOES. AND Y'KNOW WHAT? THAT DOESN'T SURPRISE ME--I'M SURE HE KNOWS HOW TO WORK A BONE...

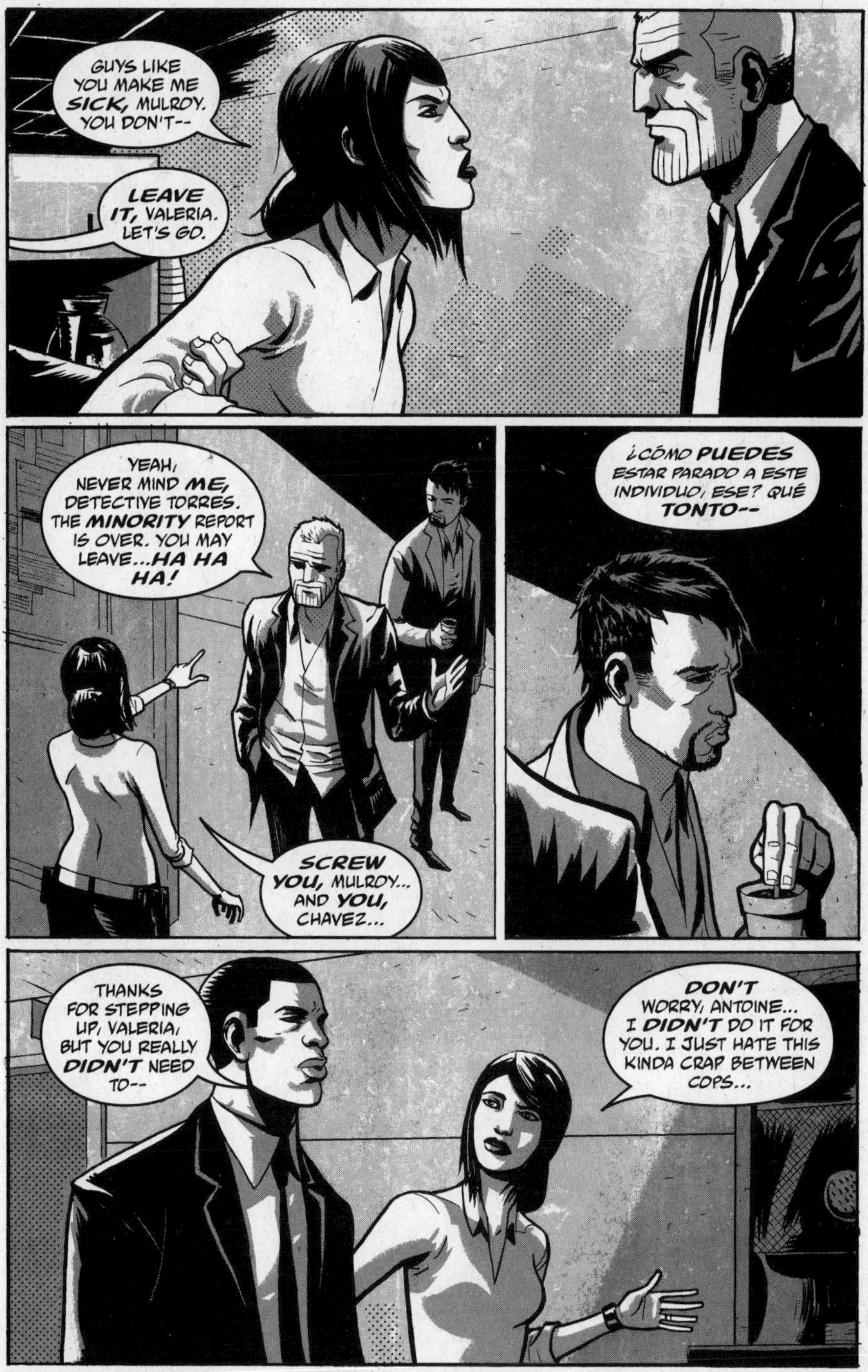
GUYS LIKE YOU MAKE ME SICK, MULROY. YOU DON'T--
LEAVE IT, VALERIA. LET'S GO.
YEAH, NEVER MIND ME, DETECTIVE TORRES. THE MINORITY REPORT IS OVER. YOU MAY LEAVE...HA HA HA!
SCREW YOU, MULROY... AND YOU, CHAVEZ...
¿CÓMO PUEDES ESTAR PARADO A ESTE INDIVIDUO, ESE? QUÉ TONTO--
THANKS FOR STEPPING UP, VALERIA, BUT YOU REALLY DIDN'T NEED TO--
DON'T WORRY, ANTOINE... I DIDN'T DO IT FOR YOU. I JUST HATE THIS KINDA CRAP BETWEEN COPS...

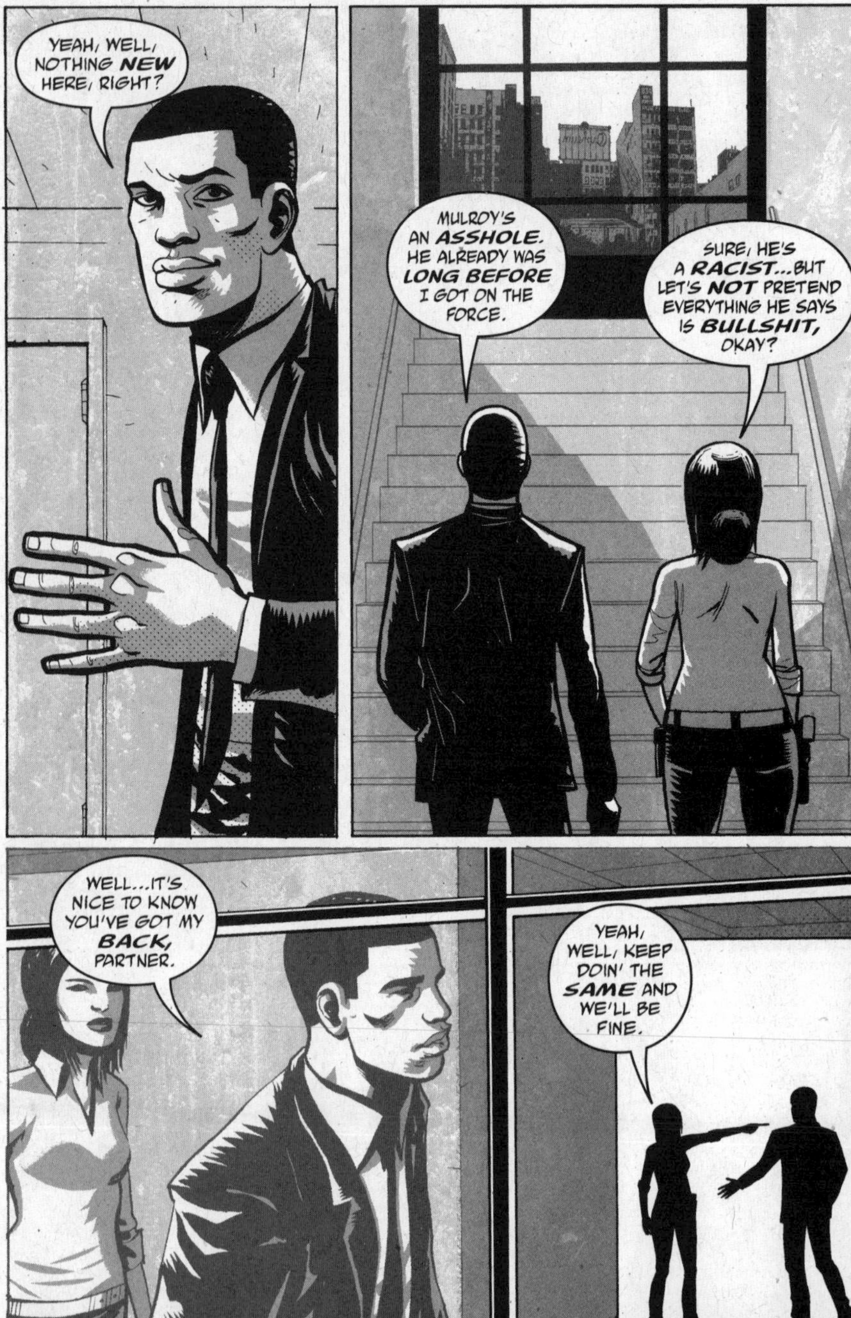
YEAH, WELL, NOTHING NEW HERE, RIGHT?
MULROY'S AN ASSHOLE. HE ALREADY WAS LONG BEFORE I GOT ON THE FORCE.
SURE, HE'S A RACIST...BUT LET'S NOT PRETEND EVERYTHING HE SAYS IS BULLSHIT, OKAY?
WELL...IT'S NICE TO KNOW YOU'VE GOT MY BACK, PARTNER.
YEAH, WELL, KEEP DOIN' THE SAME AND WE'LL BE FINE.

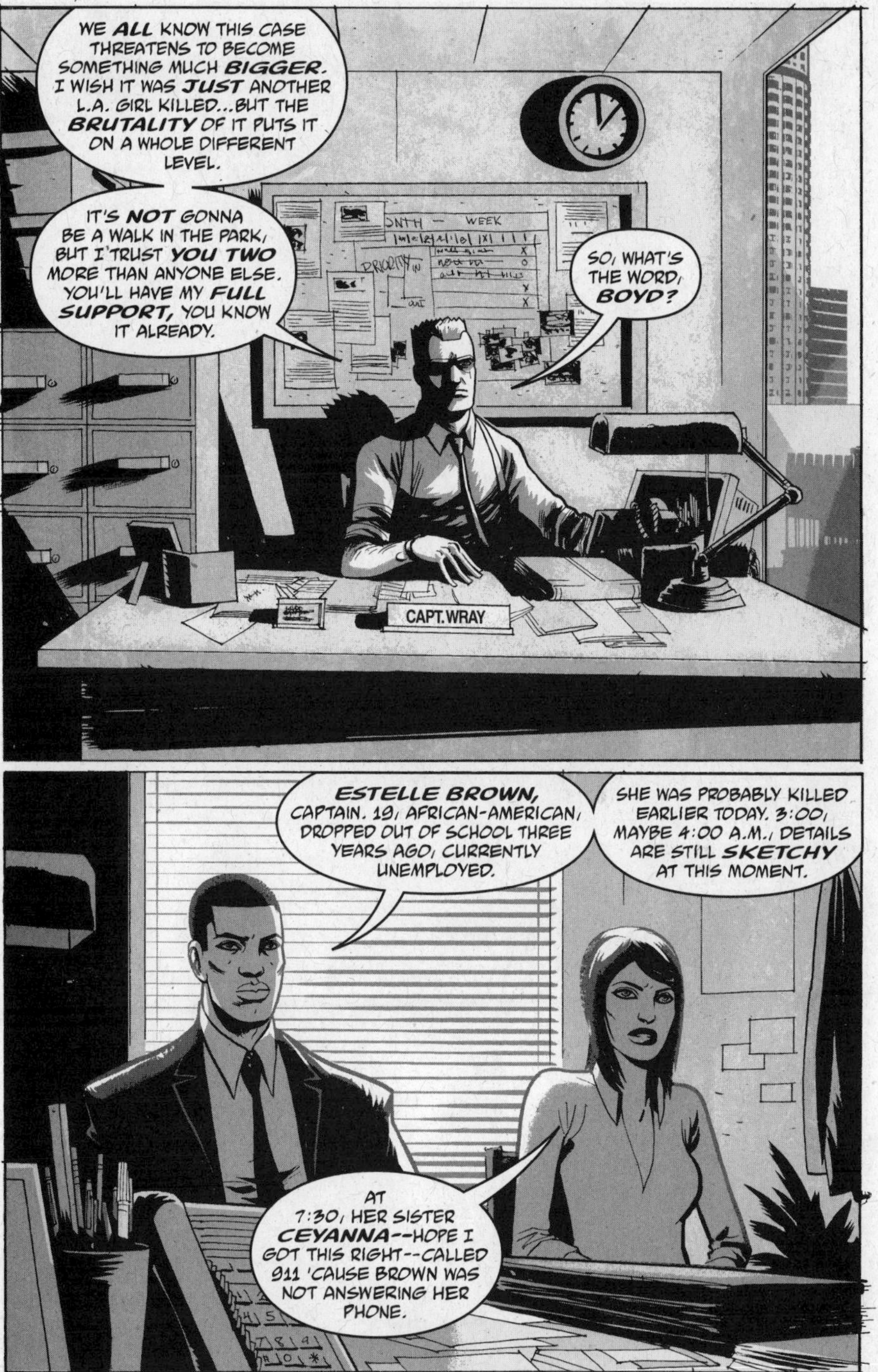
WE ALL KNOW THIS CASE THREATENS TO BECOME SOMETHING MUCH BIGGER. I WISH IT WAS JUST ANOTHER L.A. GIRL KILLED...BUT THE BRUTALITY OF IT PUTS IT ON A WHOLE DIFFERENT LEVEL.
IT'S NOT GONNA BE A WALK IN THE PARK, BUT I TRUST YOU TWO MORE THAN ANYONE ELSE. YOU'LL HAVE MY FULL SUPPORT, YOU KNOW IT ALREADY.
SO, WHAT'S THE WORD, BOYD?
CAPT. WRAY
ESTELLE BROWN, CAPTAIN. 19, AFRICAN-AMERICAN, DROPPED OUT OF SCHOOL THREE YEARS AGO, CURRENTLY UNEMPLOYED.
SHE WAS PROBABLY KILLED EARLIER TODAY. 3:00, MAYBE 4:00 A.M., DETAILS ARE STILL SKETCHY AT THIS MOMENT.
AT 7:30, HER SISTER CEYANNA--HOPE I GOT THIS RIGHT--CALLED 911 'CAUSE BROWN WAS NOT ANSWERING HER PHONE.

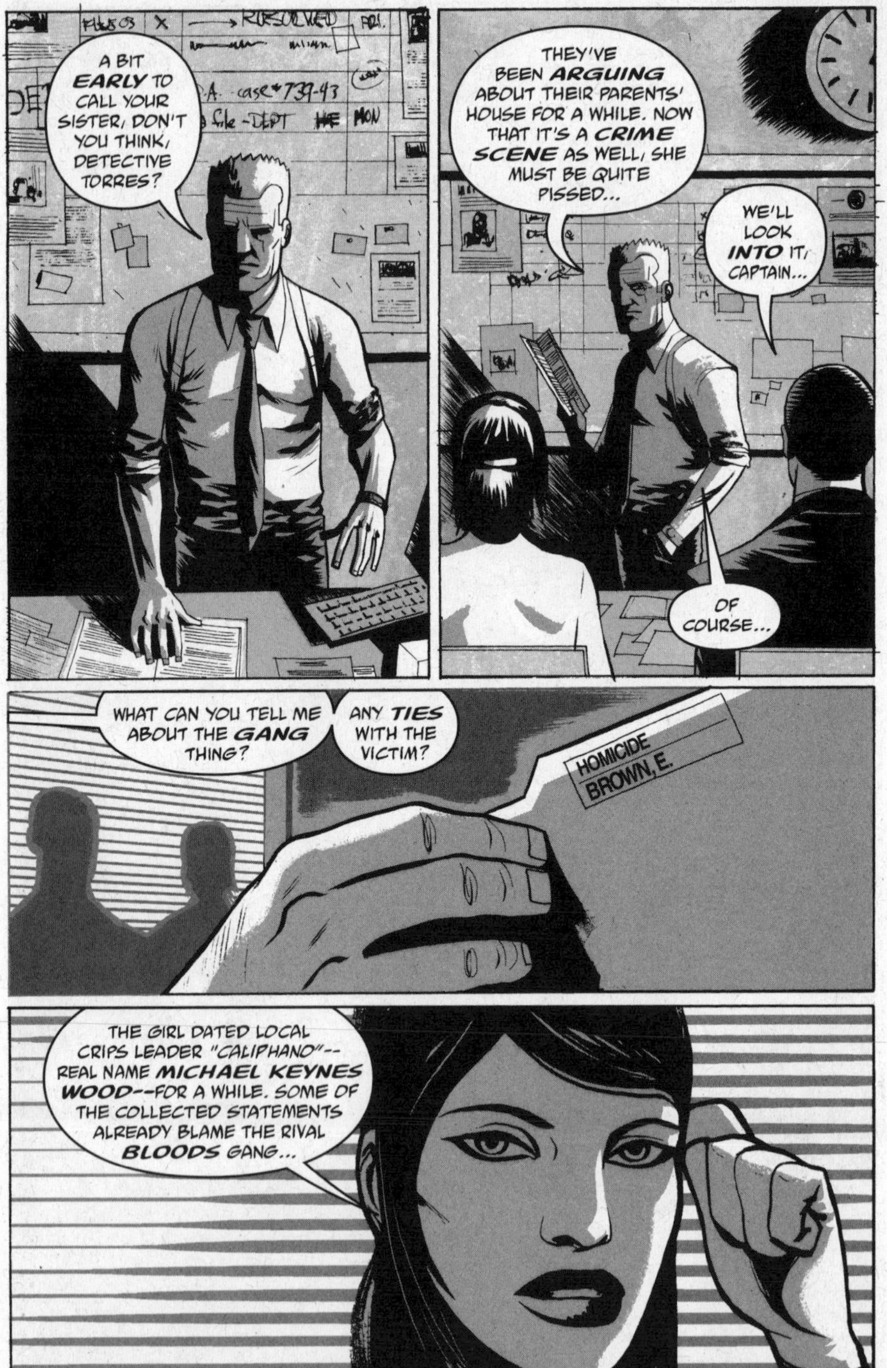
A BIT EARLY TO CALL YOUR SISTER, DON'T YOU THINK, DETECTIVE TORRES?
THEY'VE BEEN ARGUING ABOUT THEIR PARENTS' HOUSE FOR A WHILE. NOW THAT IT'S A CRIME SCENE AS WELL, SHE MUST BE QUITE PISSED...
WE'LL LOOK INTO IT, CAPTAIN...
OF COURSE...
WHAT CAN YOU TELL ME ABOUT THE GANG THING?
ANY TIES WITH THE VICTIM?
HOMICIDE
BROWN, E.
THE GIRL DATED LOCAL CRIPS LEADER "CALIPHANO"-- REAL NAME MICHAEL KEYNES WOOD--FOR A WHILE. SOME OF THE COLLECTED STATEMENTS ALREADY BLAME THE RIVAL BLOODS GANG...

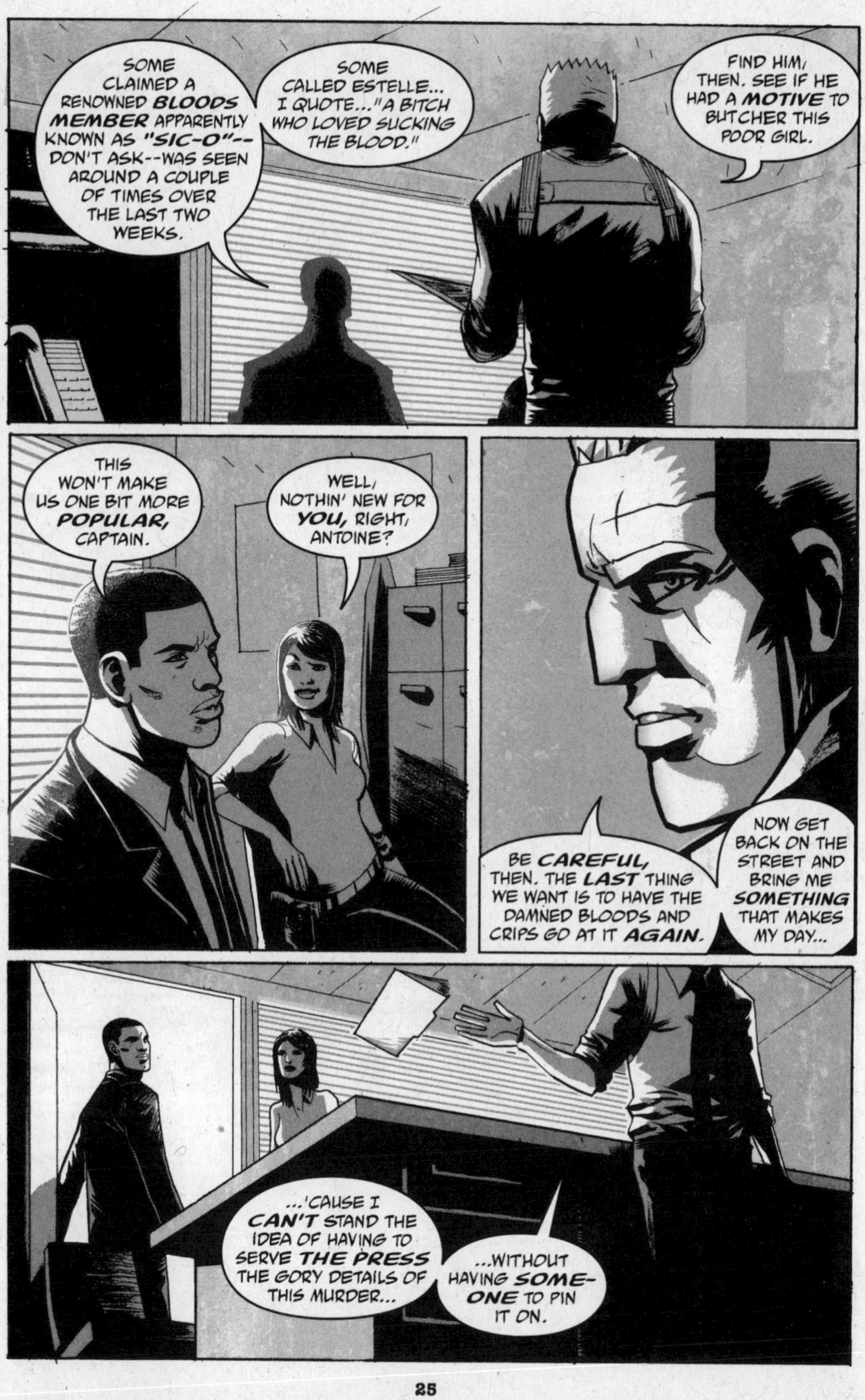

SOME CLAIMED A RENOWNED BLOODS MEMBER APPARENTLY KNOWN AS "SIC-O"--DON'T ASK--WAS SEEN AROUND A COUPLE OF TIMES OVER THE LAST TWO WEEKS.
SOME CALLED ESTELLE... I QUOTE..."A BITCH WHO LOVED SUCKING THE BLOOD."
FIND HIM, THEN. SEE IF HE HAD A MOTIVE TO BUTCHER THIS POOR GIRL.
THIS WON'T MAKE US ONE BIT MORE POPULAR, CAPTAIN.
WELL, NOTHIN' NEW FOR YOU, RIGHT, ANTOINE?
BE CAREFUL, THEN. THE LAST THING WE WANT IS TO HAVE THE DAMNED BLOODS AND CRIPS GO AT IT AGAIN.
NOW GET BACK ON THE STREET AND BRING ME SOMETHING THAT MAKES MY DAY...
...'CAUSE I CAN'T STAND THE IDEA OF HAVING TO SERVE THE PRESS THE GORY DETAILS OF THIS MURDER...
...WITHOUT HAVING SOME-ONE TO PIN IT ON.

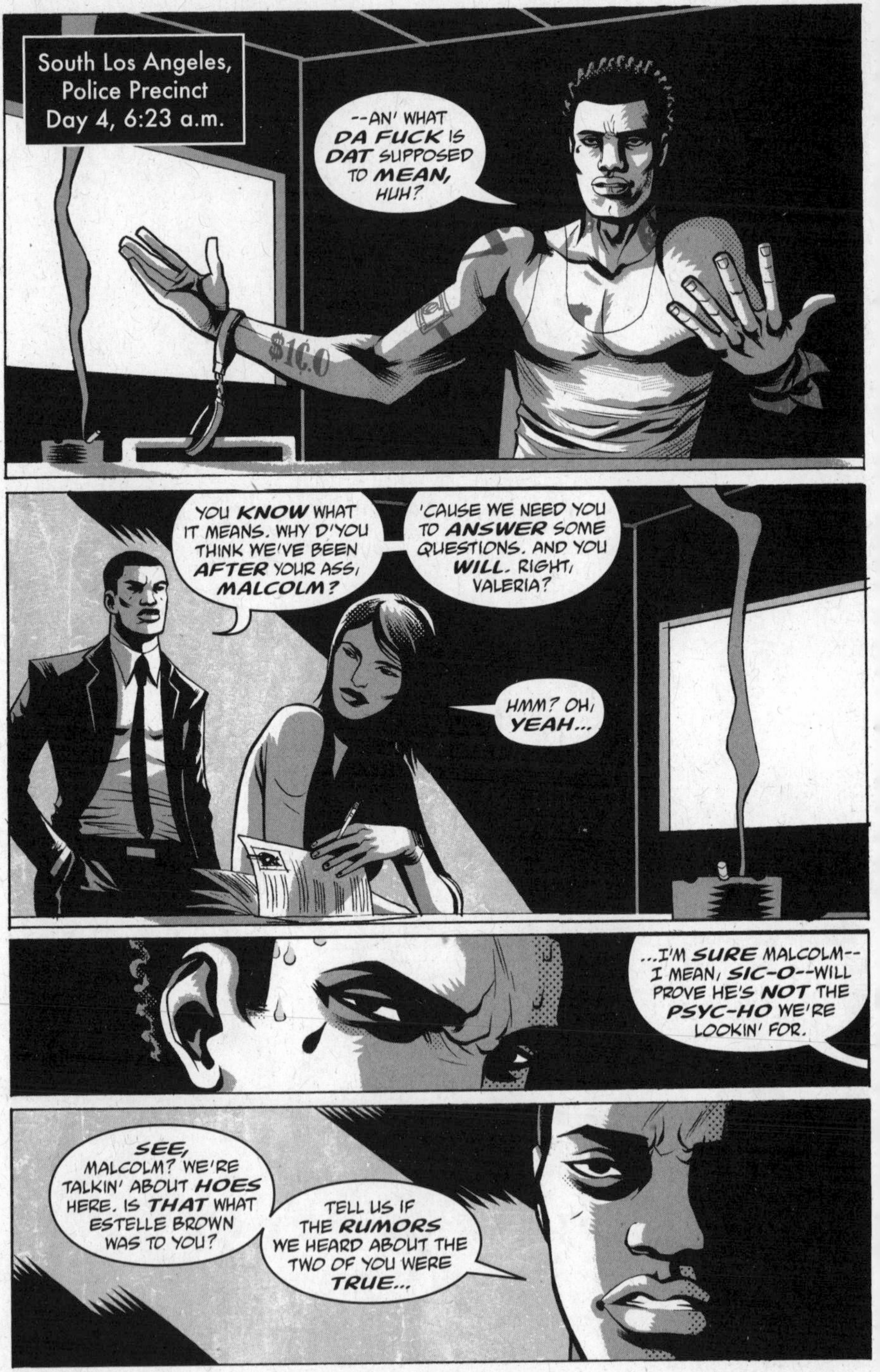
South Los Angeles, Police Precinct Day 4, 6:23 a.m.
--AN' WHAT DA FUCK IS DAT SUPPOSED TO MEAN, HUH?
$IC.O
YOU KNOW WHAT IT MEANS. WHY D'YOU THINK WE'VE BEEN AFTER YOUR ASS, MALCOLM?
'CAUSE WE NEED YOU TO ANSWER SOME QUESTIONS. AND YOU WILL. RIGHT, VALERIA?
HMM? OH, YEAH...
...I'M SURE MALCOLM-- I MEAN, SIC-O--WILL PROVE HE'S NOT THE PSYC-HO WE'RE LOOKIN' FOR.
SEE, MALCOLM? WE'RE TALKIN' ABOUT HOES HERE. IS THAT WHAT ESTELLE BROWN WAS TO YOU?
TELL US IF THE RUMORS WE HEARD ABOUT THE TWO OF YOU WERE TRUE...

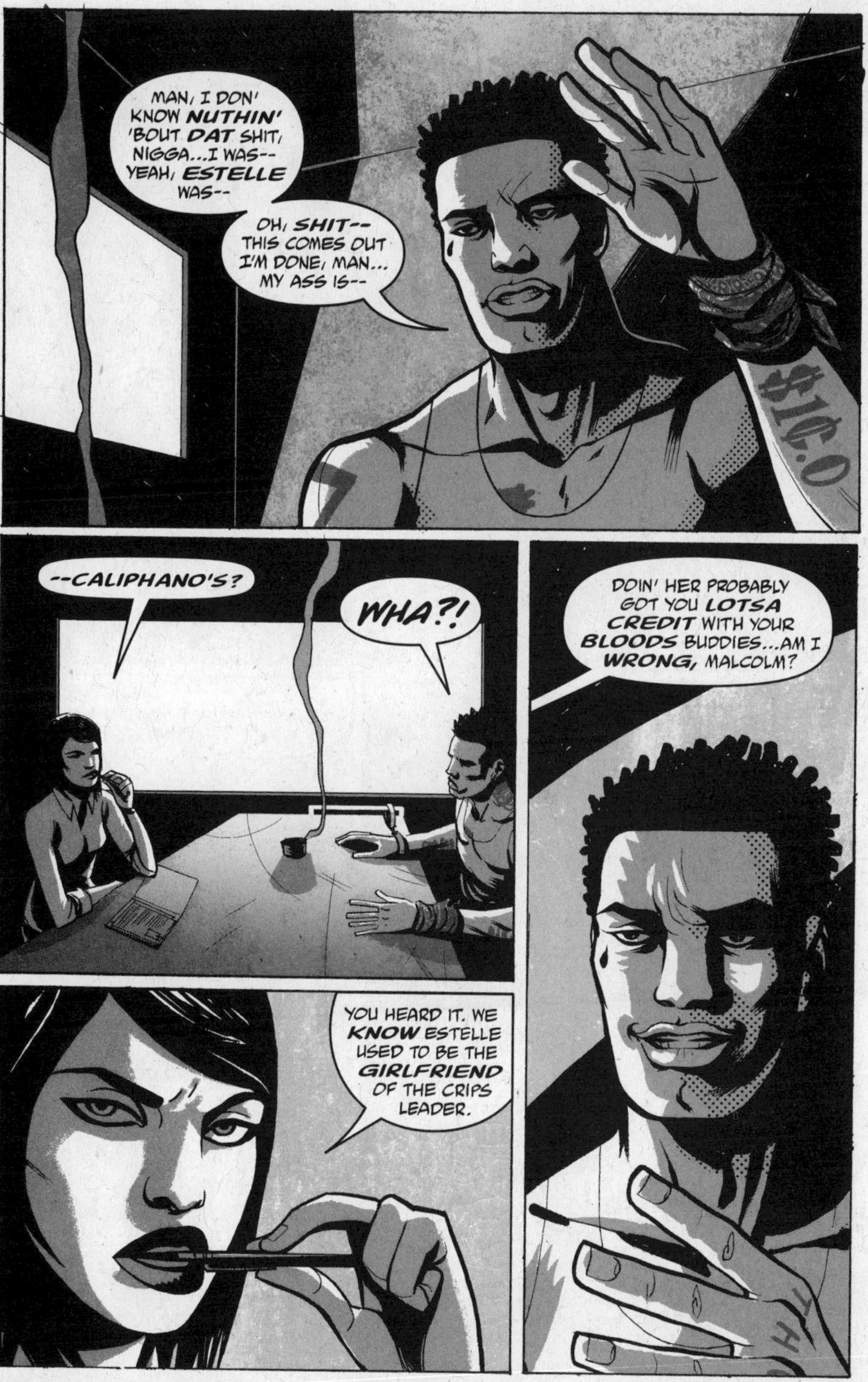
MAN, I DON' KNOW NUTHIN' 'BOUT DAT SHIT, NIGGA...I WAS-- YEAH, ESTELLE WAS--
OH, SHIT-- THIS COMES OUT I'M DONE, MAN... MY ASS IS--
--CALIPHANO'S?
WHA?!
DOIN' HER PROBABLY GOT YOU LOTSA CREDIT WITH YOUR BLOODS BUDDIES...AM I WRONG, MALCOLM?
YOU HEARD IT. WE KNOW ESTELLE USED TO BE THE GIRLFRIEND OF THE CRIPS LEADER.

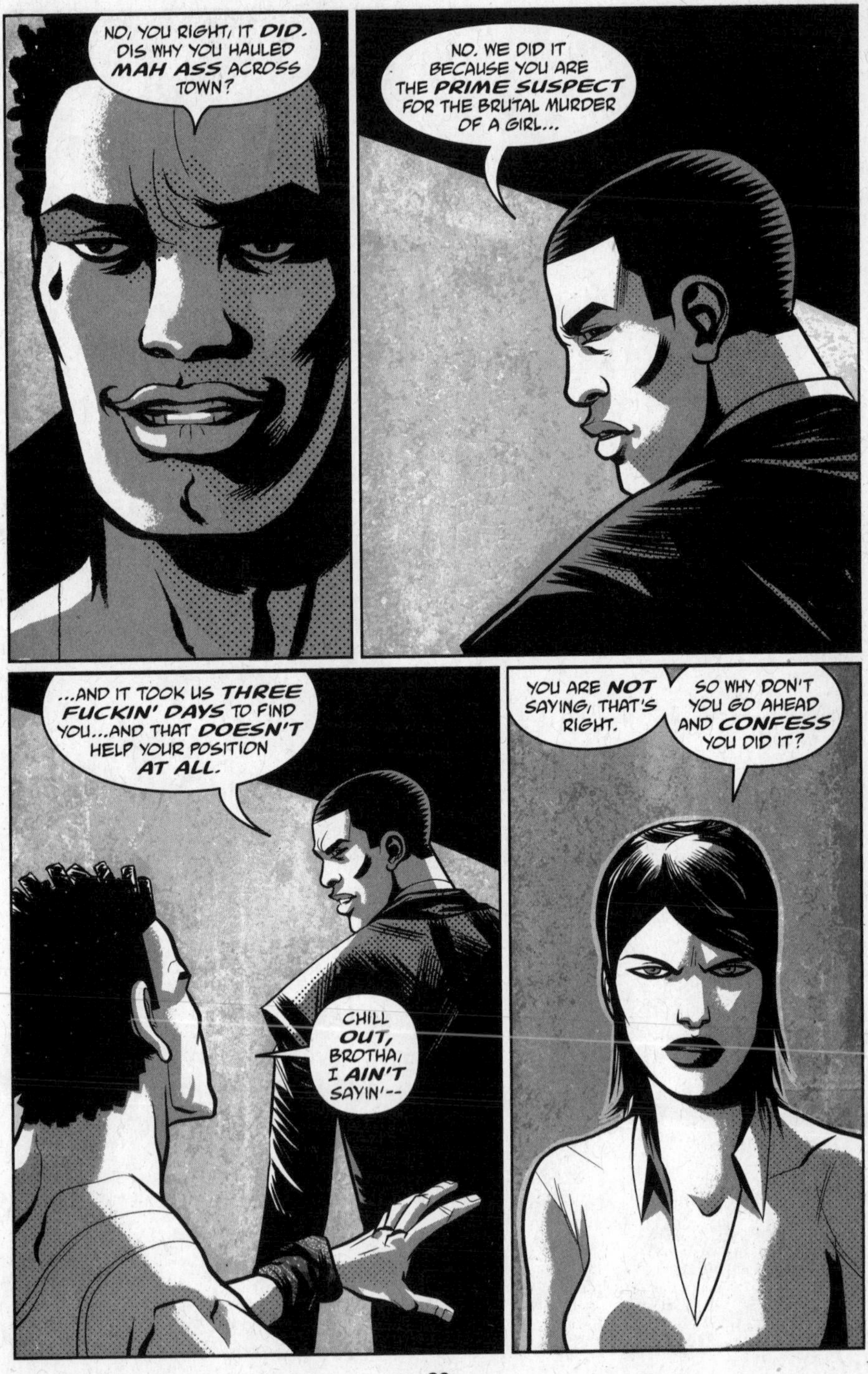
NO, YOU RIGHT, IT DID. DIS WHY YOU HAULED MAH ASS ACROSS TOWN?
NO. WE DID IT BECAUSE YOU ARE THE PRIME SUSPECT FOR THE BRUTAL MURDER OF A GIRL...
...AND IT TOOK US THREE FUCKIN' DAYS TO FIND YOU...AND THAT DOESN'T HELP YOUR POSITION AT ALL.
CHILL OUT, BROTHA, I AIN'T SAYIN'--
YOU ARE NOT SAYING, THAT'S RIGHT.
SO WHY DON'T YOU GO AHEAD AND CONFESS YOU DID IT?

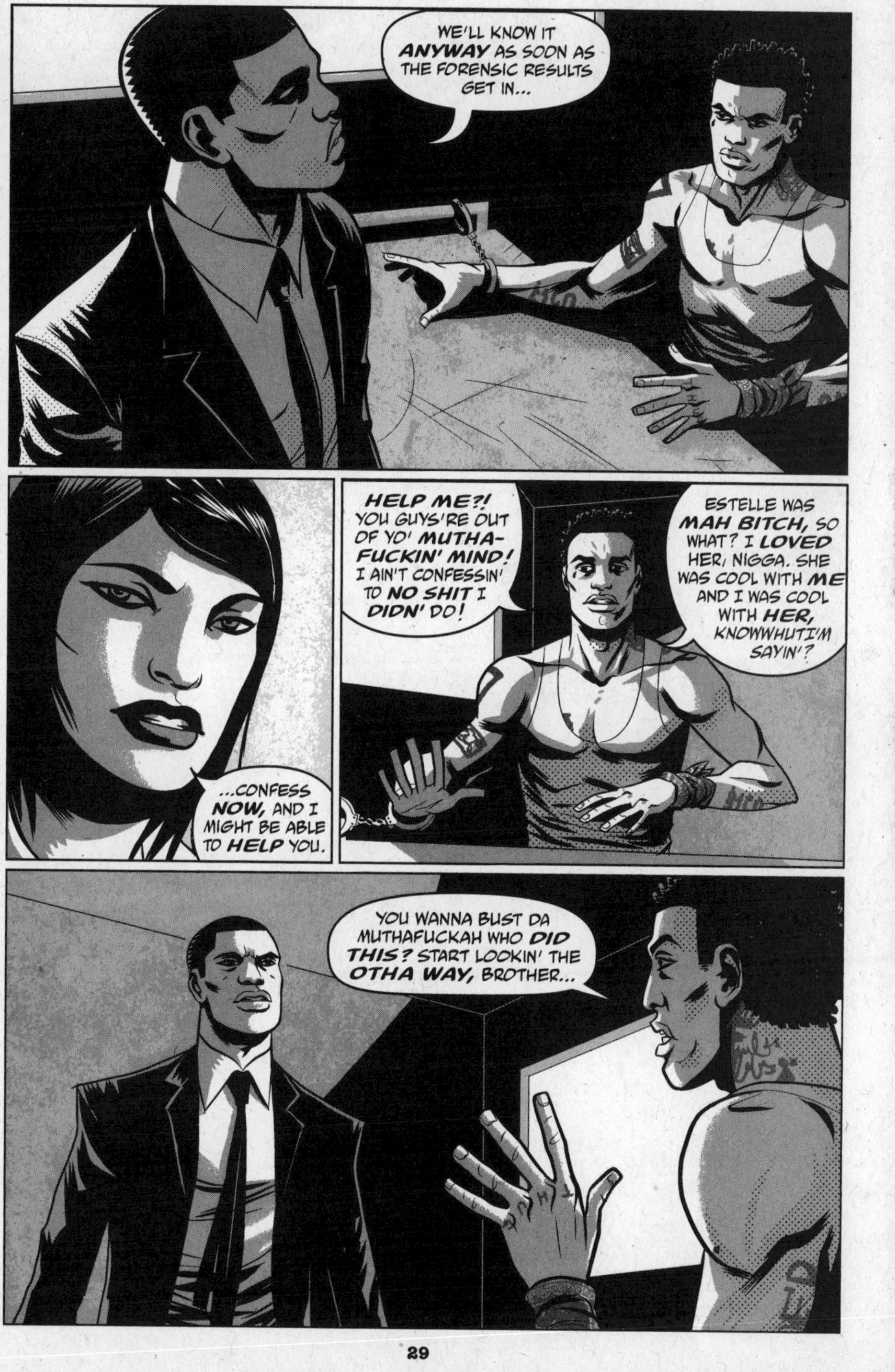
WE'LL KNOW IT ANYWAY AS SOON AS THE FORENSIC RESULTS GET IN...
...CONFESS NOW, AND I MIGHT BE ABLE TO HELP YOU.
HELP ME?! YOU GUYS'RE OUT OF YO' MUTHA-FUCKIN' MIND! I AIN'T CONFESSIN' TO NO SHIT I DIDN' DO!
ESTELLE WAS MAH BITCH, SO WHAT? I LOVED HER, NIGGA. SHE WAS COOL WITH ME AND I WAS COOL WITH HER, KNOWWHUTI'M SAYIN'?
YOU WANNA BUST DA MUTHAFUCKAH WHO DID THIS? START LOOKIN' THE OTHA WAY, BROTHER...

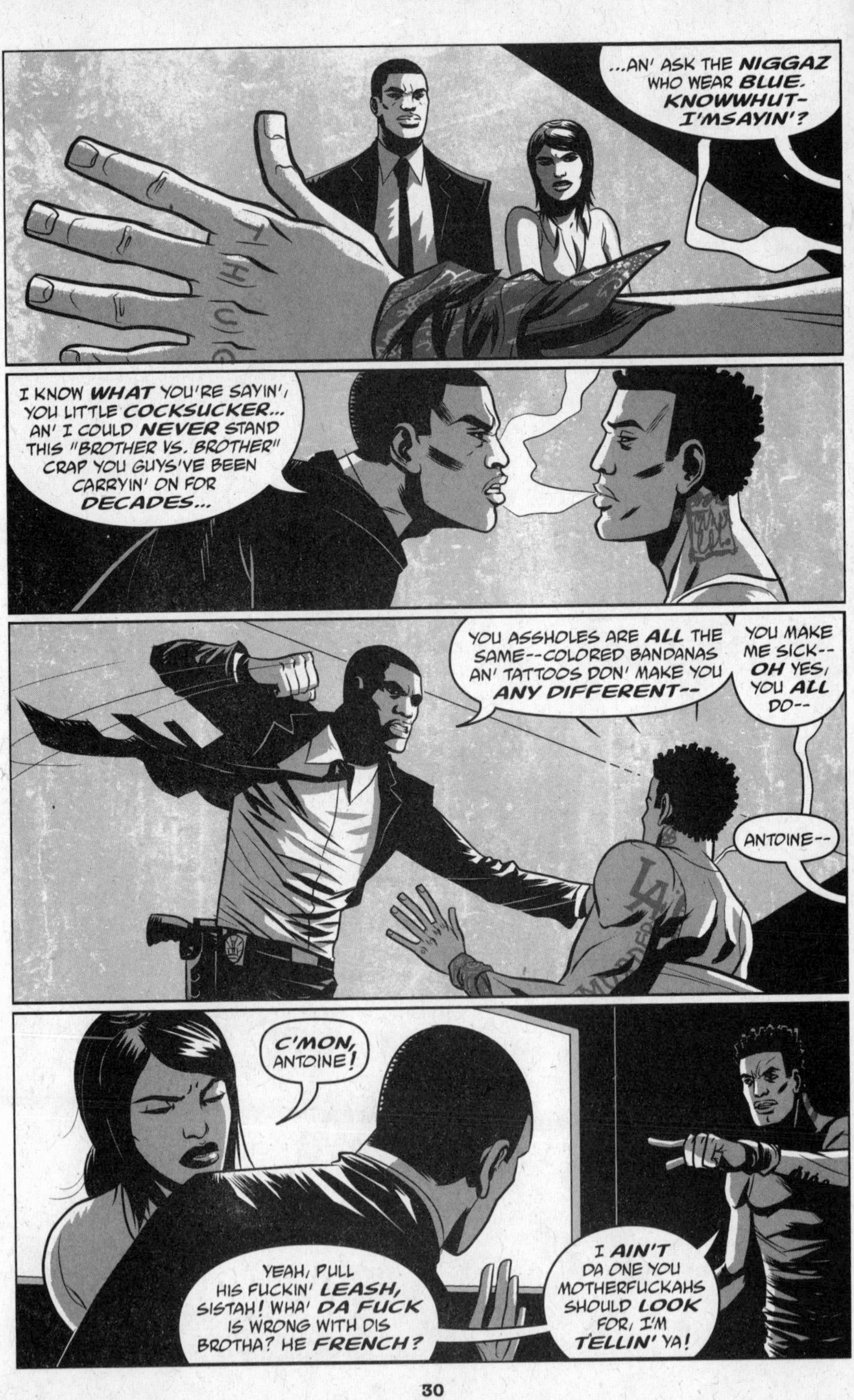
...AN' ASK THE NIGGAZ WHO WEAR BLUE. KNOWWHUT-I'MSAYIN'?
I KNOW WHAT YOU'RE SAYIN', YOU LITTLE COCKSUCKER... AN' I COULD NEVER STAND THIS "BROTHER VS. BROTHER" CRAP YOU GUYS'VE BEEN CARRYIN' ON FOR DECADES...
YOU ASSHOLES ARE ALL THE SAME--COLORED BANDANAS AN' TATTOOS DON' MAKE YOU ANY DIFFERENT--
YOU MAKE ME SICK--OH YES, YOU ALL DO--
ANTOINE--
C'MON, ANTOINE!
YEAH, PULL HIS FUCKIN' LEASH, SISTAH! WHA' DA FUCK IS WRONG WITH DIS BROTHA? HE FRENCH?
I AIN'T DA ONE YOU MOTHERFUCKAHS SHOULD LOOK FOR, I'M TELLIN' YA!

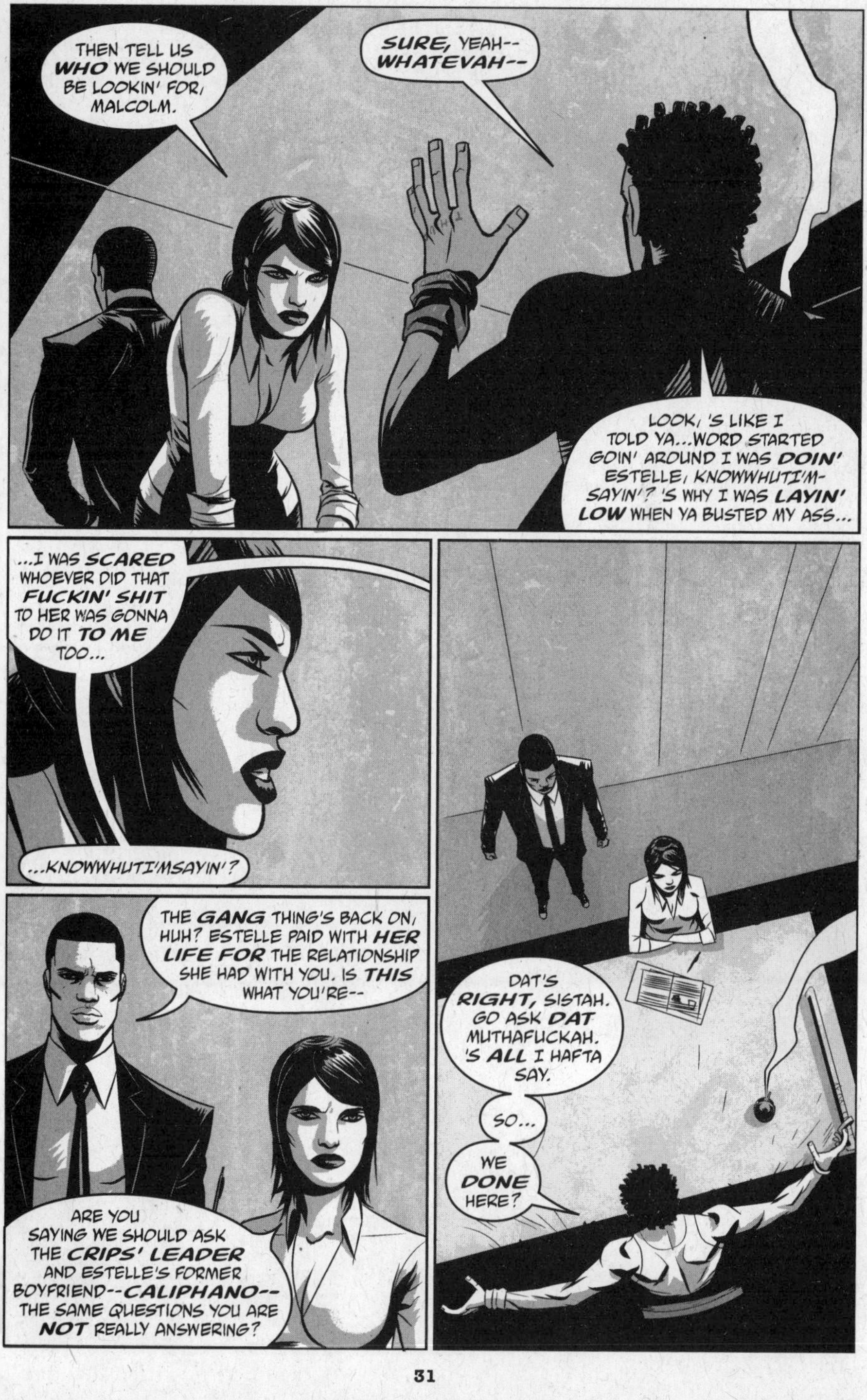
THEN TELL US WHO WE SHOULD BE LOOKIN' FOR, MALCOLM.
SURE, YEAH-- WHATEVAH--
LOOK, 'S LIKE I TOLD YA...WORD STARTED GOIN' AROUND I WAS DOIN' ESTELLE, KNOWWHUTI'M-SAYIN'? 'S WHY I WAS LAYIN' LOW WHEN YA BUSTED MY ASS...
...I WAS SCARED WHOEVER DID THAT FUCKIN' SHIT TO HER WAS GONNA DO IT TO ME TOO...
...KNOWWHUTI'MSAYIN'?
THE GANG THING'S BACK ON, HUH? ESTELLE PAID WITH HER LIFE FOR THE RELATIONSHIP SHE HAD WITH YOU. IS THIS WHAT YOU'RE--
ARE YOU SAYING WE SHOULD ASK THE CRIPS' LEADER AND ESTELLE'S FORMER BOYFRIEND--CALIPHANO-- THE SAME QUESTIONS YOU ARE NOT REALLY ANSWERING?
DAT'S RIGHT, SISTAH. GO ASK DAT MUTHAFUCKAH. 'S ALL I HAFTA SAY.
SO...
WE DONE HERE?

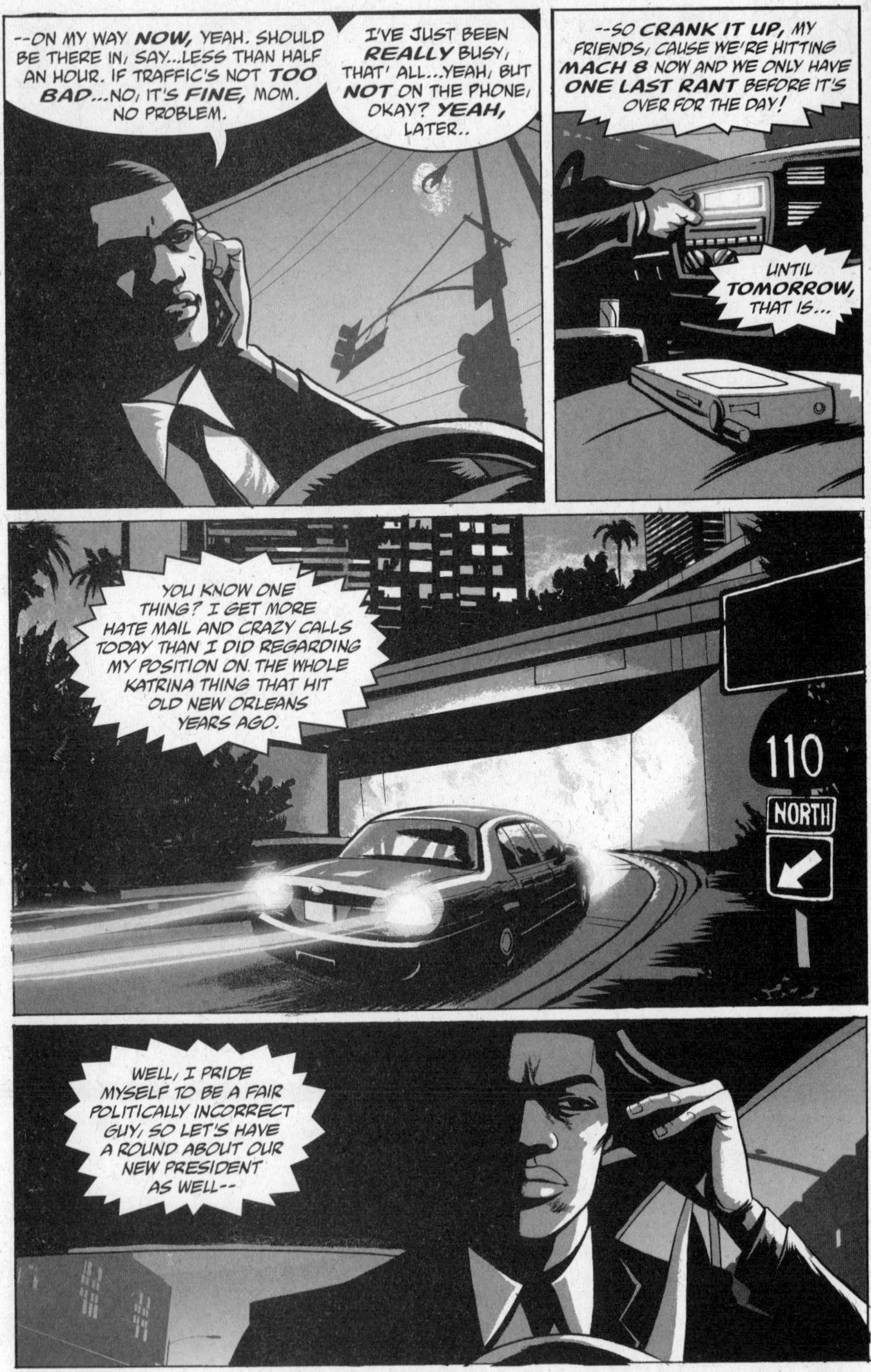
--ON MY WAY NOW, YEAH. SHOULD BE THERE IN, SAY...LESS THAN HALF AN HOUR. IF TRAFFIC'S NOT TOO BAD...NO, IT'S FINE, MOM. NO PROBLEM.
I'VE JUST BEEN REALLY BUSY, THAT' ALL...YEAH, BUT NOT ON THE PHONE, OKAY? YEAH, LATER..
--SO CRANK IT UP, MY FRIENDS, CAUSE WE'RE HITTING MACH 8 NOW AND WE ONLY HAVE ONE LAST RANT BEFORE IT'S OVER FOR THE DAY!
UNTIL TOMORROW, THAT IS...
YOU KNOW ONE THING? I GET MORE HATE MAIL AND CRAZY CALLS TODAY THAN I DID REGARDING MY POSITION ON THE WHOLE KATRINA THING THAT HIT OLD NEW ORLEANS YEARS AGO.
110
NORTH
WELL, I PRIDE MYSELF TO BE A FAIR POLITICALLY INCORRECT GUY, SO LET'S HAVE A ROUND ABOUT OUR NEW PRESIDENT AS WELL--

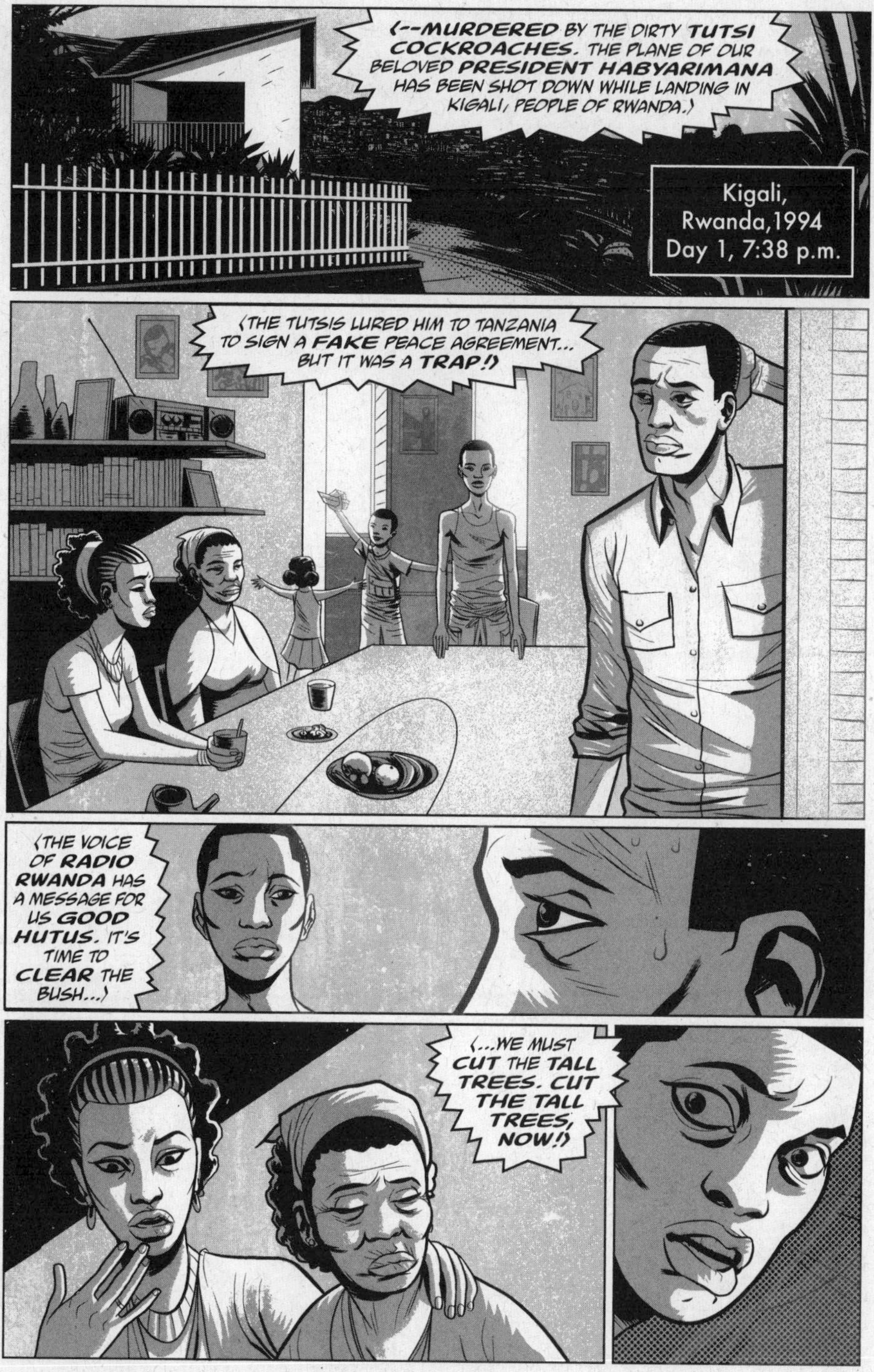
‹--MURDERED BY THE DIRTY TUTSI COCKROACHES. THE PLANE OF OUR BELOVED PRESIDENT HABYARIMANA HAS BEEN SHOT DOWN WHILE LANDING IN KIGALI, PEOPLE OF RWANDA.›
Kigali, Rwanda, 1994 Day 1, 7:38 p.m.
‹THE TUTSIS LURED HIM TO TANZANIA TO SIGN A FAKE PEACE AGREEMENT... BUT IT WAS A TRAP!›
‹THE VOICE OF RADIO RWANDA HAS A MESSAGE FOR US GOOD HUTUS. IT'S TIME TO CLEAR THE BUSH...›
‹...WE MUST CUT THE TALL TREES. CUT THE TALL TREES, NOW!›

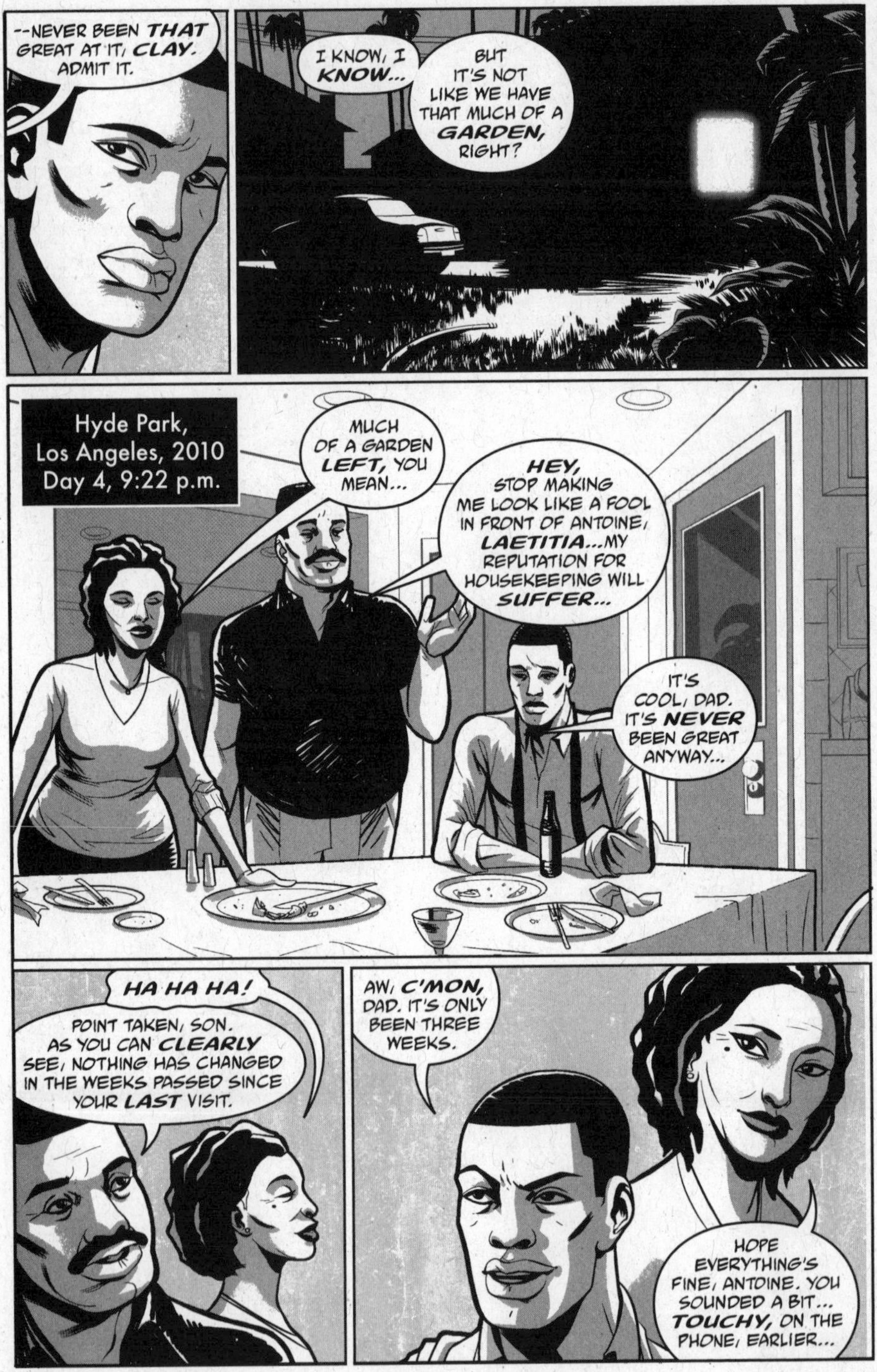
--NEVER BEEN THAT GREAT AT IT, CLAY. ADMIT IT.
I KNOW, I KNOW...
BUT IT'S NOT LIKE WE HAVE THAT MUCH OF A GARDEN, RIGHT?
Hyde Park, Los Angeles, 2010 Day 4, 9:22 p.m.
MUCH OF A GARDEN LEFT, YOU MEAN...
HEY, STOP MAKING ME LOOK LIKE A FOOL IN FRONT OF ANTOINE, LAETITIA...MY REPUTATION FOR HOUSEKEEPING WILL SUFFER...
IT'S COOL, DAD. IT'S NEVER BEEN GREAT ANYWAY...
HA HA HA!
POINT TAKEN, SON. AS YOU CAN CLEARLY SEE, NOTHING HAS CHANGED IN THE WEEKS PASSED SINCE YOUR LAST VISIT.
AW, C'MON, DAD. IT'S ONLY BEEN THREE WEEKS.
HOPE EVERYTHING'S FINE, ANTOINE. YOU SOUNDED A BIT... TOUCHY, ON THE PHONE, EARLIER...

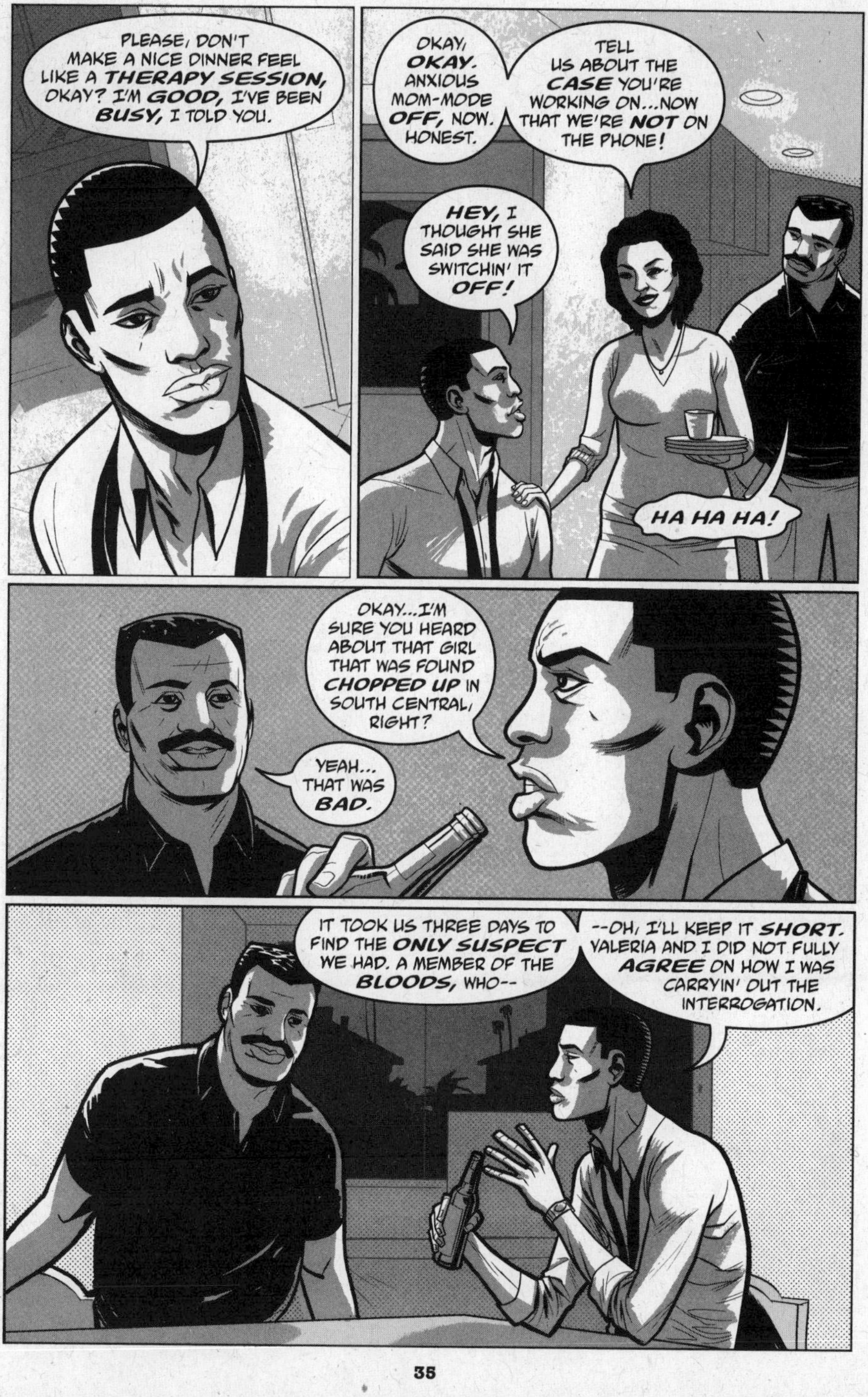
PLEASE, DON'T MAKE A NICE DINNER FEEL LIKE A **THERAPY SESSION,** OKAY? I'M **GOOD,** I'VE BEEN **BUSY,** I TOLD YOU.
OKAY, **OKAY.** ANXIOUS MOM-MODE **OFF,** NOW. HONEST.
TELL US ABOUT THE **CASE** YOU'RE WORKING ON...NOW THAT WE'RE **NOT** ON THE PHONE!
HEY, I THOUGHT SHE SAID SHE WAS SWITCHIN' IT **OFF!**
HA HA HA!
OKAY...I'M SURE YOU HEARD ABOUT THAT GIRL THAT WAS FOUND **CHOPPED UP** IN SOUTH CENTRAL, RIGHT?
YEAH... THAT WAS **BAD.**
IT TOOK US THREE DAYS TO FIND THE **ONLY SUSPECT** WE HAD. A MEMBER OF THE **BLOODS,** WHO--
--OH, I'LL KEEP IT **SHORT.** VALERIA AND I DID NOT FULLY **AGREE** ON HOW I WAS CARRYIN' OUT THE INTERROGATION.

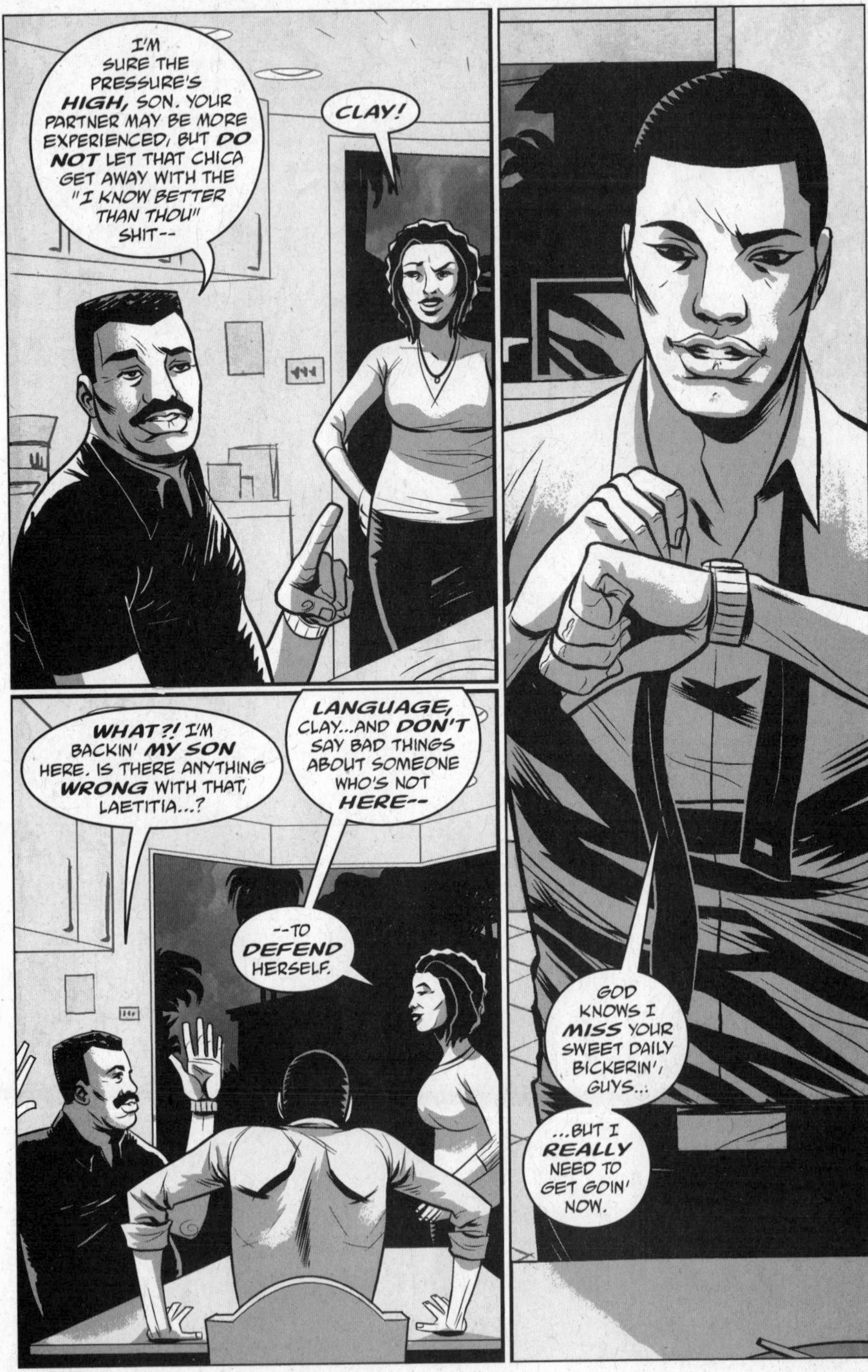
I'M SURE THE PRESSURE'S **HIGH,** SON. YOUR PARTNER MAY BE MORE EXPERIENCED, BUT **DO NOT** LET THAT CHICA GET AWAY WITH THE "I KNOW BETTER THAN THOU" SHIT--
CLAY!
GOD KNOWS I **MISS** YOUR SWEET DAILY BICKERIN', GUYS...
...BUT I **REALLY** NEED TO GET GOIN' NOW.
WHAT?! I'M BACKIN' **MY SON** HERE. IS THERE ANYTHING **WRONG** WITH THAT, LAETITIA...?
LANGUAGE, CLAY...AND **DON'T** SAY BAD THINGS ABOUT SOMEONE WHO'S NOT **HERE--**
--TO **DEFEND** HERSELF.

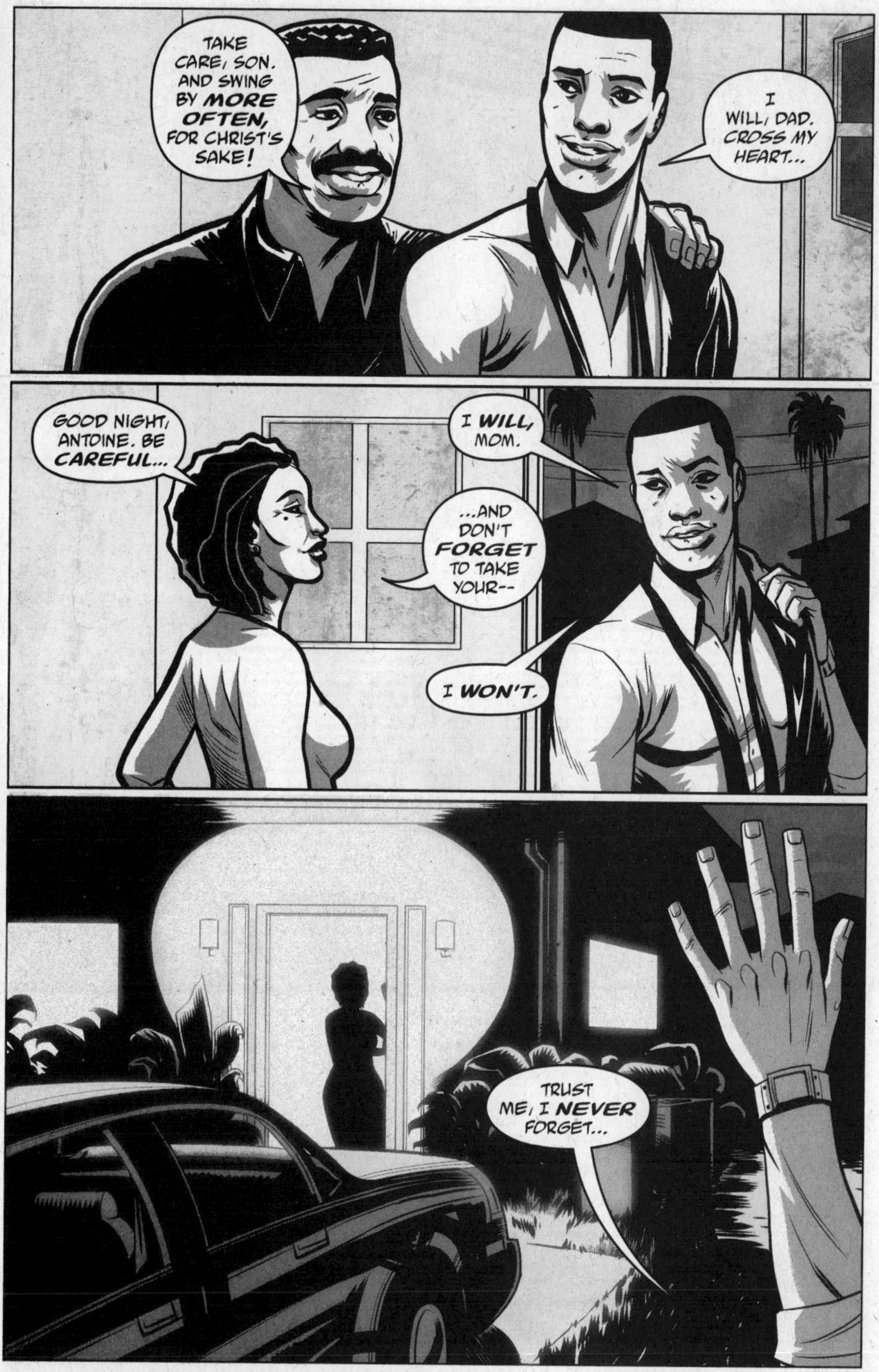
TAKE CARE, SON. AND SWING BY **MORE OFTEN,** FOR CHRIST'S SAKE!
I WILL, DAD. CROSS MY HEART...
GOOD NIGHT, ANTOINE. BE **CAREFUL...**
I **WILL,** MOM.
...AND DON'T **FORGET** TO TAKE YOUR--
I **WON'T.**
TRUST ME, I **NEVER** FORGET...

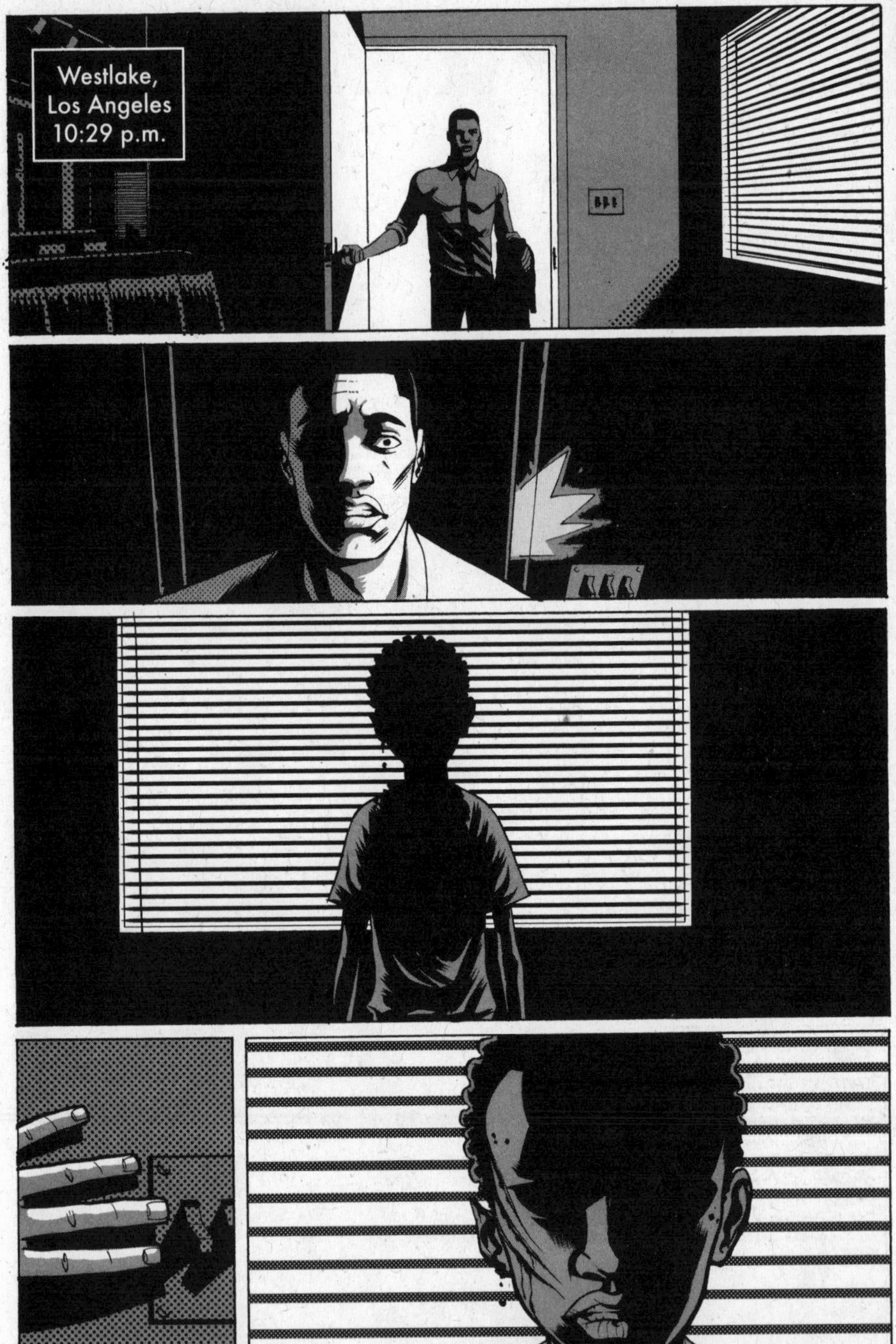
Westlake,
Los Angeles
10:29 p.m.

--OMETHING IS DEFINITELY ON TONIGHT, MY FRIENDS...

...AN' YOU KNOW YOU CAN *TRUST* OL' JACK MACK, 'SPECIALLY NOW THAT WE'RE HITTIN' *MACK 9* AND, AS USUAL, WE'RE BACK *LIVE!*

WELL, IT LOOKS LIKE OUR RESPECTABLE LAW ENFORCERS ARE GOING *KU-RAZEEE* AFTER THE SOUTH CENTRAL *CHOP* SUEY.

JACK'S GOT HIS *SOURCES,* Y'KNOW? AND THOSE SOURCES ARE GIVIN' HIM JUICY AND GORY *DETAILS* ABOUT THE MURDER THAT APPEARS TO BE *RRREALLY* STIRRIN' UP THE HOOD...

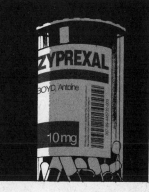

ZYPREXAL

BOYD, Antoine

10 mg

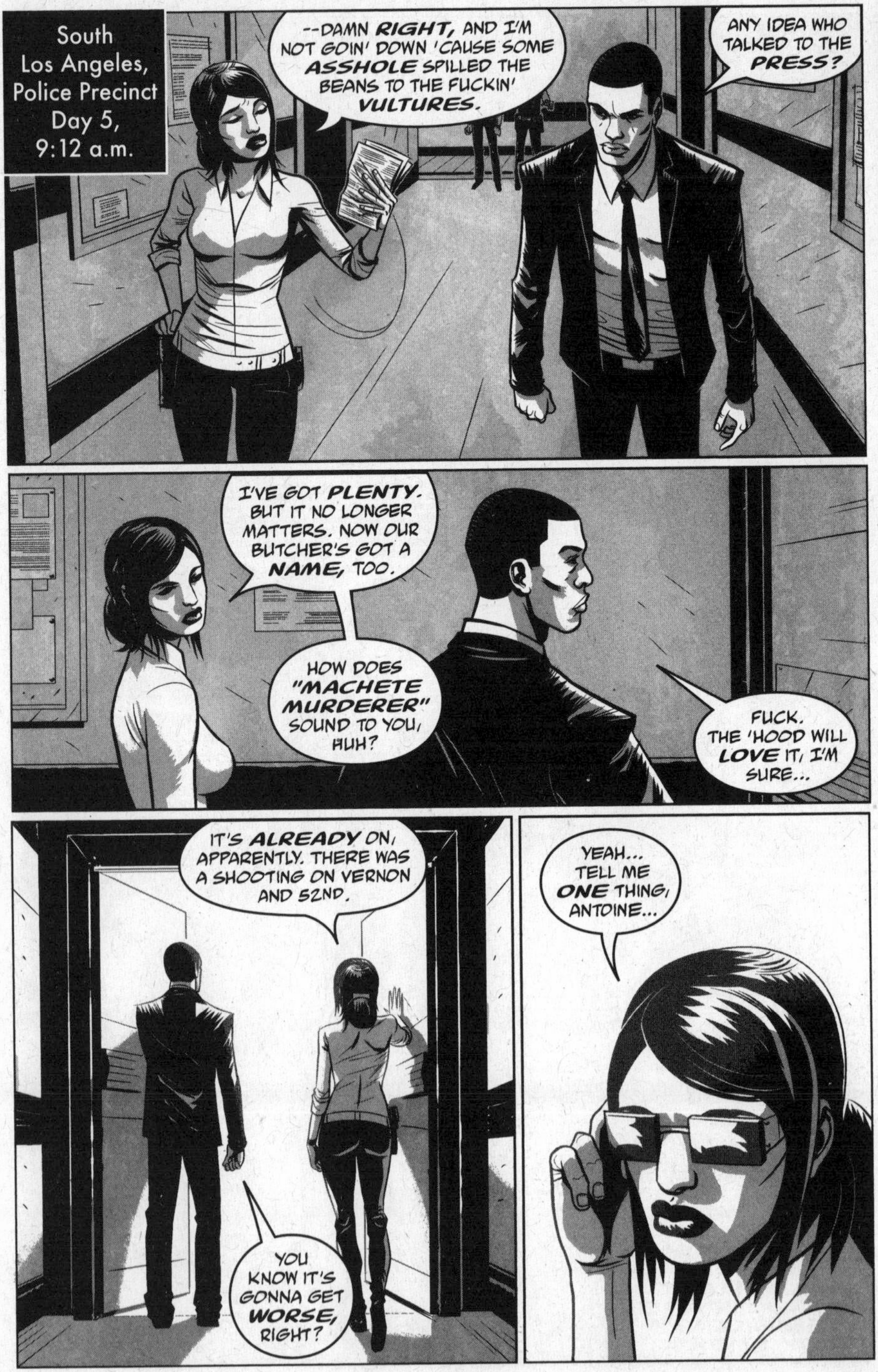
South Los Angeles, Police Precinct Day 5, 9:12 a.m.
--DAMN RIGHT, AND I'M NOT GOIN' DOWN 'CAUSE SOME ASSHOLE SPILLED THE BEANS TO THE FUCKIN' VULTURES.
ANY IDEA WHO TALKED TO THE PRESS?
I'VE GOT PLENTY. BUT IT NO LONGER MATTERS. NOW OUR BUTCHER'S GOT A NAME, TOO.
HOW DOES "MACHETE MURDERER" SOUND TO YOU, HUH?
FUCK. THE 'HOOD WILL LOVE IT, I'M SURE...
IT'S ALREADY ON, APPARENTLY. THERE WAS A SHOOTING ON VERNON AND 52ND.
YOU KNOW IT'S GONNA GET WORSE, RIGHT?
YEAH... TELL ME ONE THING, ANTOINE...

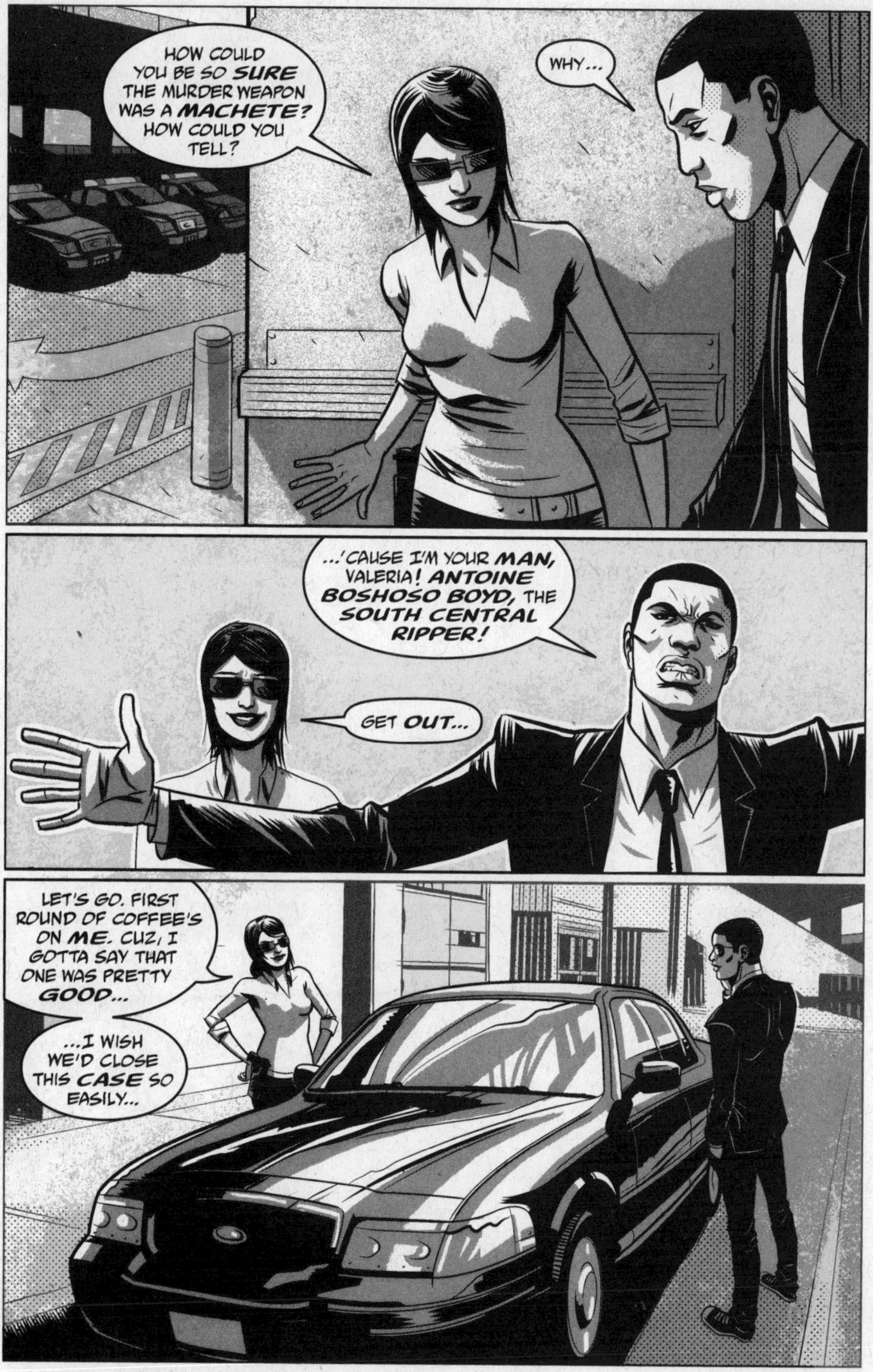
HOW COULD YOU BE SO SURE THE MURDER WEAPON WAS A MACHETE? HOW COULD YOU TELL?
WHY...
...'CAUSE I'M YOUR MAN, VALERIA! ANTOINE BOSHOSO BOYD, THE SOUTH CENTRAL RIPPER!
GET OUT...
LET'S GO. FIRST ROUND OF COFFEE'S ON ME. CUZ, I GOTTA SAY THAT ONE WAS PRETTY GOOD...
...I WISH WE'D CLOSE THIS CASE SO EASILY...

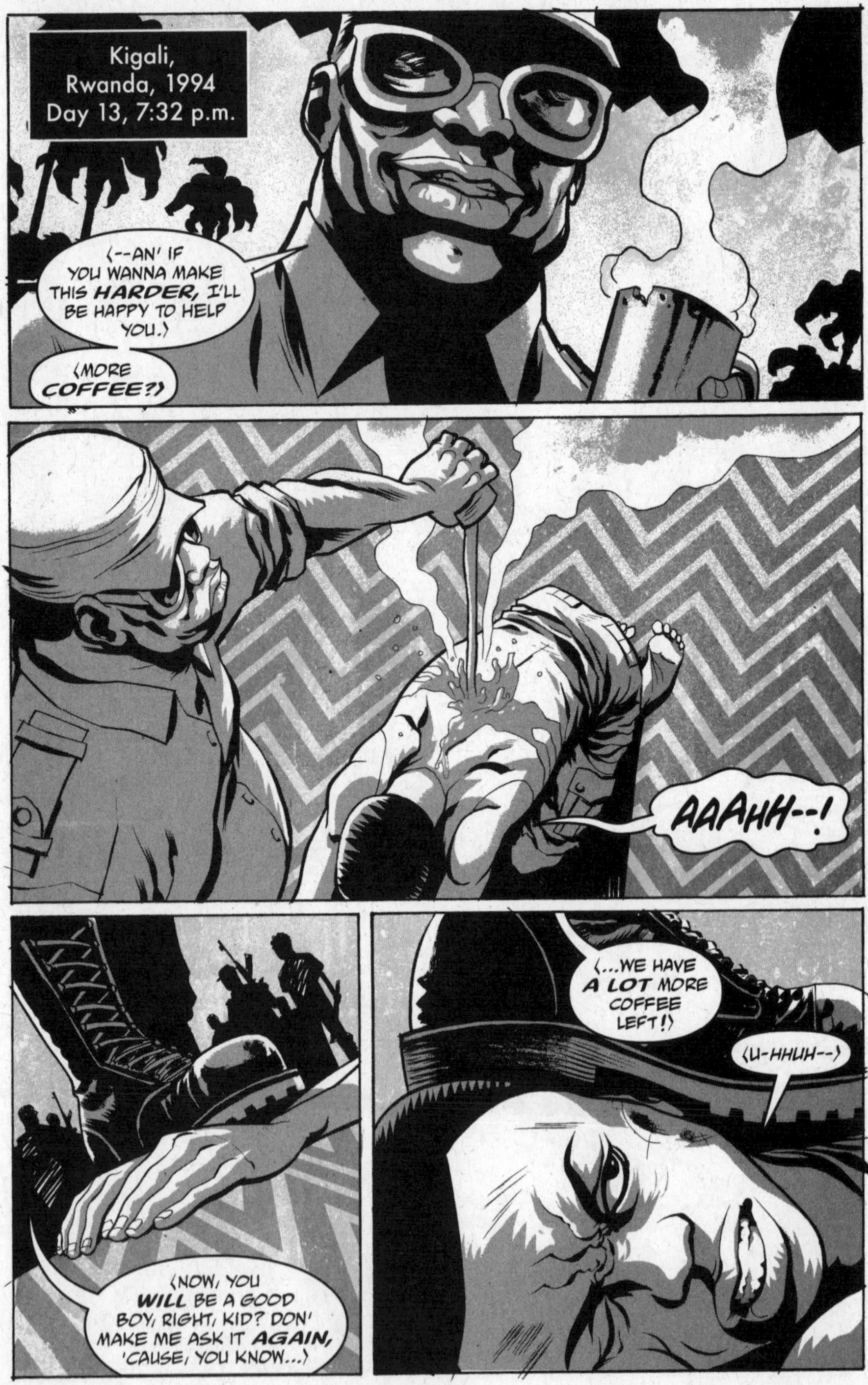
Kigali, Rwanda, 1994 Day 13, 7:32 p.m.
⟨--AN' IF YOU WANNA MAKE THIS **HARDER,** I'LL BE HAPPY TO HELP YOU.⟩
⟨MORE **COFFEE?**⟩
AAAHH--!
⟨NOW, YOU **WILL** BE A GOOD BOY, RIGHT, KID? DON' MAKE ME ASK IT **AGAIN,** 'CAUSE, YOU KNOW...⟩
⟨...WE HAVE **A LOT** MORE COFFEE LEFT!⟩
⟨U-HHUH--⟩

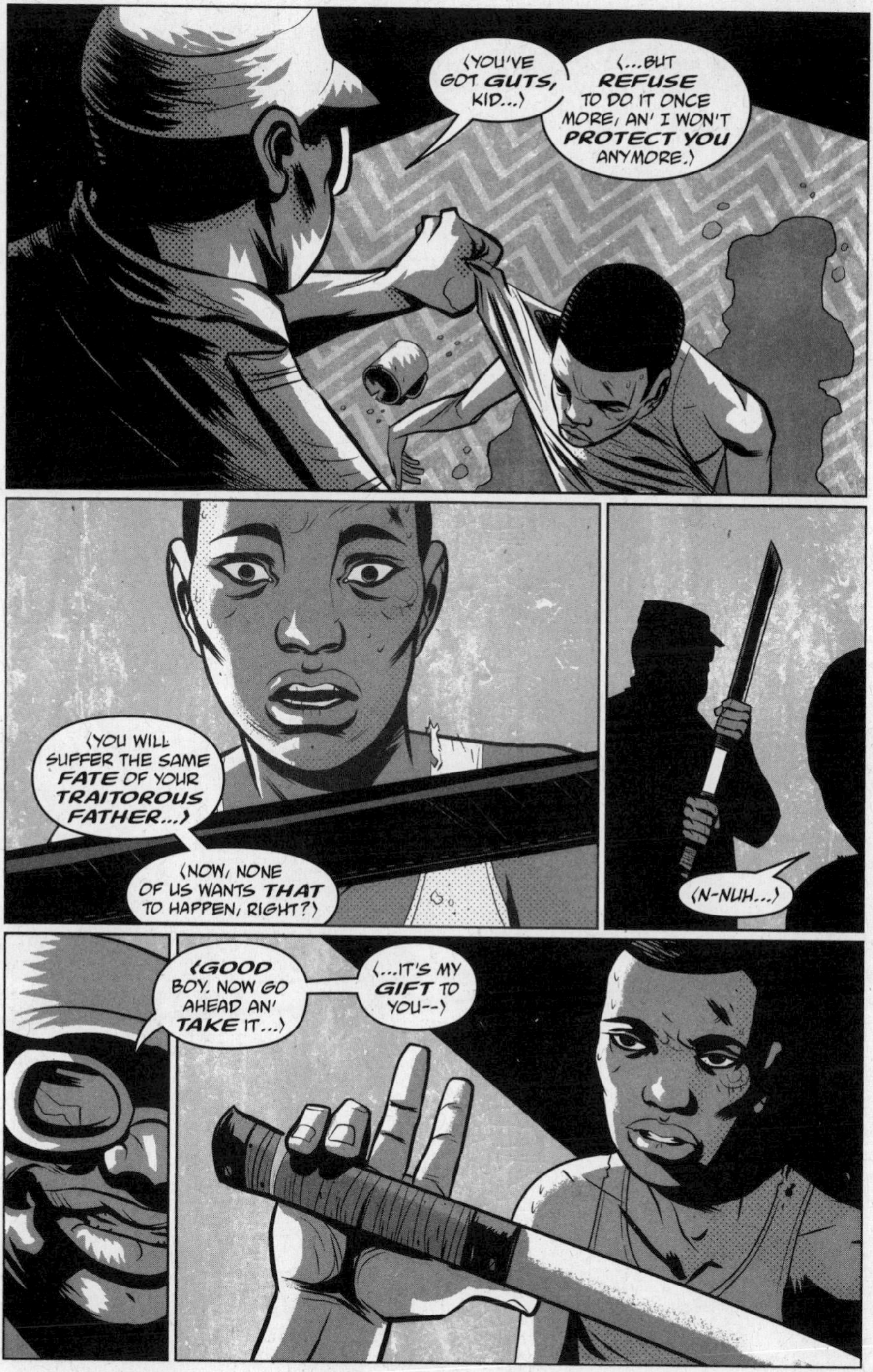
⟨YOU'VE GOT **GUTS**, KID...⟩
⟨...BUT **REFUSE** TO DO IT ONCE MORE, AN' I WON'T **PROTECT YOU** ANYMORE.⟩
⟨YOU WILL SUFFER THE SAME **FATE** OF YOUR **TRAITOROUS FATHER...**⟩
⟨NOW, NONE OF US WANTS **THAT** TO HAPPEN, RIGHT?⟩
⟨N-NUH...⟩
⟨**GOOD** BOY. NOW GO AHEAD AN' **TAKE** IT...⟩
⟨...IT'S MY **GIFT** TO YOU--⟩

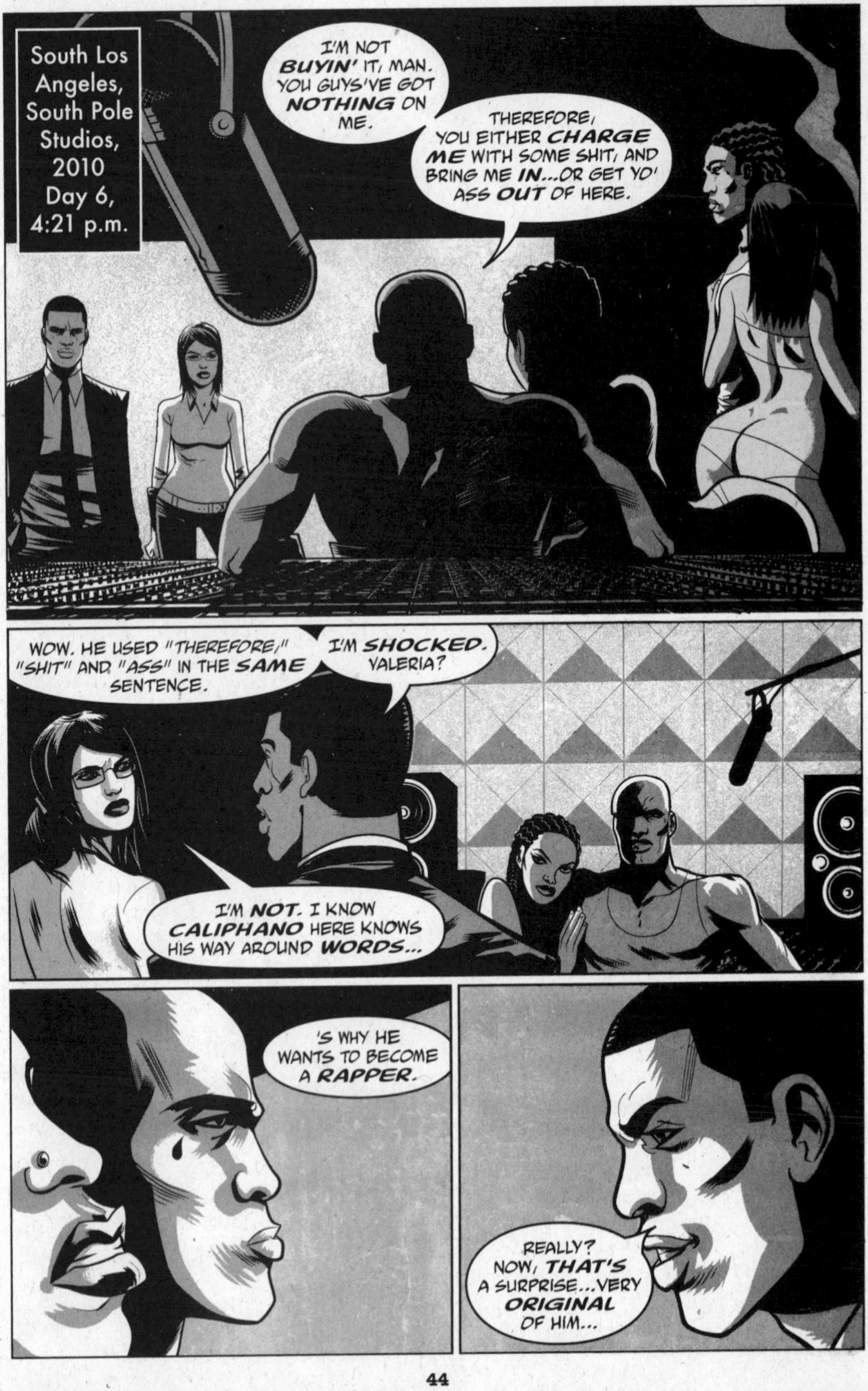
South Los Angeles, South Pole Studios, 2010 Day 6, 4:21 p.m.
I'M NOT BUYIN' IT, MAN. YOU GUYS'VE GOT NOTHING ON ME.
THEREFORE, YOU EITHER CHARGE ME WITH SOME SHIT, AND BRING ME IN...OR GET YO' ASS OUT OF HERE.
WOW. HE USED "THEREFORE," "SHIT" AND "ASS" IN THE SAME SENTENCE.
I'M SHOCKED. VALERIA?
I'M NOT. I KNOW CALIPHANO HERE KNOWS HIS WAY AROUND WORDS...
'S WHY HE WANTS TO BECOME A RAPPER.
REALLY? NOW, THAT'S A SURPRISE...VERY ORIGINAL OF HIM...

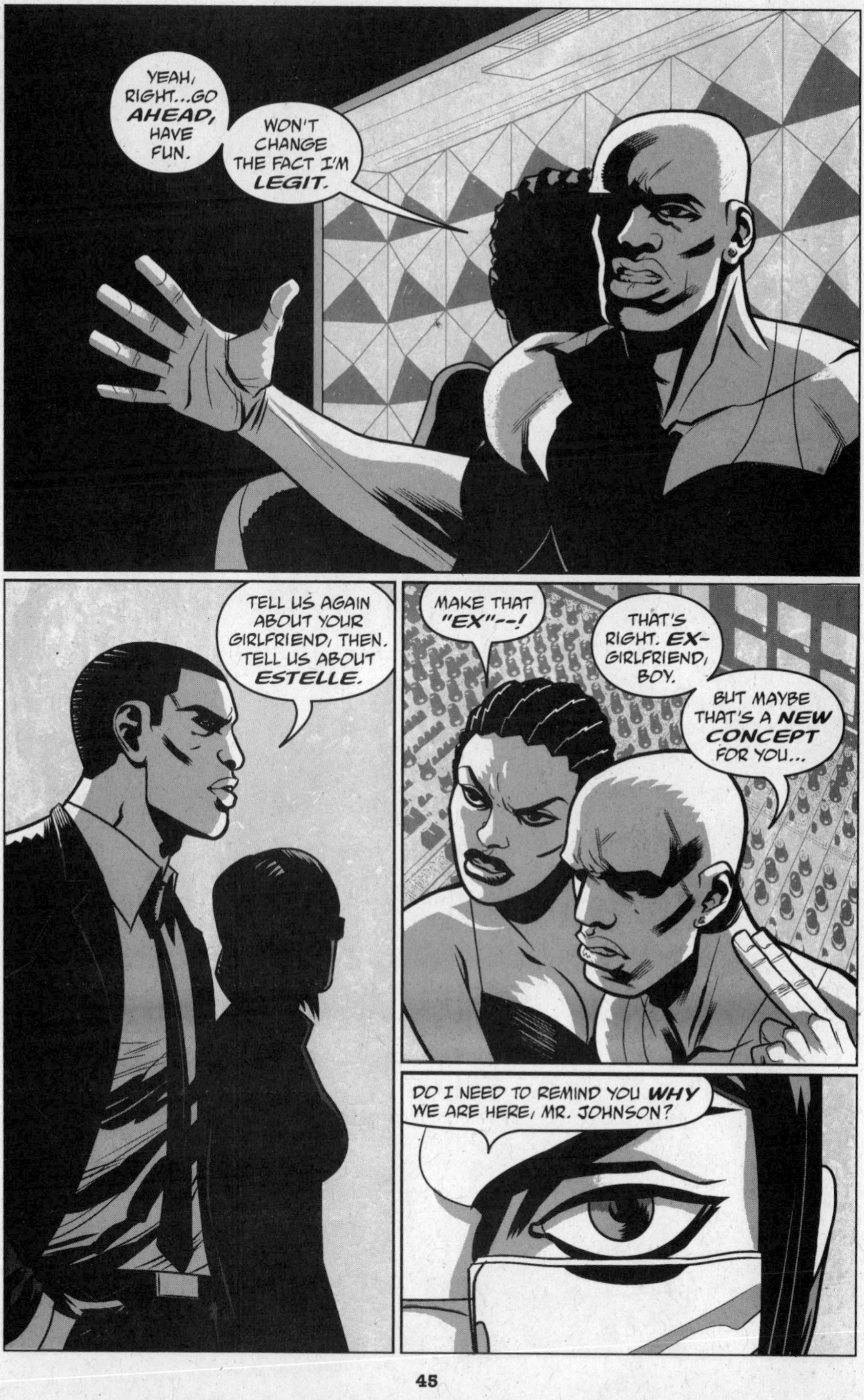
YEAH, RIGHT...GO AHEAD, HAVE FUN.
WON'T CHANGE THE FACT I'M LEGIT.
TELL US AGAIN ABOUT YOUR GIRLFRIEND, THEN. TELL US ABOUT ESTELLE.
MAKE THAT "EX"--!
THAT'S RIGHT. EX-GIRLFRIEND, BOY.
BUT MAYBE THAT'S A NEW CONCEPT FOR YOU...
DO I NEED TO REMIND YOU WHY WE ARE HERE, MR. JOHNSON?

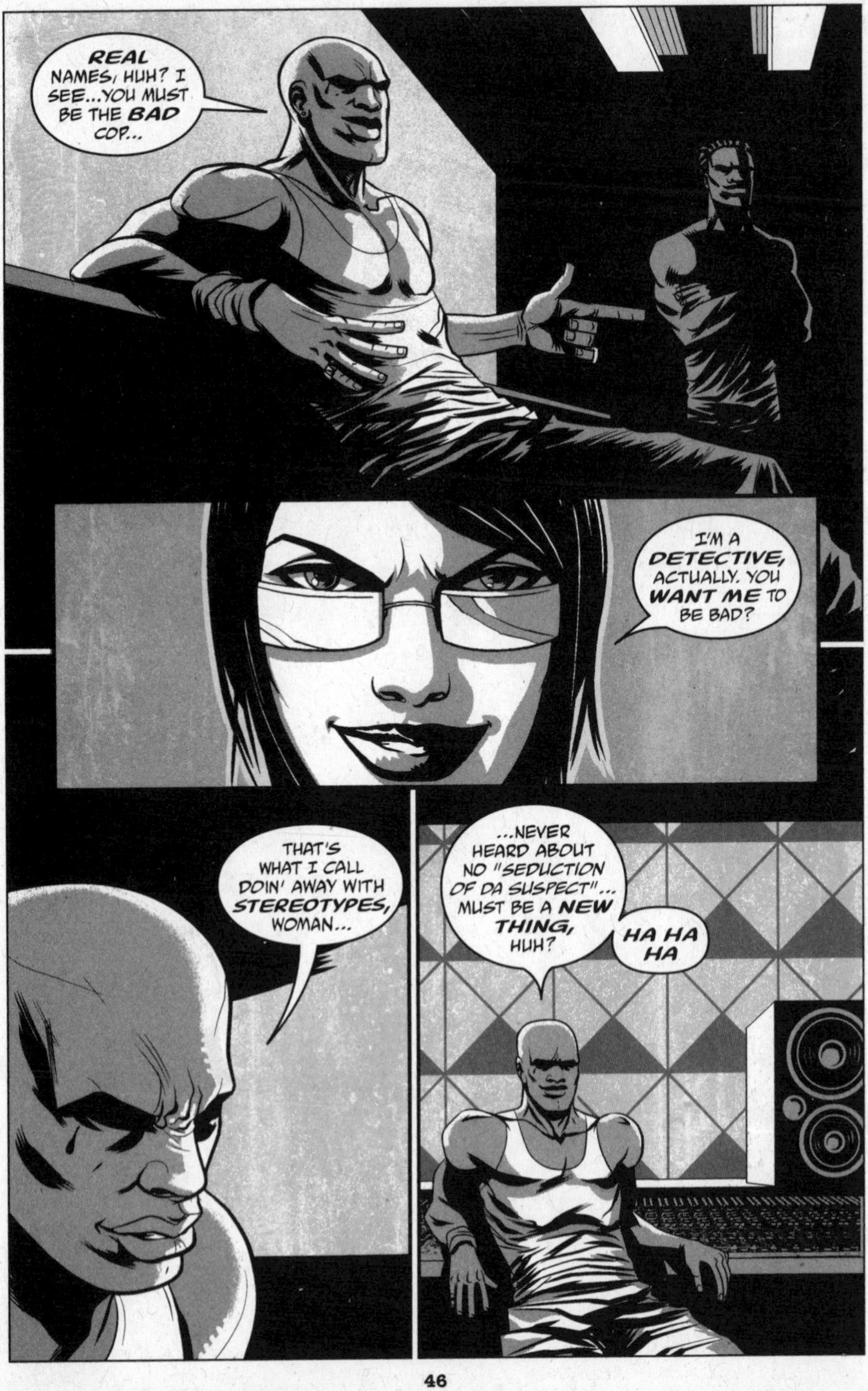
REAL NAMES, HUH? I SEE...YOU MUST BE THE BAD COP...
I'M A DETECTIVE, ACTUALLY. YOU WANT ME TO BE BAD?
THAT'S WHAT I CALL DOIN' AWAY WITH STEREOTYPES, WOMAN...
...NEVER HEARD ABOUT NO "SEDUCTION OF DA SUSPECT"... MUST BE A NEW THING, HUH?
HA HA HA

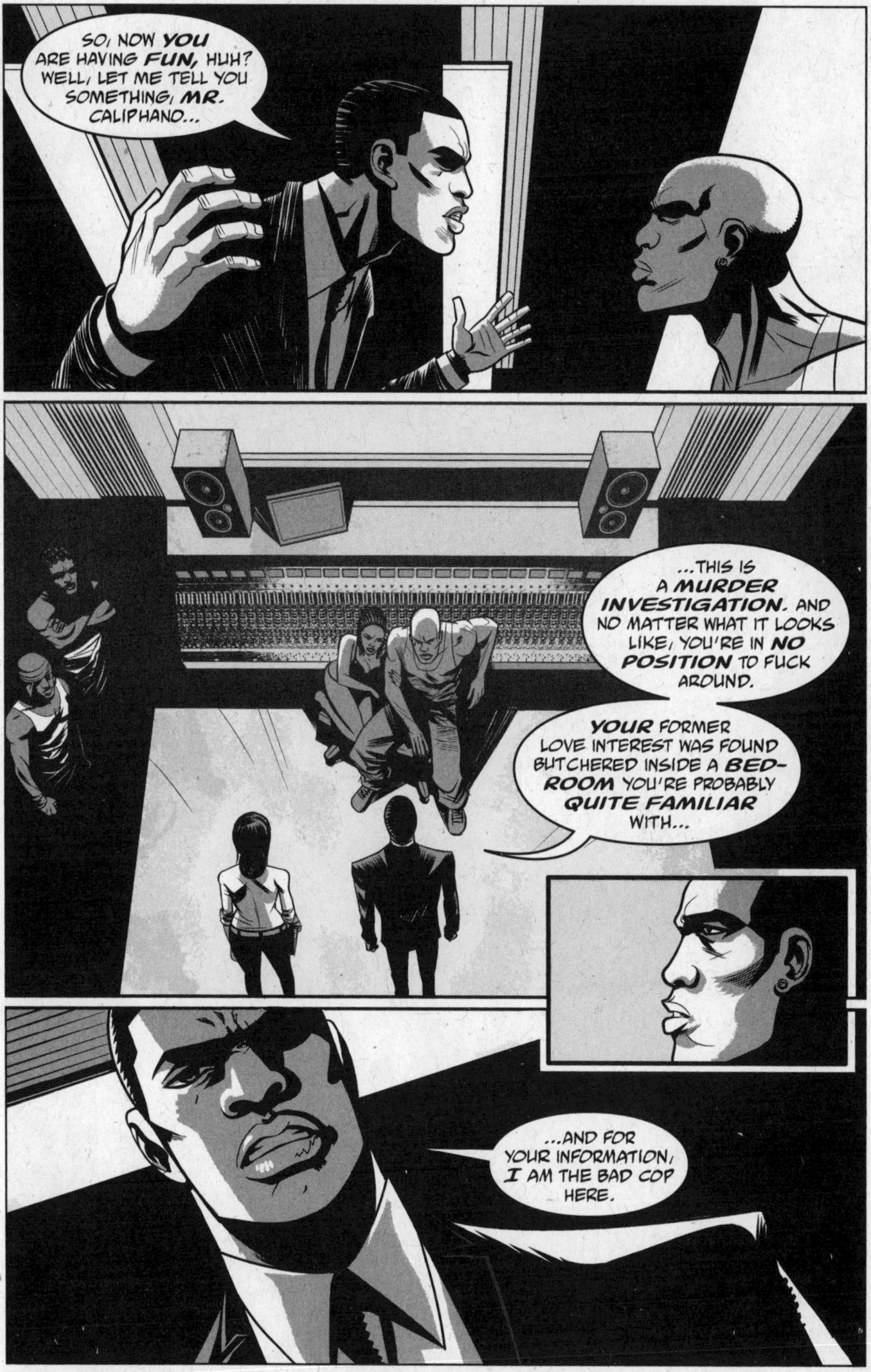
SO, NOW YOU ARE HAVING FUN, HUH? WELL, LET ME TELL YOU SOMETHING, MR. CALIPHANO...
...THIS IS A MURDER INVESTIGATION. AND NO MATTER WHAT IT LOOKS LIKE, YOU'RE IN NO POSITION TO FUCK AROUND.
YOUR FORMER LOVE INTEREST WAS FOUND BUTCHERED INSIDE A BED-ROOM YOU'RE PROBABLY QUITE FAMILIAR WITH...
...AND FOR YOUR INFORMATION, I AM THE BAD COP HERE.

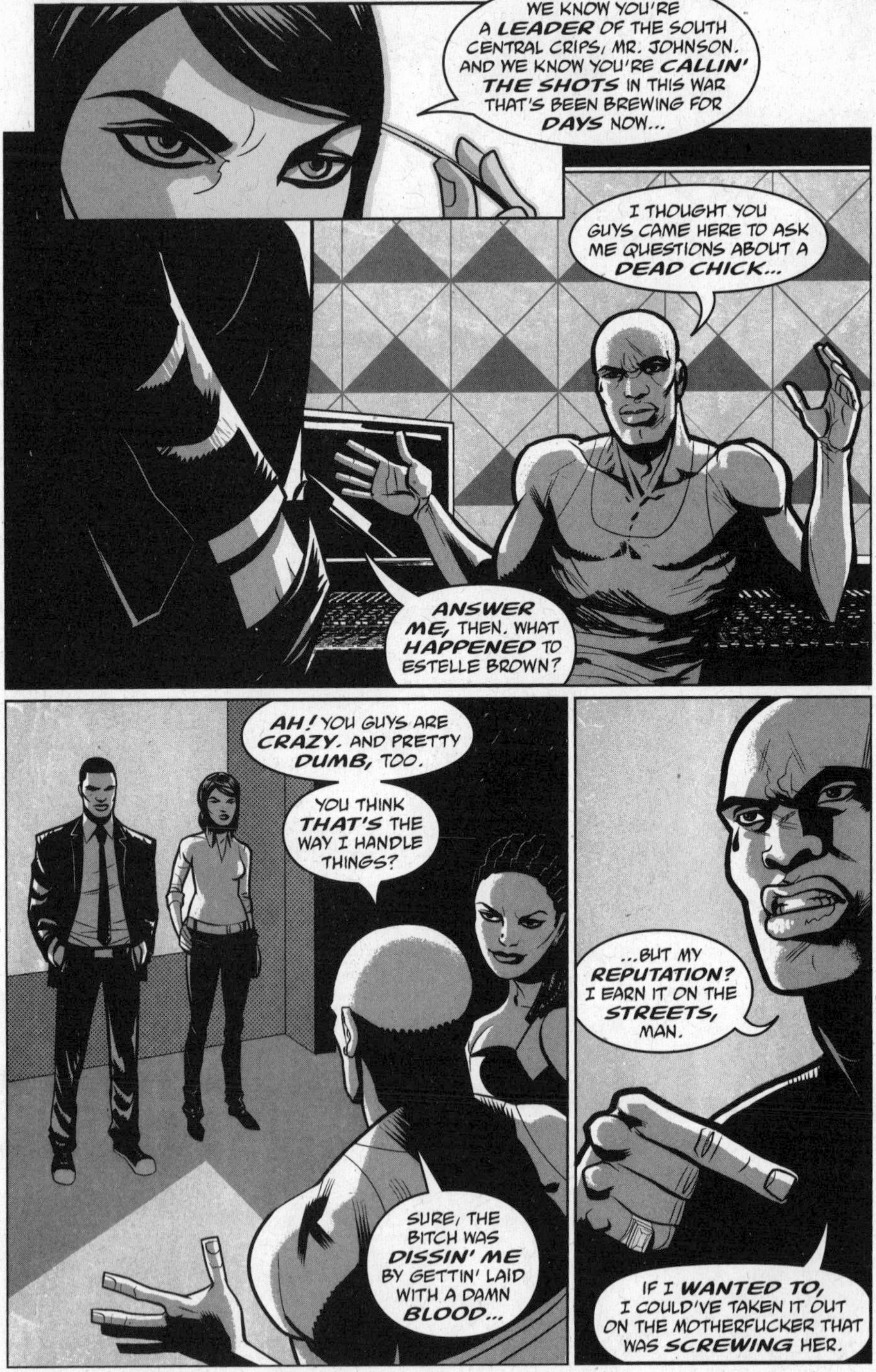
WE KNOW YOU'RE A LEADER OF THE SOUTH CENTRAL CRIPS, MR. JOHNSON. AND WE KNOW YOU'RE CALLIN' THE SHOTS IN THIS WAR THAT'S BEEN BREWING FOR DAYS NOW...
I THOUGHT YOU GUYS CAME HERE TO ASK ME QUESTIONS ABOUT A DEAD CHICK...
ANSWER ME, THEN. WHAT HAPPENED TO ESTELLE BROWN?
AH! YOU GUYS ARE CRAZY. AND PRETTY DUMB, TOO.
YOU THINK THAT'S THE WAY I HANDLE THINGS?
SURE, THE BITCH WAS DISSIN' ME BY GETTIN' LAID WITH A DAMN BLOOD...
...BUT MY REPUTATION? I EARN IT ON THE STREETS, MAN.
IF I WANTED TO, I COULD'VE TAKEN IT OUT ON THE MOTHERFUCKER THAT WAS SCREWING HER.

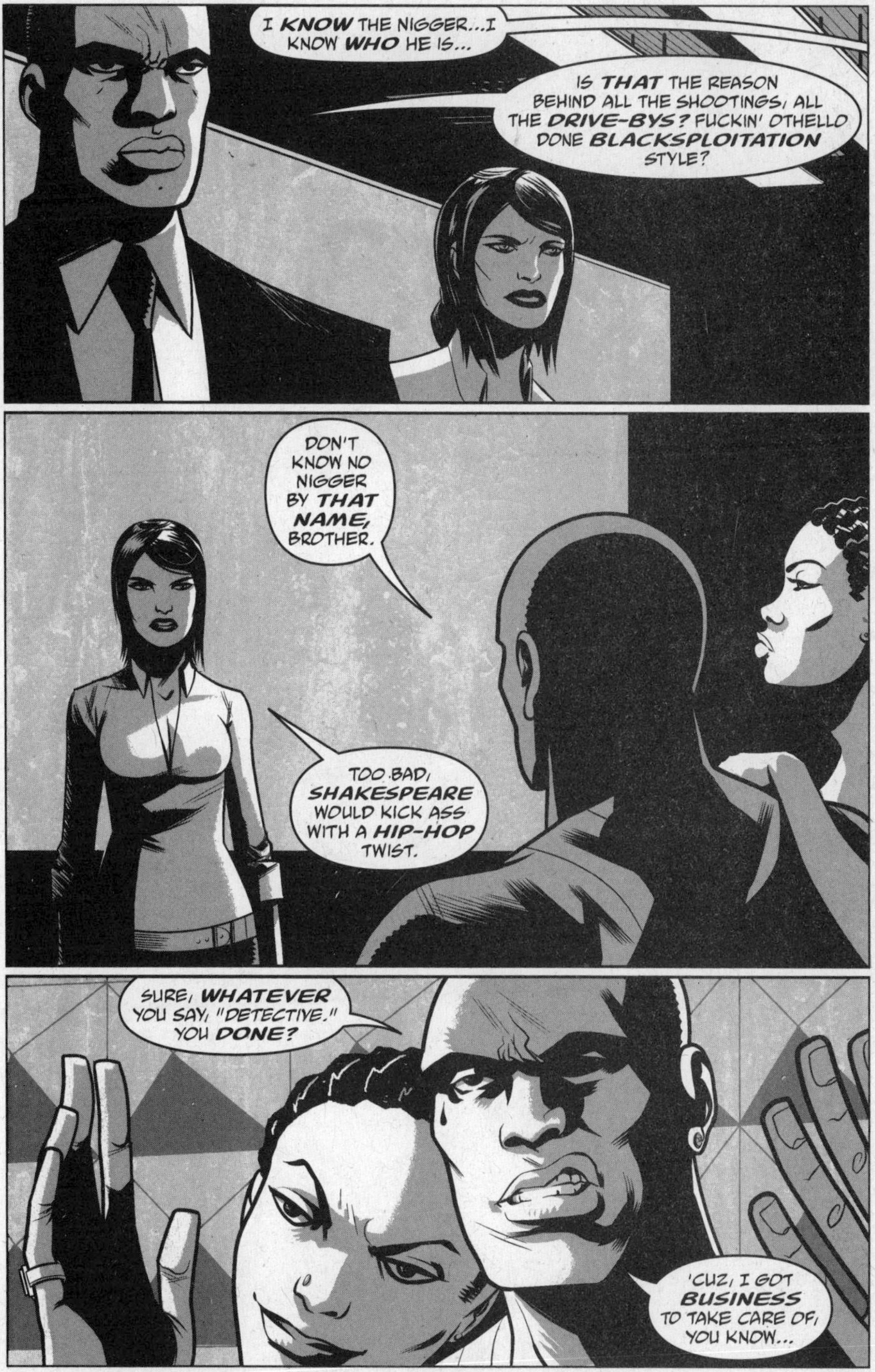
I KNOW THE NIGGER...I KNOW WHO HE IS...
IS THAT THE REASON BEHIND ALL THE SHOOTINGS, ALL THE DRIVE-BYS? FUCKIN' OTHELLO DONE BLACKSPLOITATION STYLE?
DON'T KNOW NO NIGGER BY THAT NAME, BROTHER.
TOO BAD, SHAKESPEARE WOULD KICK ASS WITH A HIP-HOP TWIST.
SURE, WHATEVER YOU SAY, "DETECTIVE." YOU DONE?
'CUZ, I GOT BUSINESS TO TAKE CARE OF, YOU KNOW...

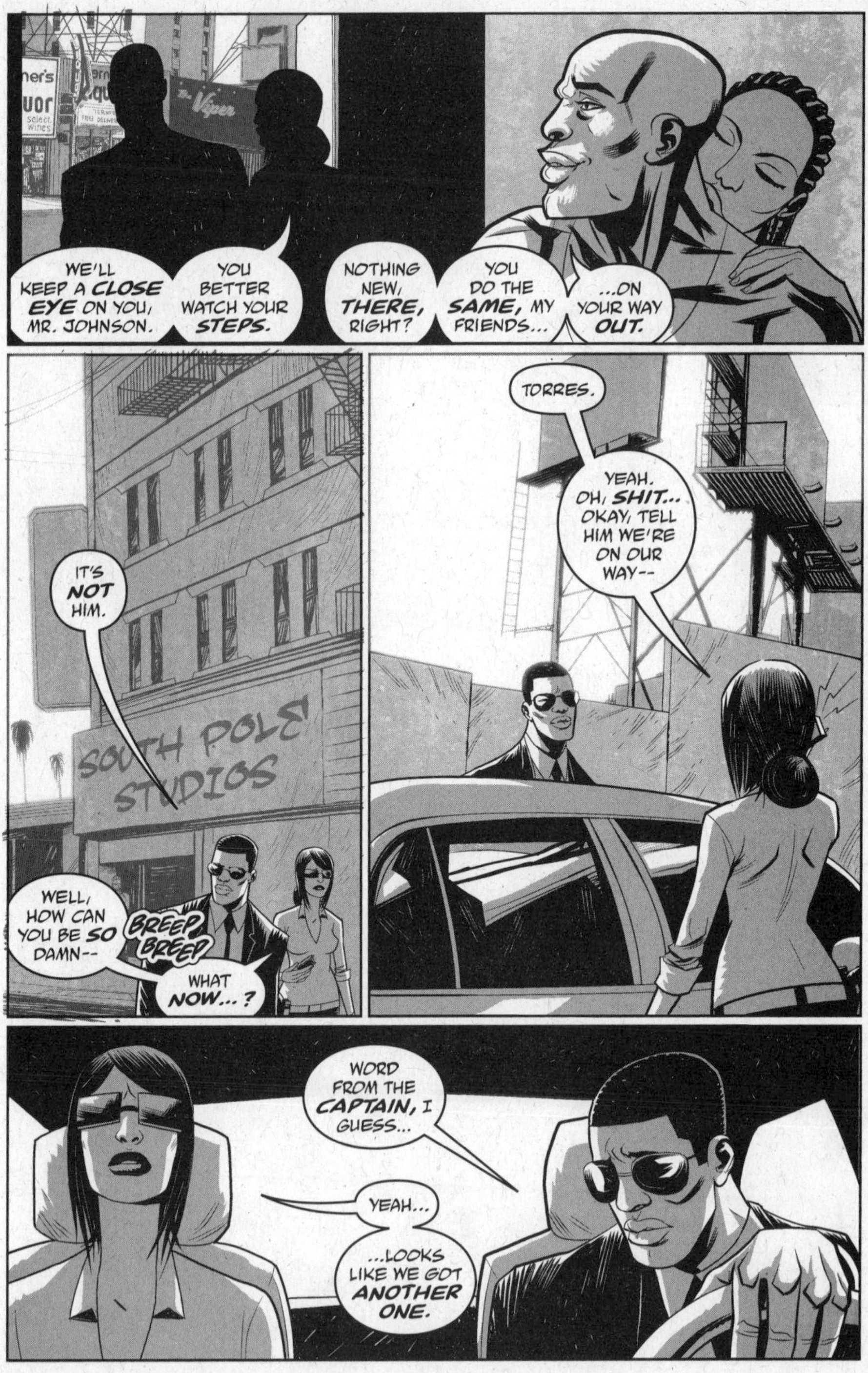

WE'LL KEEP A CLOSE EYE ON YOU, MR. JOHNSON.
YOU BETTER WATCH YOUR STEPS.
NOTHING NEW, THERE, RIGHT?
YOU DO THE SAME, MY FRIENDS...
...ON YOUR WAY OUT.
SOUTH POLE STUDIOS
IT'S NOT HIM.
WELL, HOW CAN YOU BE SO DAMN--
BREEP BREEP
WHAT NOW...?
TORRES.
YEAH. OH, SHIT... OKAY, TELL HIM WE'RE ON OUR WAY--
WORD FROM THE CAPTAIN, I GUESS...
YEAH...
...LOOKS LIKE WE GOT ANOTHER ONE.

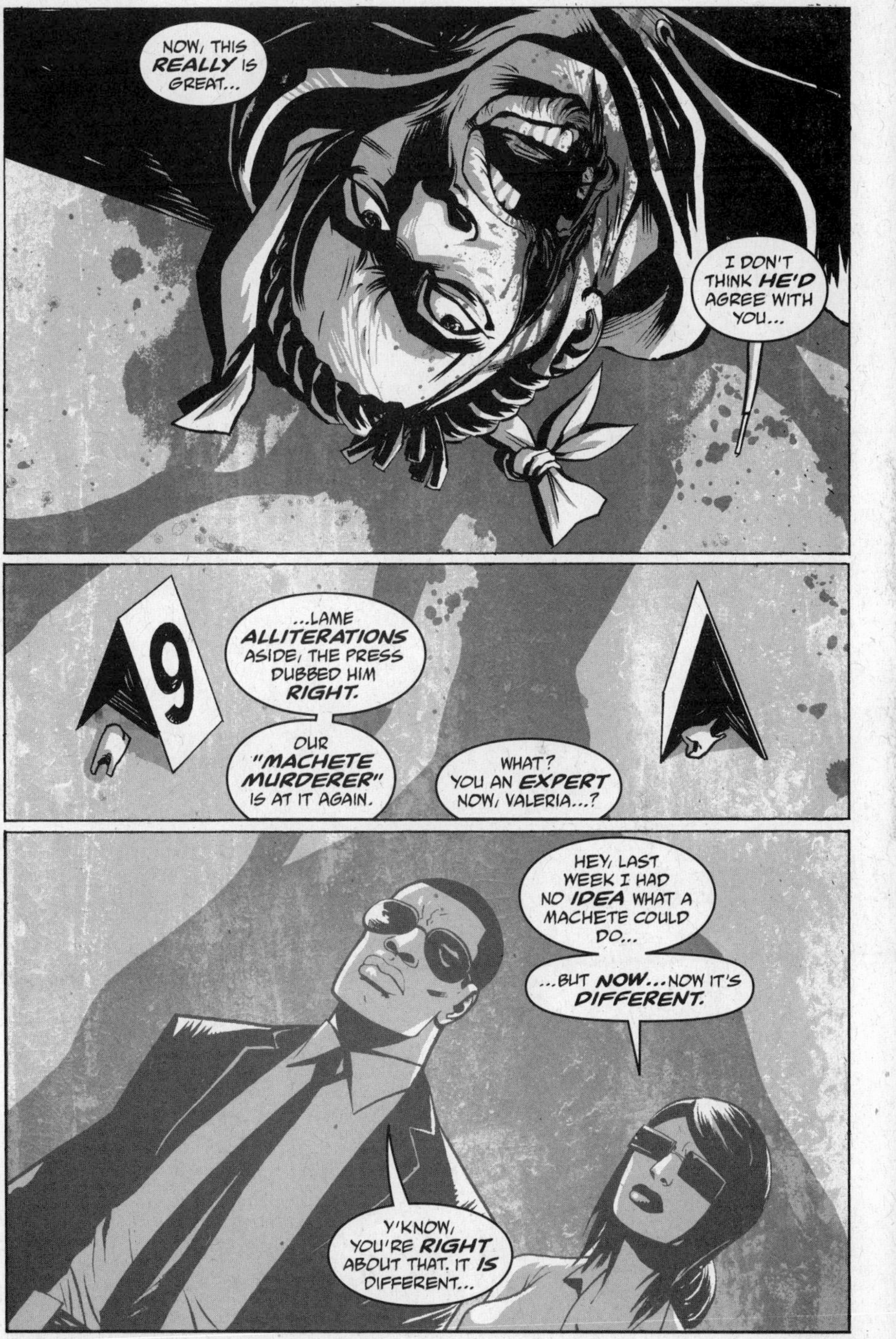
NOW, THIS REALLY IS GREAT...
I DON'T THINK HE'D AGREE WITH YOU...
...LAME ALLITERATIONS ASIDE, THE PRESS DUBBED HIM RIGHT.
OUR "MACHETE MURDERER" IS AT IT AGAIN.
WHAT? YOU AN EXPERT NOW, VALERIA...?
HEY, LAST WEEK I HAD NO IDEA WHAT A MACHETE COULD DO...
...BUT NOW...NOW IT'S DIFFERENT.
Y'KNOW, YOU'RE RIGHT ABOUT THAT. IT IS DIFFERENT...

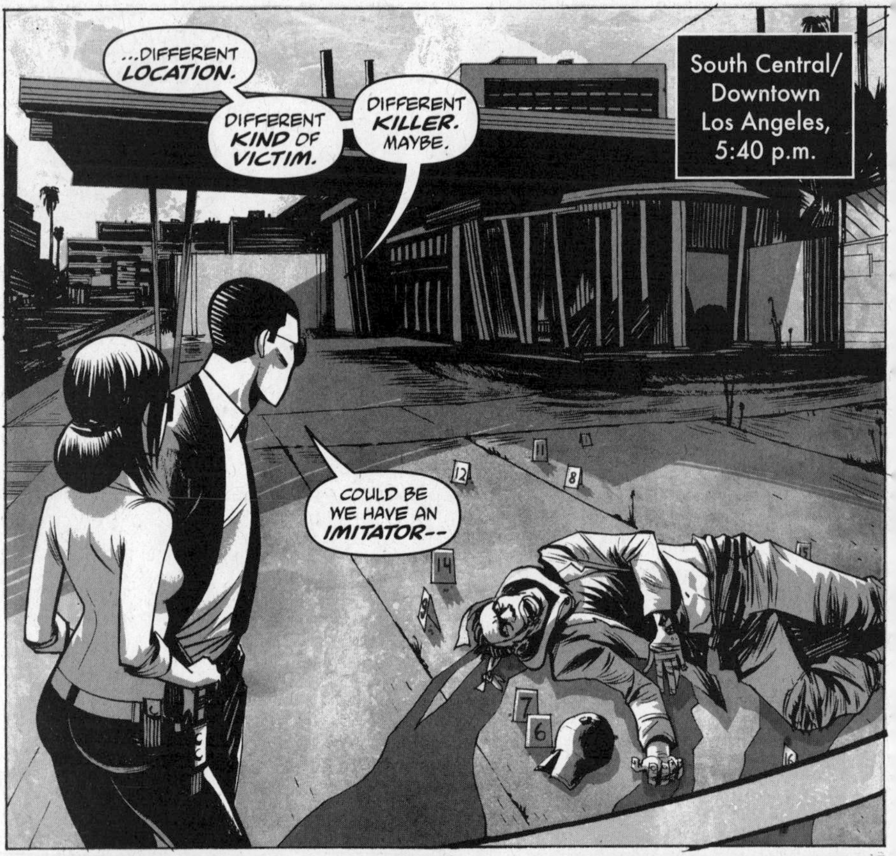
South Central/ Downtown Los Angeles, 5:40 p.m.
...DIFFERENT LOCATION.
DIFFERENT KIND OF VICTIM.
DIFFERENT KILLER. MAYBE.
COULD BE WE HAVE AN IMITATOR--

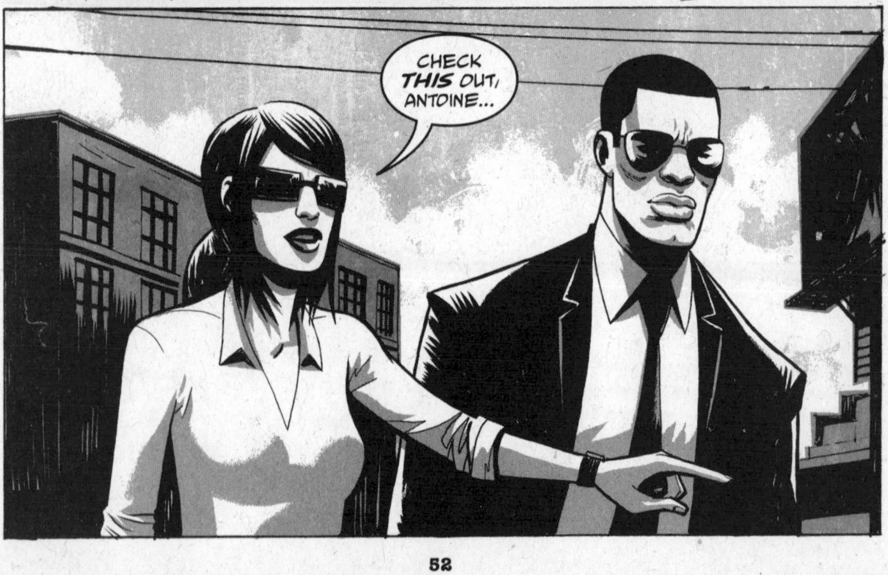
CHECK THIS OUT, ANTOINE...

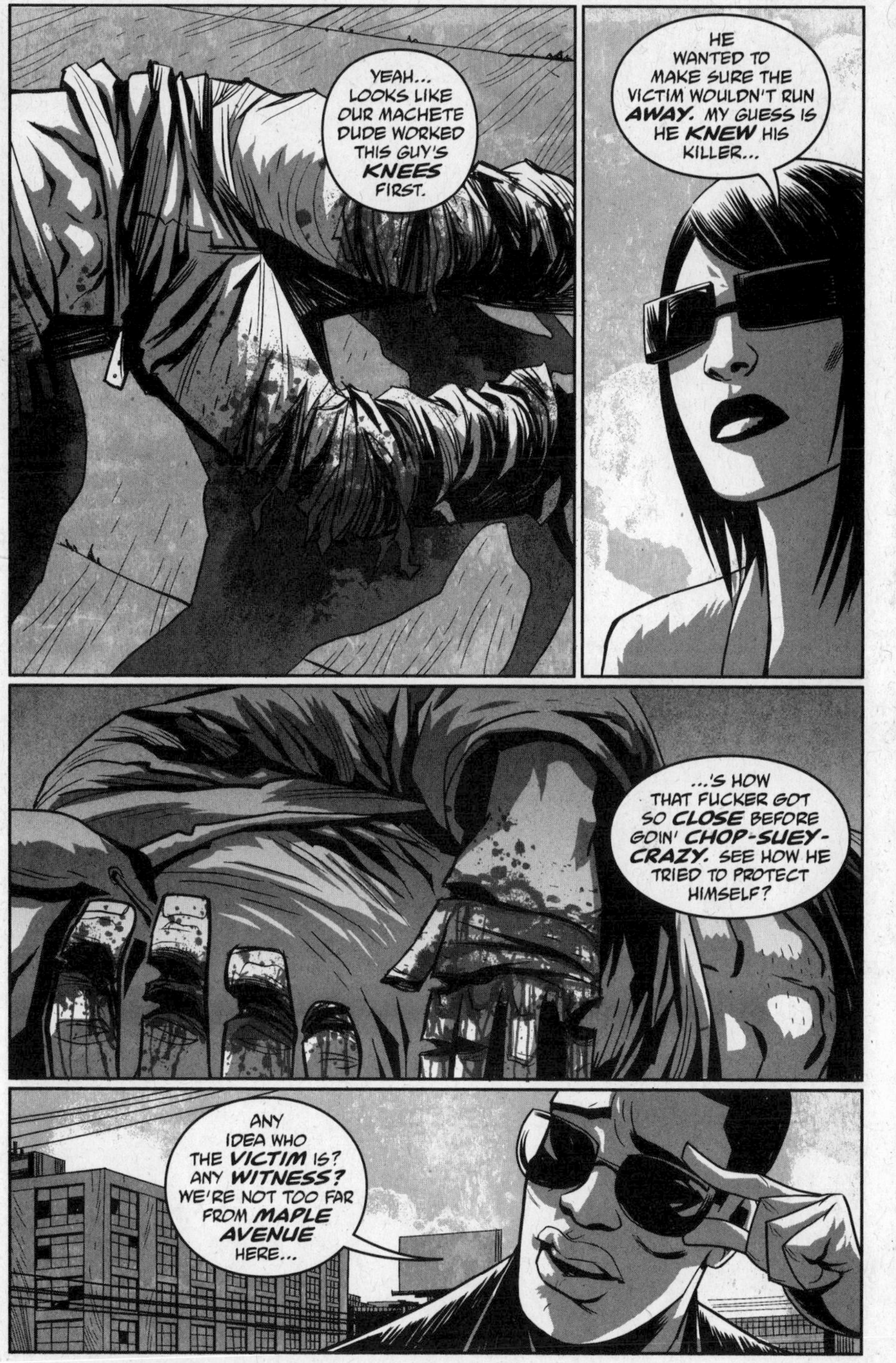
YEAH... LOOKS LIKE OUR MACHETE DUDE WORKED THIS GUY'S KNEES FIRST.
HE WANTED TO MAKE SURE THE VICTIM WOULDN'T RUN AWAY. MY GUESS IS HE KNEW HIS KILLER...
...'S HOW THAT FUCKER GOT SO CLOSE BEFORE GOIN' CHOP-SUEY-CRAZY. SEE HOW HE TRIED TO PROTECT HIMSELF?
ANY IDEA WHO THE VICTIM IS? ANY WITNESS? WE'RE NOT TOO FAR FROM MAPLE AVENUE HERE...

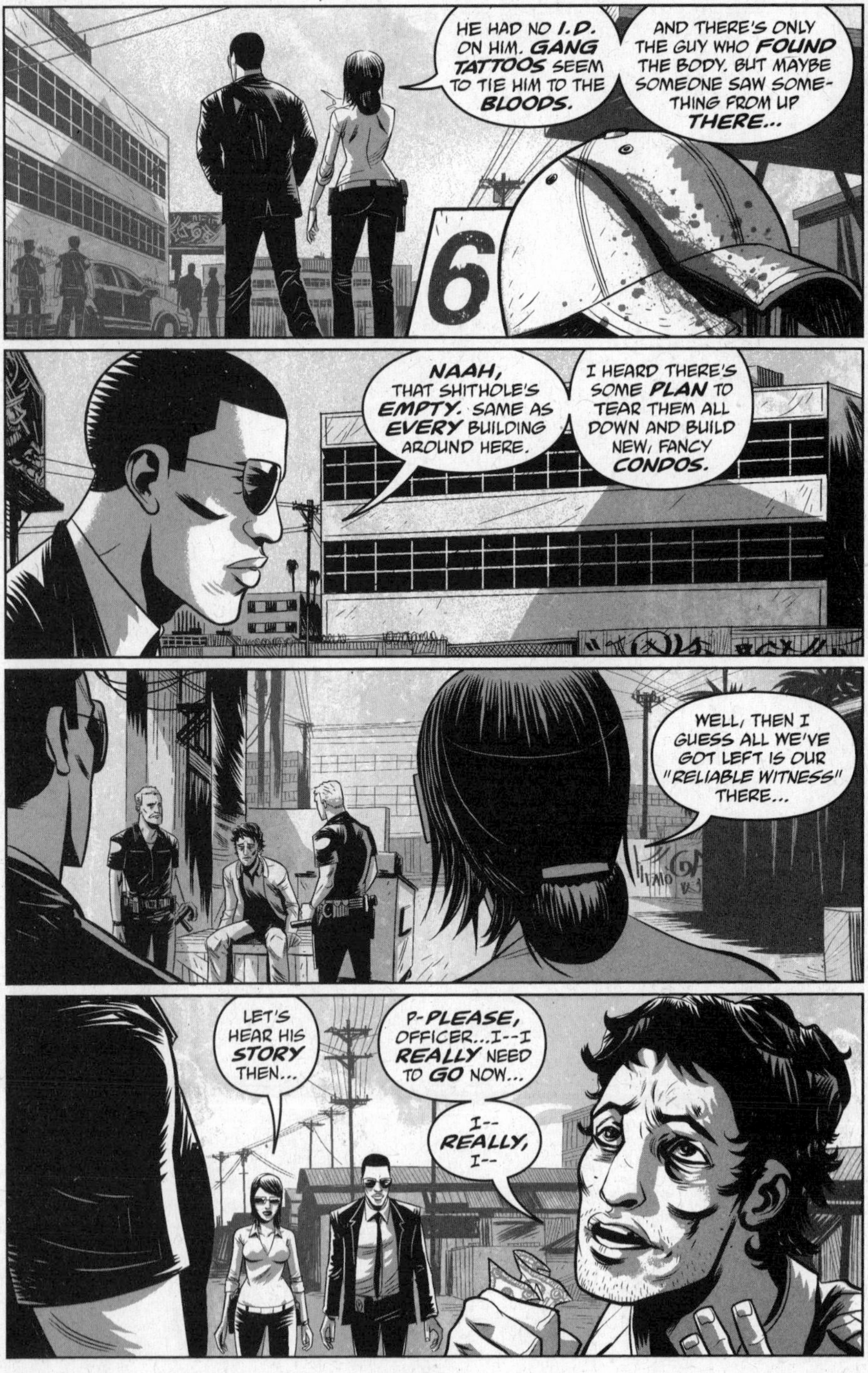
HE HAD NO I.D. ON HIM. GANG TATTOOS SEEM TO TIE HIM TO THE BLOODS.
AND THERE'S ONLY THE GUY WHO FOUND THE BODY. BUT MAYBE SOMEONE SAW SOME-THING FROM UP THERE...
6
NAAH, THAT SHITHOLE'S EMPTY. SAME AS EVERY BUILDING AROUND HERE.
I HEARD THERE'S SOME PLAN TO TEAR THEM ALL DOWN AND BUILD NEW, FANCY CONDOS.
WELL, THEN I GUESS ALL WE'VE GOT LEFT IS OUR "RELIABLE WITNESS" THERE...
LET'S HEAR HIS STORY THEN...
P-PLEASE, OFFICER...I--I REALLY NEED TO GO NOW...
I-- REALLY, I--

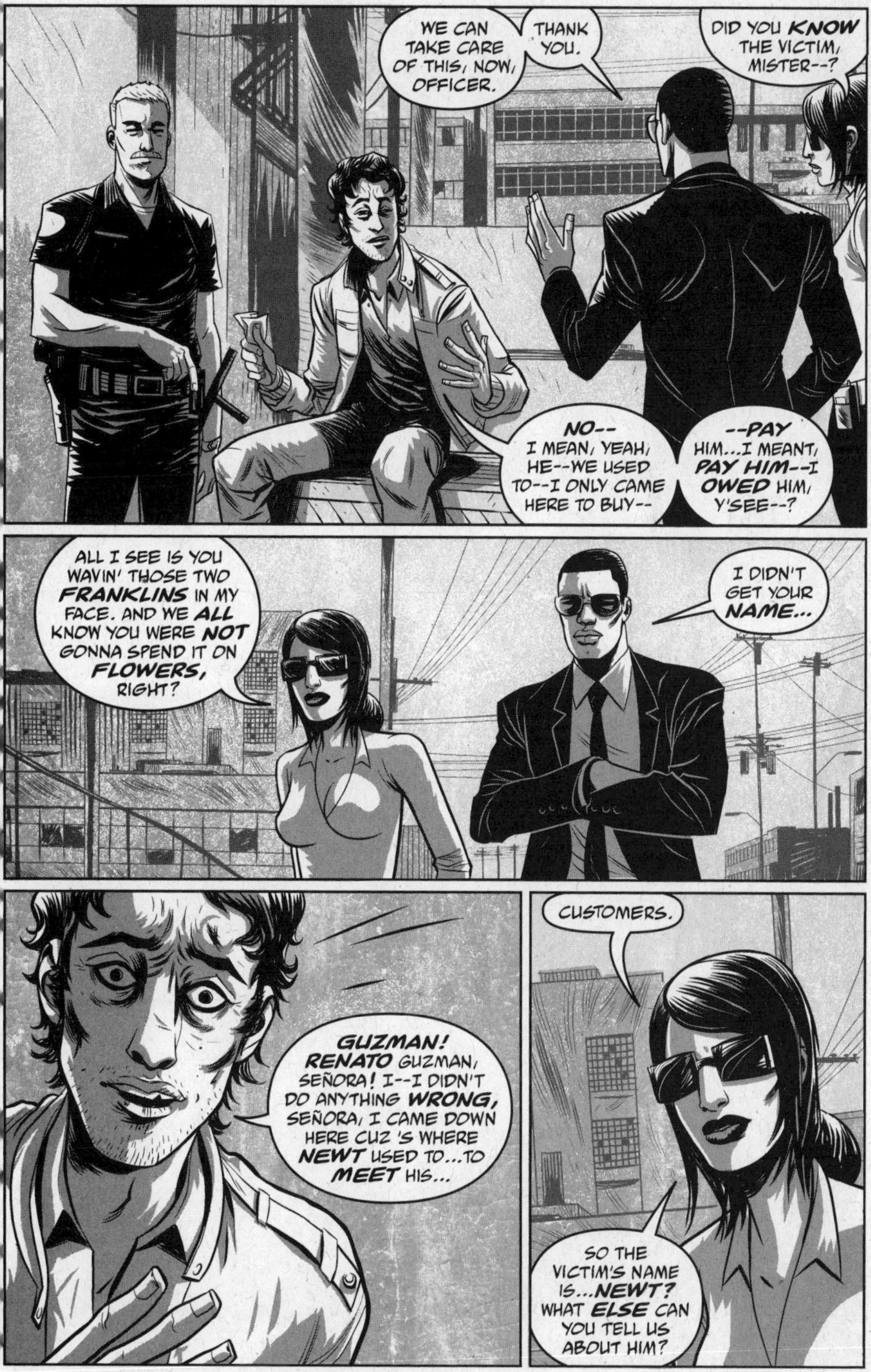
WE CAN TAKE CARE OF THIS, NOW, OFFICER.
THANK YOU.
DID YOU KNOW THE VICTIM, MISTER--?
NO-- I MEAN, YEAH, HE--WE USED TO--I ONLY CAME HERE TO BUY--
--PAY HIM...I MEANT, PAY HIM--I OWED HIM, Y'SEE--?
ALL I SEE IS YOU WAVIN' THOSE TWO FRANKLINS IN MY FACE. AND WE ALL KNOW YOU WERE NOT GONNA SPEND IT ON FLOWERS, RIGHT?
I DIDN'T GET YOUR NAME...
GUZMAN! RENATO GUZMAN, SEÑORA! I--I DIDN'T DO ANYTHING WRONG, SEÑORA, I CAME DOWN HERE CUZ 'S WHERE NEWT USED TO...TO MEET HIS...
CUSTOMERS.
SO THE VICTIM'S NAME IS...NEWT? WHAT ELSE CAN YOU TELL US ABOUT HIM?

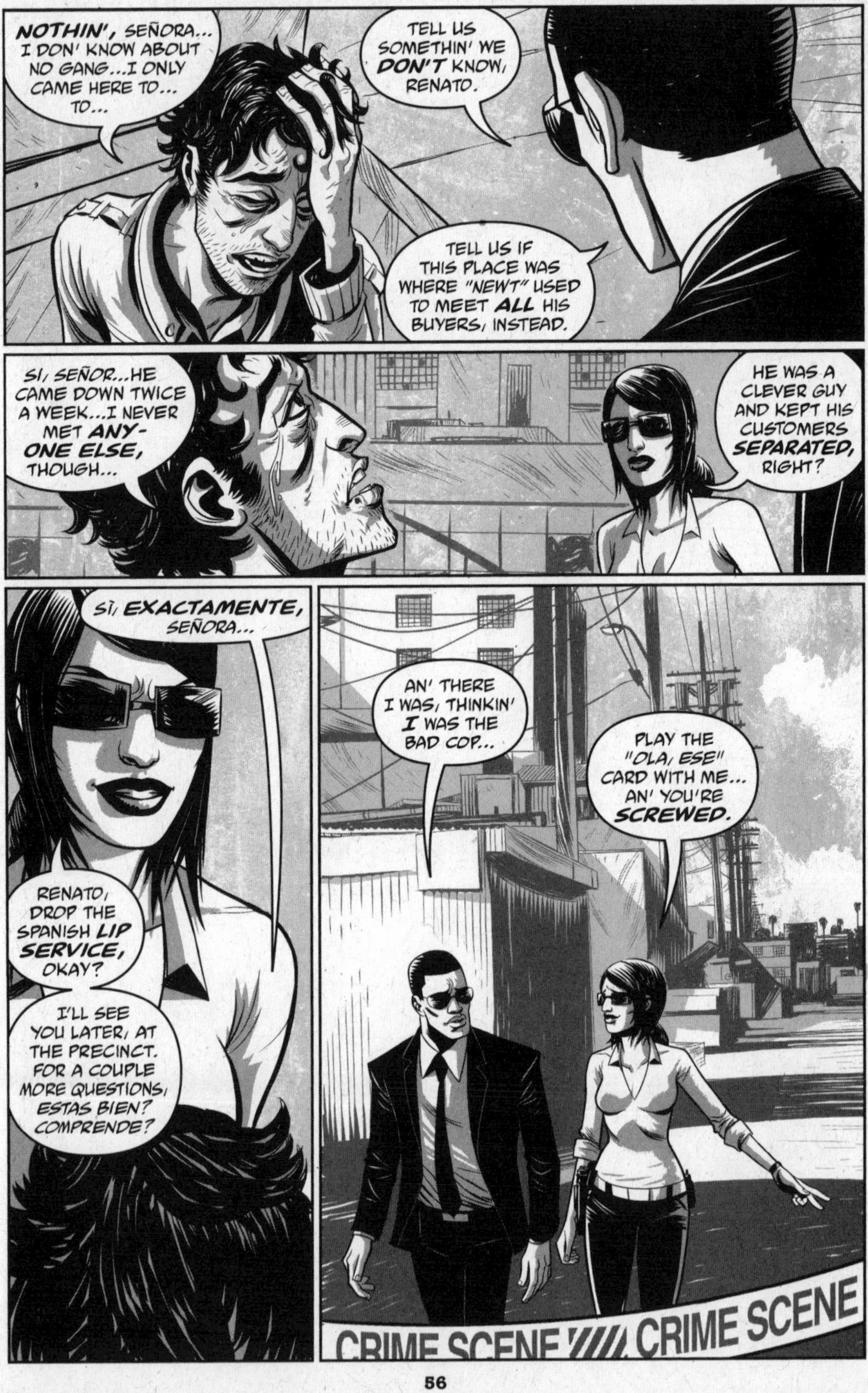
NOTHIN', SEÑORA... I DON' KNOW ABOUT NO GANG...I ONLY CAME HERE TO... TO...
TELL US SOMETHIN' WE DON'T KNOW, RENATO.
TELL US IF THIS PLACE WAS WHERE "NEWT" USED TO MEET ALL HIS BUYERS, INSTEAD.
SI, SEÑOR...HE CAME DOWN TWICE A WEEK...I NEVER MET ANY-ONE ELSE, THOUGH...
HE WAS A CLEVER GUY AND KEPT HIS CUSTOMERS SEPARATED, RIGHT?
SÌ, EXACTAMENTE, SEÑORA...
RENATO, DROP THE SPANISH LIP SERVICE, OKAY?
I'LL SEE YOU LATER, AT THE PRECINCT. FOR A COUPLE MORE QUESTIONS, ESTAS BIEN? COMPRENDE?
AN' THERE I WAS, THINKIN' I WAS THE BAD COP...
PLAY THE "OLA, ESE" CARD WITH ME... AN' YOU'RE SCREWED.
CRIME SCENE
CRIME SCENE

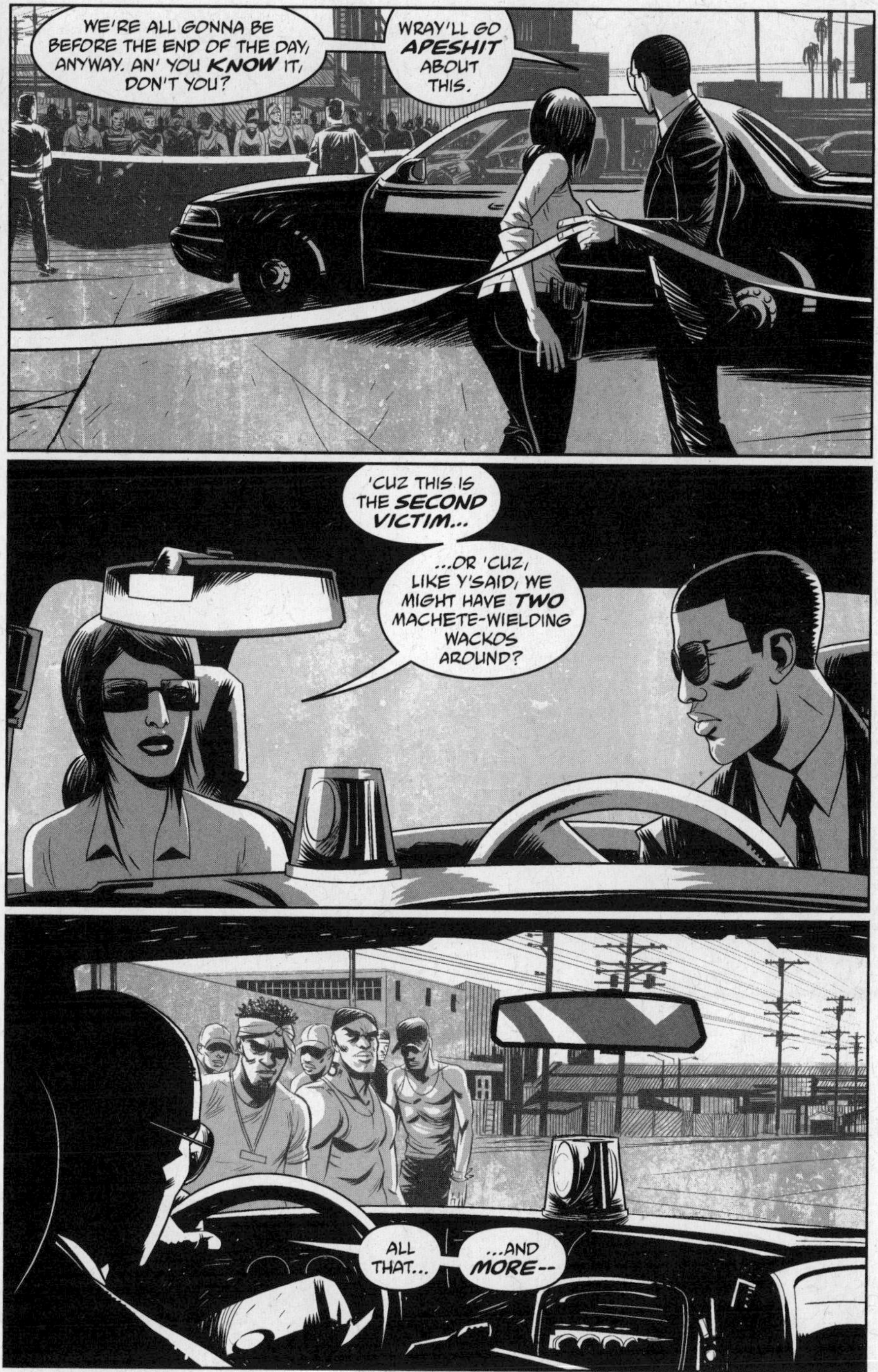
WE'RE ALL GONNA BE BEFORE THE END OF THE DAY, ANYWAY. AN' YOU KNOW IT, DON'T YOU?
WRAY'LL GO APESHIT ABOUT THIS.
'CUZ THIS IS THE SECOND VICTIM...
...OR 'CUZ, LIKE Y'SAID, WE MIGHT HAVE TWO MACHETE-WIELDING WACKOS AROUND?
ALL THAT...
...AND MORE--

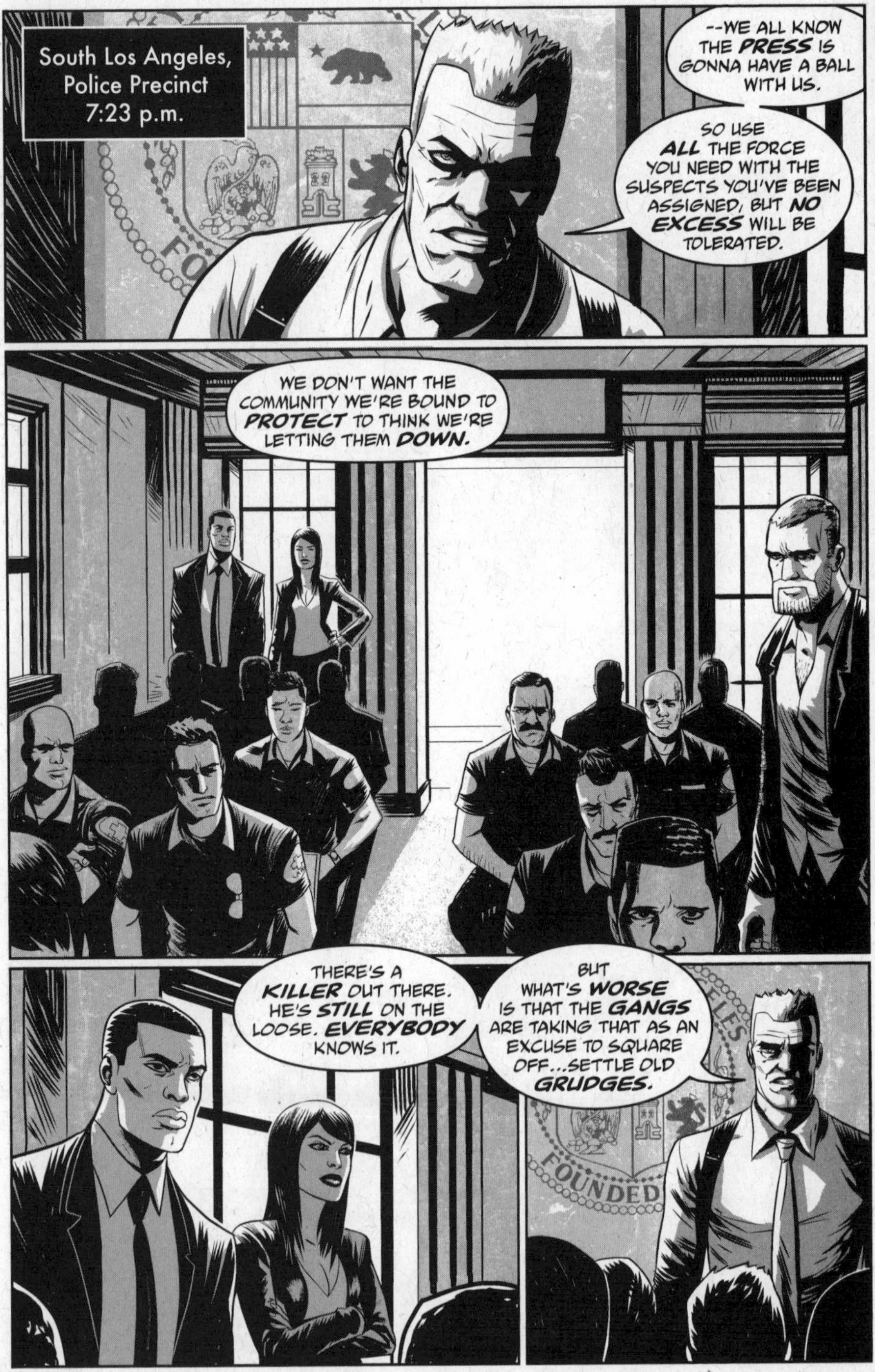
South Los Angeles,
Police Precinct
7:23 p.m.
--WE ALL KNOW THE PRESS IS GONNA HAVE A BALL WITH US.
SO USE ALL THE FORCE YOU NEED WITH THE SUSPECTS YOU'VE BEEN ASSIGNED, BUT NO EXCESS WILL BE TOLERATED.
WE DON'T WANT THE COMMUNITY WE'RE BOUND TO PROTECT TO THINK WE'RE LETTING THEM DOWN.
THERE'S A KILLER OUT THERE. HE'S STILL ON THE LOOSE. EVERYBODY KNOWS IT.
BUT WHAT'S WORSE IS THAT THE GANGS ARE TAKING THAT AS AN EXCUSE TO SQUARE OFF...SETTLE OLD GRUDGES.
FOUNDED

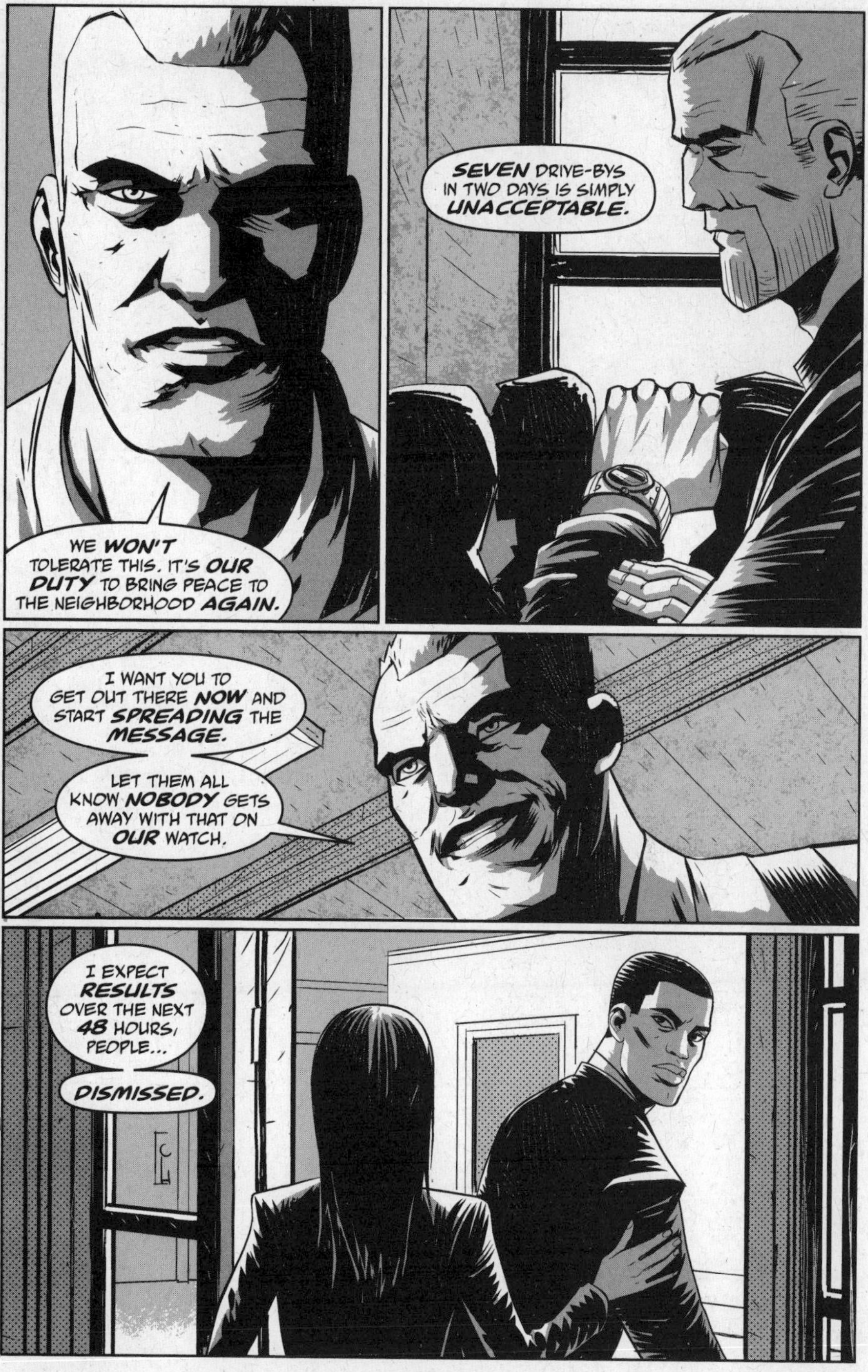
WE WON'T TOLERATE THIS. IT'S OUR DUTY TO BRING PEACE TO THE NEIGHBORHOOD AGAIN.
SEVEN DRIVE-BYS IN TWO DAYS IS SIMPLY UNACCEPTABLE.
I WANT YOU TO GET OUT THERE NOW AND START SPREADING THE MESSAGE.
LET THEM ALL KNOW NOBODY GETS AWAY WITH THAT ON OUR WATCH.
I EXPECT RESULTS OVER THE NEXT 48 HOURS, PEOPLE...
DISMISSED.

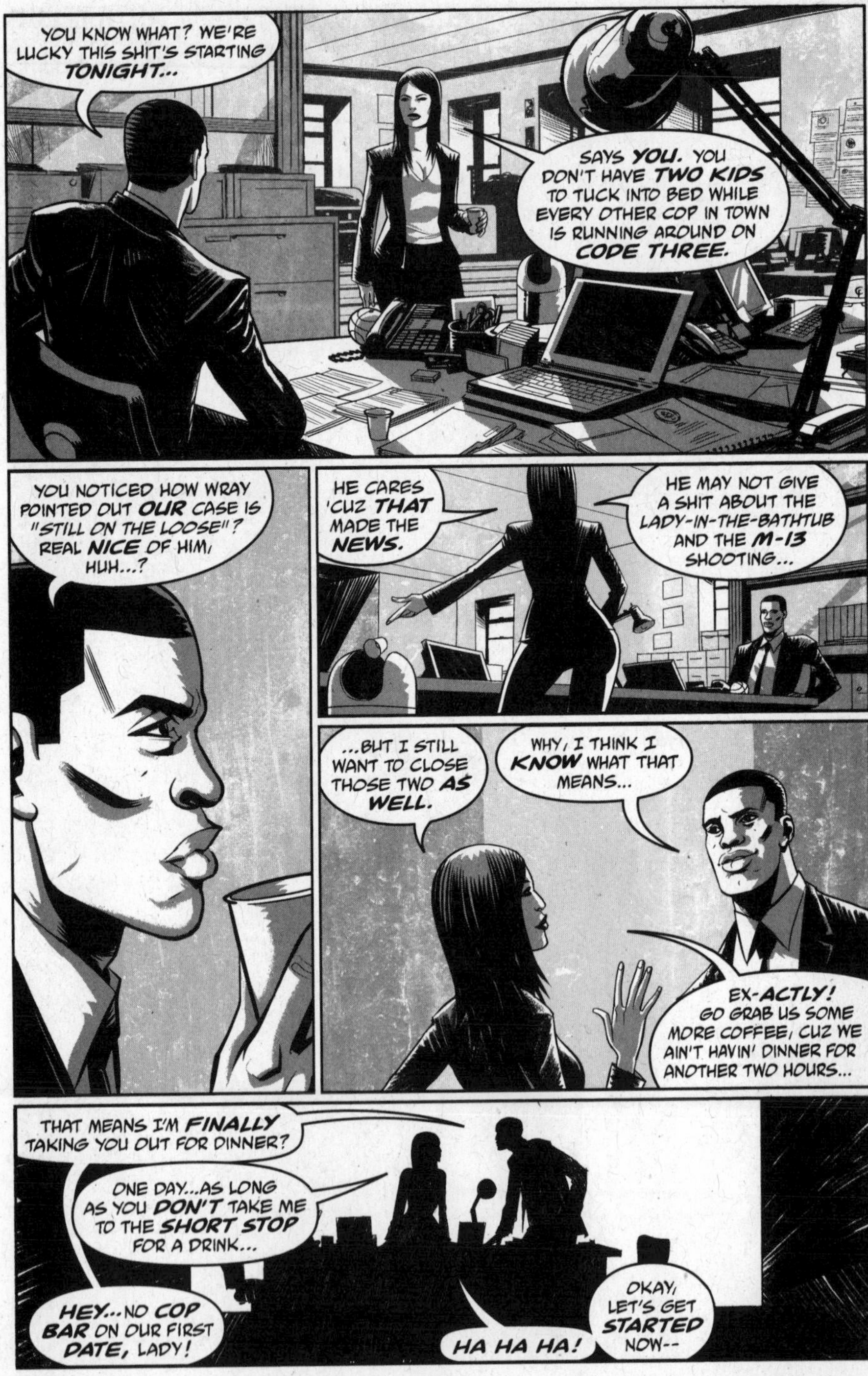

YOU KNOW WHAT? WE'RE LUCKY THIS SHIT'S STARTING TONIGHT...
SAYS YOU. YOU DON'T HAVE TWO KIDS TO TUCK INTO BED WHILE EVERY OTHER COP IN TOWN IS RUNNING AROUND ON CODE THREE.
YOU NOTICED HOW WRAY POINTED OUT OUR CASE IS "STILL ON THE LOOSE"? REAL NICE OF HIM, HUH...?
HE CARES 'CUZ THAT MADE THE NEWS.
HE MAY NOT GIVE A SHIT ABOUT THE LADY-IN-THE-BATHTUB AND THE M-13 SHOOTING...
...BUT I STILL WANT TO CLOSE THOSE TWO AS WELL.
WHY, I THINK I KNOW WHAT THAT MEANS...
EX-ACTLY! GO GRAB US SOME MORE COFFEE, CUZ WE AIN'T HAVIN' DINNER FOR ANOTHER TWO HOURS...
THAT MEANS I'M FINALLY TAKING YOU OUT FOR DINNER?
ONE DAY...AS LONG AS YOU DON'T TAKE ME TO THE SHORT STOP FOR A DRINK...
HEY...NO COP BAR ON OUR FIRST DATE, LADY!
HA HA HA!
OKAY, LET'S GET STARTED NOW--

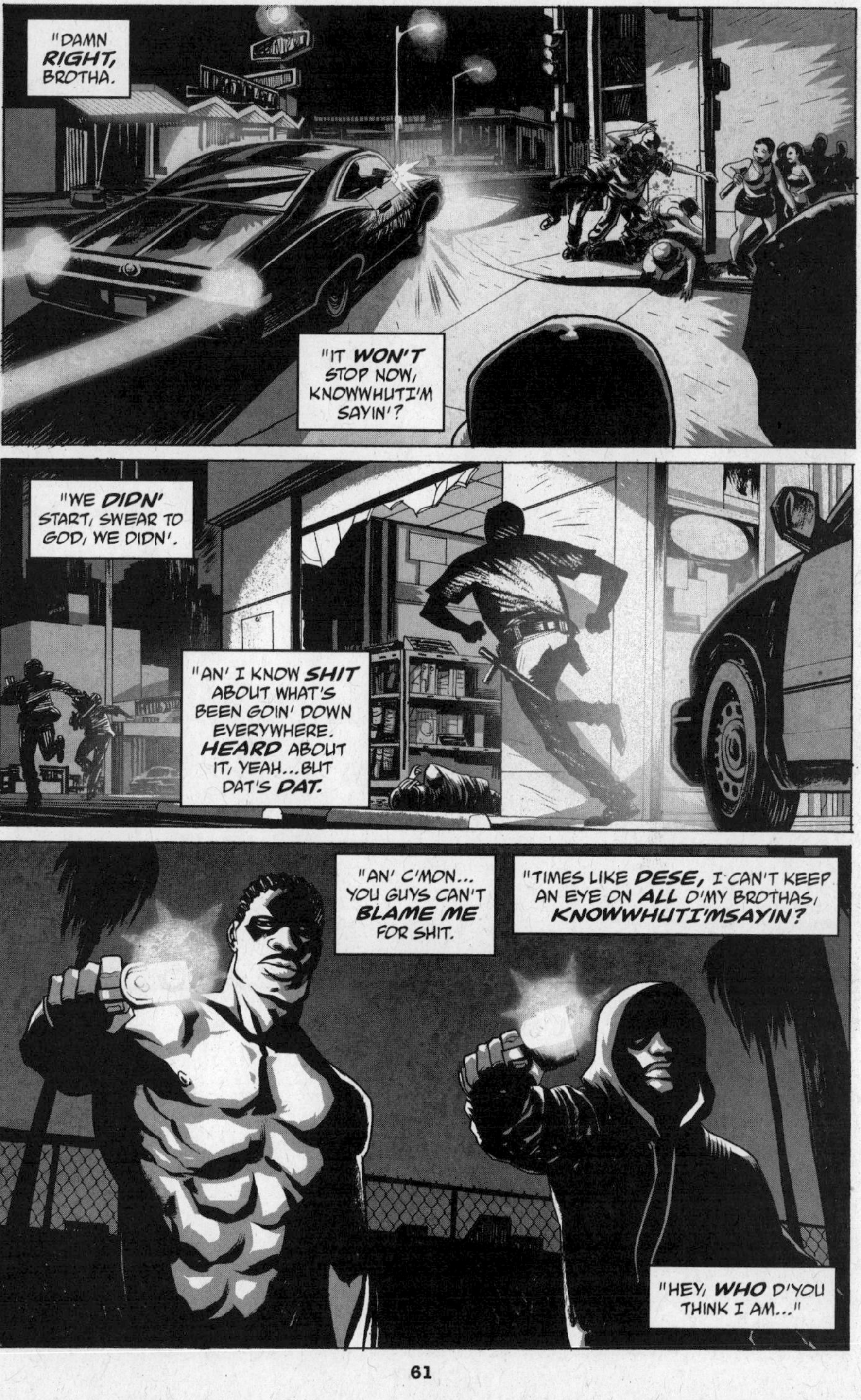
"DAMN RIGHT, BROTHA.
"IT WON'T STOP NOW, KNOWWHUTI'M SAYIN'?
"WE DIDN' START, SWEAR TO GOD, WE DIDN'.
"AN' I KNOW SHIT ABOUT WHAT'S BEEN GOIN' DOWN EVERYWHERE. HEARD ABOUT IT, YEAH...BUT DAT'S DAT.
"AN' C'MON... YOU GUYS CAN'T BLAME ME FOR SHIT.
"TIMES LIKE DESE, I CAN'T KEEP AN EYE ON ALL O'MY BROTHAS, KNOWWHUTI'MSAYIN?
"HEY, WHO D'YOU THINK I AM..."

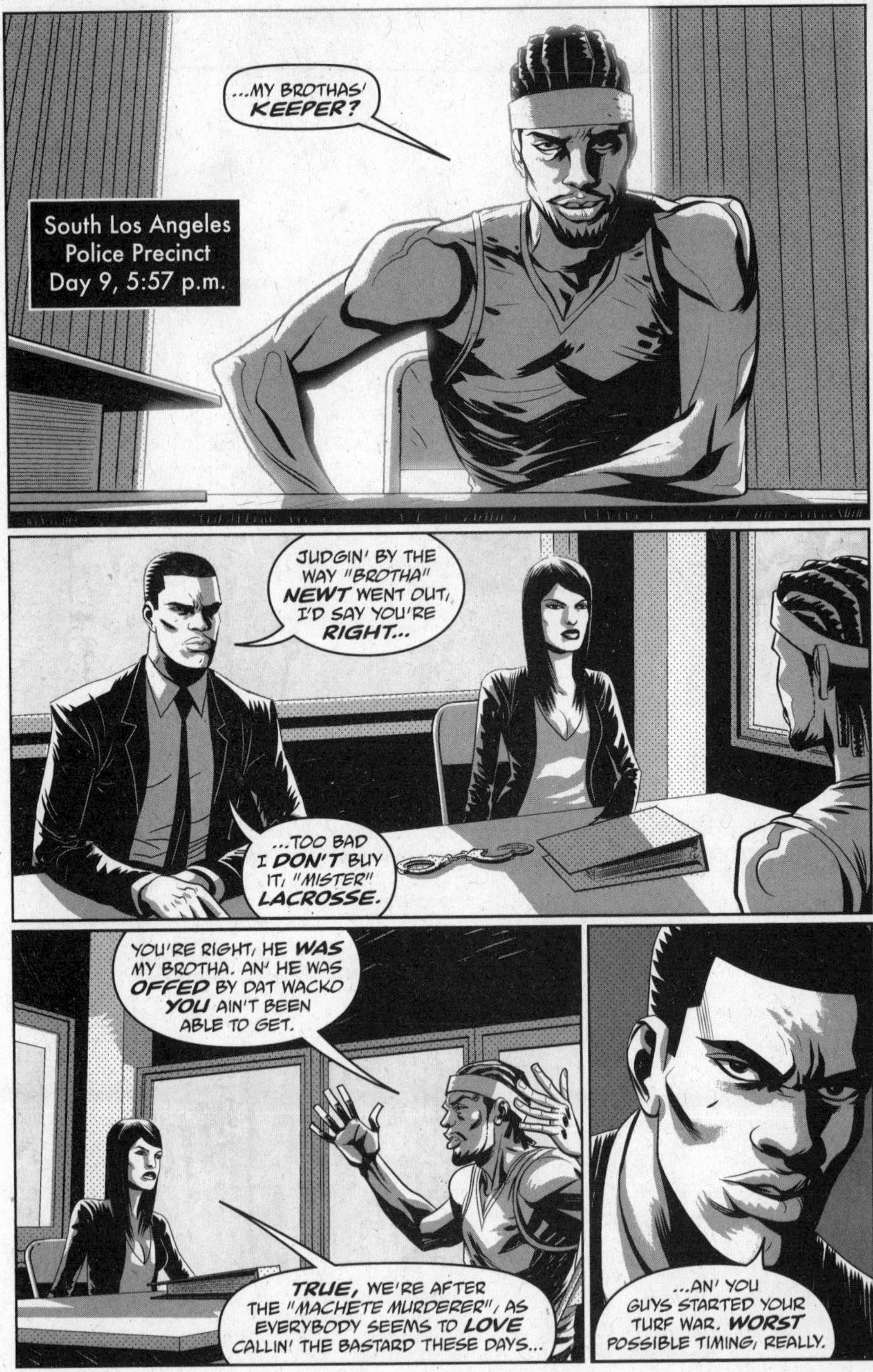
...MY BROTHAS' KEEPER?
South Los Angeles Police Precinct Day 9, 5:57 p.m.
JUDGIN' BY THE WAY "BROTHA" NEWT WENT OUT, I'D SAY YOU'RE RIGHT...
...TOO BAD I DON'T BUY IT, "MISTER" LACROSSE.
YOU'RE RIGHT, HE WAS MY BROTHA. AN' HE WAS OFFED BY DAT WACKO YOU AIN'T BEEN ABLE TO GET.
TRUE, WE'RE AFTER THE "MACHETE MURDERER", AS EVERYBODY SEEMS TO LOVE CALLIN' THE BASTARD THESE DAYS...
...AN' YOU GUYS STARTED YOUR TURF WAR. WORST POSSIBLE TIMING, REALLY.

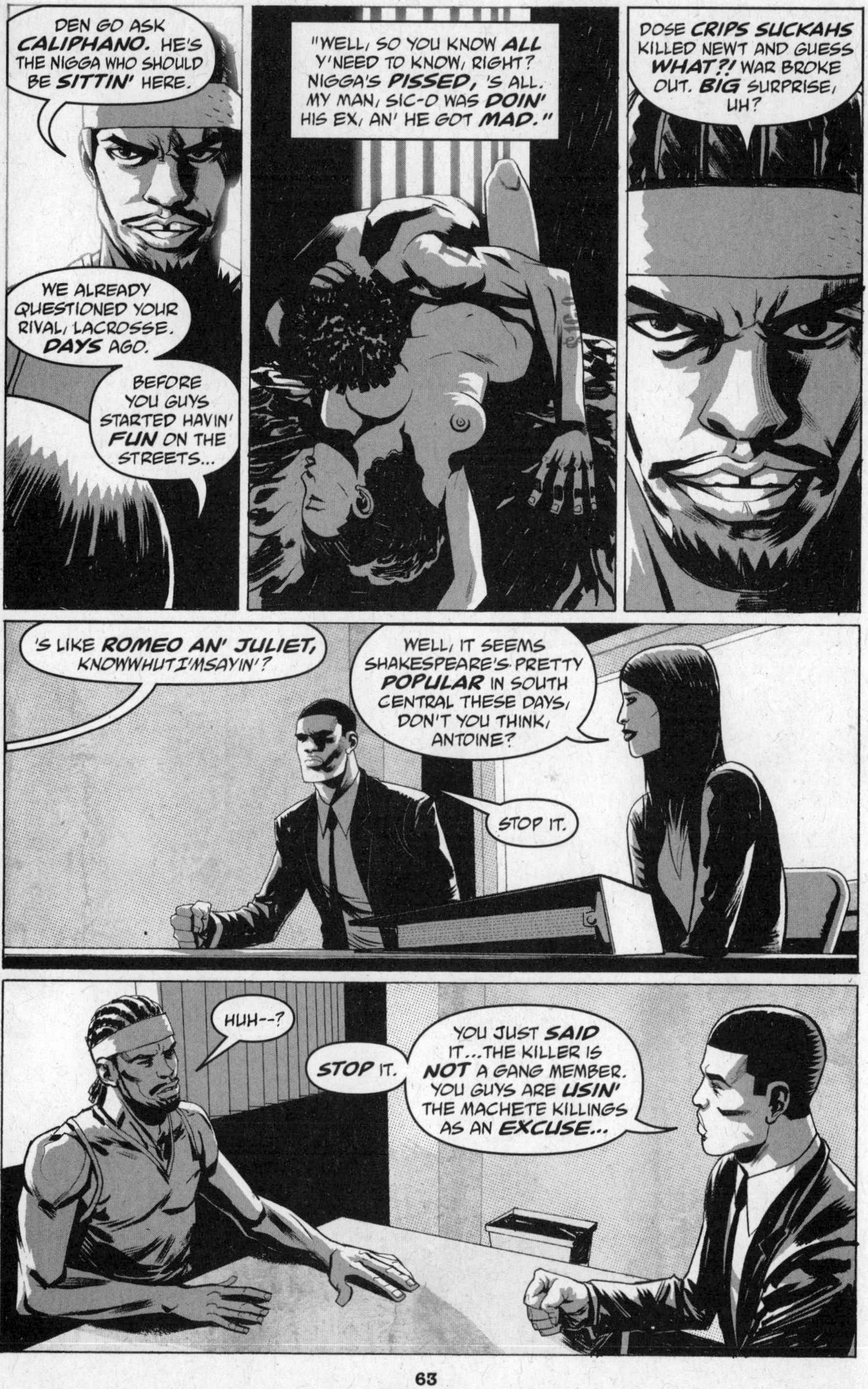
DEN GO ASK CALIPHANO. HE'S THE NIGGA WHO SHOULD BE SITTIN' HERE.
WE ALREADY QUESTIONED YOUR RIVAL, LACROSSE. DAYS AGO.
BEFORE YOU GUYS STARTED HAVIN' FUN ON THE STREETS...
"WELL, SO YOU KNOW ALL Y'NEED TO KNOW, RIGHT? NIGGA'S PISSED, 'S ALL. MY MAN, SIC-O WAS DOIN' HIS EX, AN' HE GOT MAD."
DOSE CRIPS SUCKAHS KILLED NEWT AND GUESS WHAT?! WAR BROKE OUT. BIG SURPRISE, UH?
'S LIKE ROMEO AN' JULIET, KNOWWHUTI'MSAYIN'?
WELL, IT SEEMS SHAKESPEARE'S PRETTY POPULAR IN SOUTH CENTRAL THESE DAYS, DON'T YOU THINK, ANTOINE?
STOP IT.
HUH--?
STOP IT.
YOU JUST SAID IT...THE KILLER IS NOT A GANG MEMBER. YOU GUYS ARE USIN' THE MACHETE KILLINGS AS AN EXCUSE...

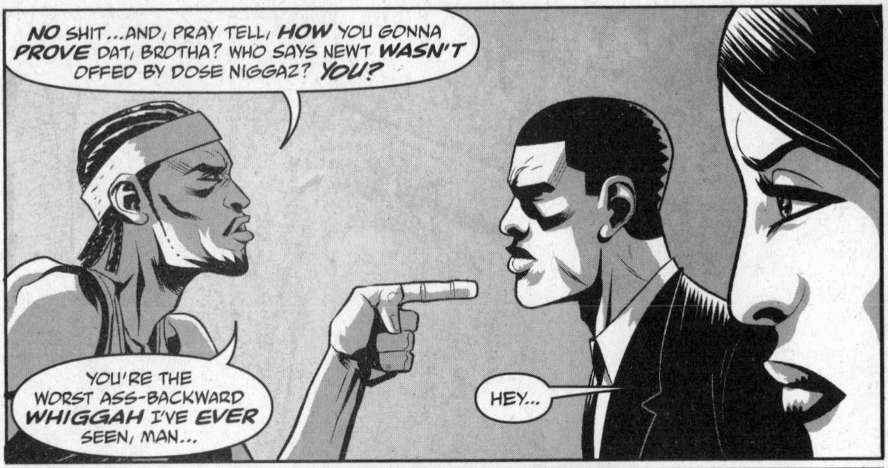
NO SHIT...AND, PRAY TELL, HOW YOU GONNA PROVE DAT, BROTHA? WHO SAYS NEWT WASN'T OFFED BY DOSE NIGGAZ? YOU?
YOU'RE THE WORST ASS-BACKWARD WHIGGAH I'VE EVER SEEN, MAN...
HEY...

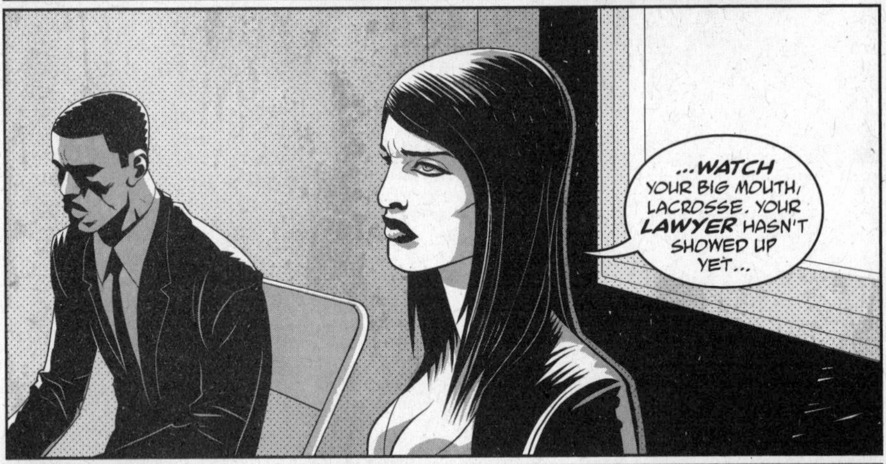
...WATCH YOUR BIG MOUTH, LACROSSE. YOUR LAWYER HASN'T SHOWED UP YET...

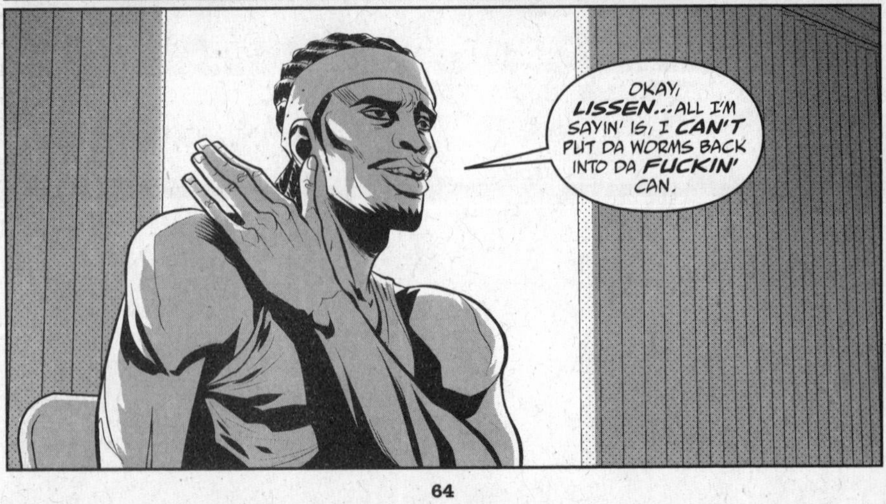
OKAY, LISSEN...ALL I'M SAYIN' IS, I CAN'T PUT DA WORMS BACK INTO DA FUCKIN' CAN.

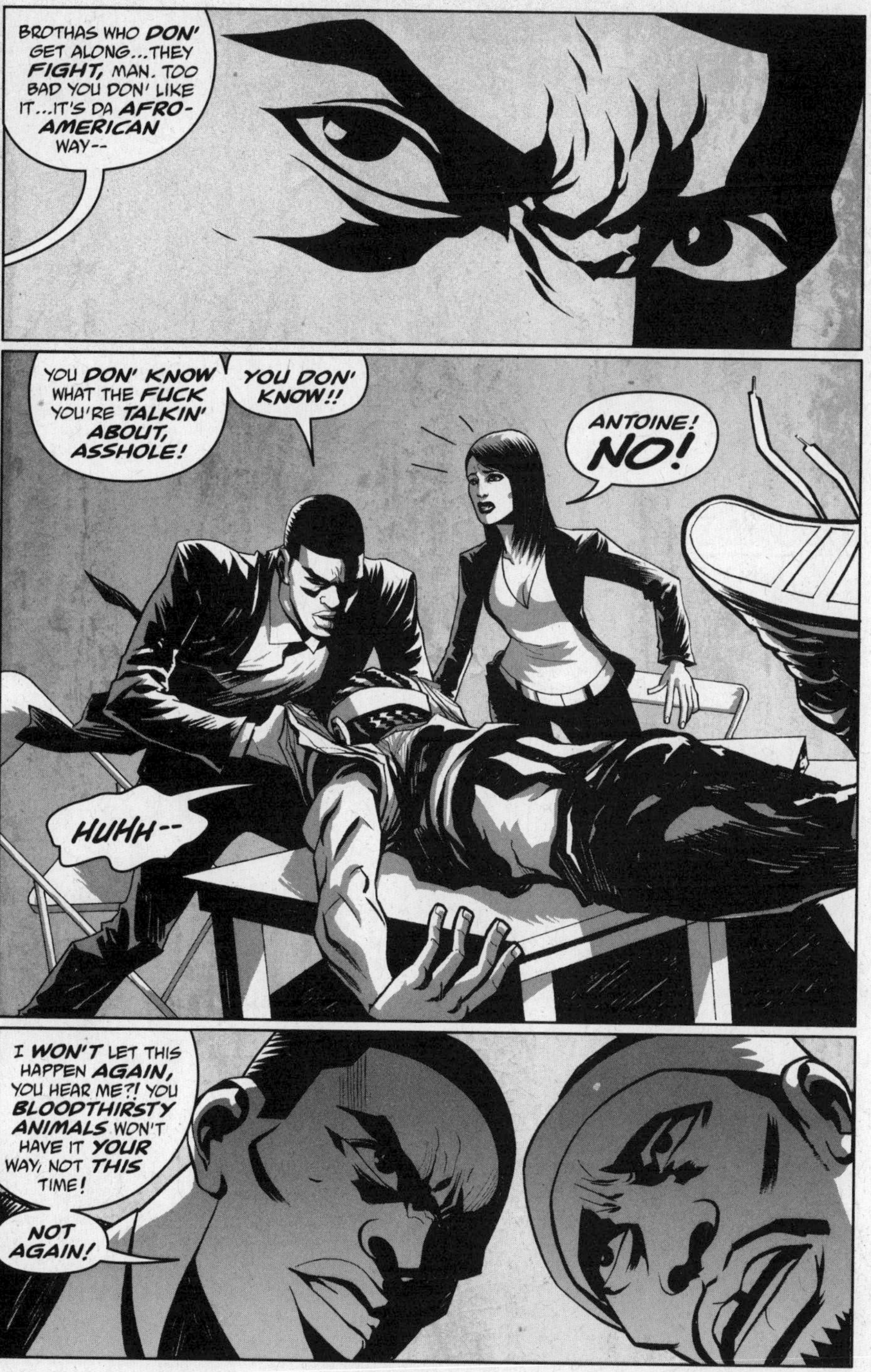
BROTHAS WHO DON' GET ALONG...THEY FIGHT, MAN. TOO BAD YOU DON' LIKE IT...IT'S DA AFRO-AMERICAN WAY--
YOU DON' KNOW WHAT THE FUCK YOU'RE TALKIN' ABOUT, ASSHOLE!
YOU DON' KNOW!!
ANTOINE! NO!
HUHH--
I WON'T LET THIS HAPPEN AGAIN, YOU HEAR ME?! YOU BLOODTHIRSTY ANIMALS WON'T HAVE IT YOUR WAY, NOT THIS TIME!
NOT AGAIN!

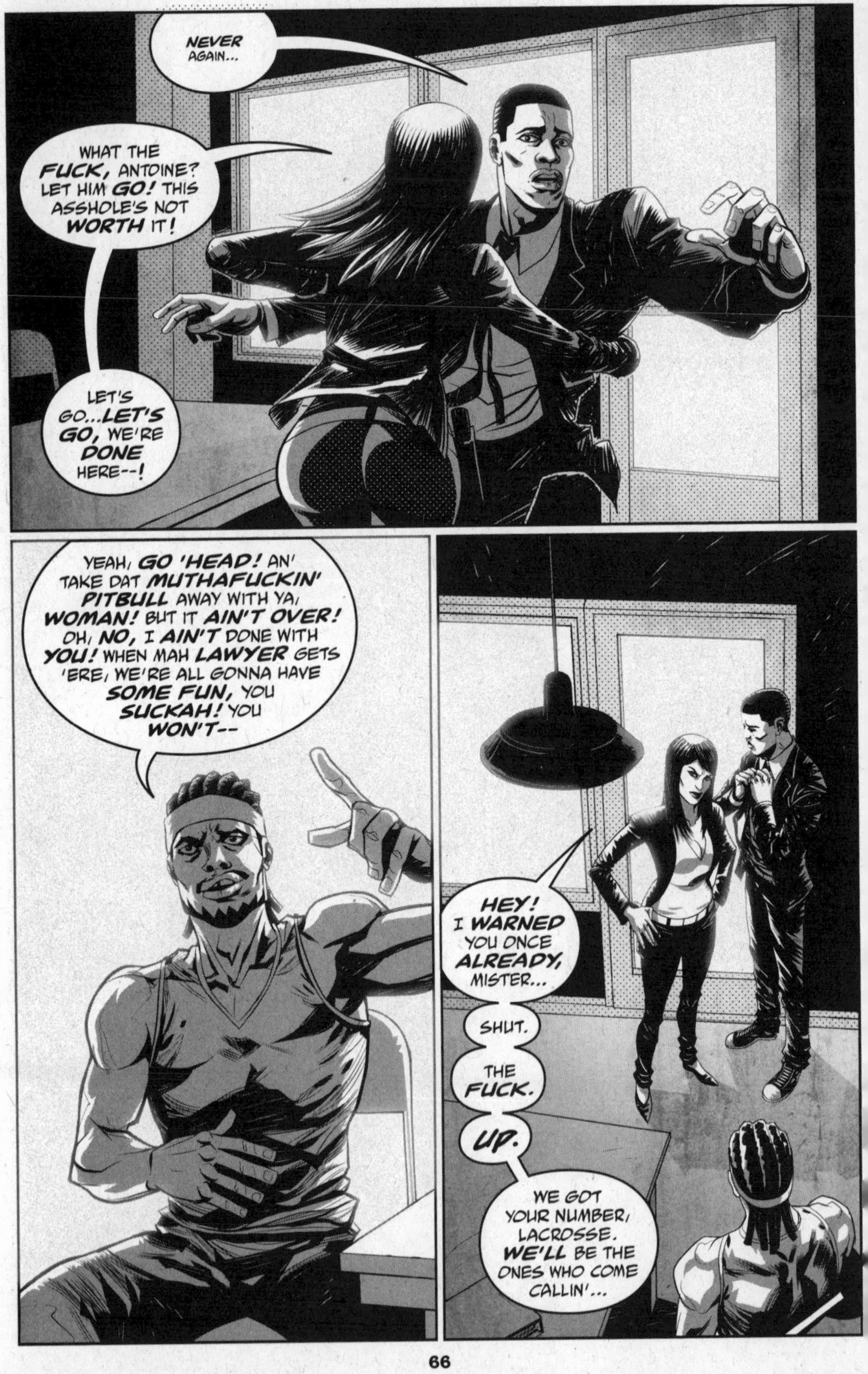
NEVER AGAIN...
WHAT THE FUCK, ANTOINE? LET HIM GO! THIS ASSHOLE'S NOT WORTH IT!
LET'S GO...LET'S GO, WE'RE DONE HERE--!
YEAH, GO 'HEAD! AN' TAKE DAT MUTHAFUCKIN' PITBULL AWAY WITH YA, WOMAN! BUT IT AIN'T OVER! OH, NO, I AIN'T DONE WITH YOU! WHEN MAH LAWYER GETS 'ERE, WE'RE ALL GONNA HAVE SOME FUN, YOU SUCKAH! YOU WON'T--
HEY! I WARNED YOU ONCE ALREADY, MISTER...
SHUT.
THE FUCK.
UP.
WE GOT YOUR NUMBER, LACROSSE. WE'LL BE THE ONES WHO COME CALLIN'...

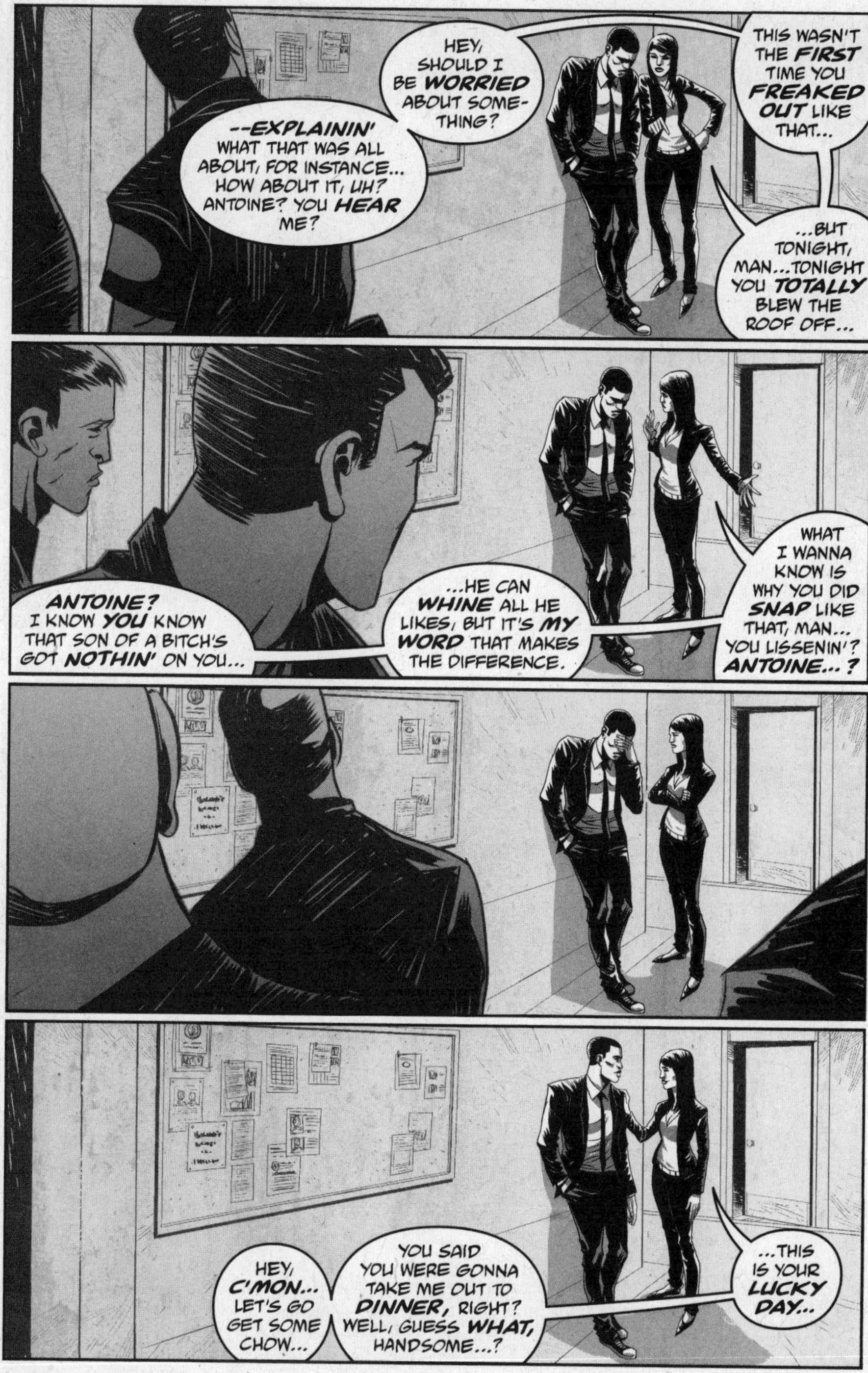
--EXPLAININ' WHAT THAT WAS ALL ABOUT, FOR INSTANCE... HOW ABOUT IT, UH? ANTOINE? YOU HEAR ME?
HEY, SHOULD I BE WORRIED ABOUT SOME-THING?
THIS WASN'T THE FIRST TIME YOU FREAKED OUT LIKE THAT...
...BUT TONIGHT, MAN...TONIGHT YOU TOTALLY BLEW THE ROOF OFF...
ANTOINE? I KNOW YOU KNOW THAT SON OF A BITCH'S GOT NOTHIN' ON YOU...
...HE CAN WHINE ALL HE LIKES, BUT IT'S MY WORD THAT MAKES THE DIFFERENCE.
WHAT I WANNA KNOW IS WHY YOU DID SNAP LIKE THAT, MAN... YOU LISSENIN'? ANTOINE...?
HEY, C'MON... LET'S GO GET SOME CHOW...
YOU SAID YOU WERE GONNA TAKE ME OUT TO DINNER, RIGHT? WELL, GUESS WHAT, HANDSOME...?
...THIS IS YOUR LUCKY DAY...

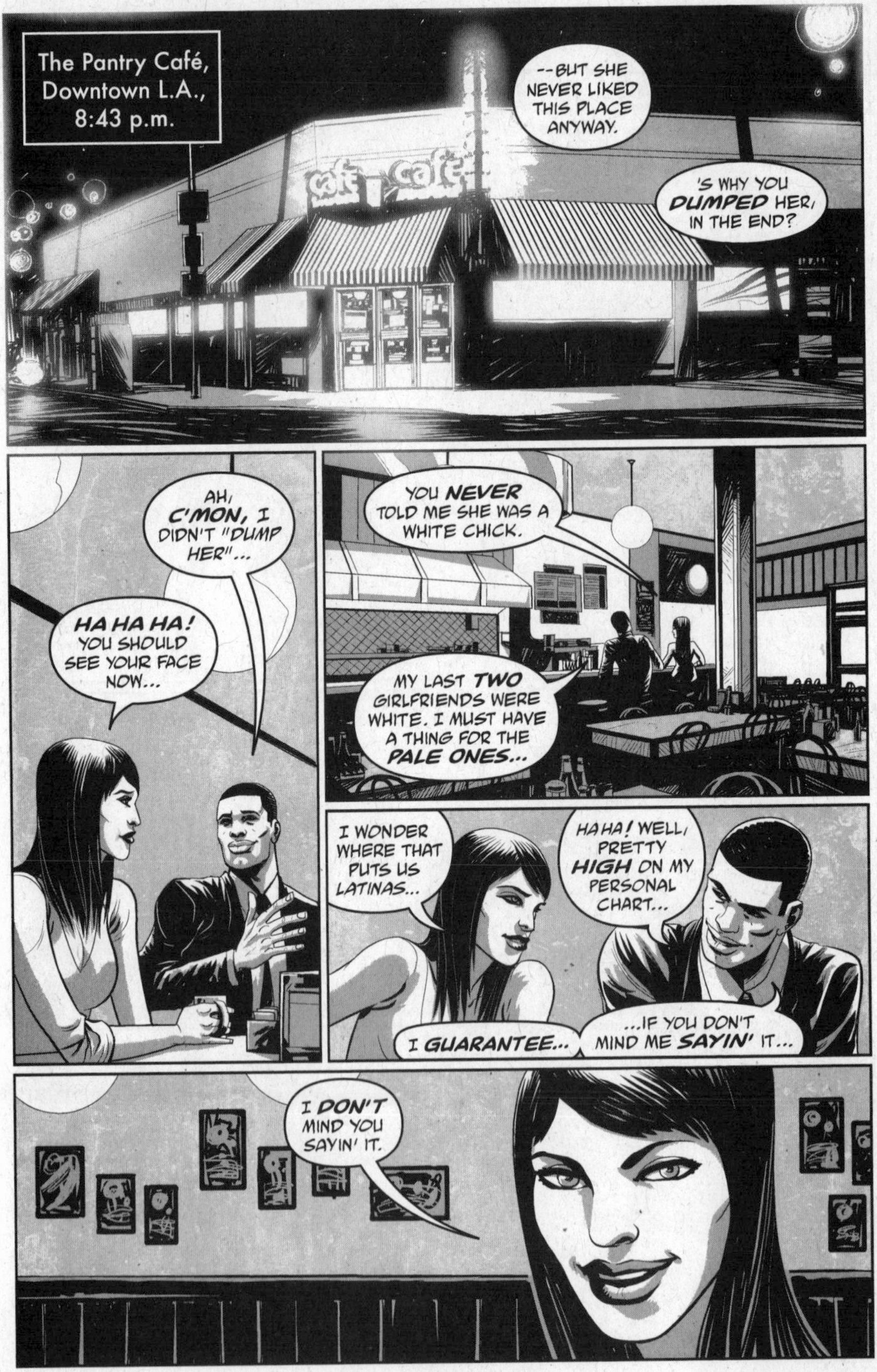
The Pantry Café, Downtown L.A., 8:43 p.m.
--BUT SHE NEVER LIKED THIS PLACE ANYWAY.
'S WHY YOU DUMPED HER, IN THE END?
AH, C'MON, I DIDN'T "DUMP HER"...
HA HA HA! YOU SHOULD SEE YOUR FACE NOW...
YOU NEVER TOLD ME SHE WAS A WHITE CHICK.
MY LAST TWO GIRLFRIENDS WERE WHITE. I MUST HAVE A THING FOR THE PALE ONES...
I WONDER WHERE THAT PUTS US LATINAS...
HA HA! WELL, PRETTY HIGH ON MY PERSONAL CHART...
...IF YOU DON'T MIND ME SAYIN' IT...
I GUARANTEE...
I DON'T MIND YOU SAYIN' IT.

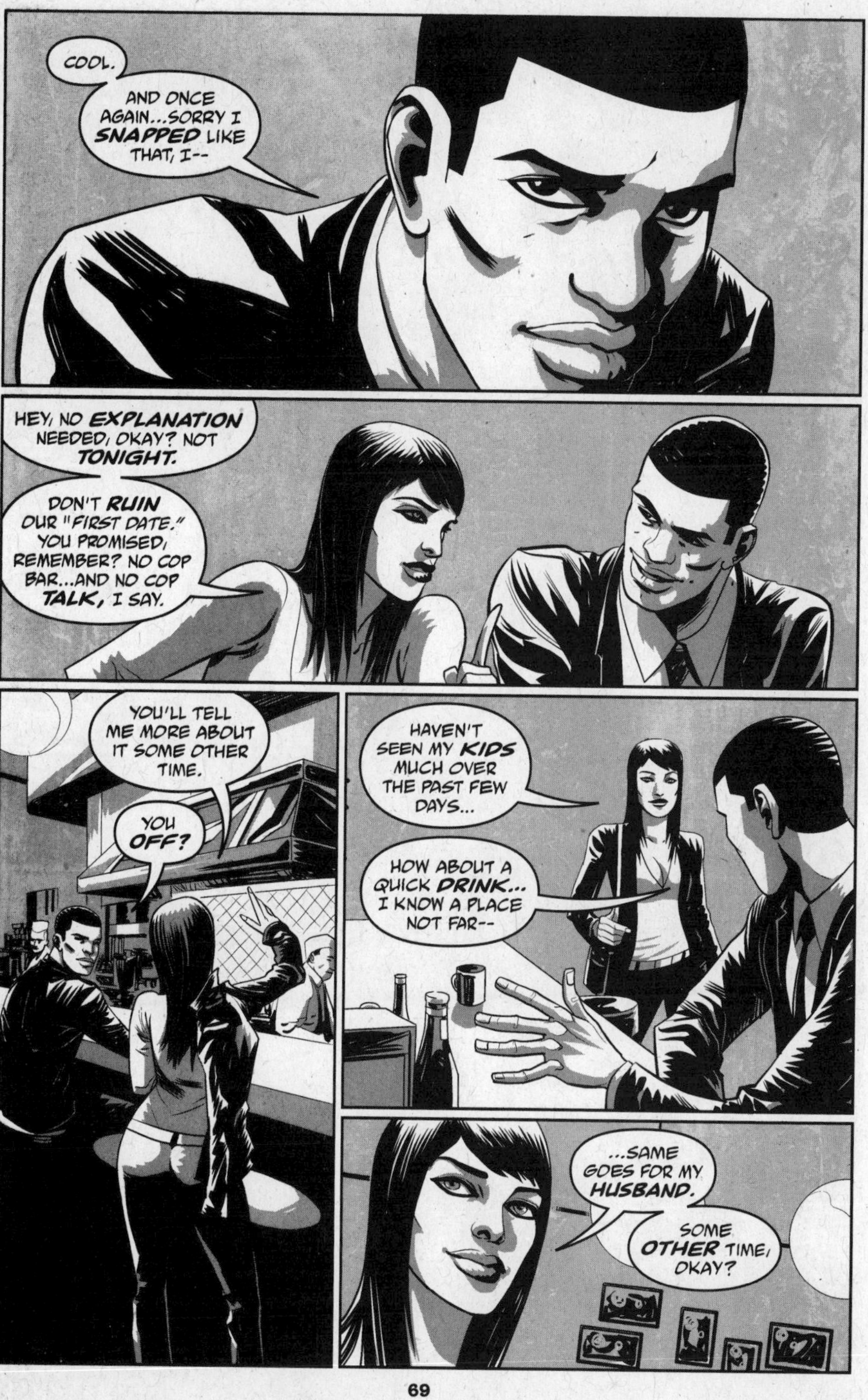
COOL.
AND ONCE AGAIN...SORRY I SNAPPED LIKE THAT, I--
HEY, NO EXPLANATION NEEDED, OKAY? NOT TONIGHT.
DON'T RUIN OUR "FIRST DATE." YOU PROMISED, REMEMBER? NO COP BAR...AND NO COP TALK, I SAY.
YOU'LL TELL ME MORE ABOUT IT SOME OTHER TIME.
YOU OFF?
HAVEN'T SEEN MY KIDS MUCH OVER THE PAST FEW DAYS...
HOW ABOUT A QUICK DRINK... I KNOW A PLACE NOT FAR--
...SAME GOES FOR MY HUSBAND.
SOME OTHER TIME, OKAY?

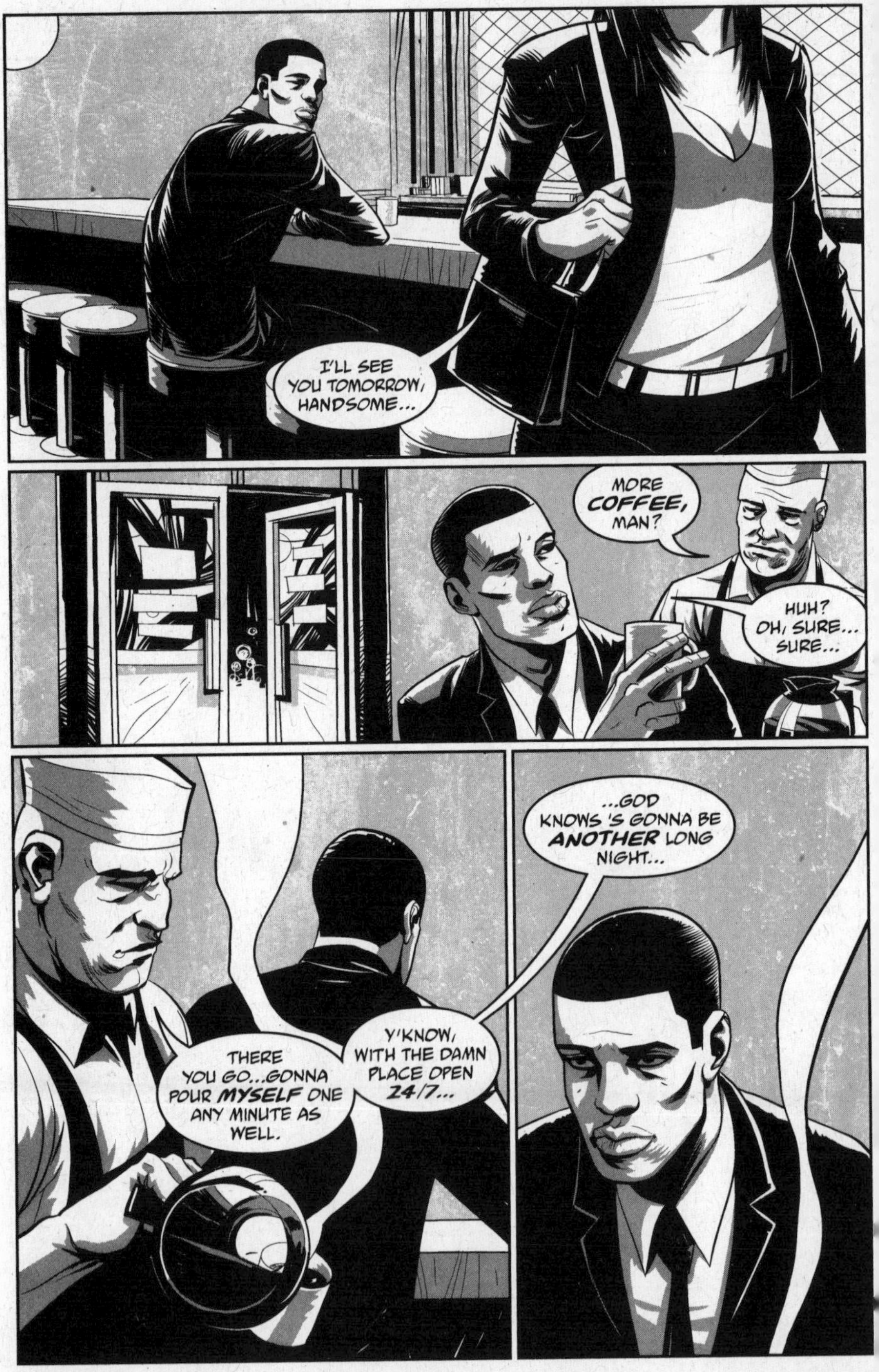
I'LL SEE YOU TOMORROW, HANDSOME...
MORE COFFEE, MAN?
HUH? OH, SURE... SURE...
THERE YOU GO...GONNA POUR MYSELF ONE ANY MINUTE AS WELL.
Y'KNOW, WITH THE DAMN PLACE OPEN 24/7...
...GOD KNOWS 'S GONNA BE ANOTHER LONG NIGHT...

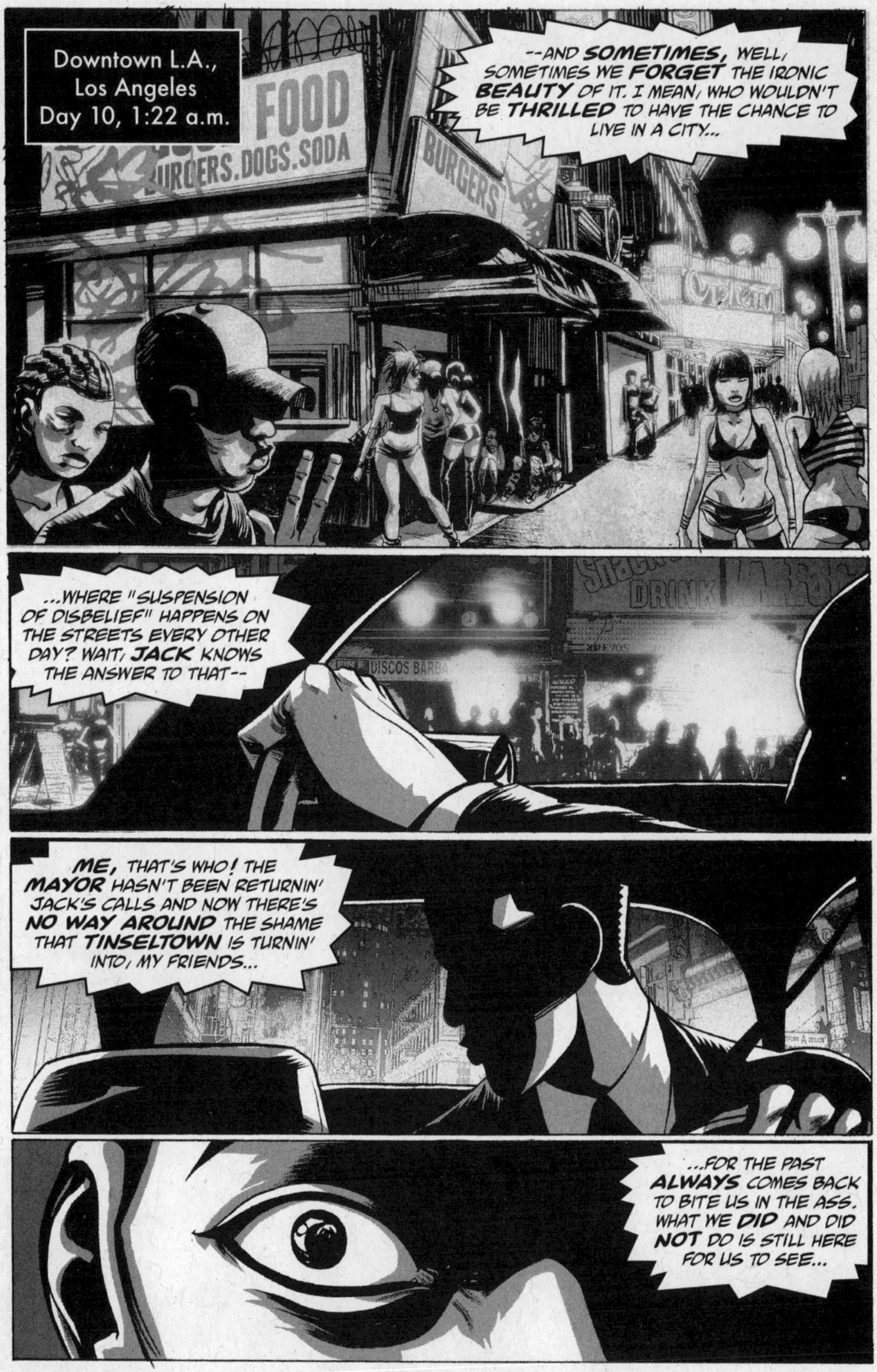

Downtown L.A., Los Angeles Day 10, 1:22 a.m.
FOOD
BURGERS.DOGS.SODA
BURGERS
--AND SOMETIMES, WELL, SOMETIMES WE FORGET THE IRONIC BEAUTY OF IT. I MEAN, WHO WOULDN'T BE THRILLED TO HAVE THE CHANCE TO LIVE IN A CITY...
...WHERE "SUSPENSION OF DISBELIEF" HAPPENS ON THE STREETS EVERY OTHER DAY? WAIT, JACK KNOWS THE ANSWER TO THAT--
DRINK
DISCOS BARBA
ME, THAT'S WHO! THE MAYOR HASN'T BEEN RETURNIN' JACK'S CALLS AND NOW THERE'S NO WAY AROUND THE SHAME THAT TINSELTOWN IS TURNIN' INTO, MY FRIENDS...
...FOR THE PAST ALWAYS COMES BACK TO BITE US IN THE ASS. WHAT WE DID AND DID NOT DO IS STILL HERE FOR US TO SEE...

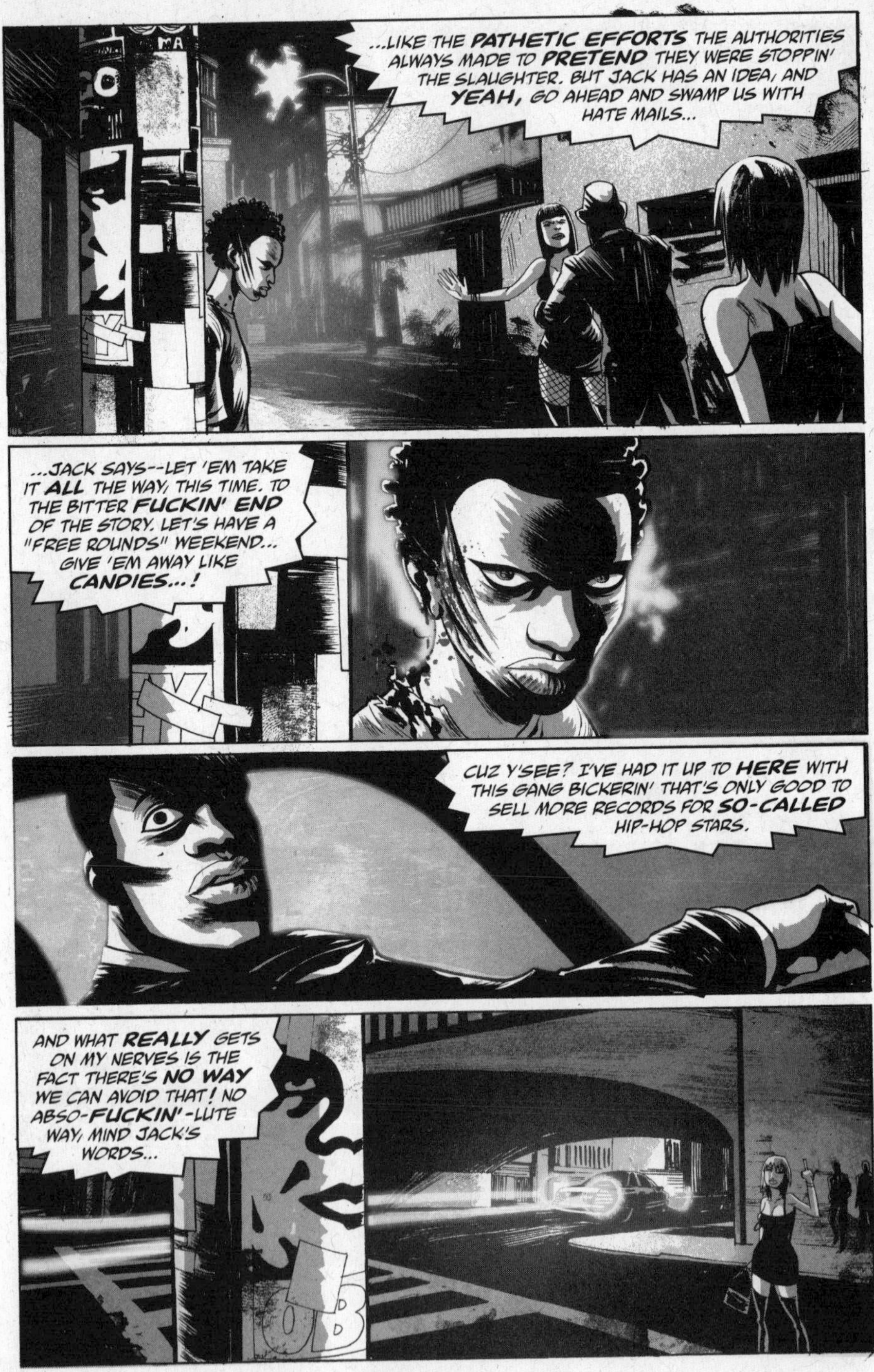
...LIKE THE PATHETIC EFFORTS THE AUTHORITIES ALWAYS MADE TO PRETEND THEY WERE STOPPIN' THE SLAUGHTER. BUT JACK HAS AN IDEA, AND YEAH, GO AHEAD AND SWAMP US WITH HATE MAILS...
...JACK SAYS--LET 'EM TAKE IT ALL THE WAY, THIS TIME. TO THE BITTER FUCKIN' END OF THE STORY. LET'S HAVE A "FREE ROUNDS" WEEKEND... GIVE 'EM AWAY LIKE CANDIES...!
CUZ Y'SEE? I'VE HAD IT UP TO HERE WITH THIS GANG BICKERIN' THAT'S ONLY GOOD TO SELL MORE RECORDS FOR SO-CALLED HIP-HOP STARS.
AND WHAT REALLY GETS ON MY NERVES IS THE FACT THERE'S NO WAY WE CAN AVOID THAT! NO ABSO-FUCKIN'-LUTE WAY, MIND JACK'S WORDS...

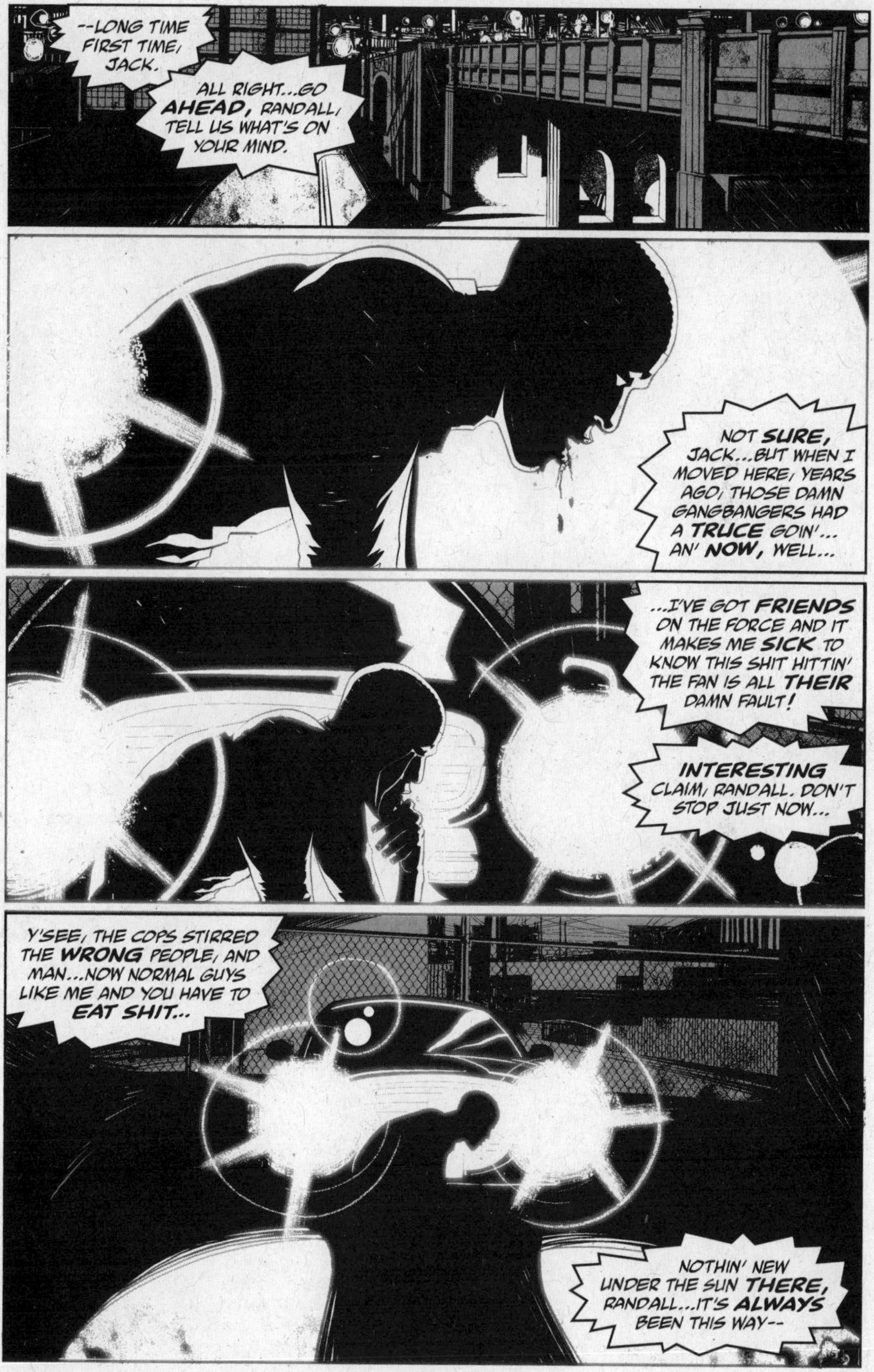
--LONG TIME FIRST TIME, JACK.
ALL RIGHT...GO AHEAD, RANDALL, TELL US WHAT'S ON YOUR MIND.
NOT SURE, JACK...BUT WHEN I MOVED HERE, YEARS AGO, THOSE DAMN GANGBANGERS HAD A TRUCE GOIN'... AN' NOW, WELL...
...I'VE GOT FRIENDS ON THE FORCE AND IT MAKES ME SICK TO KNOW THIS SHIT HITTIN' THE FAN IS ALL THEIR DAMN FAULT!
INTERESTING CLAIM, RANDALL. DON'T STOP JUST NOW...
Y'SEE, THE COPS STIRRED THE WRONG PEOPLE, AND MAN...NOW NORMAL GUYS LIKE ME AND YOU HAVE TO EAT SHIT...
NOTHIN' NEW UNDER THE SUN THERE, RANDALL...IT'S ALWAYS BEEN THIS WAY--

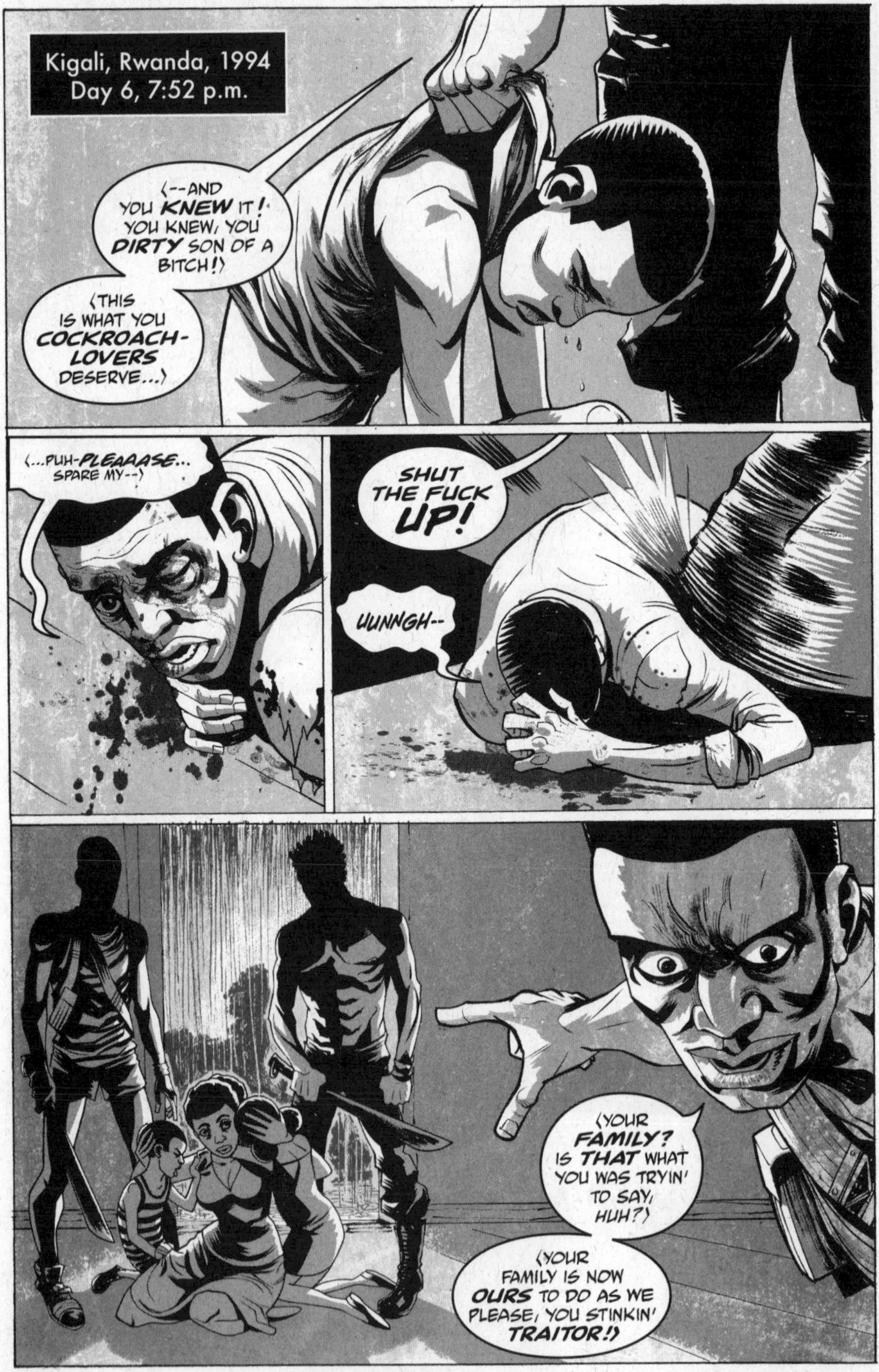
Kigali, Rwanda, 1994
Day 6, 7:52 p.m.
‹--AND YOU KNEW IT! YOU KNEW, YOU DIRTY SON OF A BITCH!›
‹THIS IS WHAT YOU COCKROACH-LOVERS DESERVE...›
‹...PUH-PLEAAASE... SPARE MY--›
SHUT THE FUCK UP!
UUNNGH--
‹YOUR FAMILY? IS THAT WHAT YOU WAS TRYIN' TO SAY, HUH?›
‹YOUR FAMILY IS NOW OURS TO DO AS WE PLEASE, YOU STINKIN' TRAITOR!›

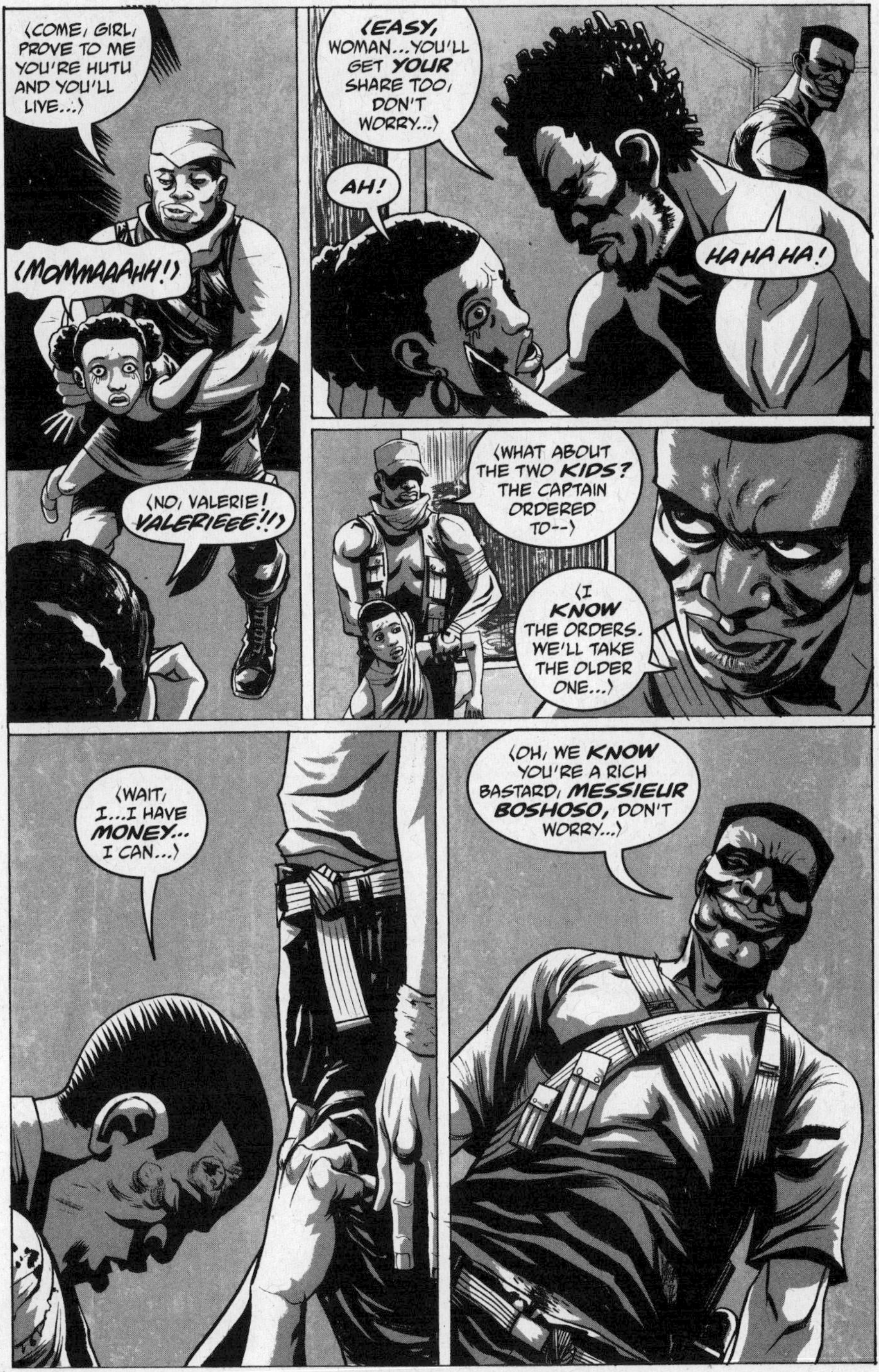
‹COME, GIRL, PROVE TO ME YOU'RE HUTU AND YOU'LL LIVE...›
‹MOMMAAAHH!›
‹NO, VALERIE! VALERIEEE!!›
‹EASY, WOMAN...YOU'LL GET YOUR SHARE TOO, DON'T WORRY...›
AH!
HA HA HA!
‹WHAT ABOUT THE TWO KIDS? THE CAPTAIN ORDERED TO--›
‹I KNOW THE ORDERS. WE'LL TAKE THE OLDER ONE...›
‹WAIT, I...I HAVE MONEY... I CAN...›
‹OH, WE KNOW YOU'RE A RICH BASTARD, MESSIEUR BOSHOSO, DON'T WORRY...›

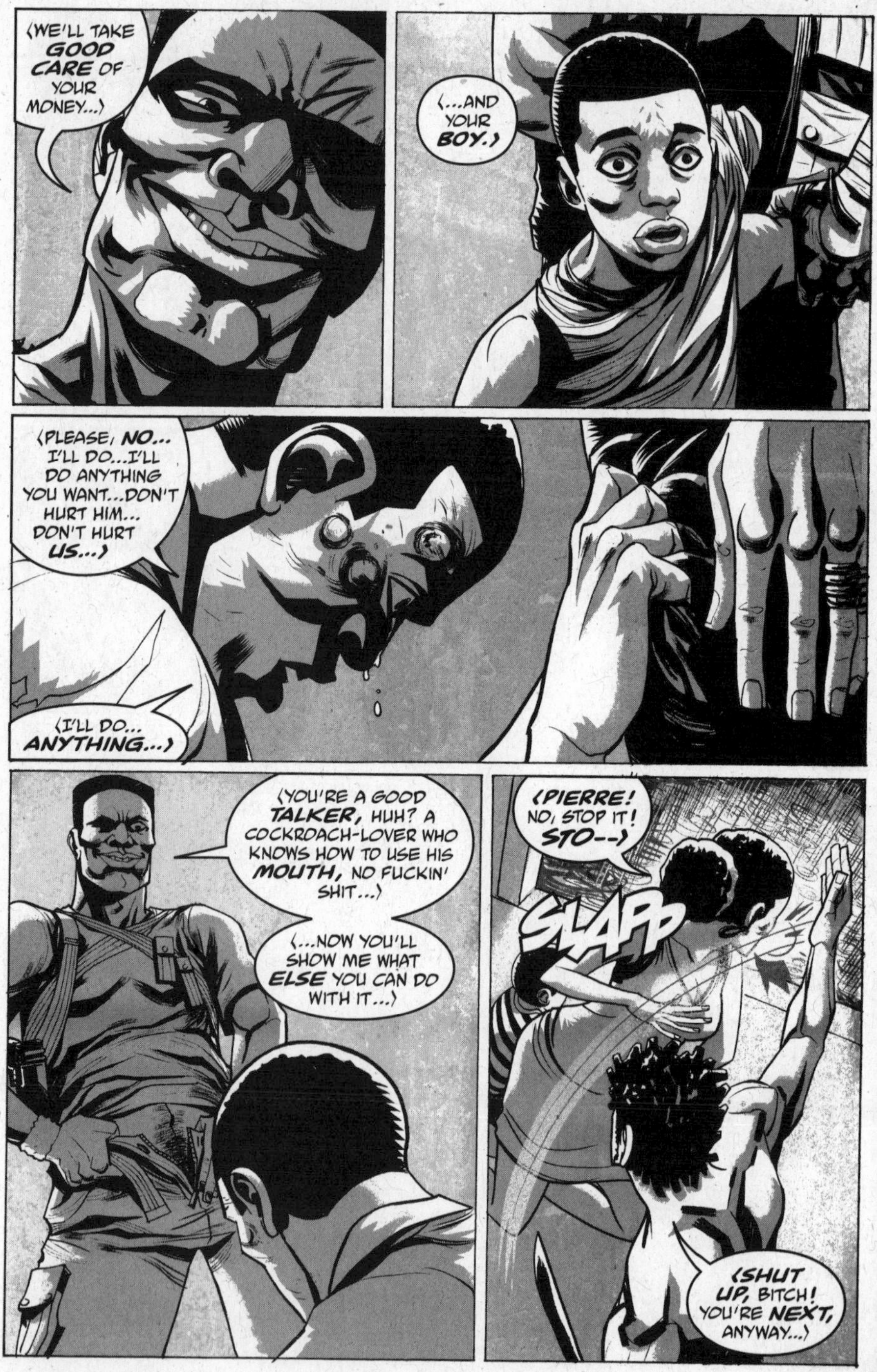
‹WE'LL TAKE GOOD CARE OF YOUR MONEY...›
‹...AND YOUR BOY.›
‹PLEASE, NO... I'LL DO...I'LL DO ANYTHING YOU WANT...DON'T HURT HIM... DON'T HURT US...›
‹I'LL DO... ANYTHING...›
‹YOU'RE A GOOD TALKER, HUH? A COCKROACH-LOVER WHO KNOWS HOW TO USE HIS MOUTH, NO FUCKIN' SHIT...›
‹...NOW YOU'LL SHOW ME WHAT ELSE YOU CAN DO WITH IT...›
‹PIERRE! NO, STOP IT! STO--›
SLAPP
‹SHUT UP, BITCH! YOU'RE NEXT, ANYWAY...›

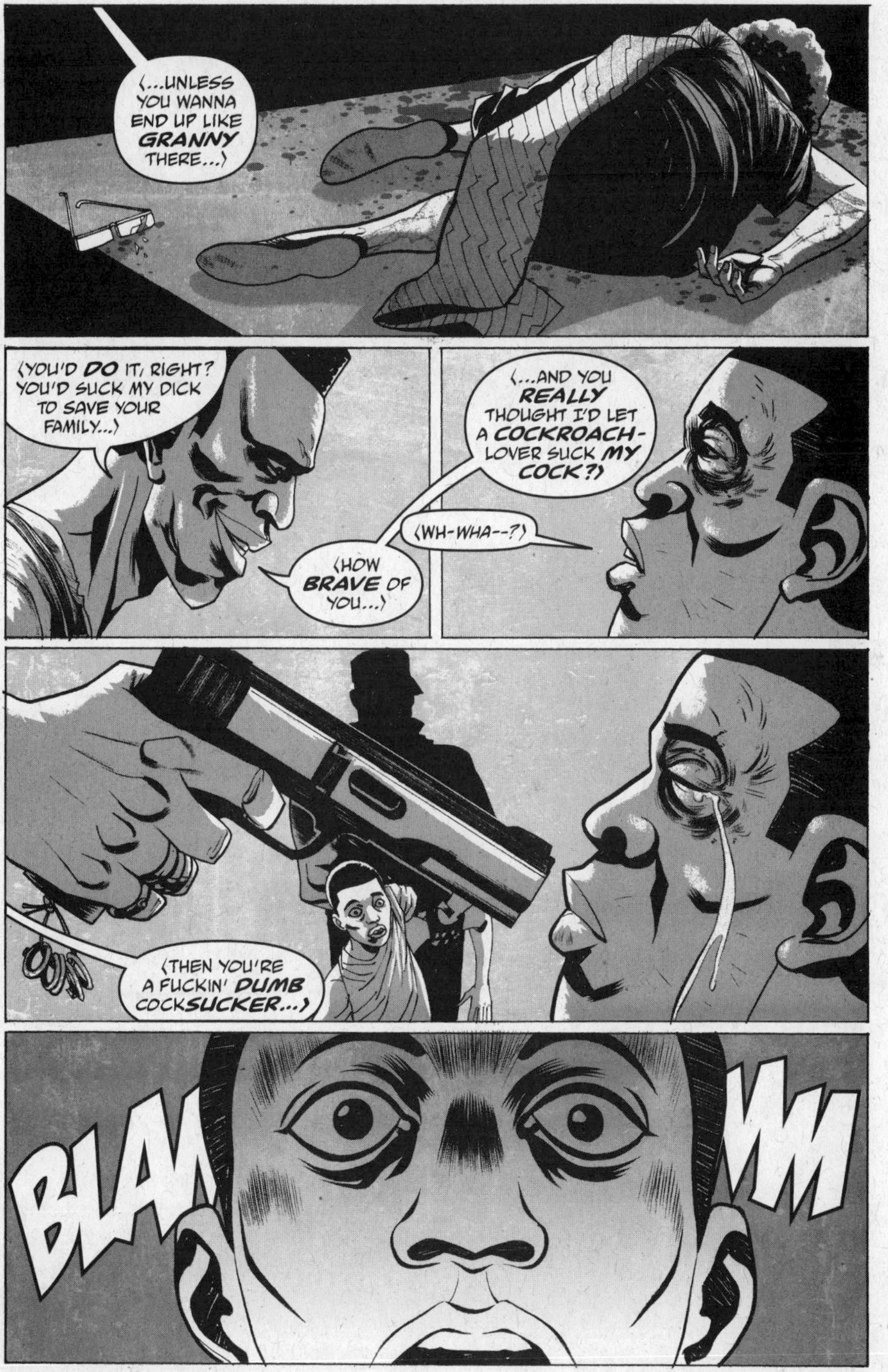
⟨...UNLESS YOU WANNA END UP LIKE GRANNY THERE...⟩
⟨YOU'D DO IT, RIGHT? YOU'D SUCK MY DICK TO SAVE YOUR FAMILY...⟩
⟨HOW BRAVE OF YOU...⟩
⟨...AND YOU REALLY THOUGHT I'D LET A COCKROACH-LOVER SUCK MY COCK?⟩
⟨WH-WHA--?⟩
⟨THEN YOU'RE A FUCKIN' DUMB COCKSUCKER...⟩
BLAMM

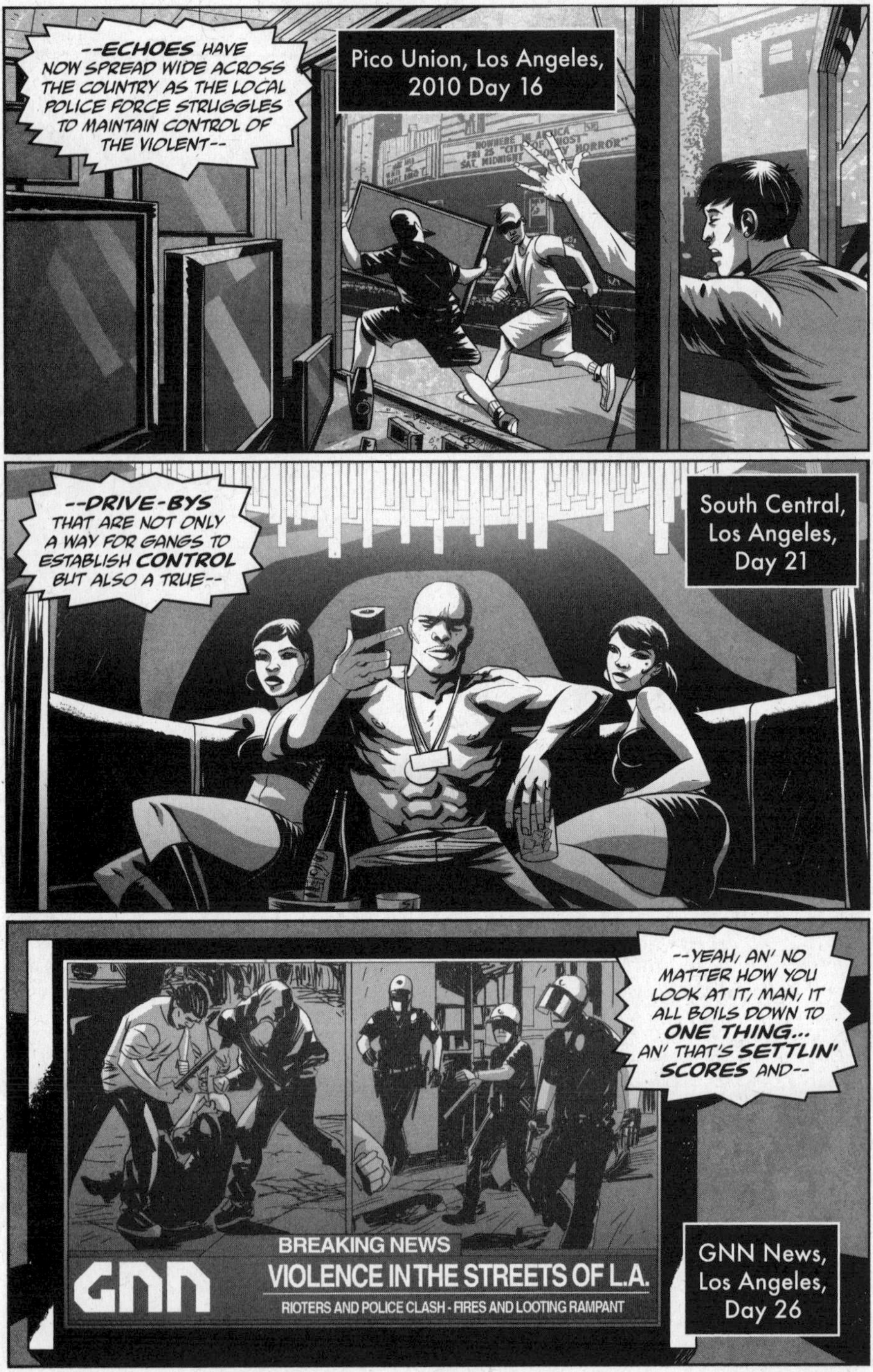
--ECHOES HAVE NOW SPREAD WIDE ACROSS THE COUNTRY AS THE LOCAL POLICE FORCE STRUGGLES TO MAINTAIN CONTROL OF THE VIOLENT--
Pico Union, Los Angeles, 2010 Day 16
--DRIVE-BYS THAT ARE NOT ONLY A WAY FOR GANGS TO ESTABLISH CONTROL BUT ALSO A TRUE--
South Central, Los Angeles, Day 21
--YEAH, AN' NO MATTER HOW YOU LOOK AT IT, MAN, IT ALL BOILS DOWN TO ONE THING... AN' THAT'S SETTLIN' SCORES AND--
BREAKING NEWS
GNN
VIOLENCE IN THE STREETS OF L.A.
RIOTERS AND POLICE CLASH - FIRES AND LOOTING RAMPANT
GNN News, Los Angeles, Day 26

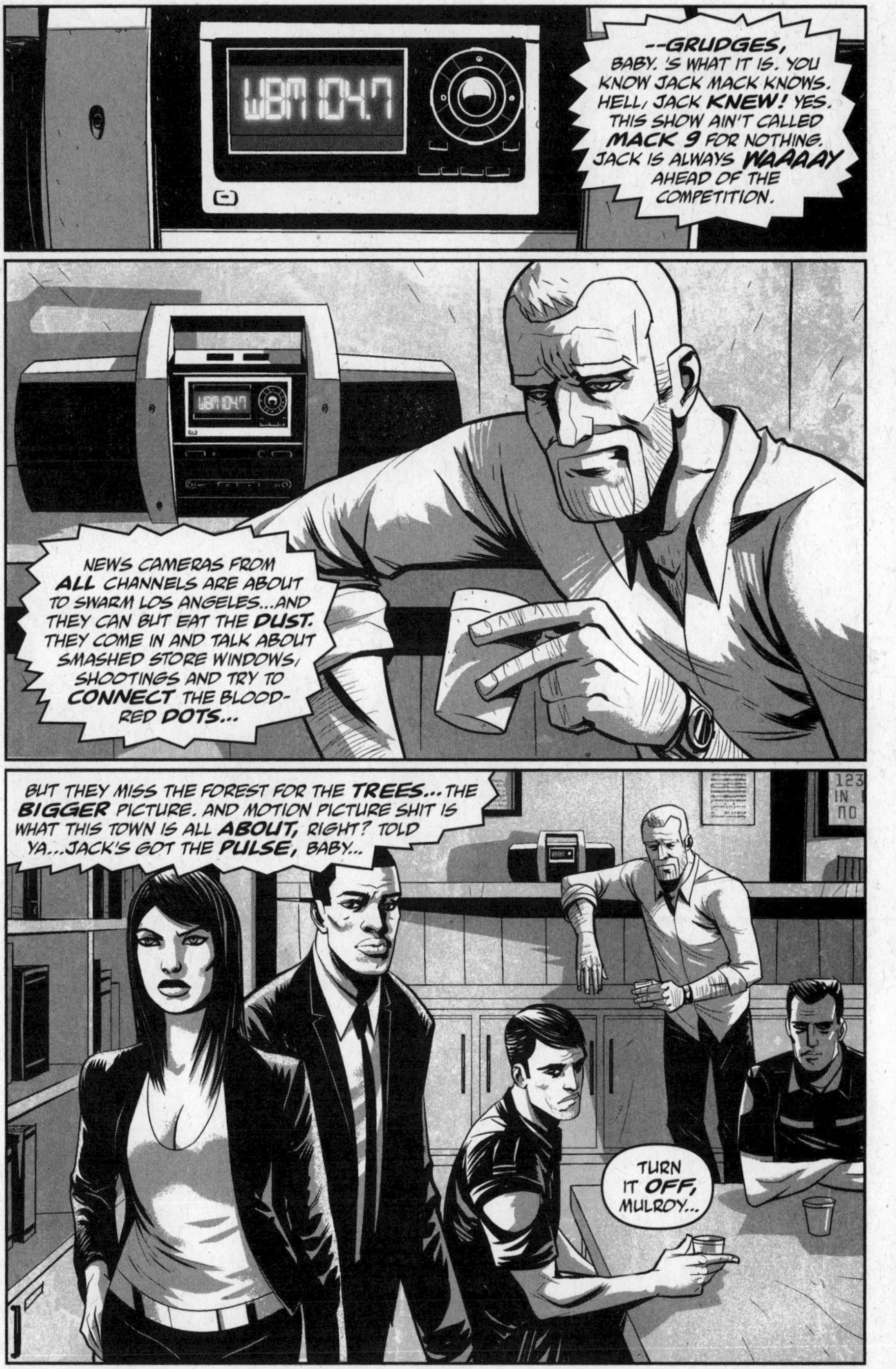
WBM 104.7
--GRUDGES, BABY. 'S WHAT IT IS. YOU KNOW JACK MACK KNOWS. HELL, JACK KNEW! YES. THIS SHOW AIN'T CALLED MACK 9 FOR NOTHING. JACK IS ALWAYS WAAAAY AHEAD OF THE COMPETITION.
WBM 104.7
NEWS CAMERAS FROM ALL CHANNELS ARE ABOUT TO SWARM LOS ANGELES...AND THEY CAN BUT EAT THE DUST. THEY COME IN AND TALK ABOUT SMASHED STORE WINDOWS, SHOOTINGS AND TRY TO CONNECT THE BLOOD-RED DOTS...
BUT THEY MISS THE FOREST FOR THE TREES...THE BIGGER PICTURE. AND MOTION PICTURE SHIT IS WHAT THIS TOWN IS ALL ABOUT, RIGHT? TOLD YA...JACK'S GOT THE PULSE, BABY...
TURN IT OFF, MULROY...

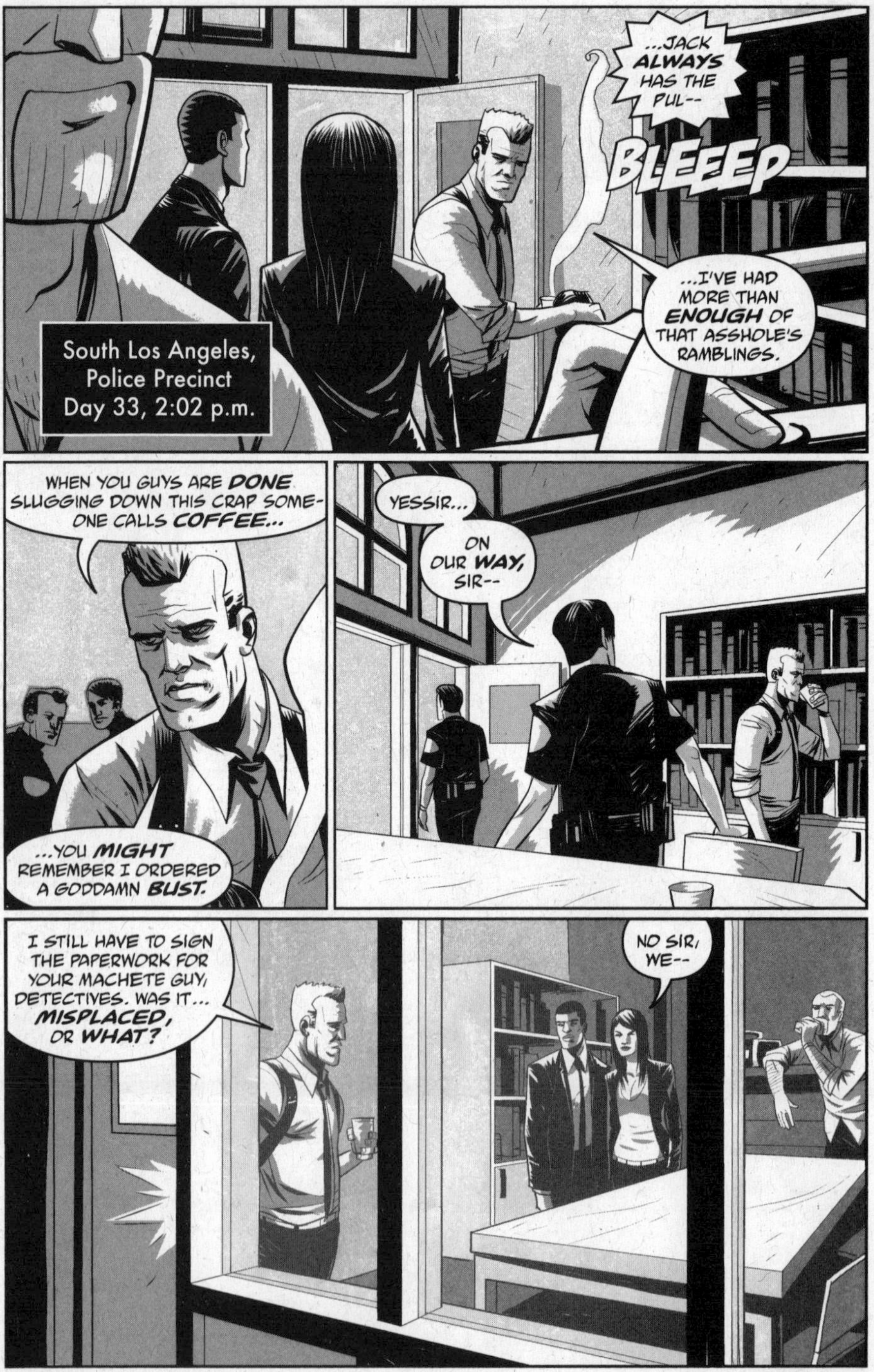
...JACK ALWAYS HAS THE PUL--
BLEEEP
...I'VE HAD MORE THAN ENOUGH OF THAT ASSHOLE'S RAMBLINGS.
South Los Angeles, Police Precinct Day 33, 2:02 p.m.
WHEN YOU GUYS ARE DONE SLUGGING DOWN THIS CRAP SOME-ONE CALLS COFFEE...
...YOU MIGHT REMEMBER I ORDERED A GODDAMN BUST.
YESSIR...
ON OUR WAY, SIR--
I STILL HAVE TO SIGN THE PAPERWORK FOR YOUR MACHETE GUY, DETECTIVES. WAS IT... MISPLACED, OR WHAT?
NO SIR, WE--

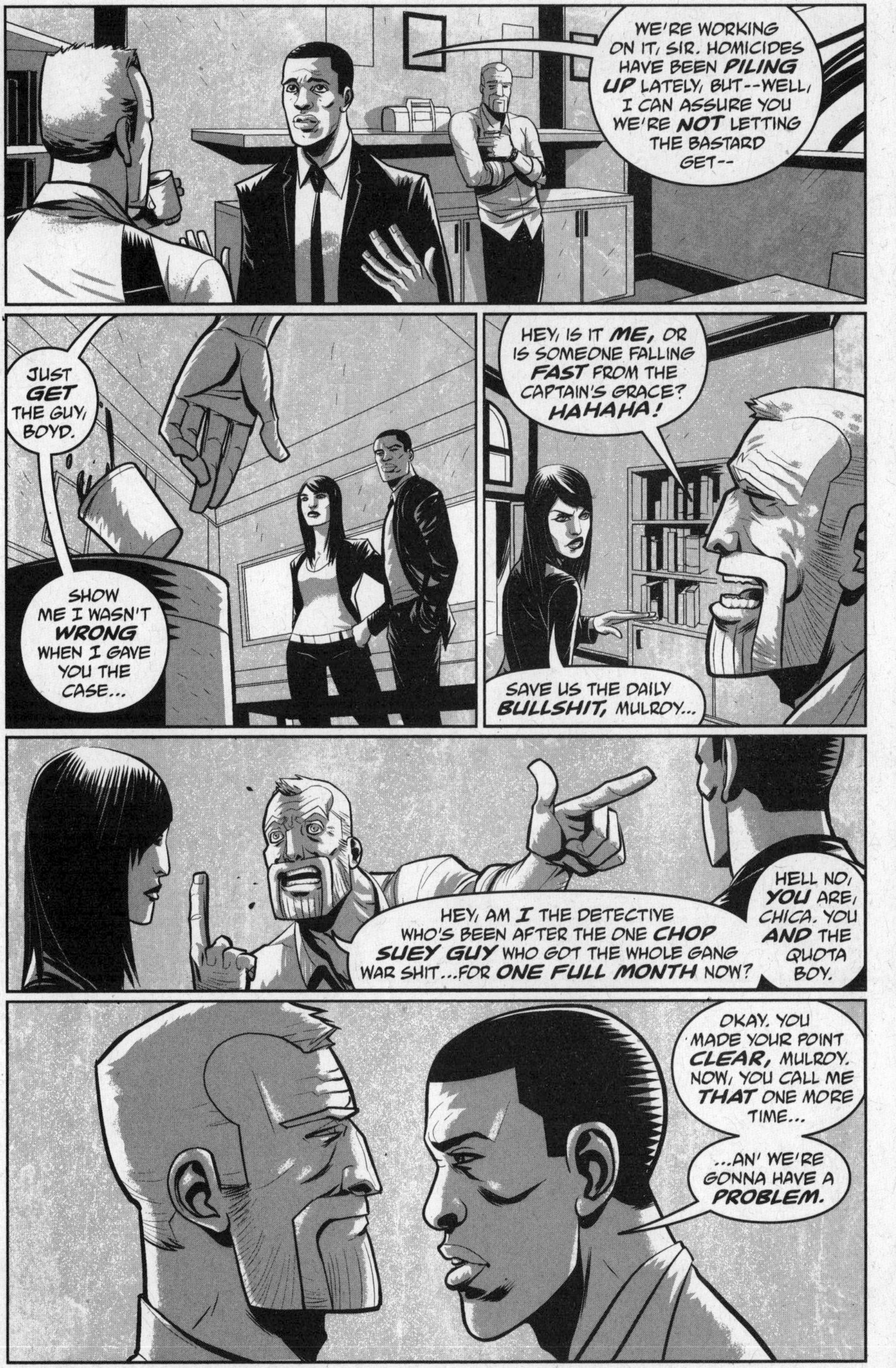
WE'RE WORKING ON IT, SIR. HOMICIDES HAVE BEEN PILING UP LATELY, BUT--WELL, I CAN ASSURE YOU WE'RE NOT LETTING THE BASTARD GET--
JUST GET THE GUY, BOYD.
SHOW ME I WASN'T WRONG WHEN I GAVE YOU THE CASE...
HEY, IS IT ME, OR IS SOMEONE FALLING FAST FROM THE CAPTAIN'S GRACE? HAHAHA!
SAVE US THE DAILY BULLSHIT, MULROY...
HEY, AM I THE DETECTIVE WHO'S BEEN AFTER THE ONE CHOP SUEY GUY WHO GOT THE WHOLE GANG WAR SHIT...FOR ONE FULL MONTH NOW?
HELL NO, YOU ARE, CHICA. YOU AND THE QUOTA BOY.
OKAY. YOU MADE YOUR POINT CLEAR, MULROY. NOW, YOU CALL ME THAT ONE MORE TIME...
...AN' WE'RE GONNA HAVE A PROBLEM.

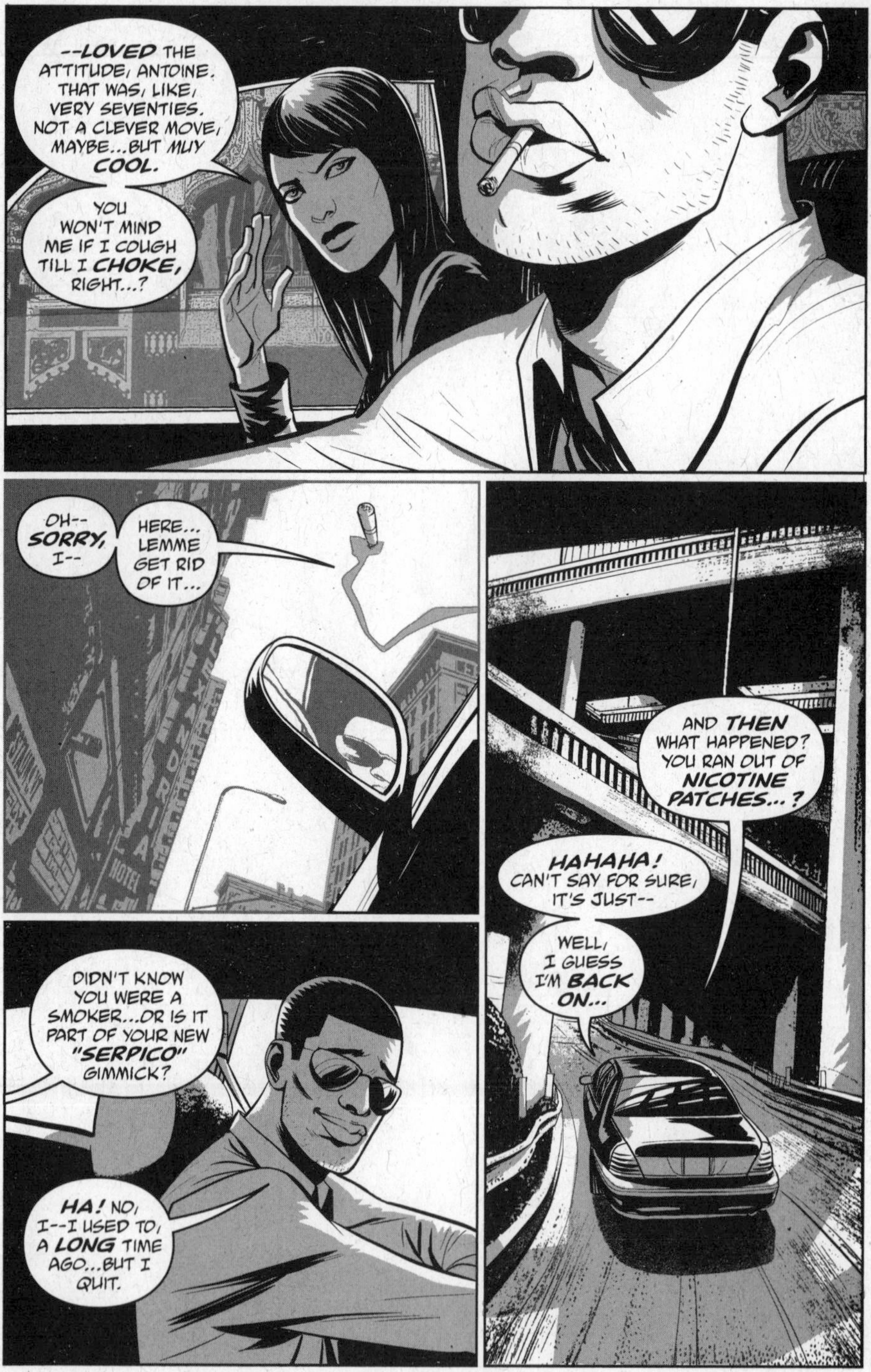
--LOVED THE ATTITUDE, ANTOINE. THAT WAS, LIKE, VERY SEVENTIES. NOT A CLEVER MOVE, MAYBE...BUT MUY COOL.
YOU WON'T MIND ME IF I COUGH TILL I CHOKE, RIGHT...?
OH-- SORRY, I--
HERE... LEMME GET RID OF IT...
DIDN'T KNOW YOU WERE A SMOKER...OR IS IT PART OF YOUR NEW "SERPICO" GIMMICK?
HA! NO, I--I USED TO, A LONG TIME AGO...BUT I QUIT.
AND THEN WHAT HAPPENED? YOU RAN OUT OF NICOTINE PATCHES...?
HAHAHA! CAN'T SAY FOR SURE, IT'S JUST--
WELL, I GUESS I'M BACK ON...

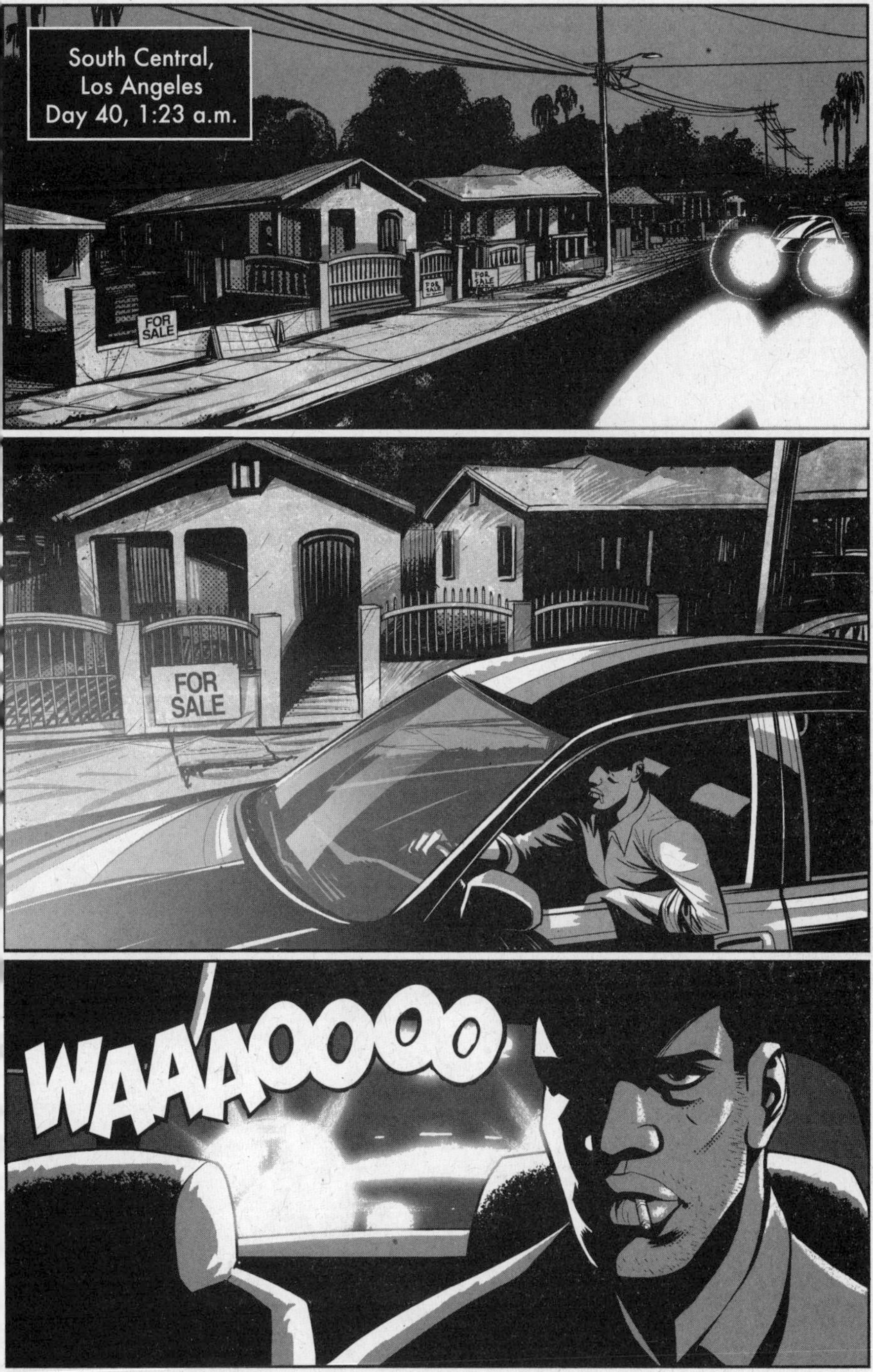
South Central, Los Angeles Day 40, 1:23 a.m.
FOR SALE
FOR SALE
FOR SALE
FOR SALE
WAAAOOOO

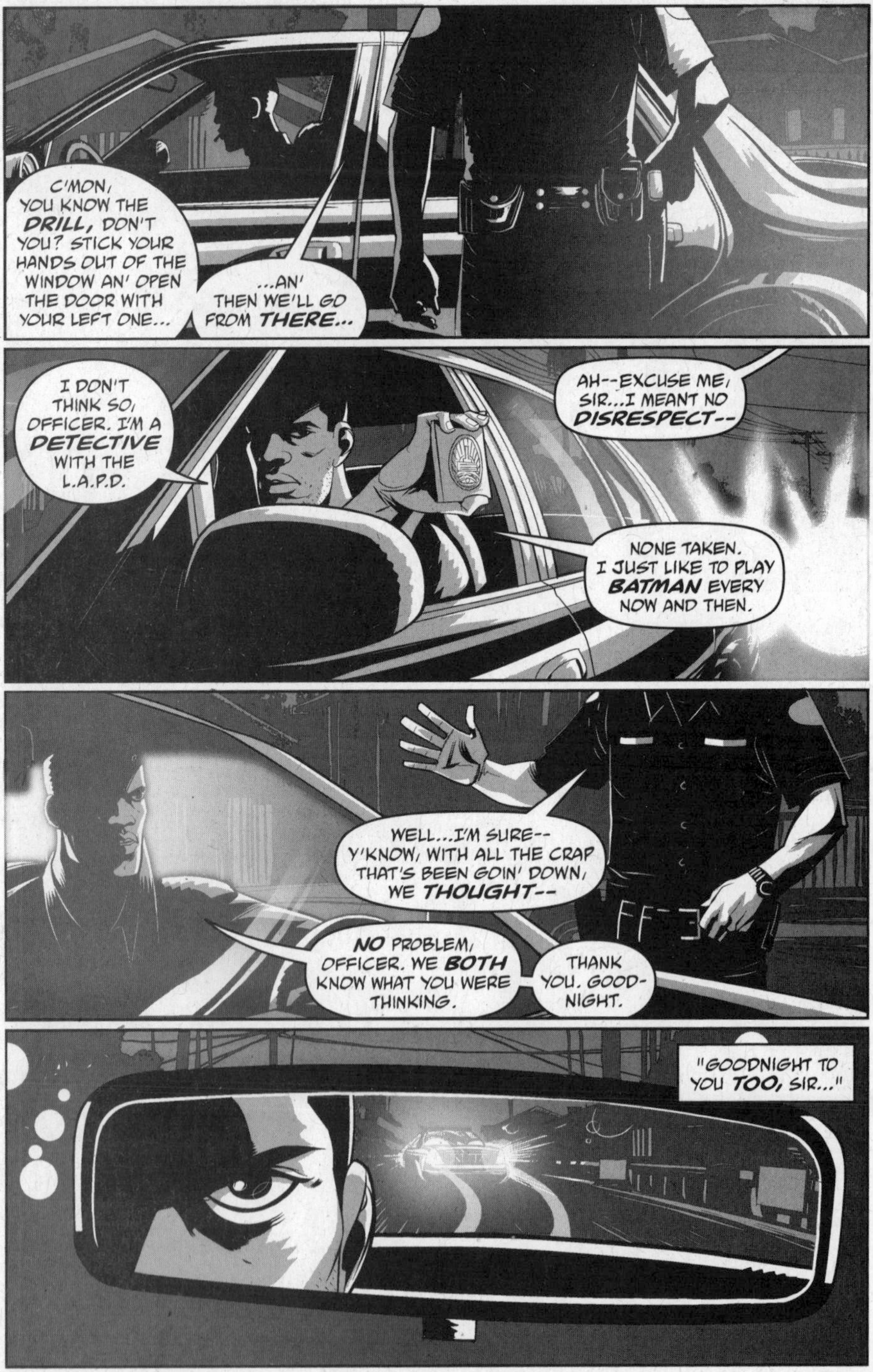
C'MON, YOU KNOW THE DRILL, DON'T YOU? STICK YOUR HANDS OUT OF THE WINDOW AN' OPEN THE DOOR WITH YOUR LEFT ONE...
...AN' THEN WE'LL GO FROM THERE...
I DON'T THINK SO, OFFICER. I'M A DETECTIVE WITH THE L.A.P.D.
AH--EXCUSE ME, SIR...I MEANT NO DISRESPECT--
NONE TAKEN. I JUST LIKE TO PLAY BATMAN EVERY NOW AND THEN.
WELL...I'M SURE-- Y'KNOW, WITH ALL THE CRAP THAT'S BEEN GOIN' DOWN, WE THOUGHT--
NO PROBLEM, OFFICER. WE BOTH KNOW WHAT YOU WERE THINKING.
THANK YOU. GOOD-NIGHT.
"GOODNIGHT TO YOU TOO, SIR..."

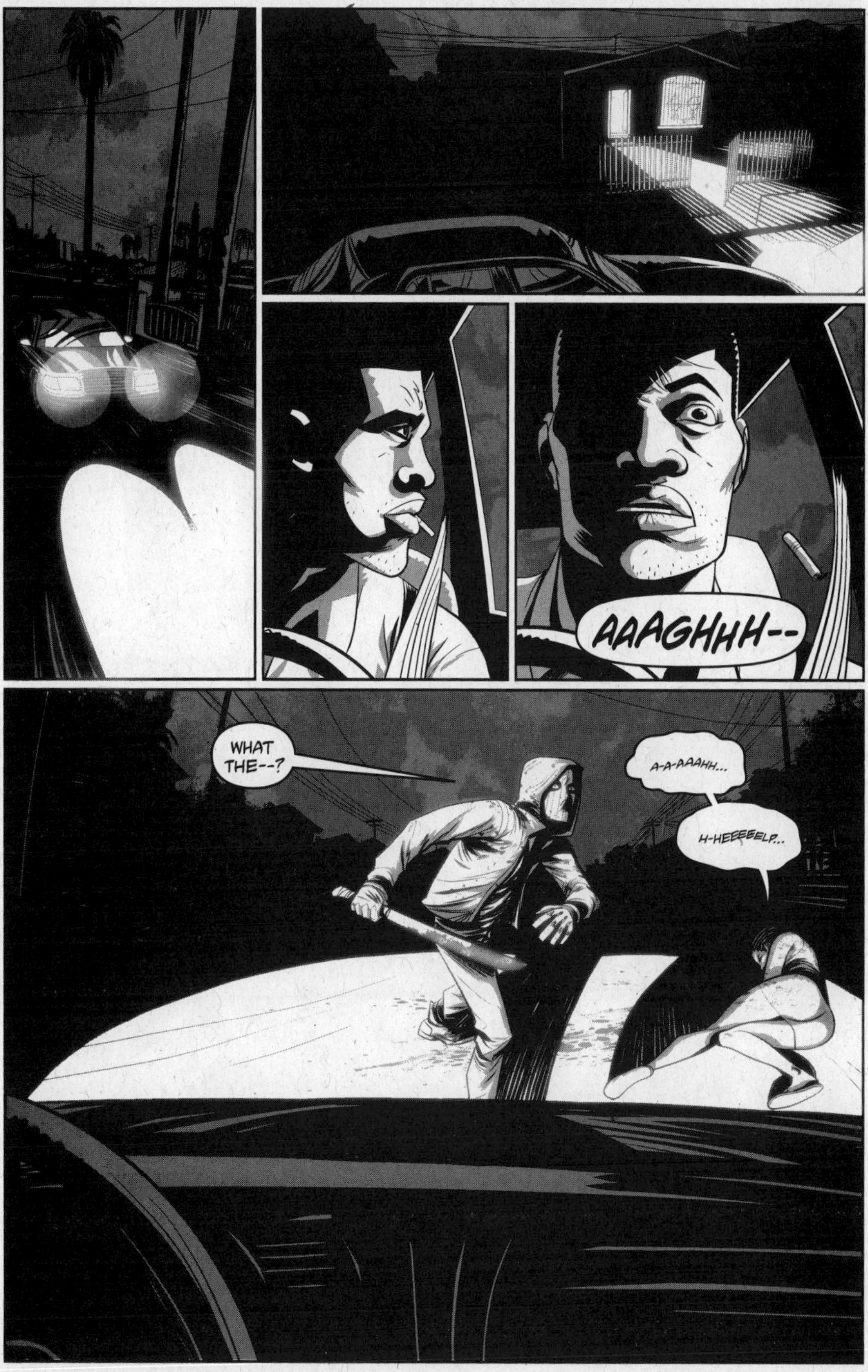
AAAGHHH--
WHAT THE--?
A-A-AAAHH...
H-HEEEEELP...

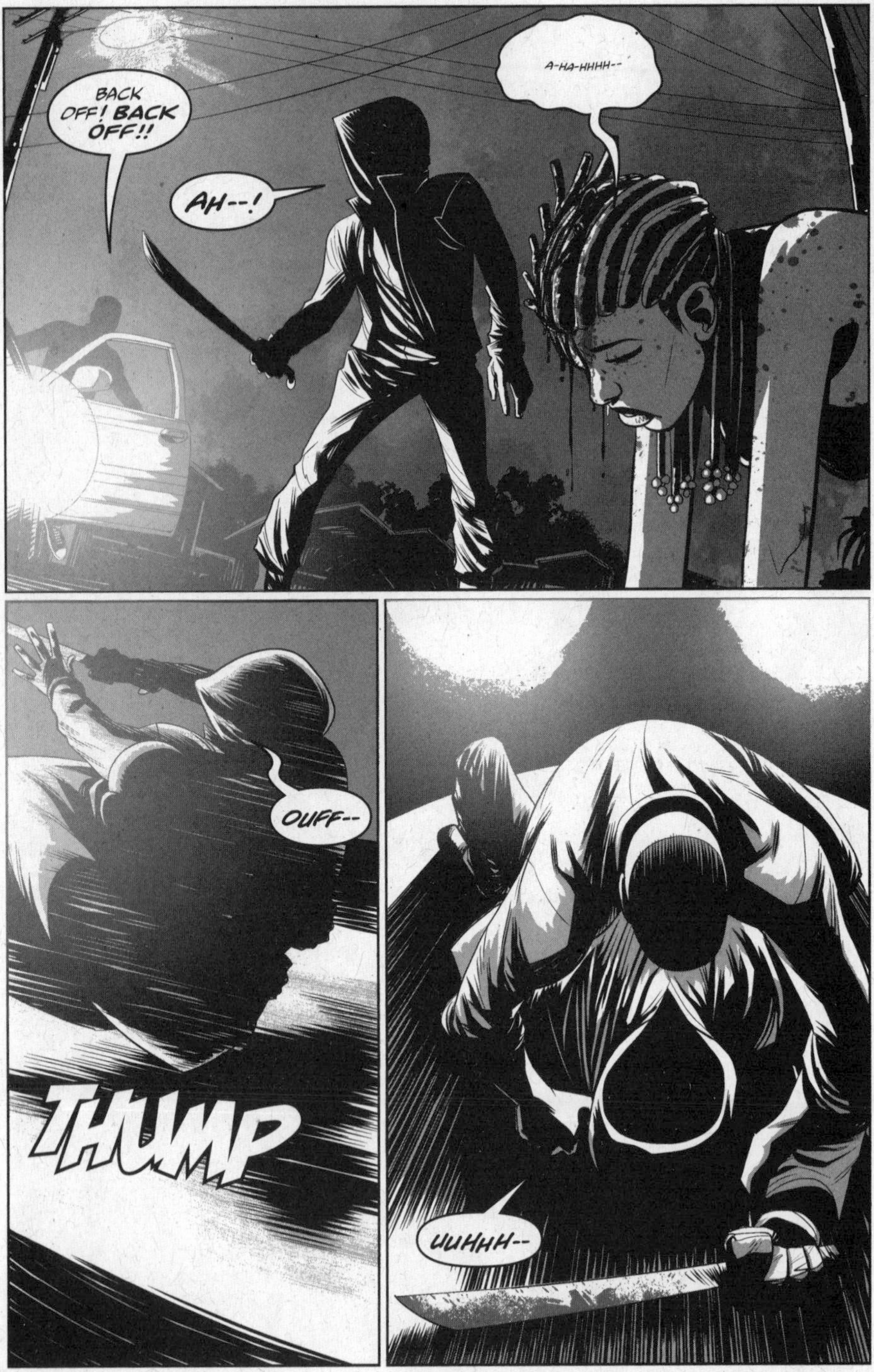
BACK OFF! BACK OFF!!
AH--!
A-HA-HHHH--
OUFF--
THUMP
UUHHH--

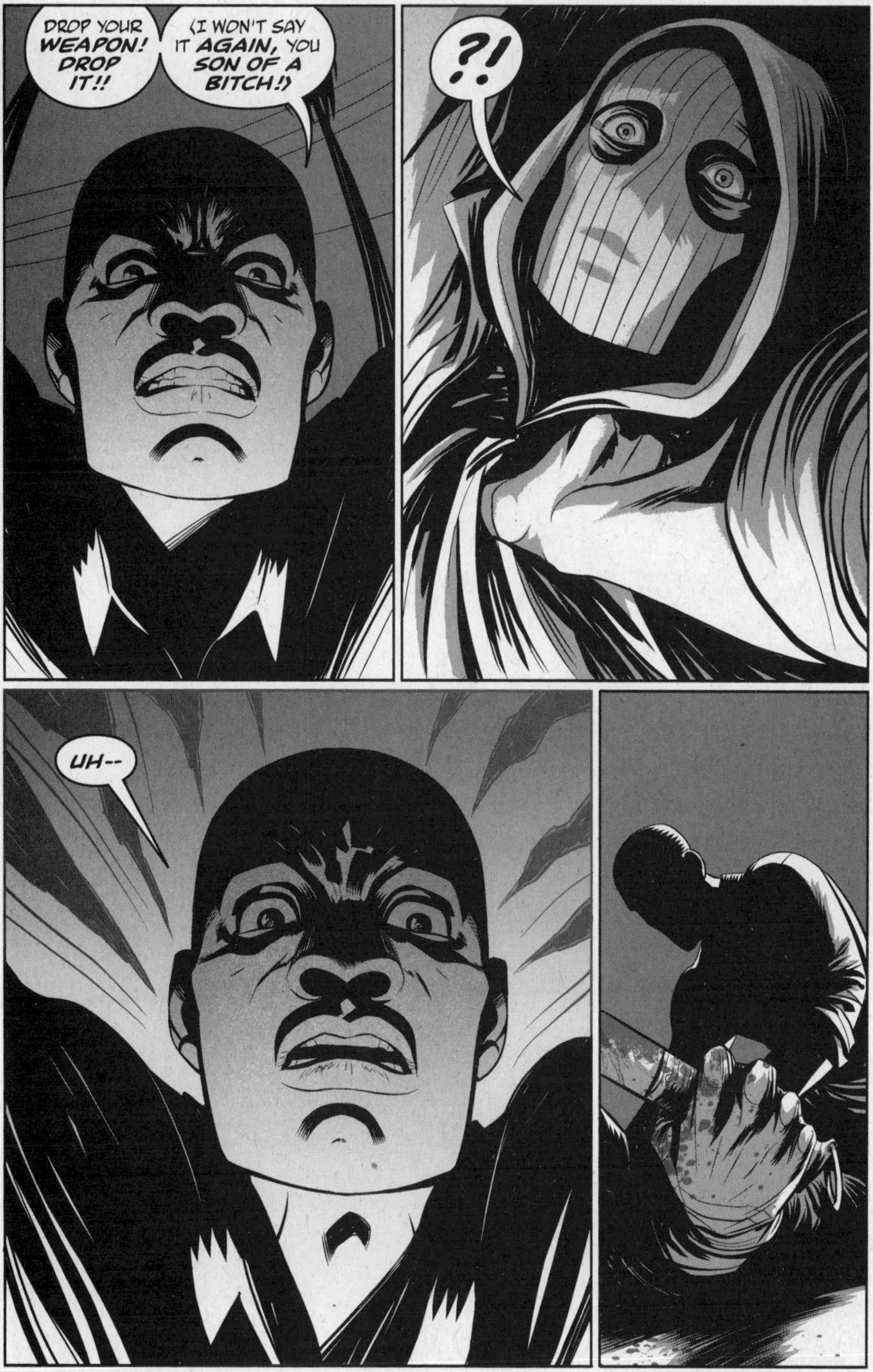
DROP YOUR WEAPON! DROP IT!!
‹I WON'T SAY IT AGAIN, YOU SON OF A BITCH!›
?!
UH--

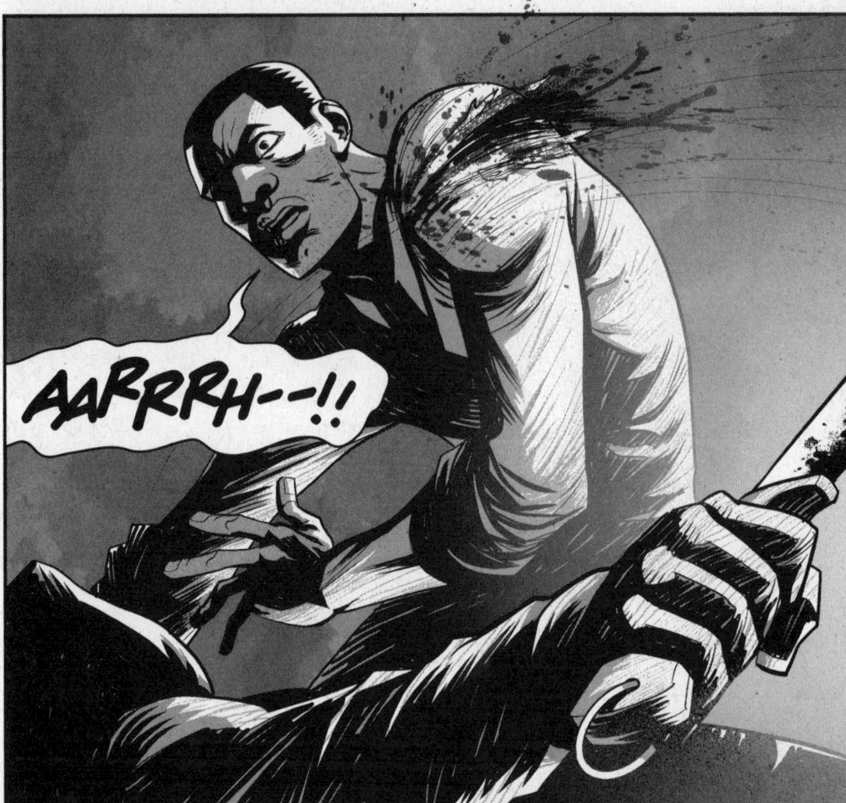
AARRRH--!!

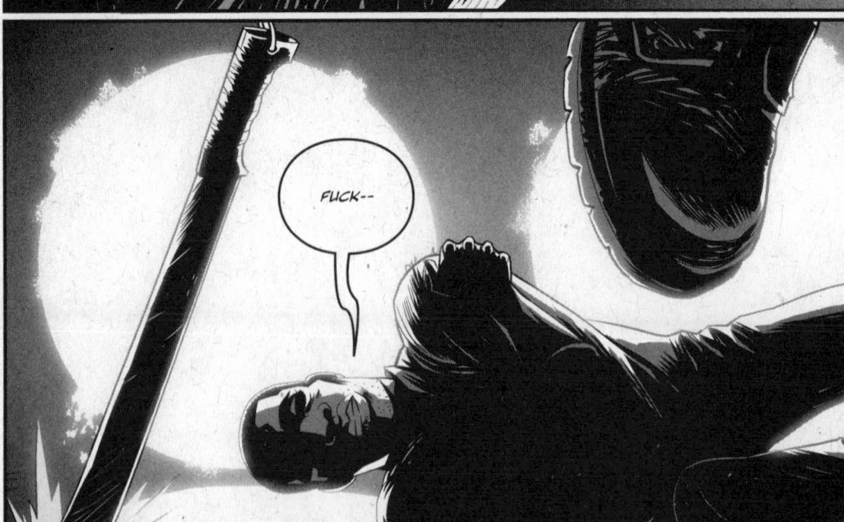
FUCK--

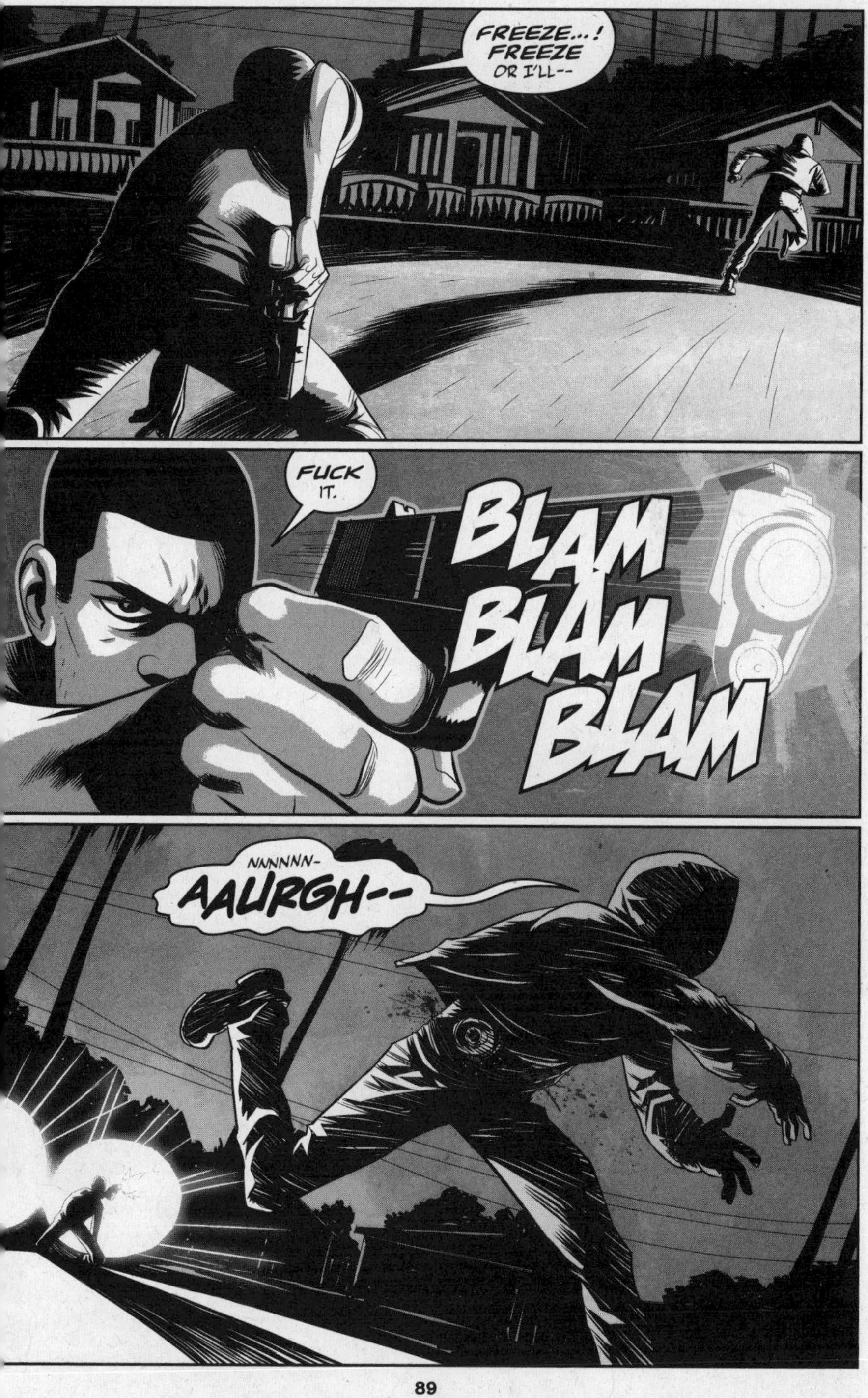
FREEZE...! FREEZE OR I'LL--
FUCK IT.
BLAM BLAM BLAM
NNNNNN- AAURGH--

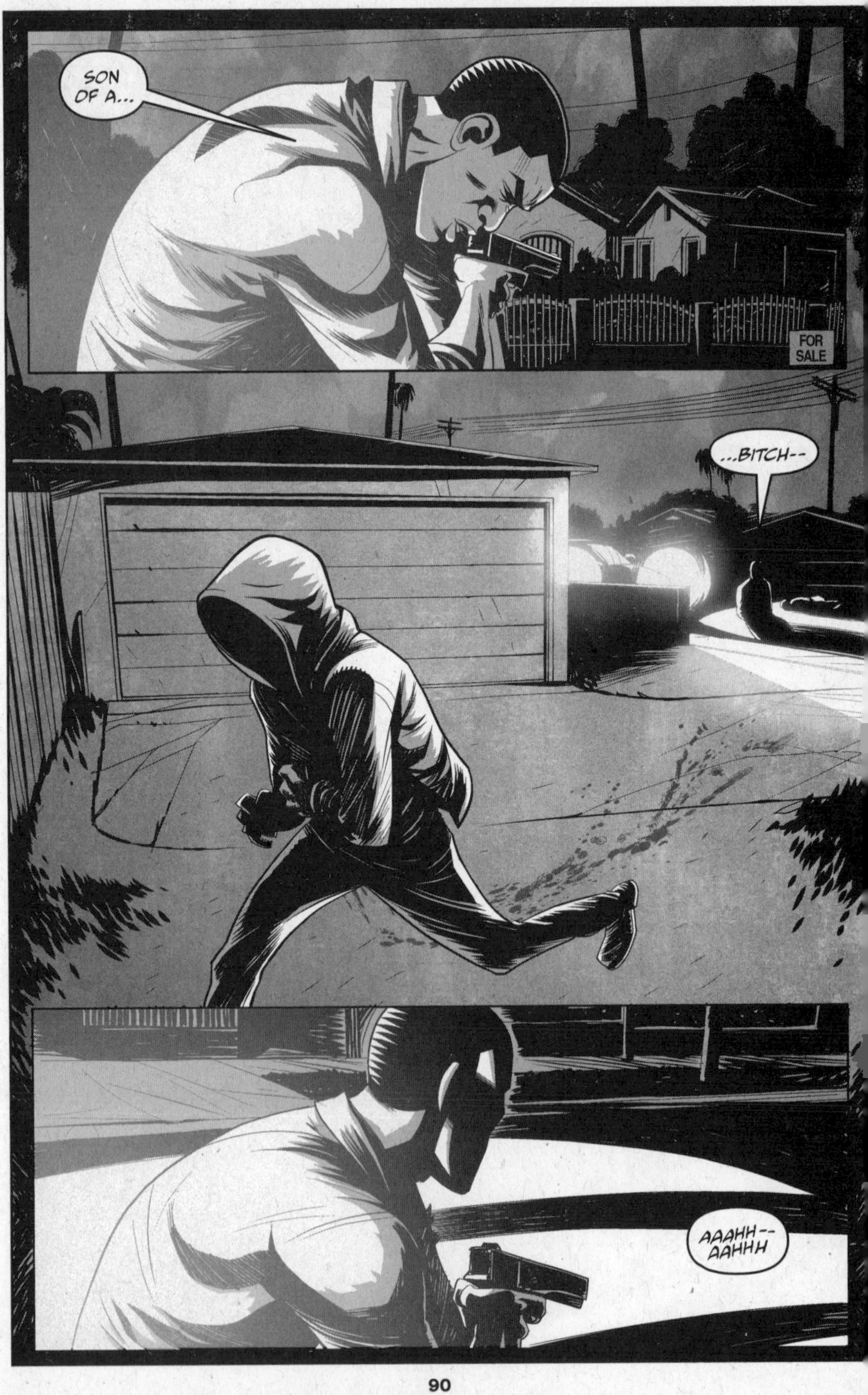
SON OF A...
FOR SALE
...BITCH--
AAAHH--
AAHHH

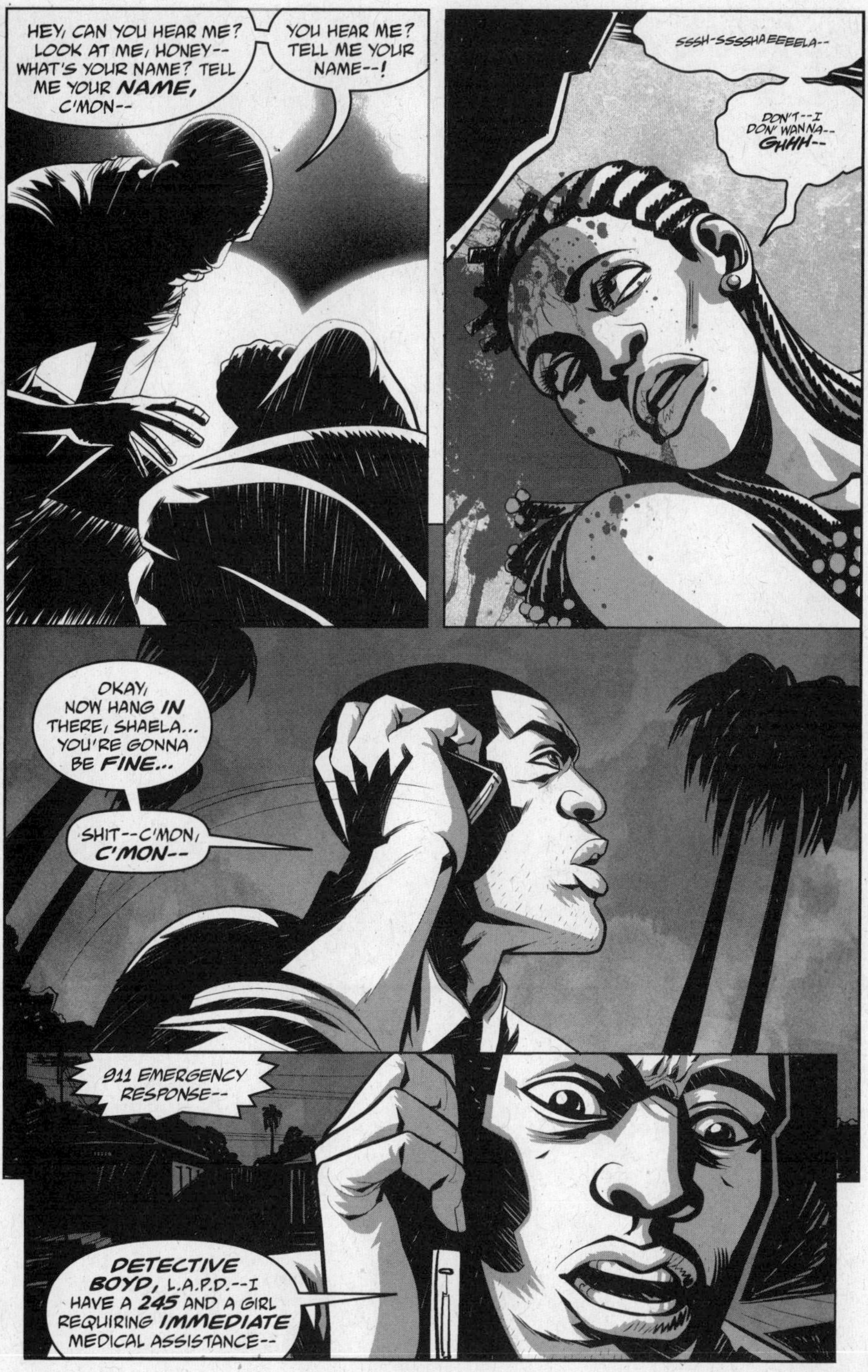
HEY, CAN YOU HEAR ME? LOOK AT ME, HONEY-- WHAT'S YOUR NAME? TELL ME YOUR NAME, C'MON--
YOU HEAR ME? TELL ME YOUR NAME--!
SSSH-SSSSHAEEEEELA--
DON'T--I DON' WANNA-- GHHH--
OKAY, NOW HANG IN THERE, SHAELA... YOU'RE GONNA BE FINE...
SHIT--C'MON, C'MON--
911 EMERGENCY RESPONSE--
DETECTIVE BOYD, L.A.P.D.--I HAVE A 245 AND A GIRL REQUIRING IMMEDIATE MEDICAL ASSISTANCE--

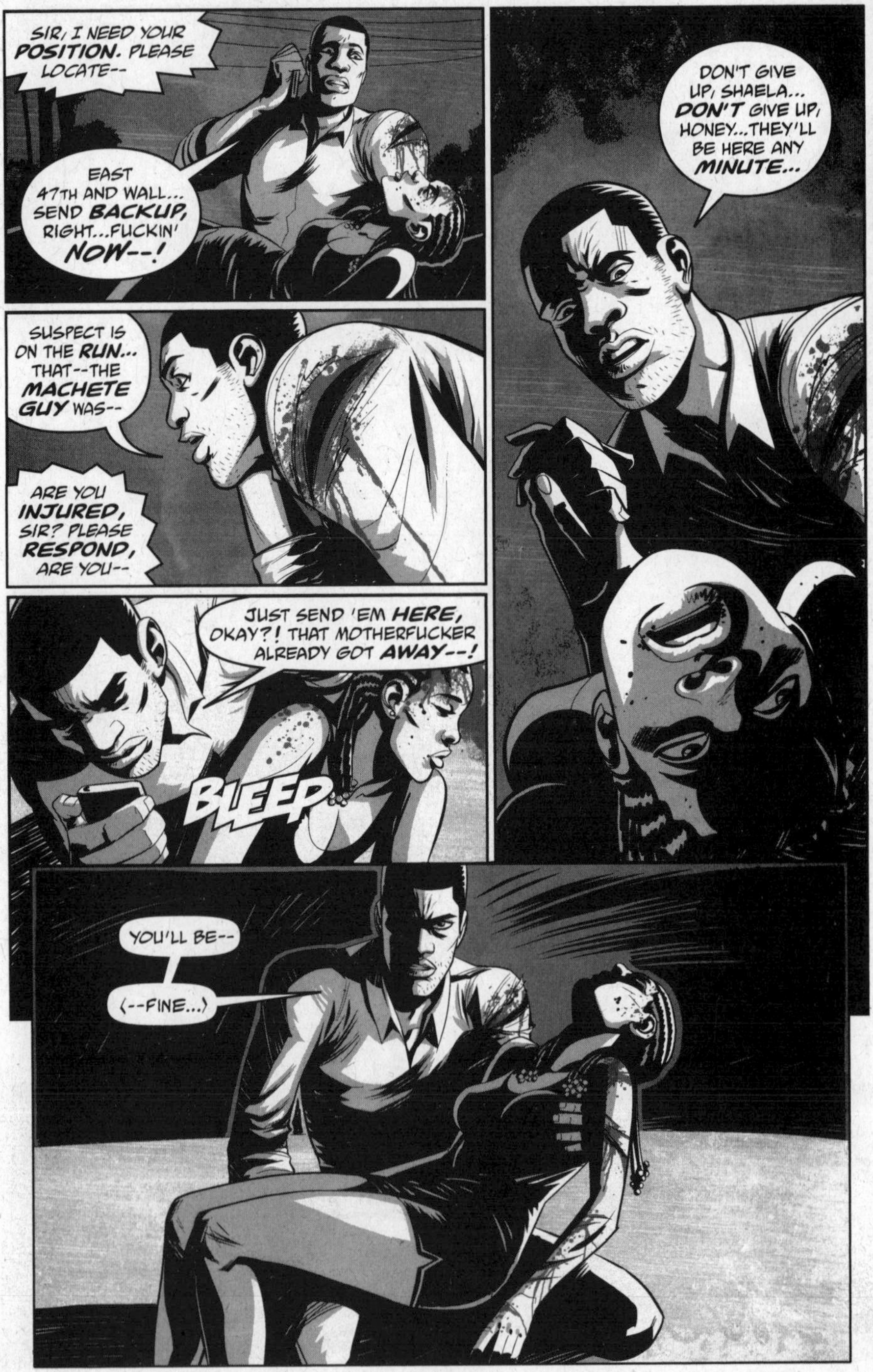
SIR, I NEED YOUR POSITION. PLEASE LOCATE--
EAST 47TH AND WALL... SEND BACKUP, RIGHT...FUCKIN' NOW--!
SUSPECT IS ON THE RUN... THAT--THE MACHETE GUY WAS--
ARE YOU INJURED, SIR? PLEASE RESPOND, ARE YOU--
JUST SEND 'EM HERE, OKAY?! THAT MOTHERFUCKER ALREADY GOT AWAY--!
BLEEP
DON'T GIVE UP, SHAELA... DON'T GIVE UP, HONEY...THEY'LL BE HERE ANY MINUTE...
YOU'LL BE--
(--FINE...)

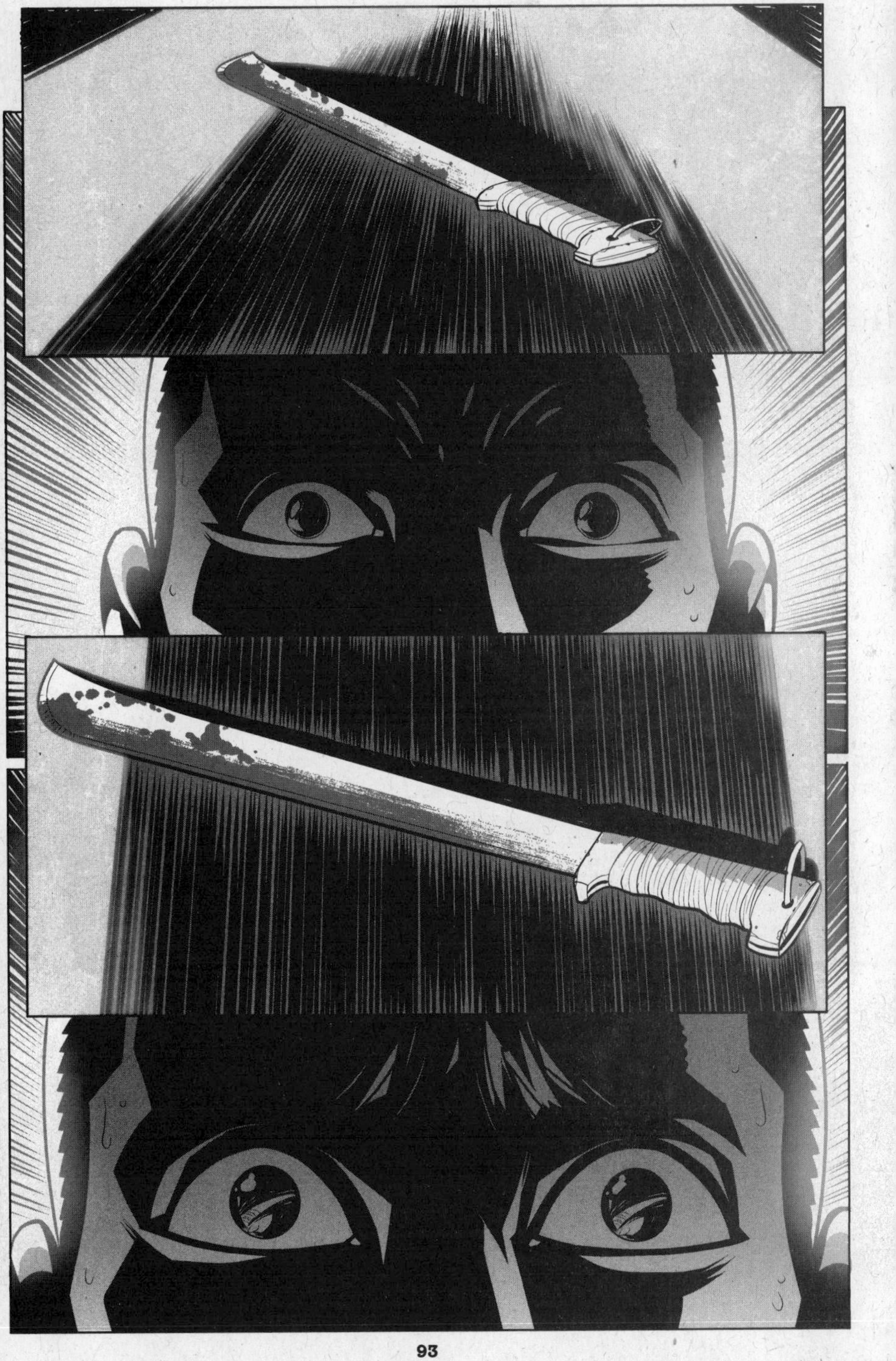

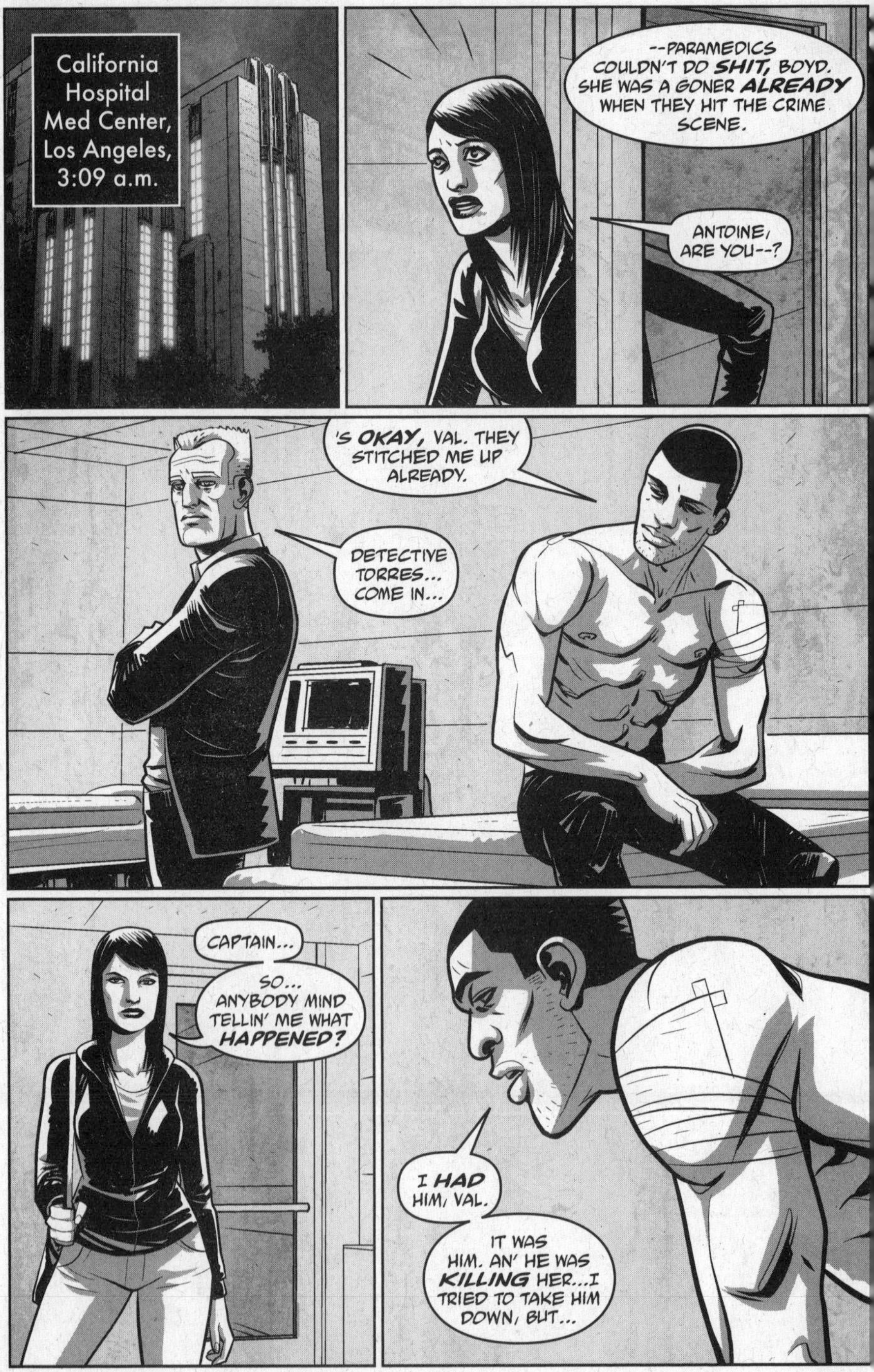
California Hospital Med Center, Los Angeles, 3:09 a.m.
--PARAMEDICS COULDN'T DO SHIT, BOYD. SHE WAS A GONER ALREADY WHEN THEY HIT THE CRIME SCENE.
ANTOINE, ARE YOU--?
'S OKAY, VAL. THEY STITCHED ME UP ALREADY.
DETECTIVE TORRES... COME IN...
CAPTAIN...
SO... ANYBODY MIND TELLIN' ME WHAT HAPPENED?
I HAD HIM, VAL.
IT WAS HIM. AN' HE WAS KILLING HER...I TRIED TO TAKE HIM DOWN, BUT...

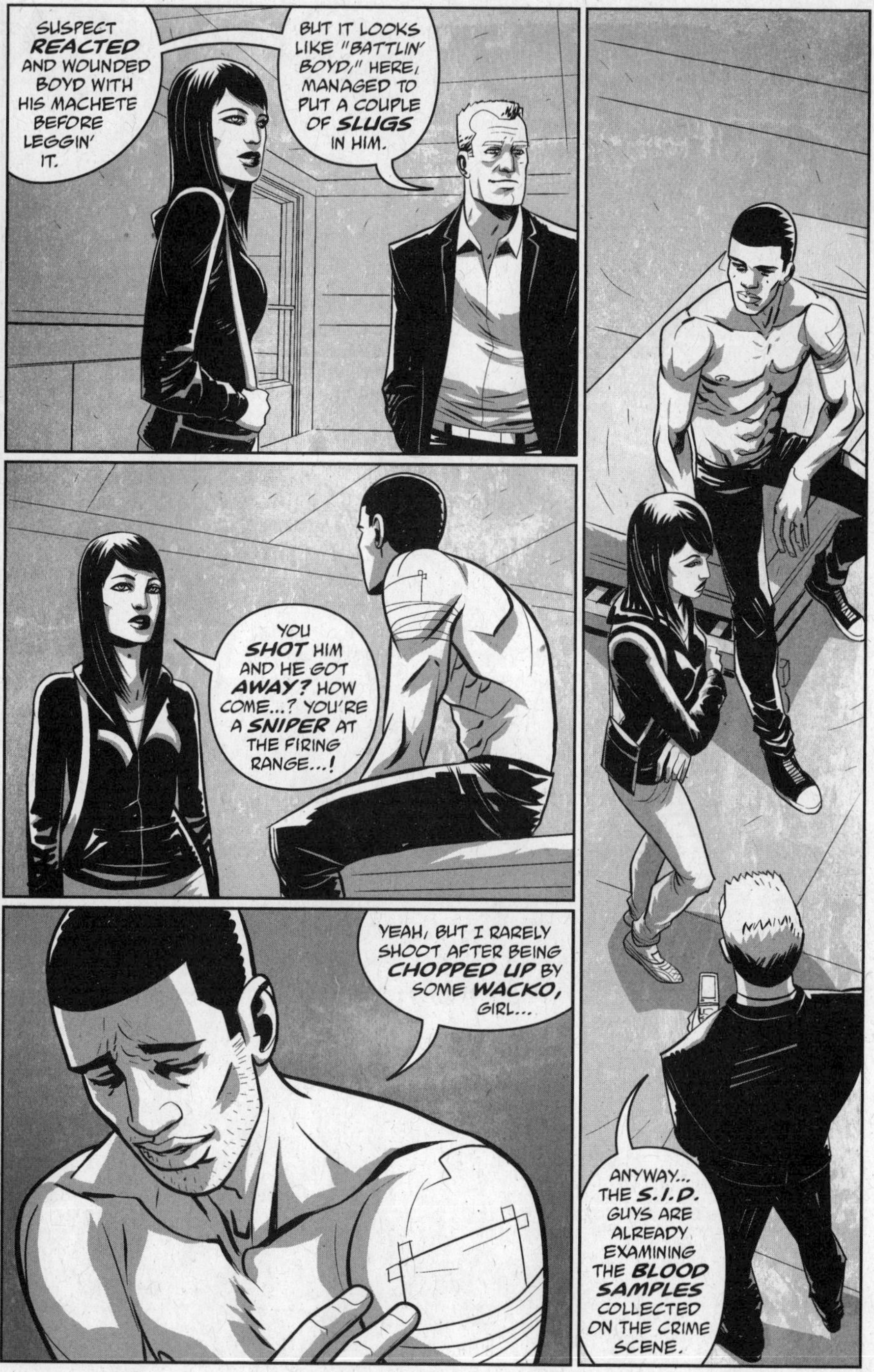
SUSPECT REACTED AND WOUNDED BOYD WITH HIS MACHETE BEFORE LEGGIN' IT.
BUT IT LOOKS LIKE "BATTLIN' BOYD," HERE, MANAGED TO PUT A COUPLE OF SLUGS IN HIM.
YOU SHOT HIM AND HE GOT AWAY? HOW COME...? YOU'RE A SNIPER AT THE FIRING RANGE...!
YEAH, BUT I RARELY SHOOT AFTER BEING CHOPPED UP BY SOME WACKO, GIRL...
ANYWAY... THE S.I.D. GUYS ARE ALREADY EXAMINING THE BLOOD SAMPLES COLLECTED ON THE CRIME SCENE.

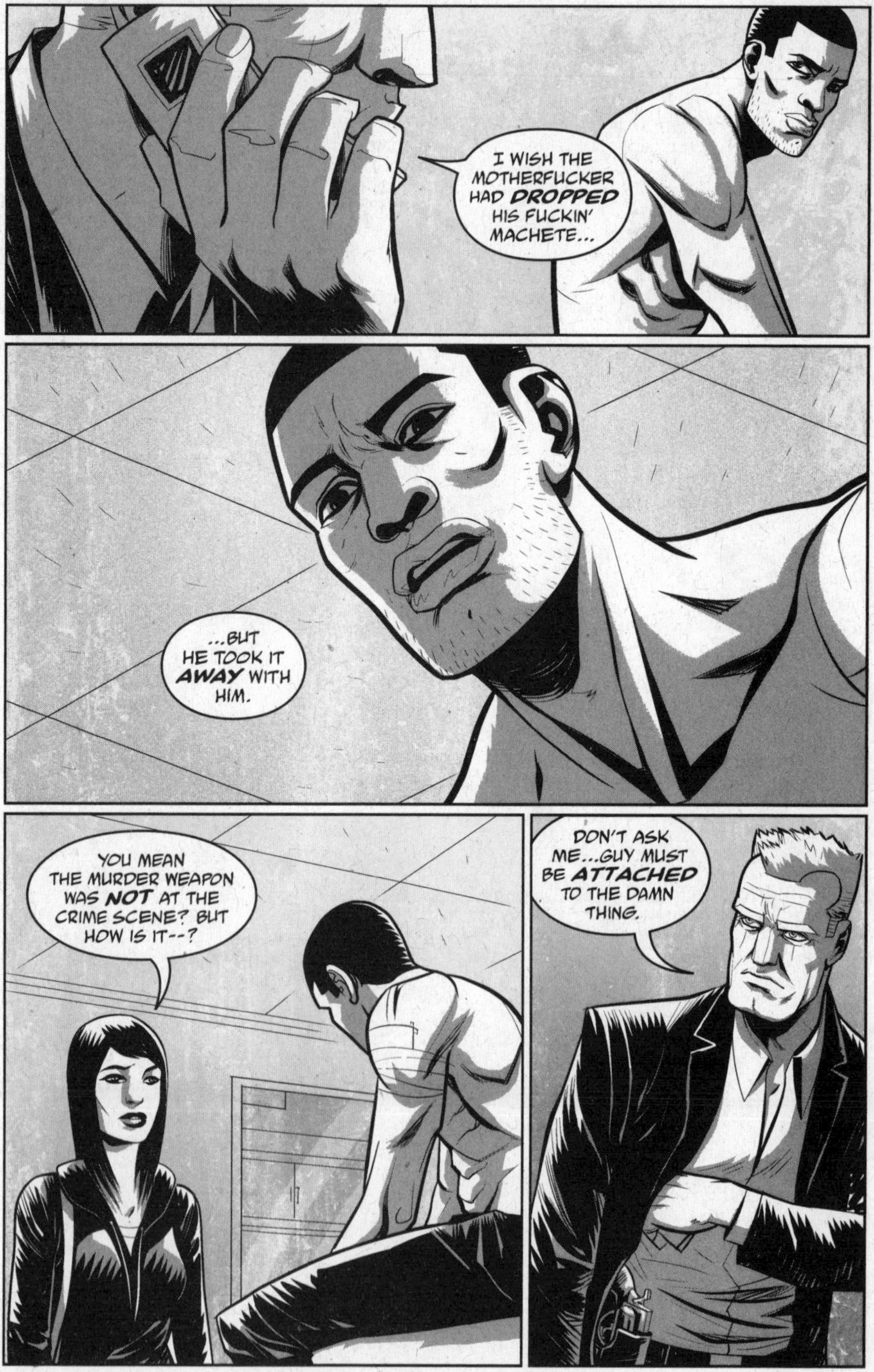
I WISH THE MOTHERFUCKER HAD DROPPED HIS FUCKIN' MACHETE...
...BUT HE TOOK IT AWAY WITH HIM.
YOU MEAN THE MURDER WEAPON WAS NOT AT THE CRIME SCENE? BUT HOW IS IT--?
DON'T ASK ME...GUY MUST BE ATTACHED TO THE DAMN THING.

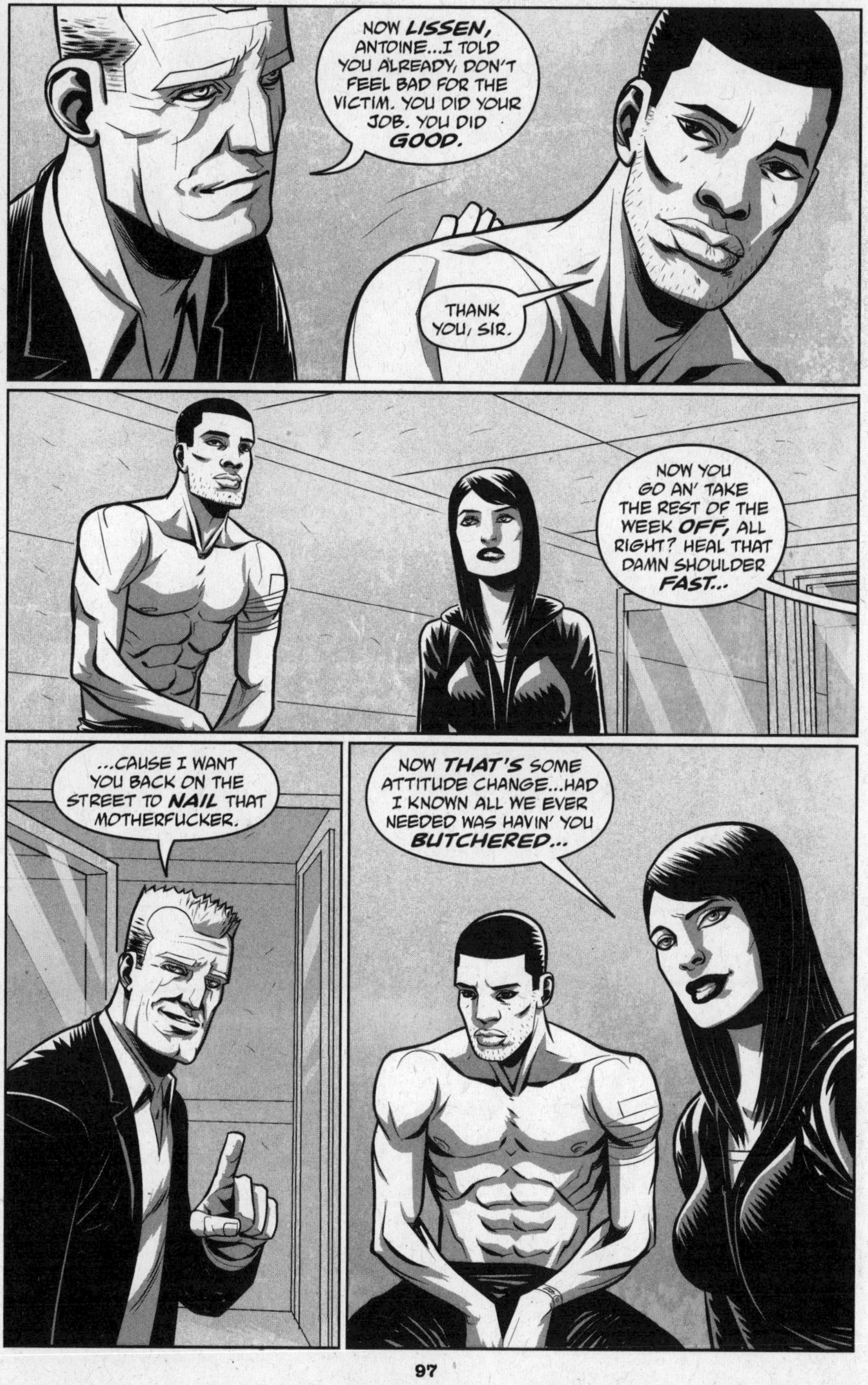
NOW LISSEN, ANTOINE...I TOLD YOU ALREADY, DON'T FEEL BAD FOR THE VICTIM. YOU DID YOUR JOB. YOU DID GOOD.
THANK YOU, SIR.
NOW YOU GO AN' TAKE THE REST OF THE WEEK OFF, ALL RIGHT? HEAL THAT DAMN SHOULDER FAST...
...CAUSE I WANT YOU BACK ON THE STREET TO NAIL THAT MOTHERFUCKER.
NOW THAT'S SOME ATTITUDE CHANGE...HAD I KNOWN ALL WE EVER NEEDED WAS HAVIN' YOU BUTCHERED...

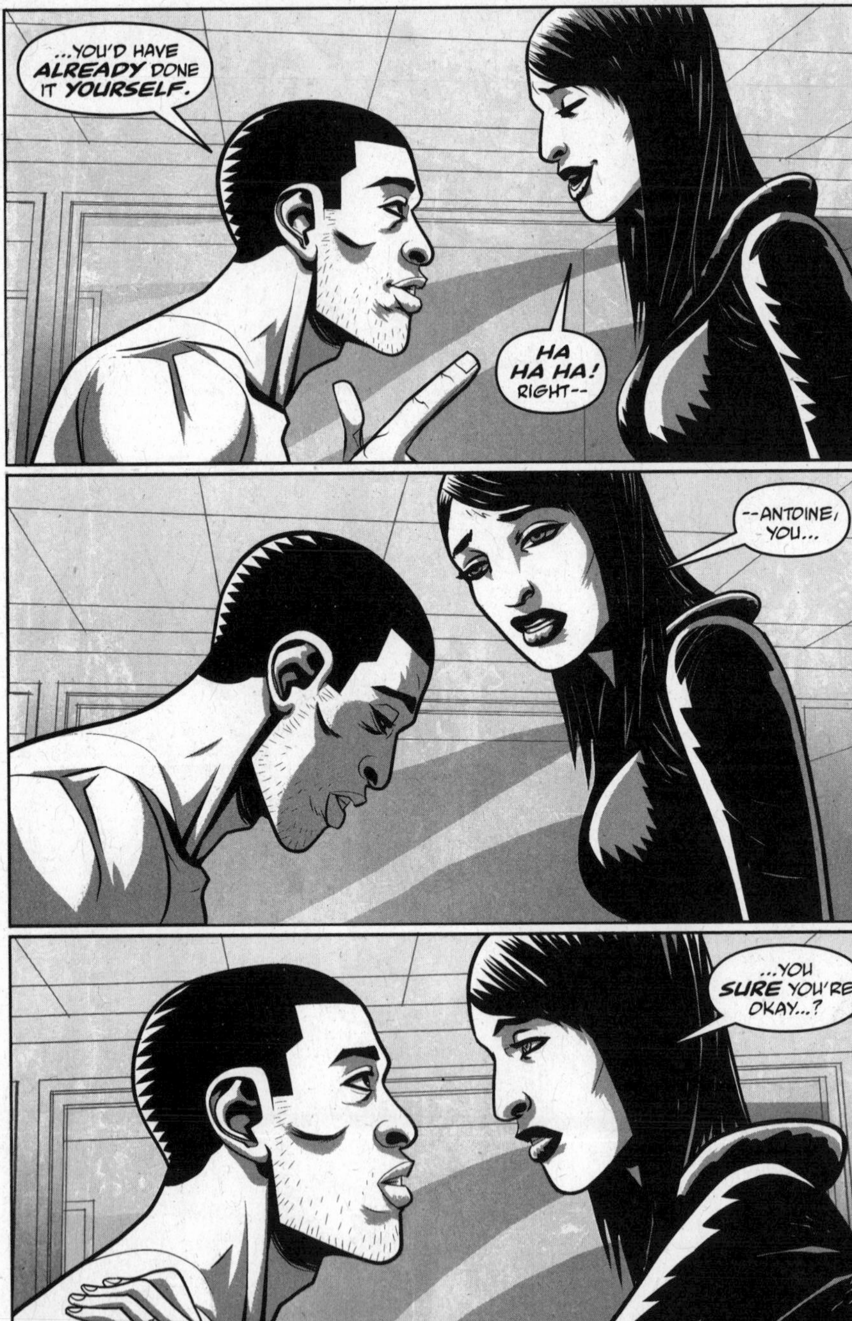
...YOU'D HAVE ALREADY DONE IT YOURSELF.
HA HA HA! RIGHT--
--ANTOINE, YOU...
...YOU SURE YOU'RE OKAY...?

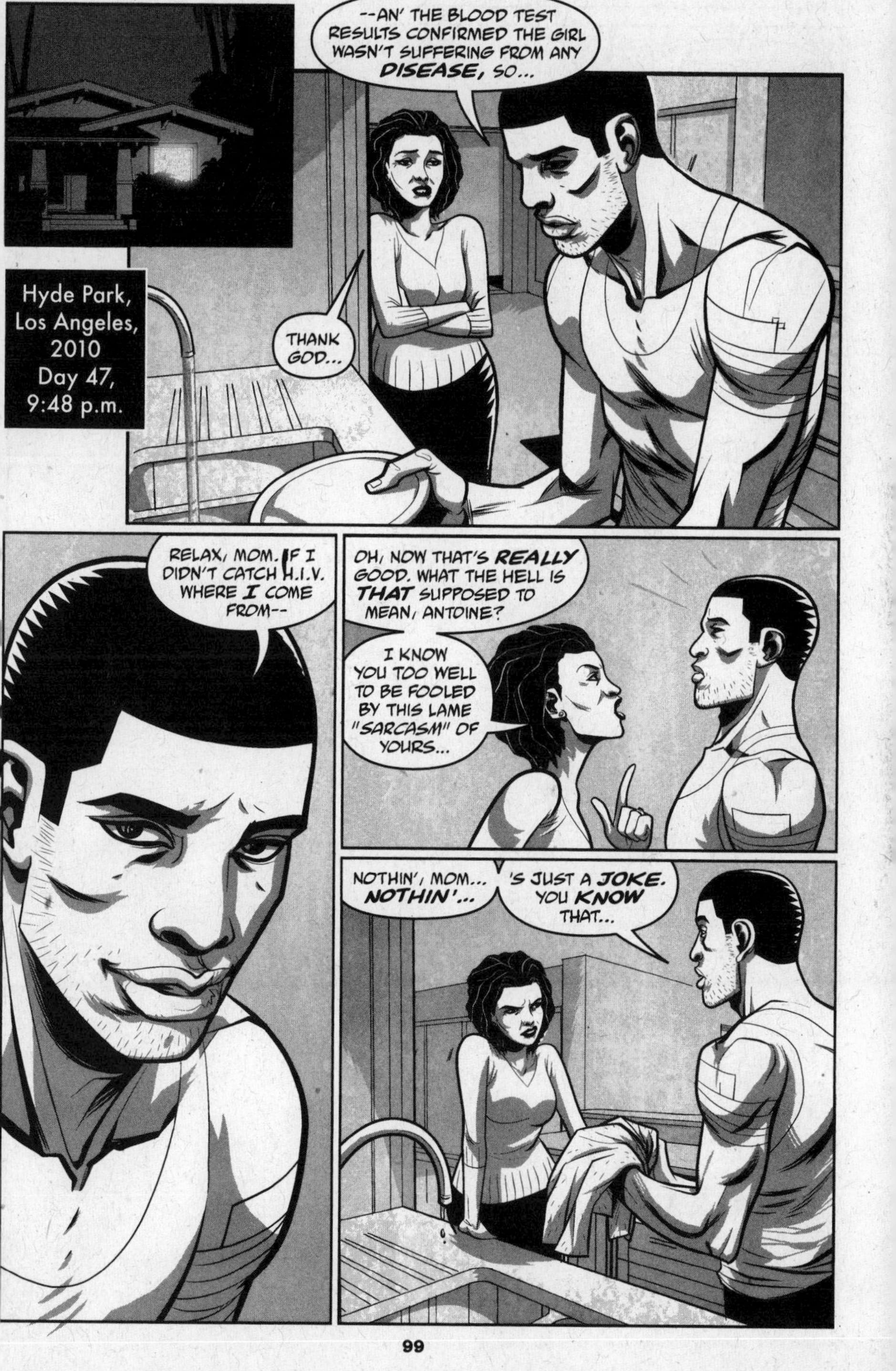
--AN' THE BLOOD TEST RESULTS CONFIRMED THE GIRL WASN'T SUFFERING FROM ANY **DISEASE,** SO...
Hyde Park, Los Angeles, 2010 Day 47, 9:48 p.m.
THANK GOD...
RELAX, MOM. IF I DIDN'T CATCH H.I.V. WHERE **I** COME FROM--
OH, NOW THAT'S **REALLY** GOOD. WHAT THE HELL IS **THAT** SUPPOSED TO MEAN, ANTOINE?
I KNOW YOU TOO WELL TO BE FOOLED BY THIS LAME "SARCASM" OF YOURS...
NOTHIN', MOM... **NOTHIN'...**
'S JUST A **JOKE.** YOU **KNOW** THAT...

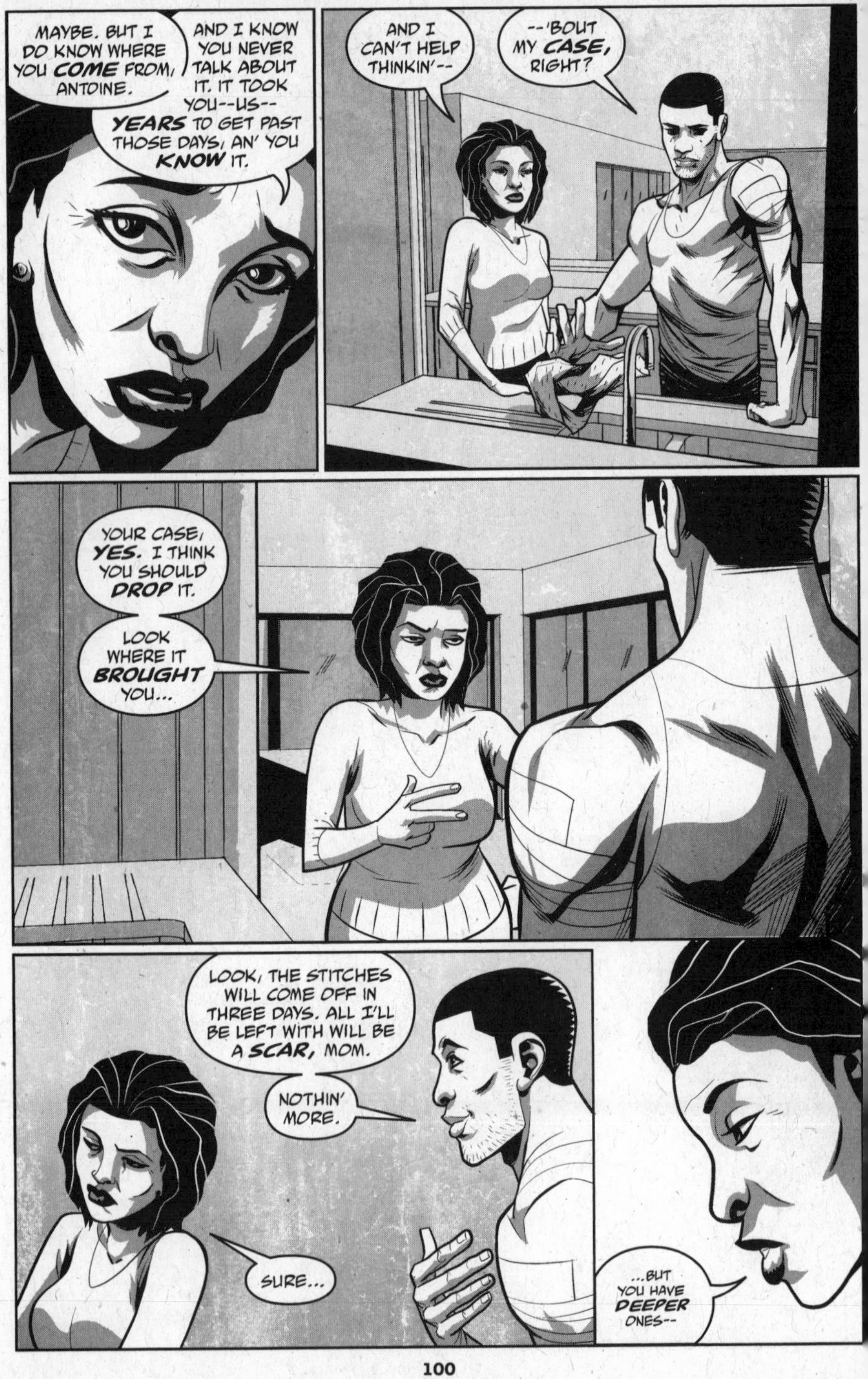
MAYBE. BUT I DO KNOW WHERE YOU COME FROM, ANTOINE.
AND I KNOW YOU NEVER TALK ABOUT IT. IT TOOK YOU--US--YEARS TO GET PAST THOSE DAYS, AN' YOU KNOW IT.
AND I CAN'T HELP THINKIN'--
--'BOUT MY CASE, RIGHT?
YOUR CASE, YES. I THINK YOU SHOULD DROP IT.
LOOK WHERE IT BROUGHT YOU...
LOOK, THE STITCHES WILL COME OFF IN THREE DAYS. ALL I'LL BE LEFT WITH WILL BE A SCAR, MOM.
NOTHIN' MORE.
SURE...
...BUT YOU HAVE DEEPER ONES--

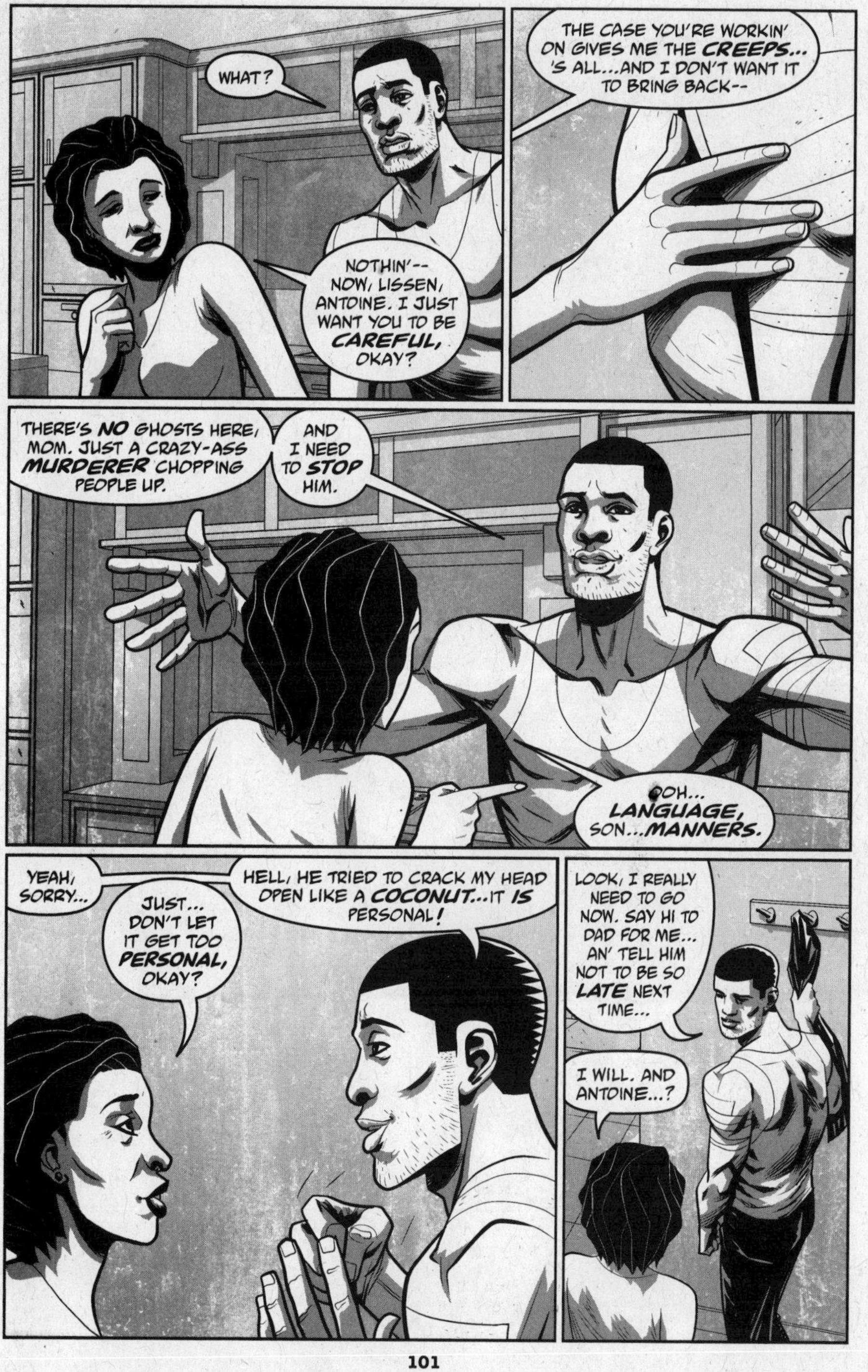
WHAT?
NOTHIN'-- NOW, LISSEN, ANTOINE. I JUST WANT YOU TO BE CAREFUL, OKAY?
THE CASE YOU'RE WORKIN' ON GIVES ME THE CREEPS... 'S ALL...AND I DON'T WANT IT TO BRING BACK--
THERE'S NO GHOSTS HERE, MOM. JUST A CRAZY-ASS MURDERER CHOPPING PEOPLE UP.
AND I NEED TO STOP HIM.
OOH... LANGUAGE, SON...MANNERS.
YEAH, SORRY...
JUST... DON'T LET IT GET TOO PERSONAL, OKAY?
HELL, HE TRIED TO CRACK MY HEAD OPEN LIKE A COCONUT...IT IS PERSONAL!
LOOK, I REALLY NEED TO GO NOW. SAY HI TO DAD FOR ME... AN' TELL HIM NOT TO BE SO LATE NEXT TIME...
I WILL. AND ANTOINE...?

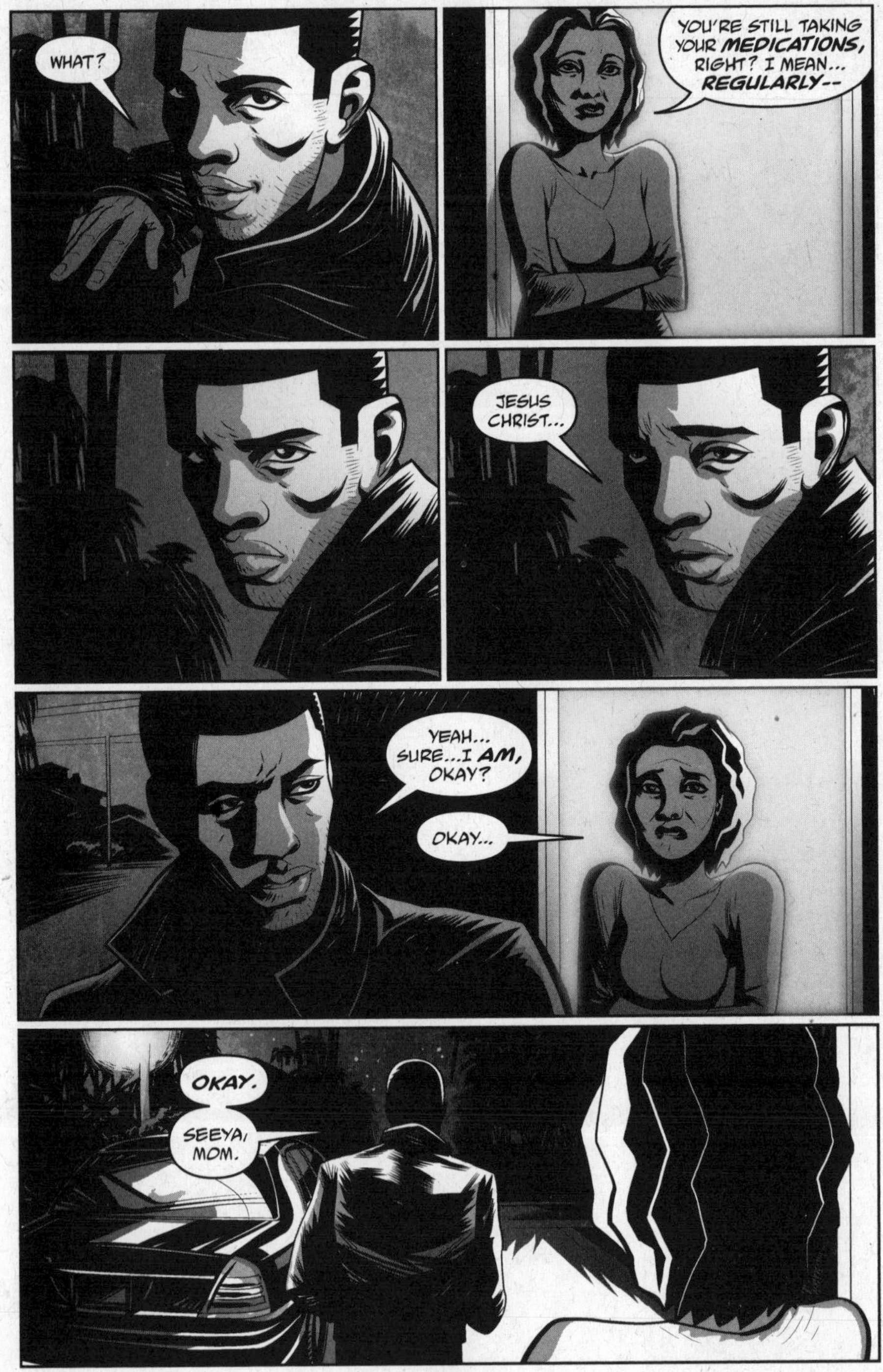
WHAT?
YOU'RE STILL TAKING YOUR MEDICATIONS, RIGHT? I MEAN... REGULARLY--
JESUS CHRIST...
YEAH... SURE...I AM, OKAY?
OKAY...
OKAY.
SEEYA, MOM.

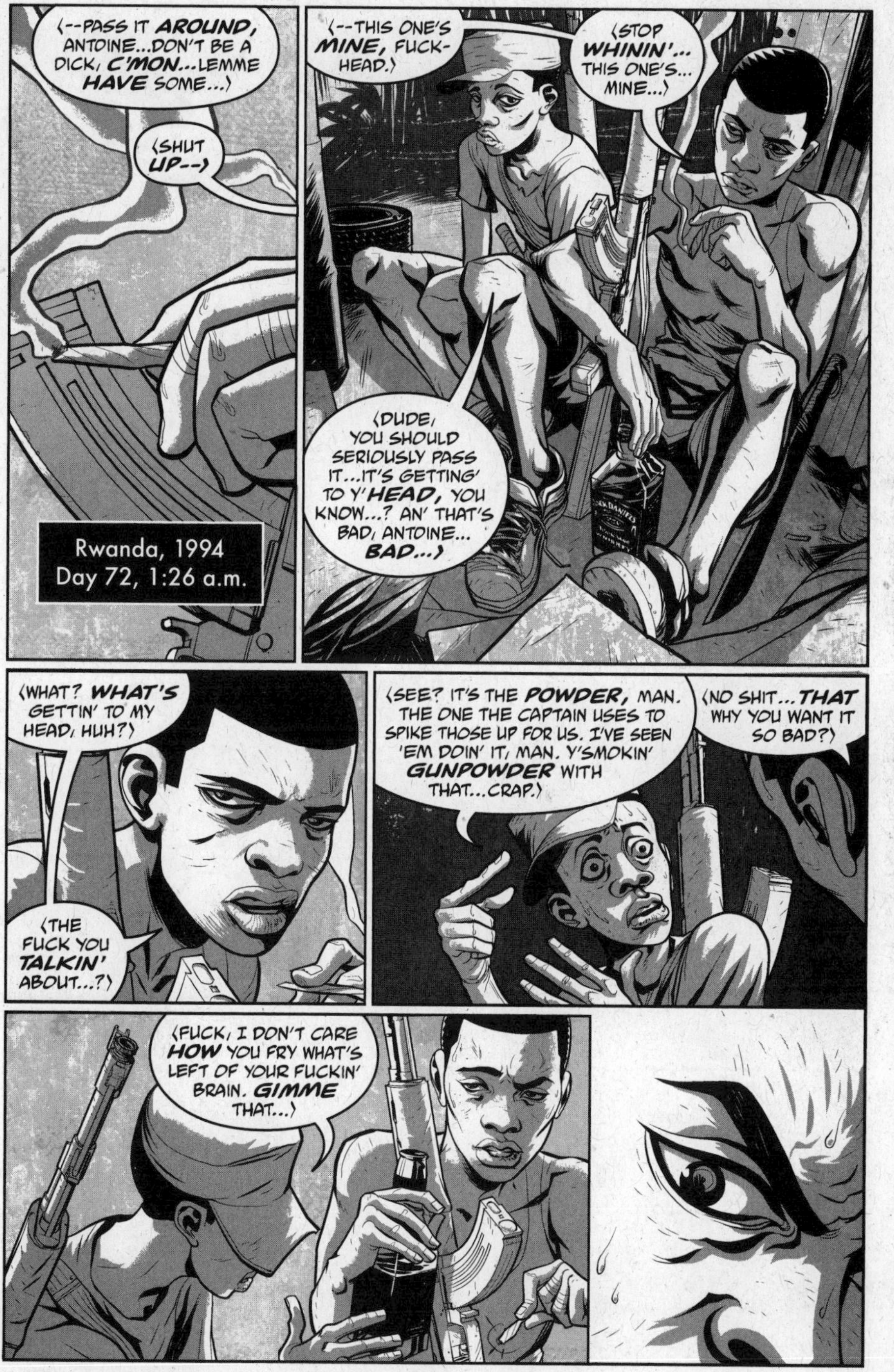
⟨--PASS IT AROUND, ANTOINE...DON'T BE A DICK, C'MON...LEMME HAVE SOME...⟩
⟨SHUT UP--⟩
Rwanda, 1994
Day 72, 1:26 a.m.
⟨--THIS ONE'S MINE, FUCK-HEAD.⟩
⟨STOP WHININ'... THIS ONE'S... MINE...⟩
⟨DUDE, YOU SHOULD SERIOUSLY PASS IT...IT'S GETTING' TO Y'HEAD, YOU KNOW...? AN' THAT'S BAD, ANTOINE... BAD...⟩
⟨WHAT? WHAT'S GETTIN' TO MY HEAD, HUH?⟩
⟨THE FUCK YOU TALKIN' ABOUT...?⟩
⟨SEE? IT'S THE POWDER, MAN. THE ONE THE CAPTAIN USES TO SPIKE THOSE UP FOR US. I'VE SEEN 'EM DOIN' IT, MAN. Y'SMOKIN' GUNPOWDER WITH THAT...CRAP.⟩
⟨NO SHIT...THAT WHY YOU WANT IT SO BAD?⟩
⟨FUCK, I DON'T CARE HOW YOU FRY WHAT'S LEFT OF YOUR FUCKIN' BRAIN. GIMME THAT...⟩

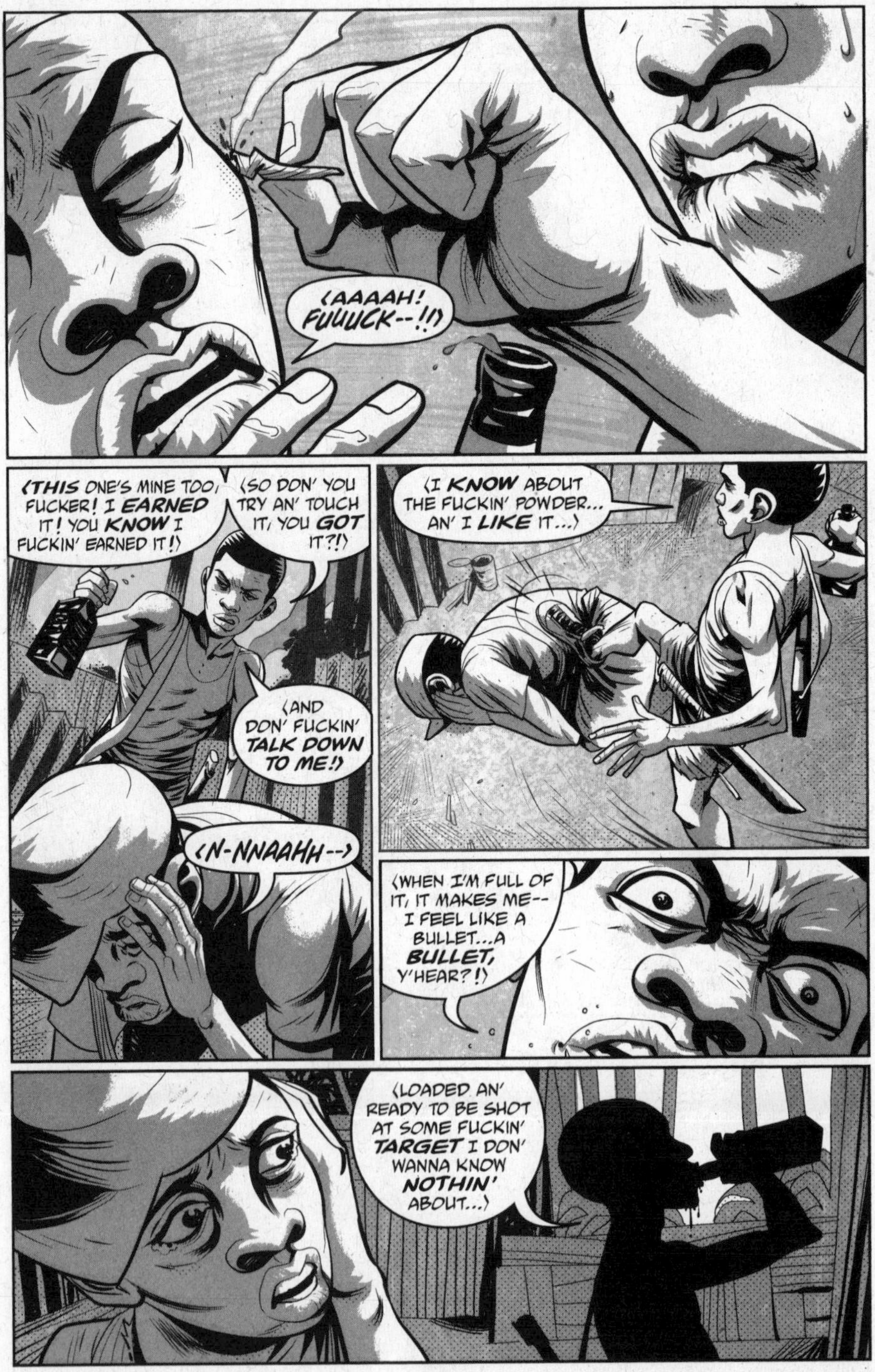
‹AAAAH! FUUUCK--!!›
‹THIS ONE'S MINE TOO, FUCKER! I EARNED IT! YOU KNOW I FUCKIN' EARNED IT!›
‹SO DON' YOU TRY AN' TOUCH IT, YOU GOT IT?!›
‹AND DON' FUCKIN' TALK DOWN TO ME!›
‹N-NNAAHH--›
‹I KNOW ABOUT THE FUCKIN' POWDER... AN' I LIKE IT...›
‹WHEN I'M FULL OF IT, IT MAKES ME-- I FEEL LIKE A BULLET...A BULLET, Y'HEAR?!›
‹LOADED AN' READY TO BE SHOT AT SOME FUCKIN' TARGET I DON' WANNA KNOW NOTHIN' ABOUT...›

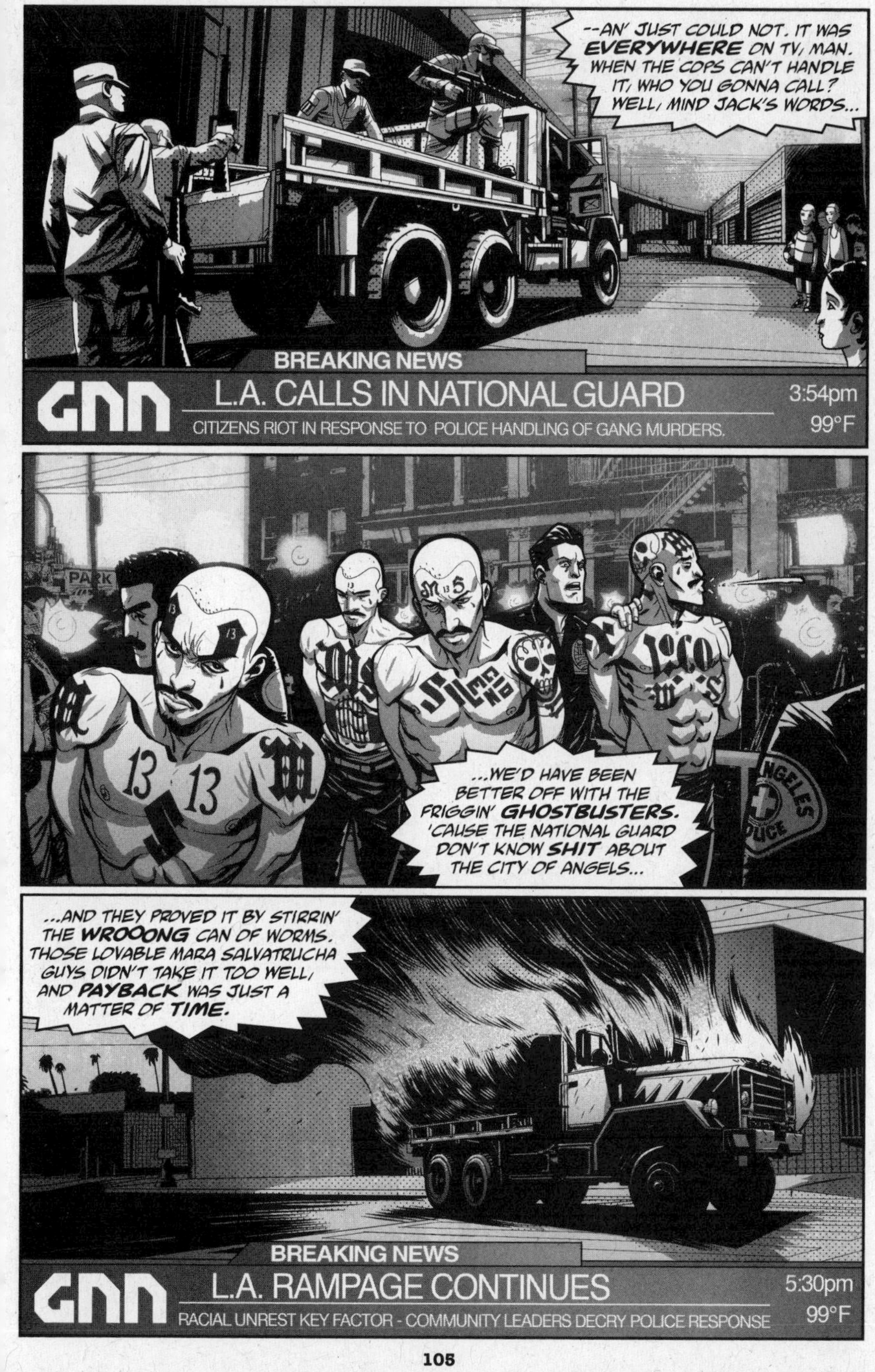
--AN' JUST COULD NOT. IT WAS EVERYWHERE ON TV, MAN. WHEN THE COPS CAN'T HANDLE IT, WHO YOU GONNA CALL? WELL, MIND JACK'S WORDS...
BREAKING NEWS
GNN
L.A. CALLS IN NATIONAL GUARD
CITIZENS RIOT IN RESPONSE TO POLICE HANDLING OF GANG MURDERS.
3:54pm
99°F
...WE'D HAVE BEEN BETTER OFF WITH THE FRIGGIN' GHOSTBUSTERS. 'CAUSE THE NATIONAL GUARD DON'T KNOW SHIT ABOUT THE CITY OF ANGELS...
...AND THEY PROVED IT BY STIRRIN' THE WROOONG CAN OF WORMS. THOSE LOVABLE MARA SALVATRUCHA GUYS DIDN'T TAKE IT TOO WELL, AND PAYBACK WAS JUST A MATTER OF TIME.
BREAKING NEWS
GNN
L.A. RAMPAGE CONTINUES
RACIAL UNREST KEY FACTOR - COMMUNITY LEADERS DECRY POLICE RESPONSE
5:30pm
99°F

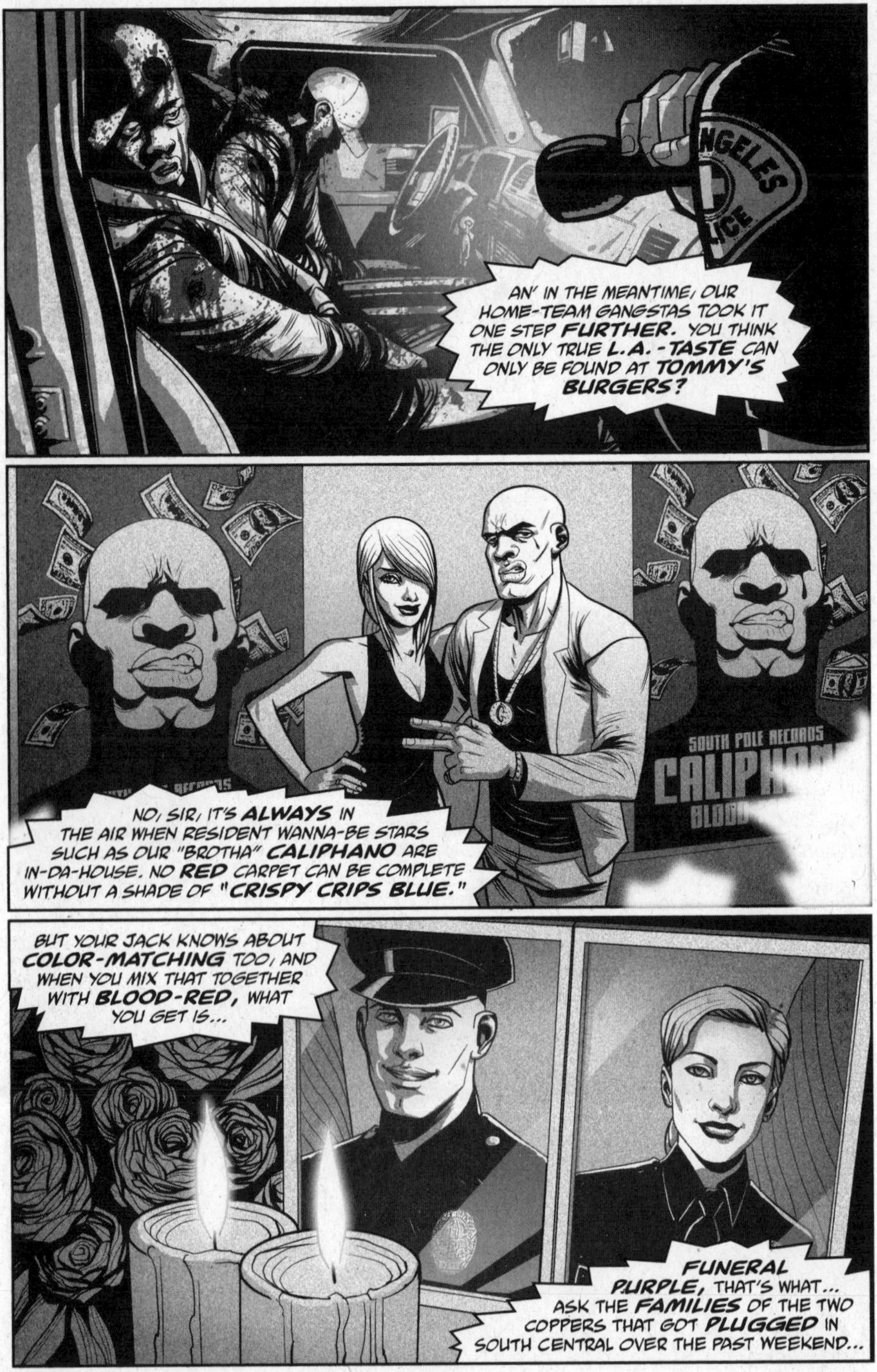
AN' IN THE MEANTIME, OUR HOME-TEAM GANGSTAS TOOK IT ONE STEP **FURTHER.** YOU THINK THE ONLY TRUE **L.A.-TASTE** CAN ONLY BE FOUND AT **TOMMY'S BURGERS?**
SOUTH POLE RECORDS
NO, SIR, IT'S **ALWAYS** IN THE AIR WHEN RESIDENT WANNA-BE STARS SUCH AS OUR "BROTHA" **CALIPHANO** ARE IN-DA-HOUSE. NO **RED** CARPET CAN BE COMPLETE WITHOUT A SHADE OF **"CRISPY CRIPS BLUE."**
BUT YOUR JACK KNOWS ABOUT **COLOR-MATCHING** TOO, AND WHEN YOU MIX THAT TOGETHER WITH **BLOOD-RED,** WHAT YOU GET IS...
FUNERAL PURPLE, THAT'S WHAT... ASK THE **FAMILIES** OF THE TWO COPPERS THAT GOT **PLUGGED** IN SOUTH CENTRAL OVER THE PAST WEEKEND...

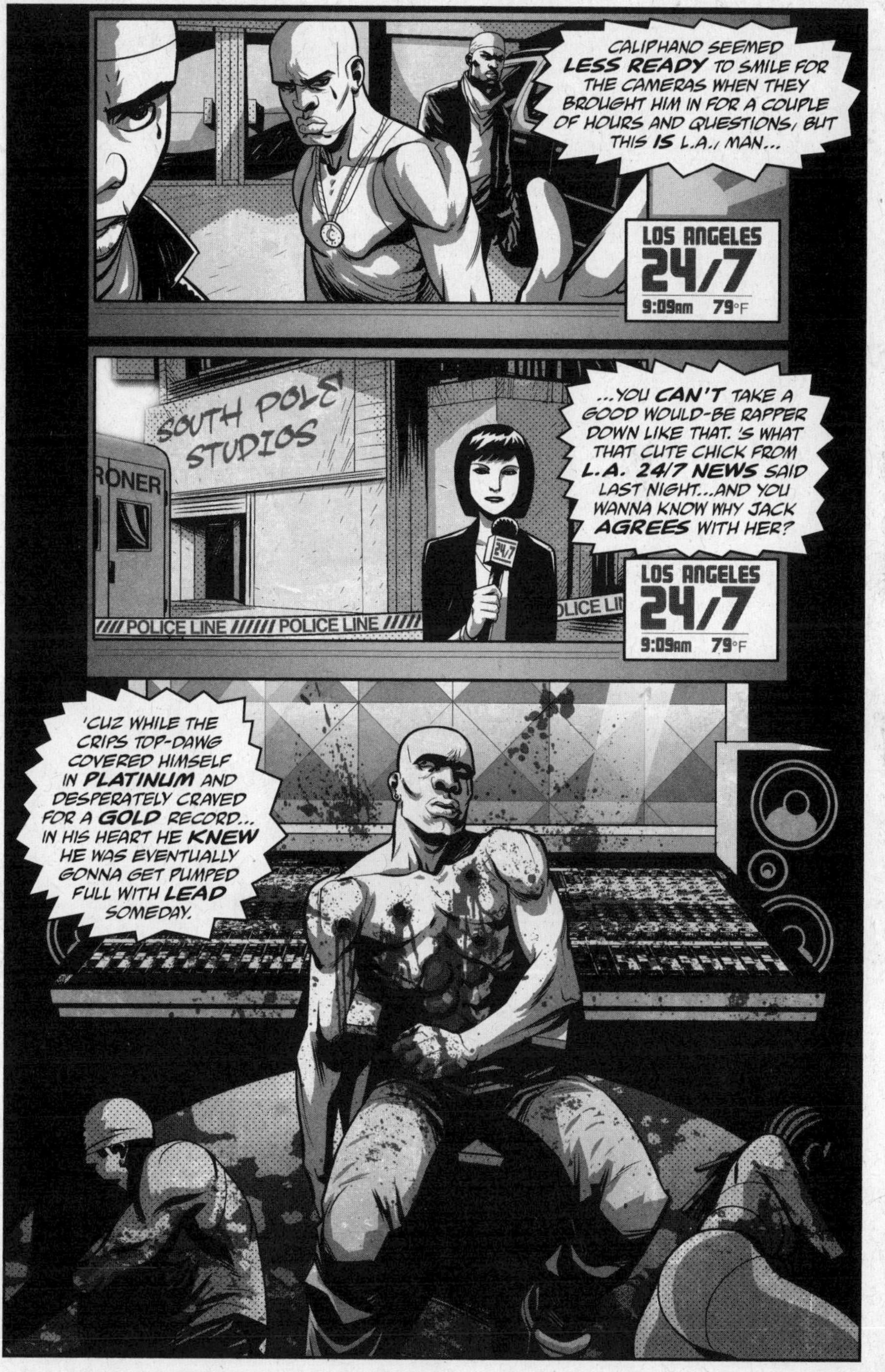
CALIPHANO SEEMED LESS READY TO SMILE FOR THE CAMERAS WHEN THEY BROUGHT HIM IN FOR A COUPLE OF HOURS AND QUESTIONS, BUT THIS IS L.A., MAN...
LOS ANGELES 24/7
9:09AM 79°F
SOUTH POLE STUDIOS
RONER
POLICE LINE
POLICE LINE
POLICE LINE
24/7
...YOU CAN'T TAKE A GOOD WOULD-BE RAPPER DOWN LIKE THAT. 'S WHAT THAT CUTE CHICK FROM L.A. 24/7 NEWS SAID LAST NIGHT...AND YOU WANNA KNOW WHY JACK AGREES WITH HER?
LOS ANGELES 24/7
9:09AM 79°F
'CUZ WHILE THE CRIPS TOP-DAWG COVERED HIMSELF IN PLATINUM AND DESPERATELY CRAVED FOR A GOLD RECORD... IN HIS HEART HE KNEW HE WAS EVENTUALLY GONNA GET PUMPED FULL WITH LEAD SOMEDAY.

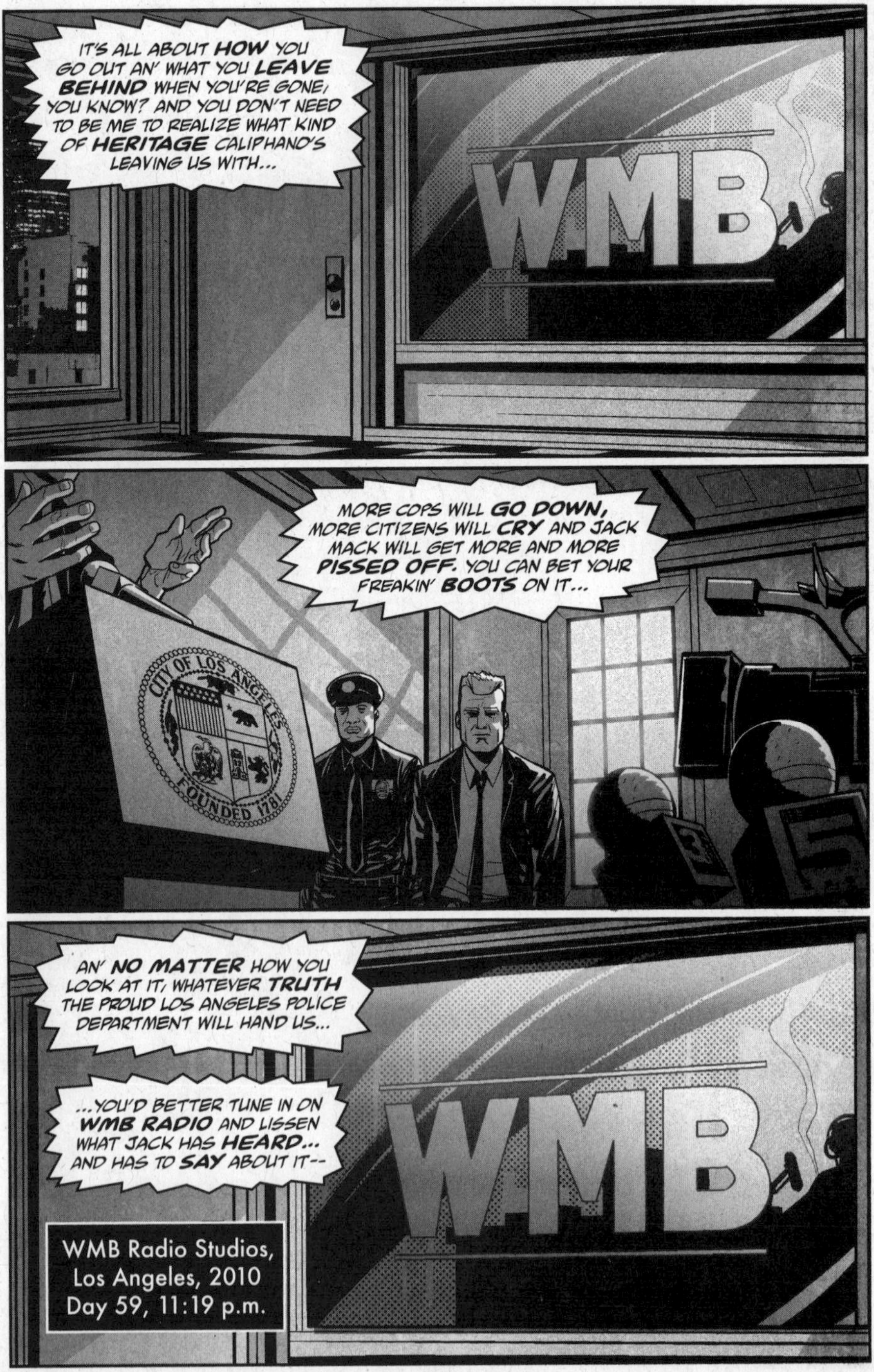
IT'S ALL ABOUT HOW YOU GO OUT AN' WHAT YOU LEAVE BEHIND WHEN YOU'RE GONE, YOU KNOW? AND YOU DON'T NEED TO BE ME TO REALIZE WHAT KIND OF HERITAGE CALIPHANO'S LEAVING US WITH...
WMB
MORE COPS WILL GO DOWN, MORE CITIZENS WILL CRY AND JACK MACK WILL GET MORE AND MORE PISSED OFF. YOU CAN BET YOUR FREAKIN' BOOTS ON IT...
CITY OF LOS ANGELES FOUNDED 1781
AN' NO MATTER HOW YOU LOOK AT IT, WHATEVER TRUTH THE PROUD LOS ANGELES POLICE DEPARTMENT WILL HAND US...
...YOU'D BETTER TUNE IN ON WMB RADIO AND LISSEN WHAT JACK HAS HEARD... AND HAS TO SAY ABOUT IT--
WMB Radio Studios, Los Angeles, 2010 Day 59, 11:19 p.m.
WMB

--WHAT I WANNA KNOW IS WHO **LEAKS** HIM ALL THE FUCKIN' DETAILS...!

South Los Angeles, Police Precinct, Day 62, 6:27 p.m.

YEAH, ME TOO.

FUCK, THAT SON OF A BITCH KNEW EVERYTHING **MINUTES** AFTER **WE** WERE TOLD!

AND JUST PICTURE WHAT EFFECT HIS **RACIST RANTS** WILL HAVE ON THE PUBLIC OPINION...

NOTHING WILL CHANGE.

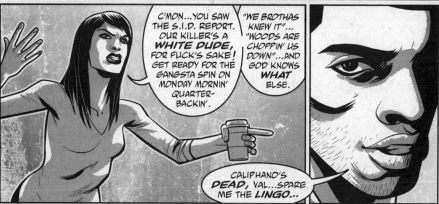

C'MON...YOU SAW THE S.I.D. REPORT. OUR KILLER'S A **WHITE DUDE,** FOR FUCK'S SAKE! GET READY FOR THE GANGSTA SPIN ON MONDAY MORNIN' QUARTER-BACKIN'.

"WE BROTHAS KNEW IT"... "WOODS ARE CHOPPIN' US DOWN"...AND GOD KNOWS **WHAT** ELSE.

CALIPHANO'S **DEAD,** VAL...SPARE ME THE **LINGO...**

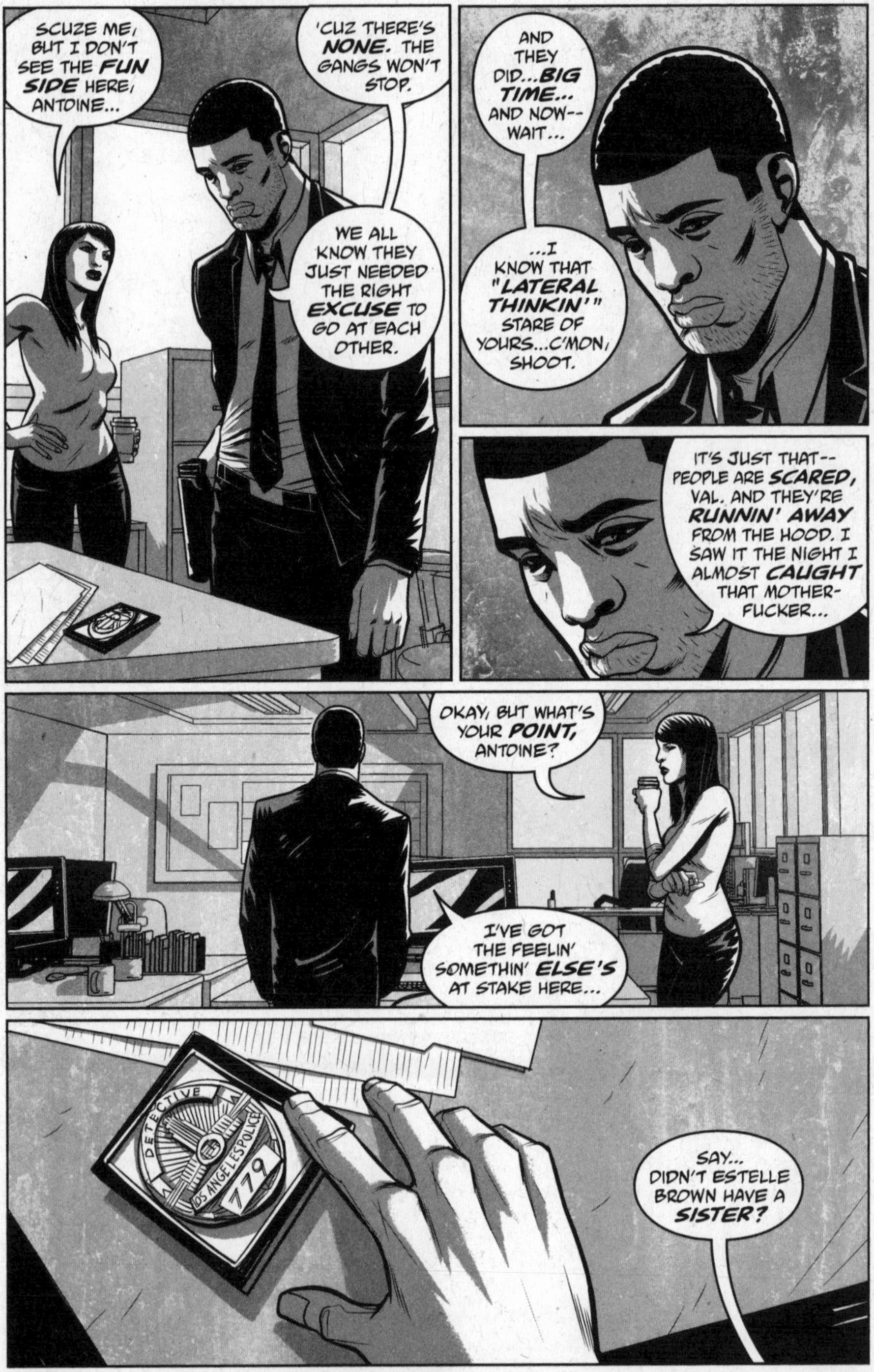
SCUZE ME, BUT I DON'T SEE THE FUN SIDE HERE, ANTOINE...
'CUZ THERE'S NONE. THE GANGS WON'T STOP.
WE ALL KNOW THEY JUST NEEDED THE RIGHT EXCUSE TO GO AT EACH OTHER.
AND THEY DID...BIG TIME... AND NOW-- WAIT...
...I KNOW THAT "LATERAL THINKIN'" STARE OF YOURS...C'MON, SHOOT.
IT'S JUST THAT-- PEOPLE ARE SCARED, VAL. AND THEY'RE RUNNIN' AWAY FROM THE HOOD. I SAW IT THE NIGHT I ALMOST CAUGHT THAT MOTHER-FUCKER...
OKAY, BUT WHAT'S YOUR POINT, ANTOINE?
I'VE GOT THE FEELIN' SOMETHIN' ELSE'S AT STAKE HERE...
DETECTIVE
LOS ANGELES POLICE
779
SAY... DIDN'T ESTELLE BROWN HAVE A SISTER?

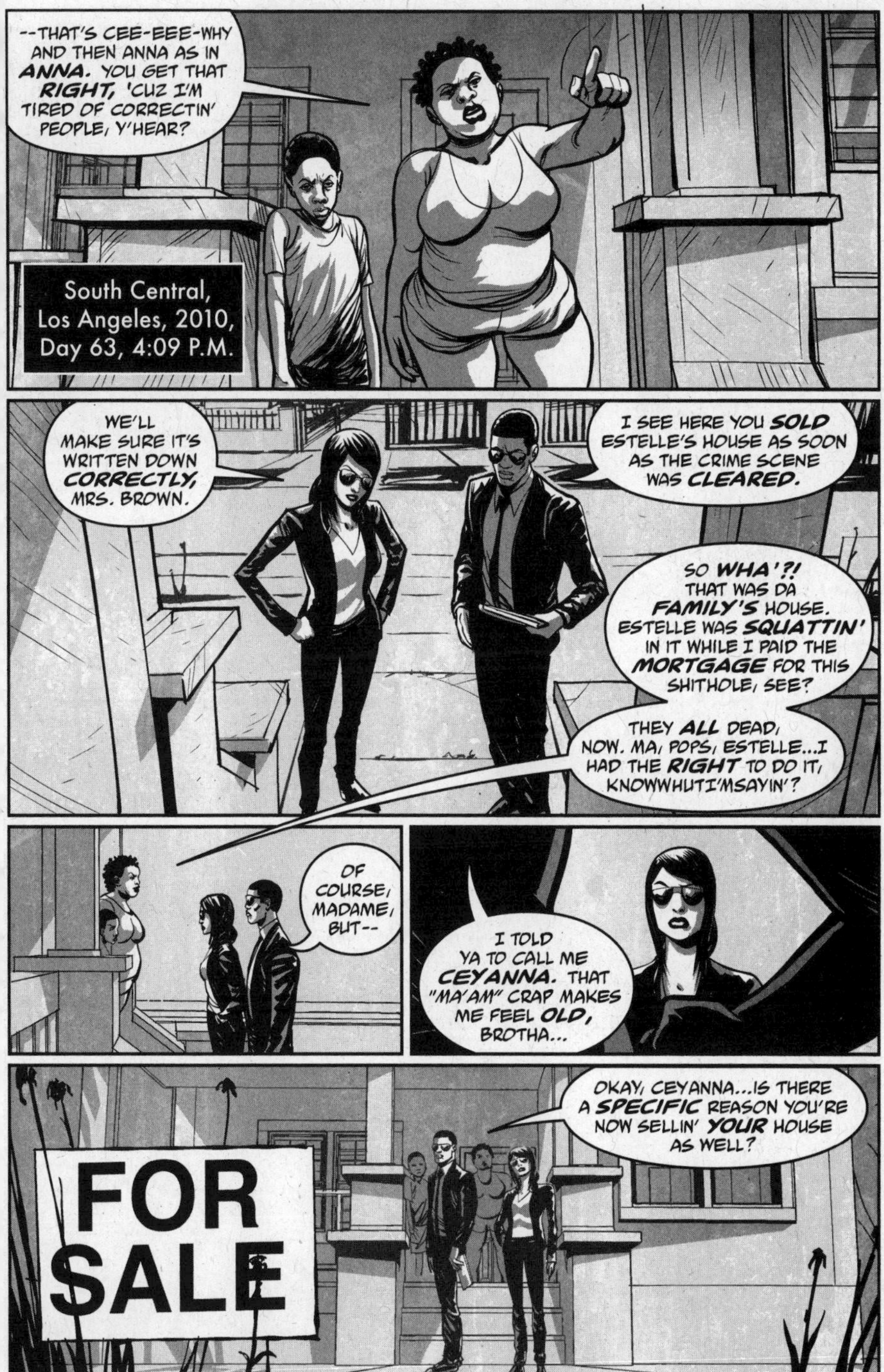
--THAT'S CEE-EEE-WHY AND THEN ANNA AS IN ANNA. YOU GET THAT RIGHT, 'CUZ I'M TIRED OF CORRECTIN' PEOPLE, Y'HEAR?
South Central, Los Angeles, 2010, Day 63, 4:09 P.M.
WE'LL MAKE SURE IT'S WRITTEN DOWN CORRECTLY, MRS. BROWN.
I SEE HERE YOU SOLD ESTELLE'S HOUSE AS SOON AS THE CRIME SCENE WAS CLEARED.
SO WHA'?! THAT WAS DA FAMILY'S HOUSE. ESTELLE WAS SQUATTIN' IN IT WHILE I PAID THE MORTGAGE FOR THIS SHITHOLE, SEE?
THEY ALL DEAD, NOW. MA, POPS, ESTELLE...I HAD THE RIGHT TO DO IT, KNOWWHUTI'MSAYIN'?
OF COURSE, MADAME, BUT--
I TOLD YA TO CALL ME CEYANNA. THAT "MA'AM" CRAP MAKES ME FEEL OLD, BROTHA...
OKAY, CEYANNA...IS THERE A SPECIFIC REASON YOU'RE NOW SELLIN' YOUR HOUSE AS WELL?
FOR SALE

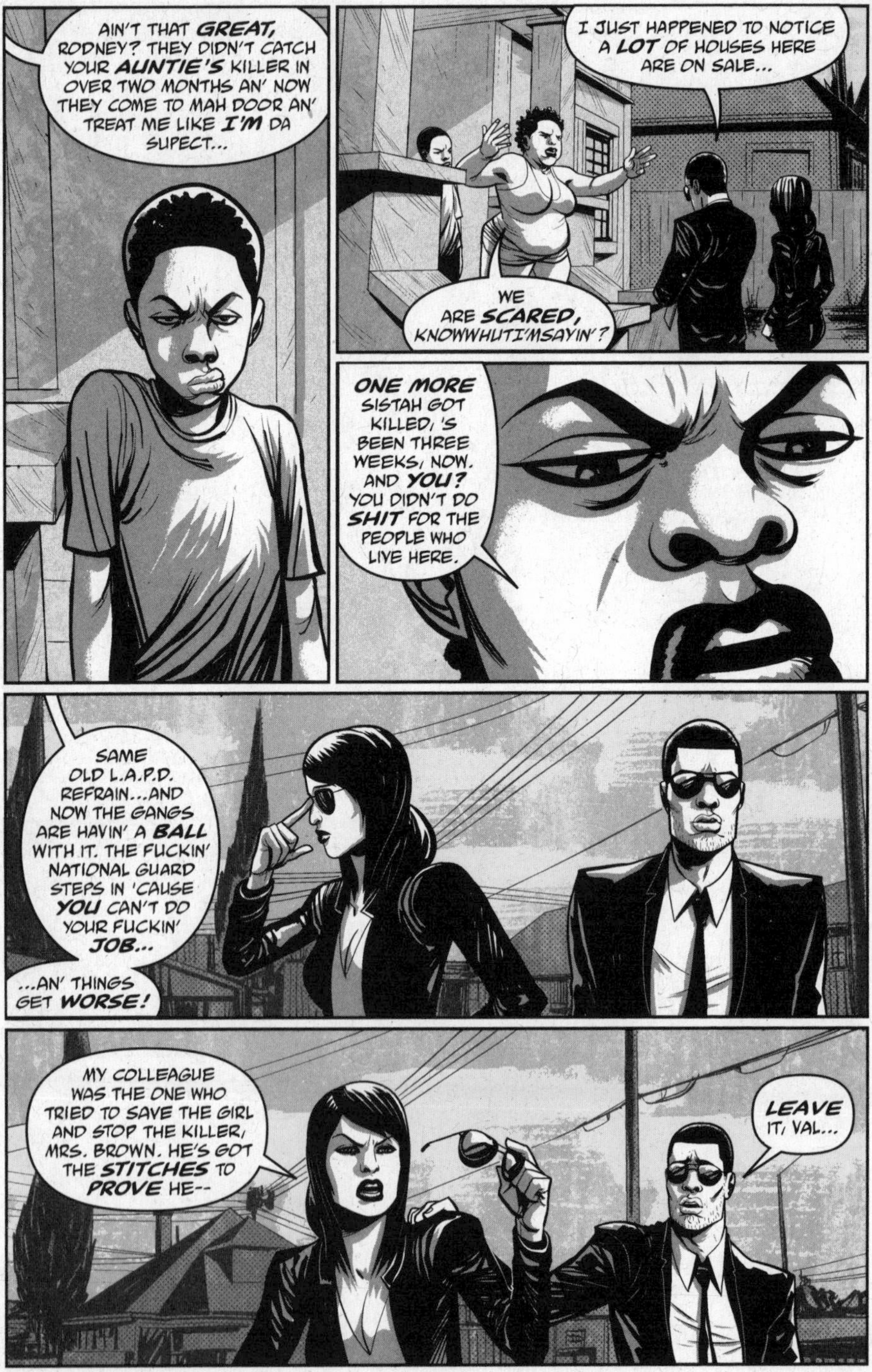
AIN'T THAT GREAT, RODNEY? THEY DIDN'T CATCH YOUR AUNTIE'S KILLER IN OVER TWO MONTHS AN' NOW THEY COME TO MAH DOOR AN' TREAT ME LIKE I'M DA SUPECT...
I JUST HAPPENED TO NOTICE A LOT OF HOUSES HERE ARE ON SALE...
WE ARE SCARED, KNOWWHUTI'MSAYIN'?
ONE MORE SISTAH GOT KILLED, 'S BEEN THREE WEEKS, NOW. AND YOU? YOU DIDN'T DO SHIT FOR THE PEOPLE WHO LIVE HERE.
SAME OLD L.A.P.D. REFRAIN...AND NOW THE GANGS ARE HAVIN' A BALL WITH IT. THE FUCKIN' NATIONAL GUARD STEPS IN 'CAUSE YOU CAN'T DO YOUR FUCKIN' JOB...
...AN' THINGS GET WORSE!
MY COLLEAGUE WAS THE ONE WHO TRIED TO SAVE THE GIRL AND STOP THE KILLER, MRS. BROWN. HE'S GOT THE STITCHES TO PROVE HE--
LEAVE IT, VAL...

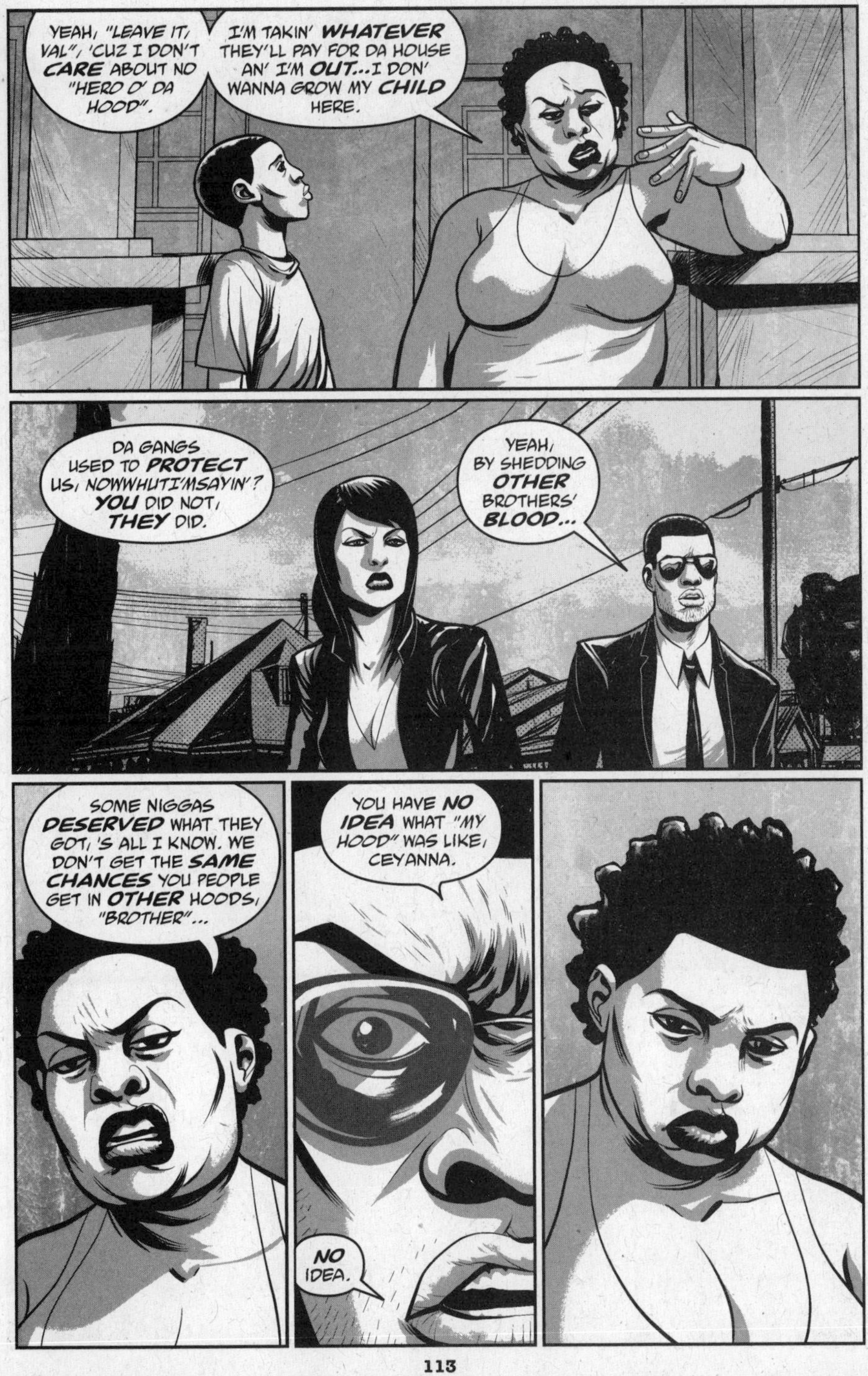
YEAH, "LEAVE IT, VAL", 'CUZ I DON'T CARE ABOUT NO "HERO O' DA HOOD".
I'M TAKIN' WHATEVER THEY'LL PAY FOR DA HOUSE AN' I'M OUT...I DON' WANNA GROW MY CHILD HERE.
DA GANGS USED TO PROTECT US, NOWWHUTI'MSAYIN'? YOU DID NOT, THEY DID.
YEAH, BY SHEDDING OTHER BROTHERS' BLOOD...
SOME NIGGAS DESERVED WHAT THEY GOT, 'S ALL I KNOW. WE DON'T GET THE SAME CHANCES YOU PEOPLE GET IN OTHER HOODS, "BROTHER"...
YOU HAVE NO IDEA WHAT "MY HOOD" WAS LIKE, CEYANNA.
NO IDEA.

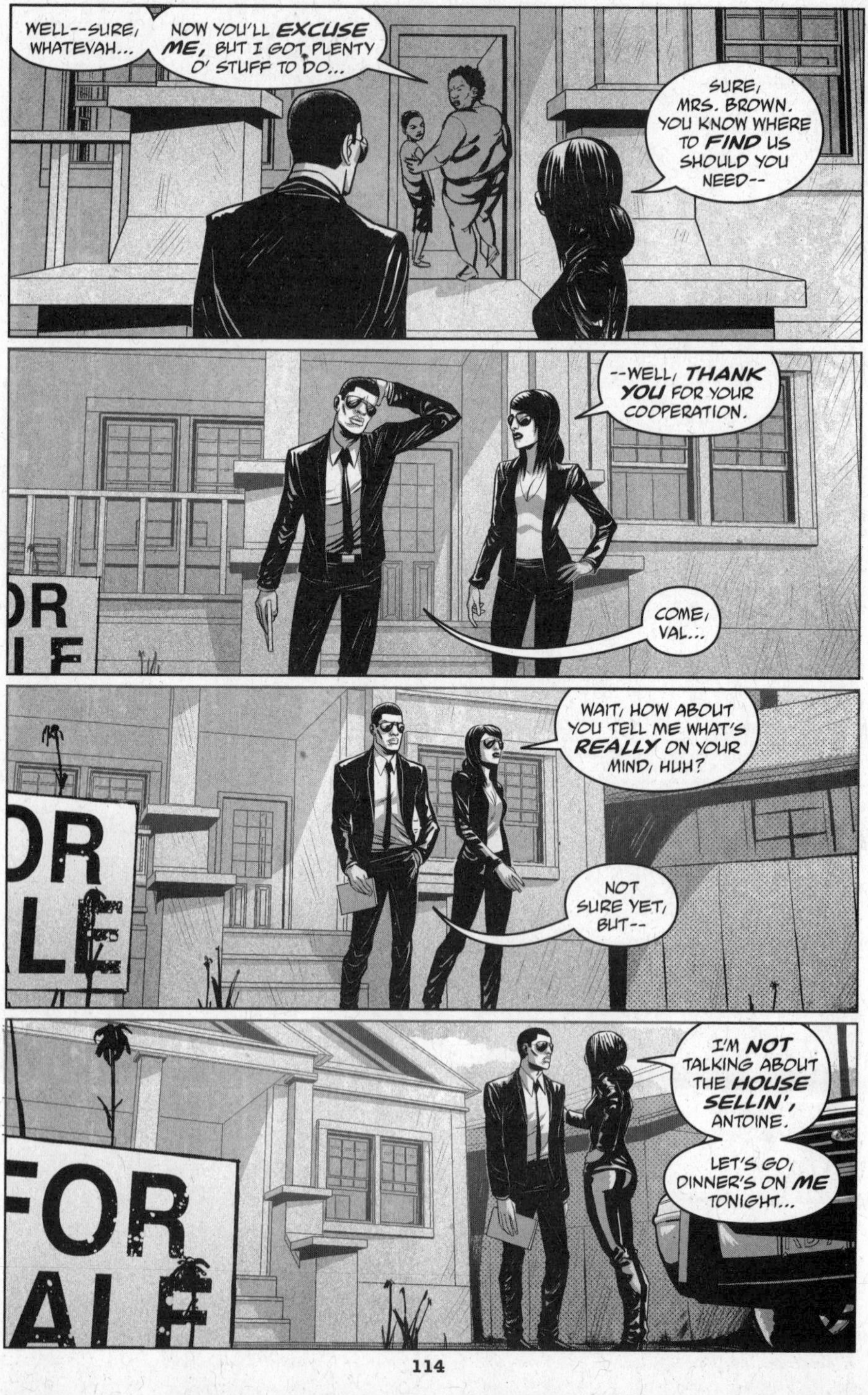
WELL--SURE, WHATEVAH...
NOW YOU'LL EXCUSE ME, BUT I GOT PLENTY O' STUFF TO DO...
SURE, MRS. BROWN. YOU KNOW WHERE TO FIND US SHOULD YOU NEED--
--WELL, THANK YOU FOR YOUR COOPERATION.
COME, VAL...
WAIT, HOW ABOUT YOU TELL ME WHAT'S REALLY ON YOUR MIND, HUH?
NOT SURE YET, BUT--
I'M NOT TALKING ABOUT THE HOUSE SELLIN', ANTOINE.
LET'S GO, DINNER'S ON ME TONIGHT...

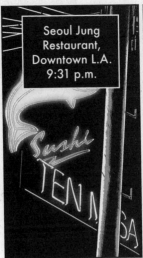

Seoul Jung Restaurant, Downtown L.A. 9:31 p.m.

GOD...I FEEL LIKE **SHIT**...

ALL **I** CARED ABOUT IN THOSE DAYS WAS **KURT COBAIN** BLOWING HIS **HEAD** OFF...

NOT YOUR FAULT, VAL. AFRICA WAS--STILL **IS**-- A **FARAWAY PLACE** FOR THE U.S.

THE SLAUGHTER WENT ON FOR MORE THAN **THREE MONTHS**...HUTUS AND TUTSIS AGAINST EACH OTHER...JUST LIKE THE **BLOODS** AND THE **CRIPS**...

WHAT WAS THE **CAUSE** OF IT ALL? **ETHNICITY? POLITICS?**

A BIT OF BOTH...AND **NONE** AT THE SAME TIME. IN THE TWENTIES, THE **BELGIAN COLONISTS** SEPARATED TWO ETHNIC GROUPS THAT SHARED THE SAME LANGUAGE AND HAD SIMILAR TRADITIONS.

BY FAVORING THE TUTSIS AND GIVING THEM BETTER **EDUCATION** AND **EMPLOYMENT**, THEY CREATED THE PRECEDENT FOR THE TENSION THAT ERUPTED IN APRIL OF 1994.

THEY NOW SAY IT LASTED **100 DAYS**.

AND IN THE END, ALMOST **ONE MILLION** TUTSIS AND MODERATE HUTUS...LIKE **MY FAMILY**...WERE SLAIN.

WHILE THE REST OF THE WORLD STOOD **STILL** AND KEPT SINGIN' "SMELLS LIKE FUCKIN' TEEN SPIRIT..."

JESUS...

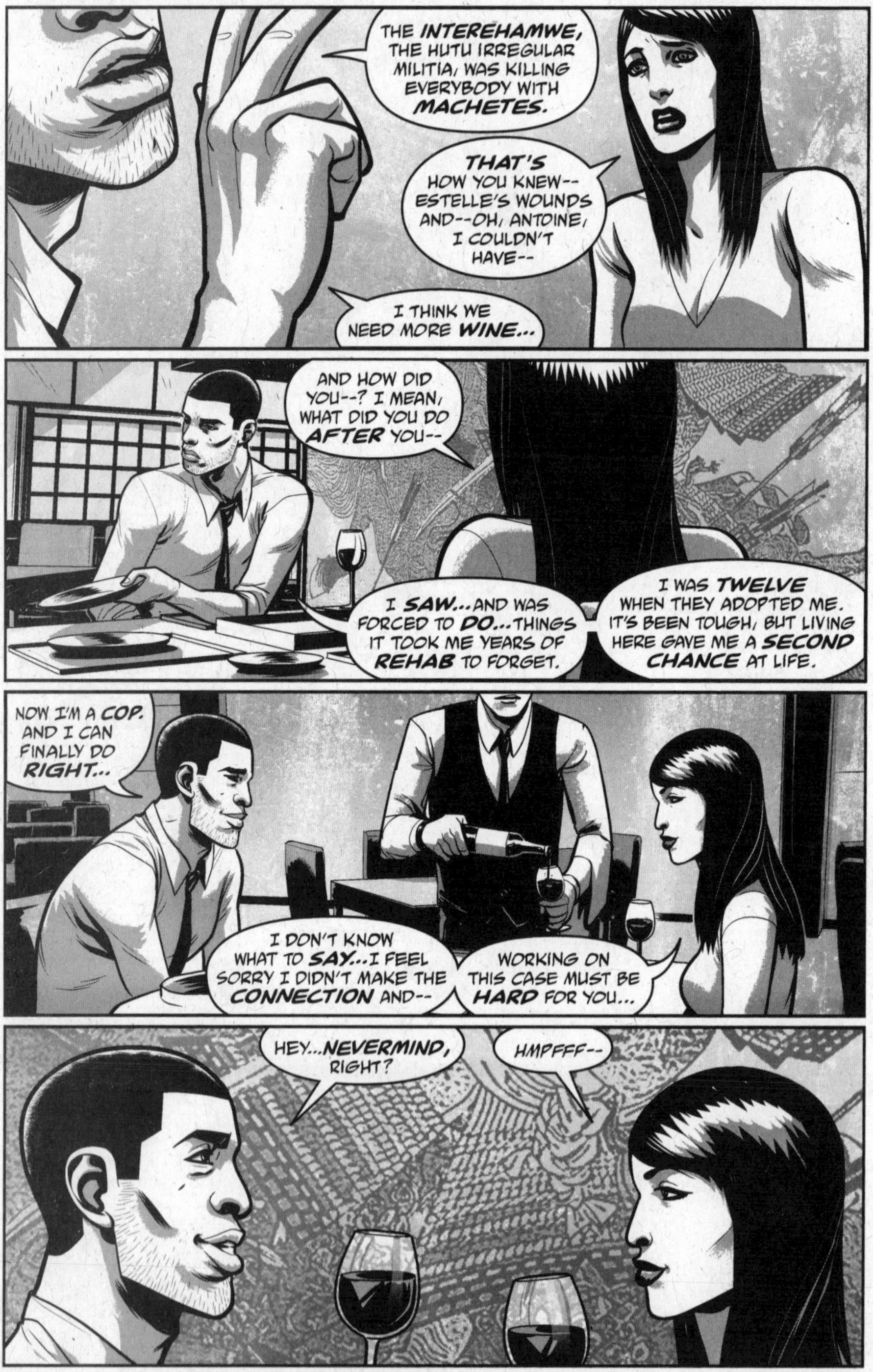
THE INTEREHAMWE, THE HUTU IRREGULAR MILITIA, WAS KILLING EVERYBODY WITH MACHETES.
THAT'S HOW YOU KNEW-- ESTELLE'S WOUNDS AND--OH, ANTOINE, I COULDN'T HAVE--
I THINK WE NEED MORE WINE...
AND HOW DID YOU--? I MEAN, WHAT DID YOU DO AFTER YOU--
I SAW...AND WAS FORCED TO DO...THINGS IT TOOK ME YEARS OF REHAB TO FORGET.
I WAS TWELVE WHEN THEY ADOPTED ME. IT'S BEEN TOUGH, BUT LIVING HERE GAVE ME A SECOND CHANCE AT LIFE.
NOW I'M A COP. AND I CAN FINALLY DO RIGHT...
I DON'T KNOW WHAT TO SAY...I FEEL SORRY I DIDN'T MAKE THE CONNECTION AND--
WORKING ON THIS CASE MUST BE HARD FOR YOU...
HEY...NEVERMIND, RIGHT?
HMPFFF--

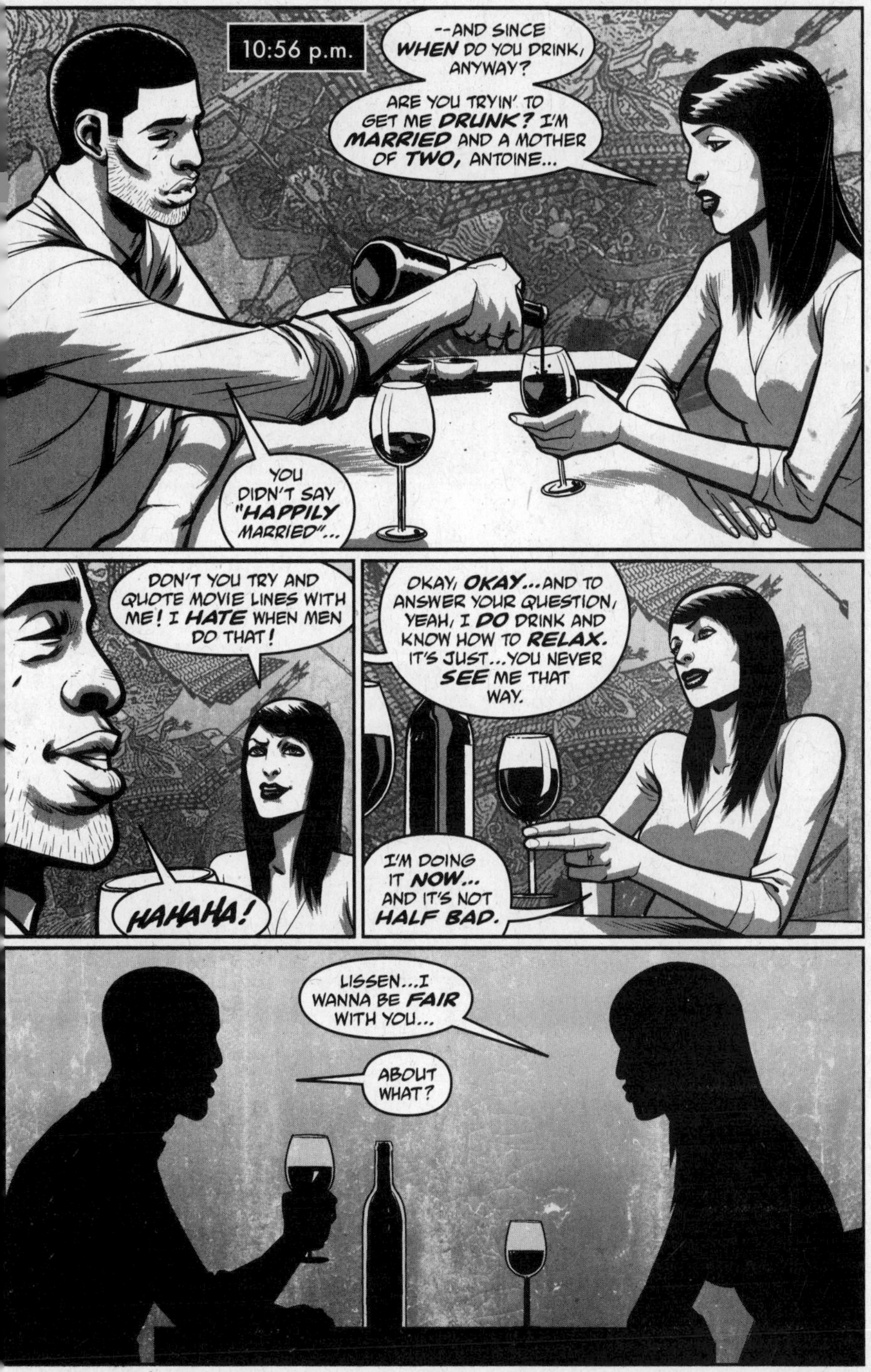
10:56 p.m.
--AND SINCE WHEN DO YOU DRINK, ANYWAY?
ARE YOU TRYIN' TO GET ME DRUNK? I'M MARRIED AND A MOTHER OF TWO, ANTOINE...
YOU DIDN'T SAY "HAPPILY MARRIED"...
DON'T YOU TRY AND QUOTE MOVIE LINES WITH ME! I HATE WHEN MEN DO THAT!
HAHAHA!
OKAY, OKAY...AND TO ANSWER YOUR QUESTION, YEAH, I DO DRINK AND KNOW HOW TO RELAX. IT'S JUST...YOU NEVER SEE ME THAT WAY.
I'M DOING IT NOW... AND IT'S NOT HALF BAD.
LISSEN...I WANNA BE FAIR WITH YOU...
ABOUT WHAT?

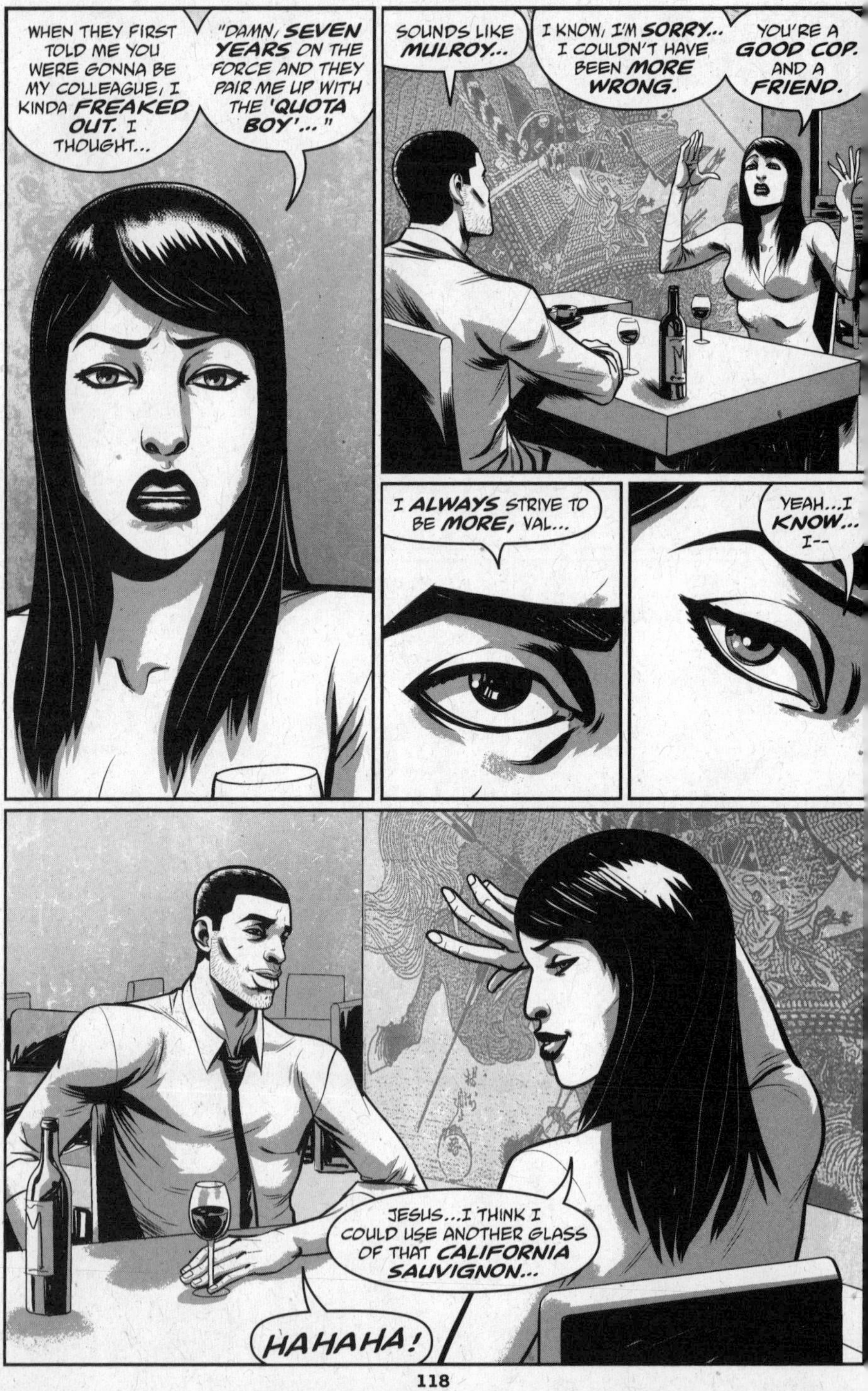
WHEN THEY FIRST TOLD ME YOU WERE GONNA BE MY COLLEAGUE, I KINDA FREAKED OUT. I THOUGHT...
"DAMN, SEVEN YEARS ON THE FORCE AND THEY PAIR ME UP WITH THE 'QUOTA BOY'..."
SOUNDS LIKE MULROY...
I KNOW, I'M SORRY... I COULDN'T HAVE BEEN MORE WRONG.
YOU'RE A GOOD COP. AND A FRIEND.
I ALWAYS STRIVE TO BE MORE, VAL...
YEAH...I KNOW... I--
JESUS...I THINK I COULD USE ANOTHER GLASS OF THAT CALIFORNIA SAUVIGNON...
HAHAHA!

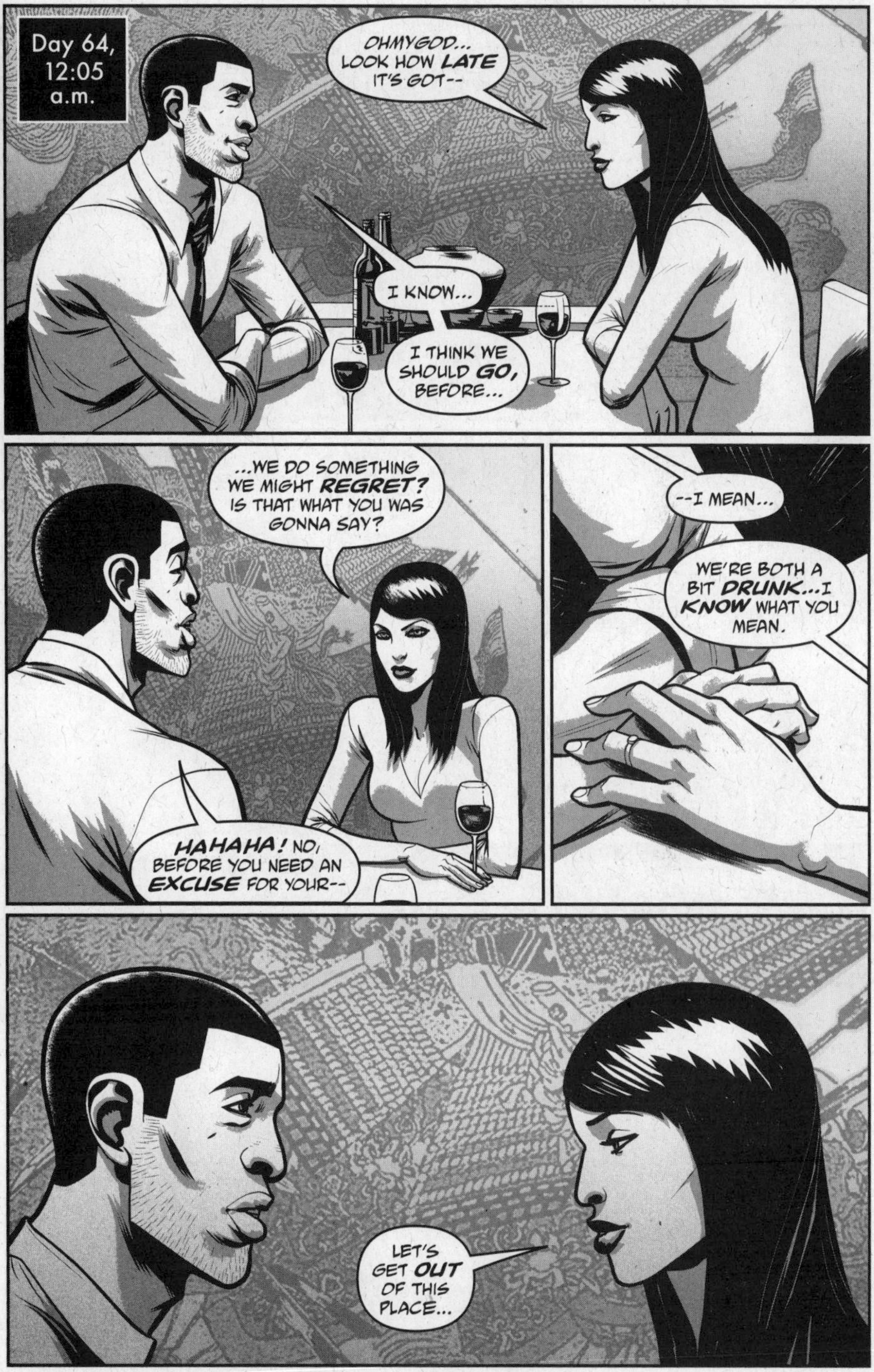
Day 64, 12:05 a.m.
OHMYGOD... LOOK HOW LATE IT'S GOT--
I KNOW...
I THINK WE SHOULD GO, BEFORE...
...WE DO SOMETHING WE MIGHT REGRET? IS THAT WHAT YOU WAS GONNA SAY?
HAHAHA! NO, BEFORE YOU NEED AN EXCUSE FOR YOUR--
--I MEAN...
WE'RE BOTH A BIT DRUNK...I KNOW WHAT YOU MEAN.
LET'S GET OUT OF THIS PLACE...

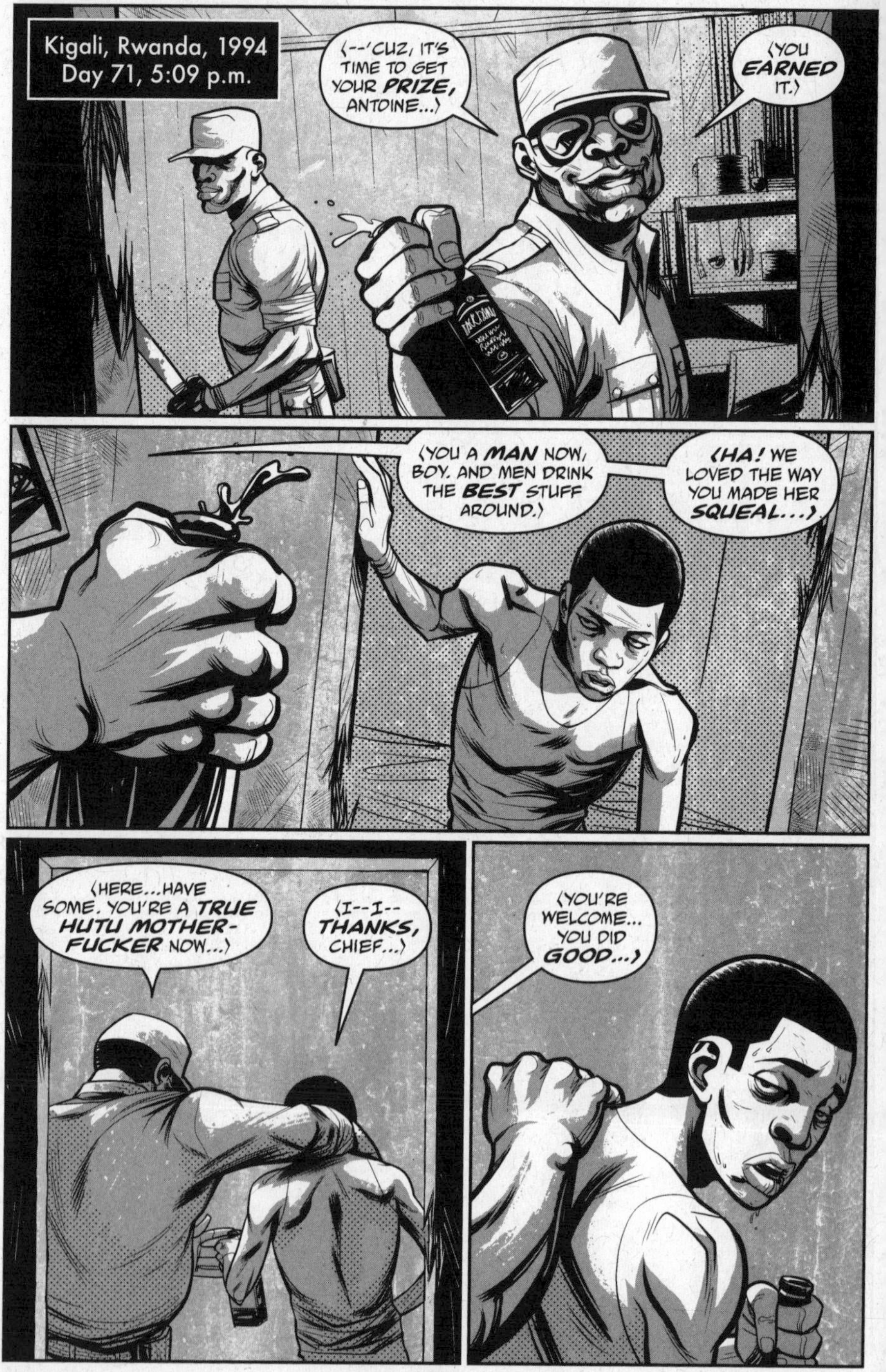
Kigali, Rwanda, 1994
Day 71, 5:09 p.m.
⟨--'CUZ, IT'S TIME TO GET YOUR PRIZE, ANTOINE...⟩
⟨YOU EARNED IT.⟩
⟨YOU A MAN NOW, BOY. AND MEN DRINK THE BEST STUFF AROUND.⟩
⟨HA! WE LOVED THE WAY YOU MADE HER SQUEAL...⟩
⟨HERE...HAVE SOME. YOU'RE A TRUE HUTU MOTHER-FUCKER NOW...⟩
⟨I--I-- THANKS, CHIEF...⟩
⟨YOU'RE WELCOME... YOU DID GOOD...⟩

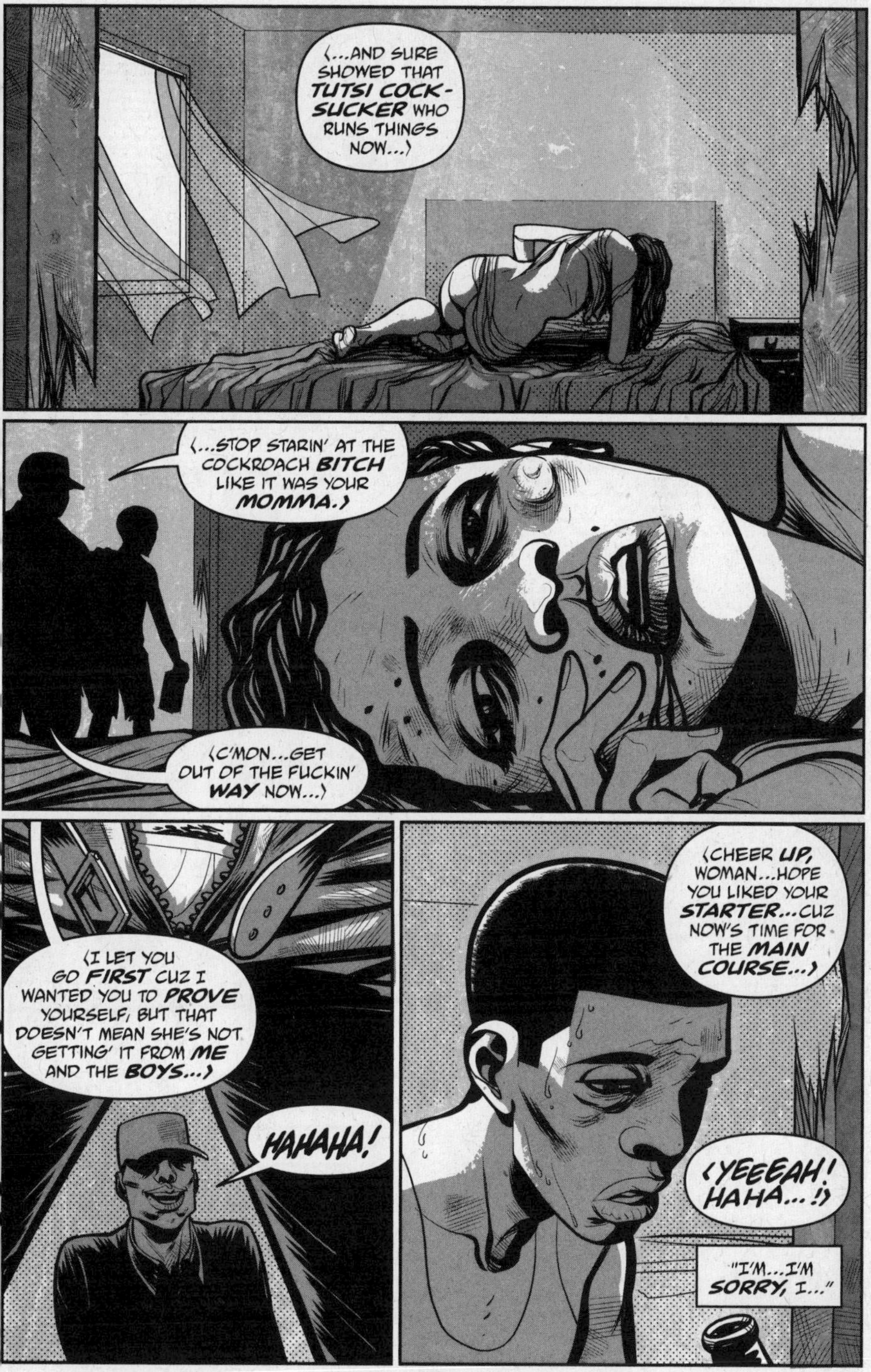

‹...AND SURE SHOWED THAT TUTSI COCK-SUCKER WHO RUNS THINGS NOW...›
‹...STOP STARIN' AT THE COCKROACH BITCH LIKE IT WAS YOUR MOMMA.›
‹C'MON...GET OUT OF THE FUCKIN' WAY NOW...›
‹I LET YOU GO FIRST CUZ I WANTED YOU TO PROVE YOURSELF, BUT THAT DOESN'T MEAN SHE'S NOT GETTING' IT FROM ME AND THE BOYS...›
HAHAHA!
‹CHEER UP, WOMAN...HOPE YOU LIKED YOUR STARTER...CUZ NOW'S TIME FOR THE MAIN COURSE...›
‹YEEEAH! HAHA...!›
"I'M...I'M SORRY, I..."

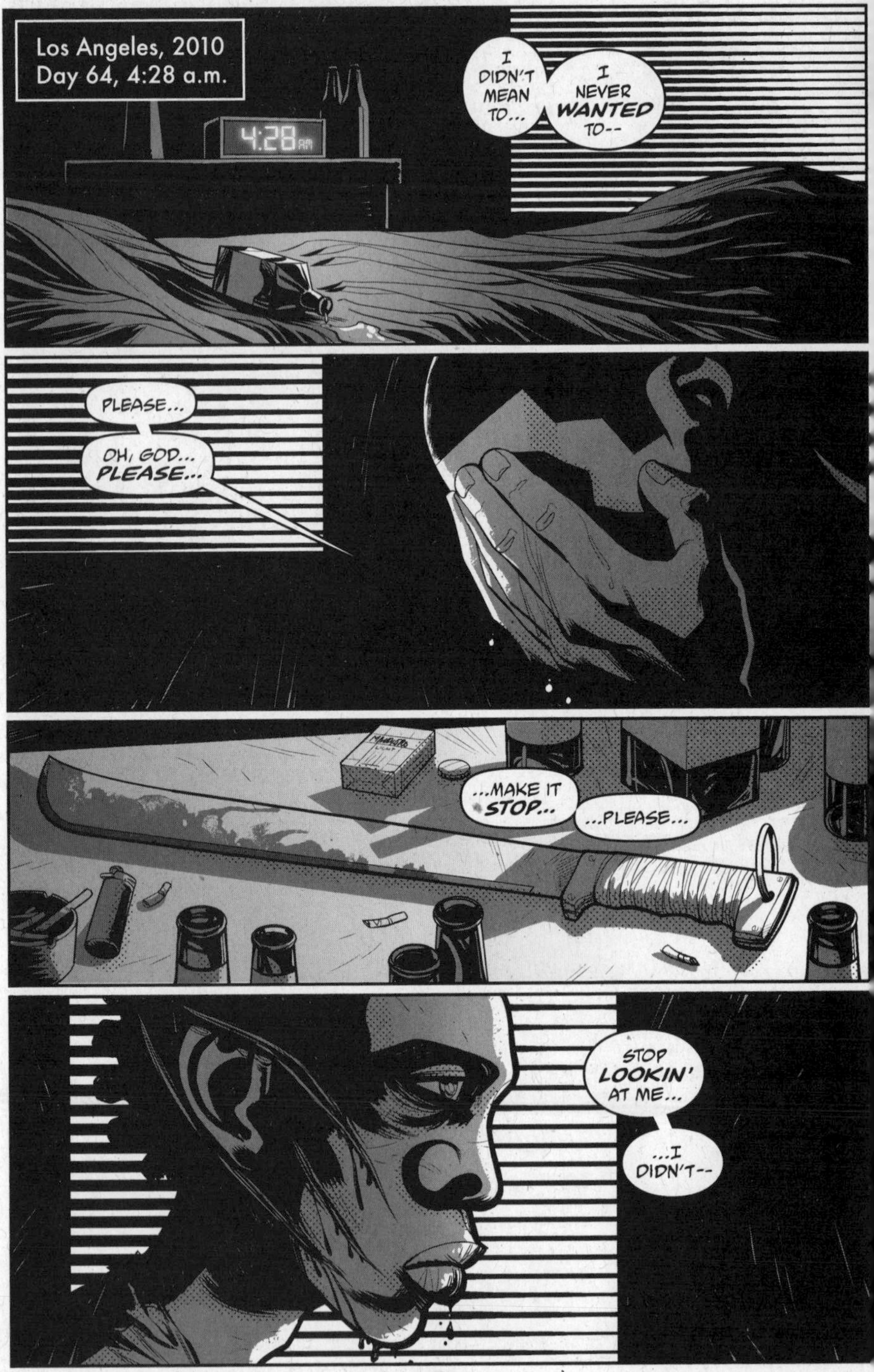
Los Angeles, 2010
Day 64, 4:28 a.m.
4:28 AM
I DIDN'T MEAN TO...
I NEVER WANTED TO--
PLEASE...
OH, GOD... PLEASE...
...MAKE IT STOP...
...PLEASE...
STOP LOOKIN' AT ME...
...I DIDN'T--

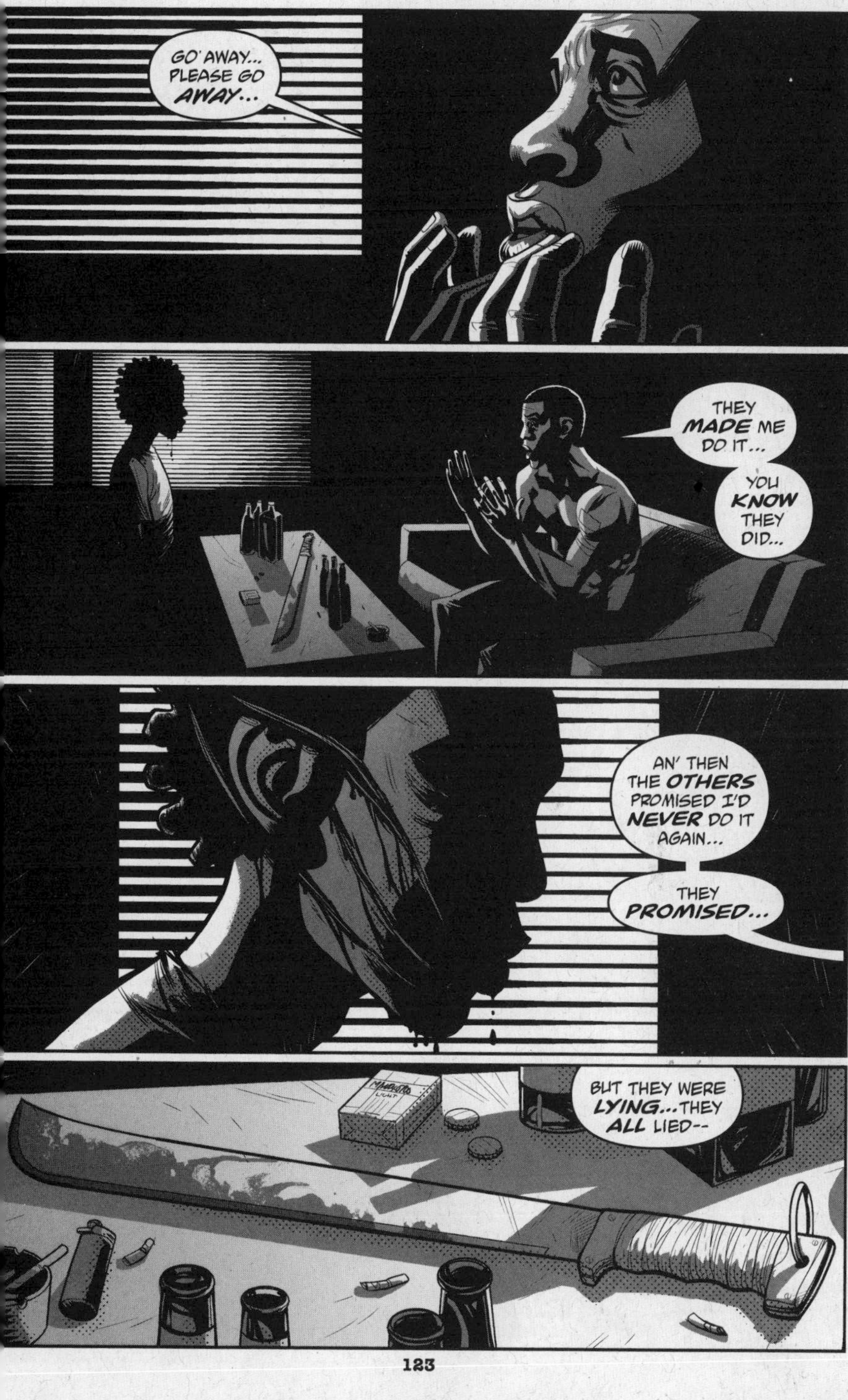
GO' AWAY... PLEASE GO AWAY...
THEY MADE ME DO IT...
YOU KNOW THEY DID...
AN' THEN THE OTHERS PROMISED I'D NEVER DO IT AGAIN...
THEY PROMISED...
BUT THEY WERE LYING... THEY ALL LIED--

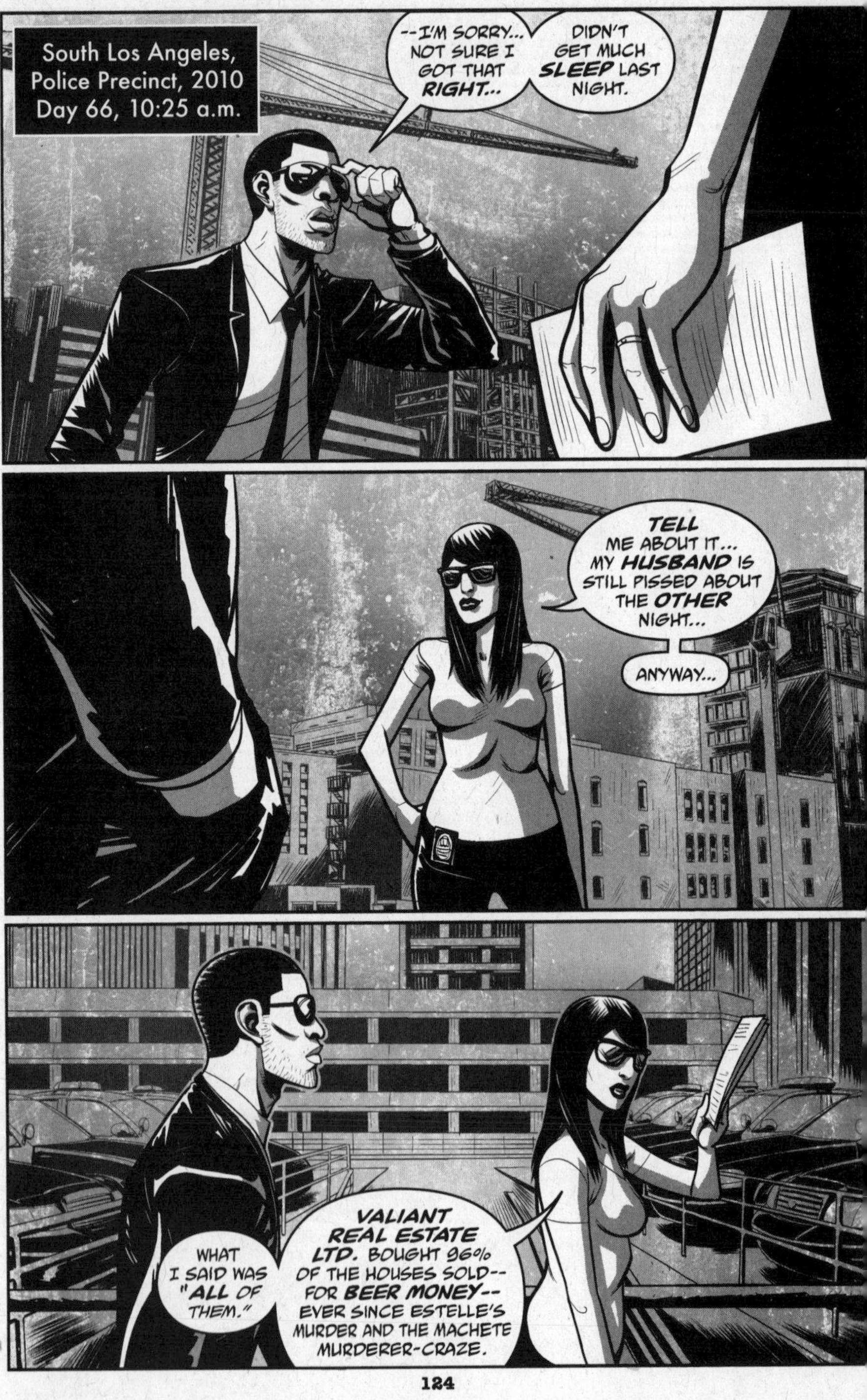
South Los Angeles, Police Precinct, 2010 Day 66, 10:25 a.m.
--I'M SORRY... NOT SURE I GOT THAT RIGHT...
DIDN'T GET MUCH SLEEP LAST NIGHT.
TELL ME ABOUT IT... MY HUSBAND IS STILL PISSED ABOUT THE OTHER NIGHT...
ANYWAY...
VALIANT REAL ESTATE LTD. BOUGHT 96% OF THE HOUSES SOLD-- FOR BEER MONEY-- EVER SINCE ESTELLE'S MURDER AND THE MACHETE MURDERER-CRAZE.
WHAT I SAID WAS "ALL OF THEM."

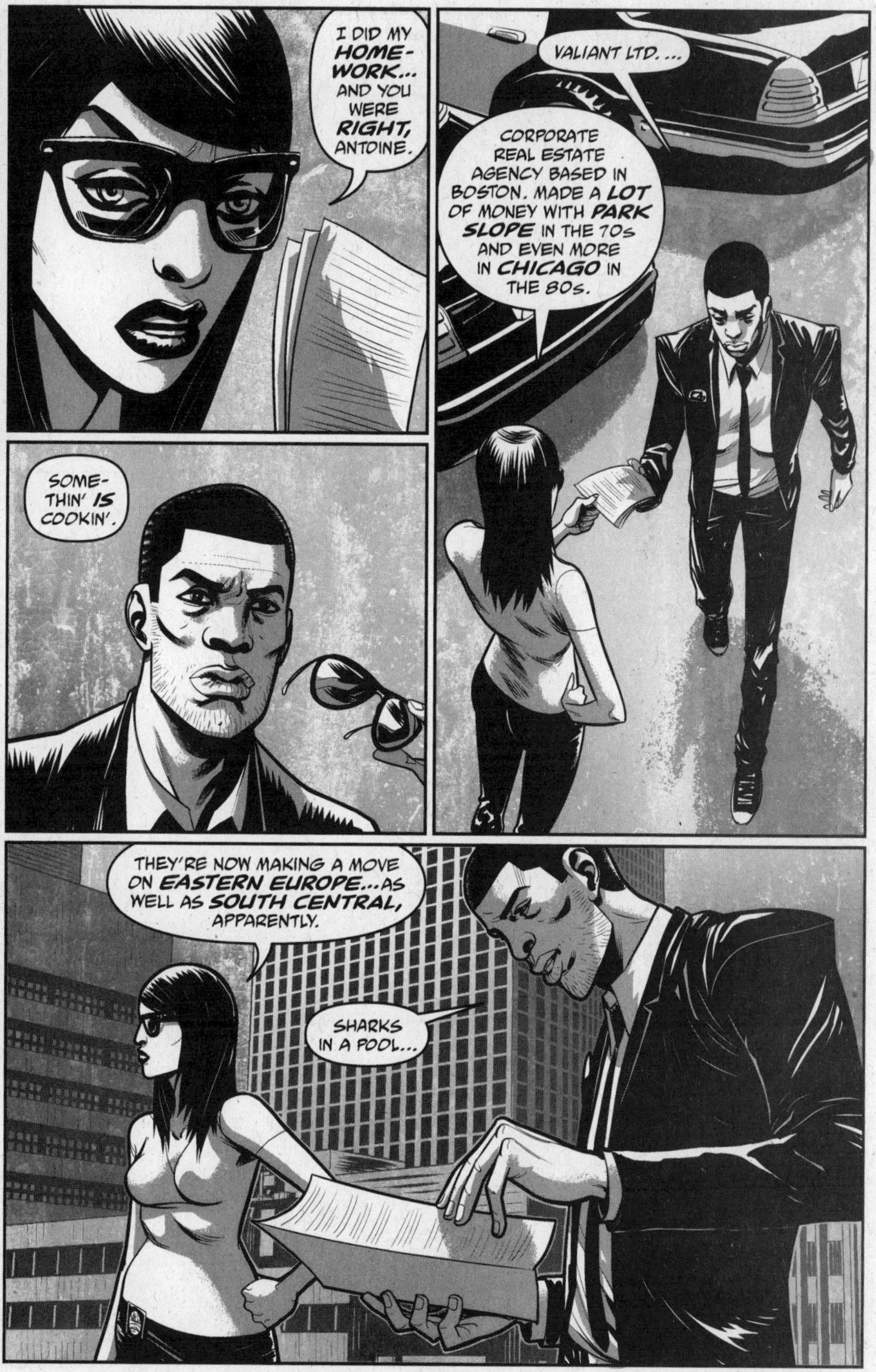
I DID MY HOME-WORK... AND YOU WERE RIGHT, ANTOINE.
VALIANT LTD. ...
CORPORATE REAL ESTATE AGENCY BASED IN BOSTON. MADE A LOT OF MONEY WITH PARK SLOPE IN THE 70s AND EVEN MORE IN CHICAGO IN THE 80s.
SOME-THIN' IS COOKIN'.
THEY'RE NOW MAKING A MOVE ON EASTERN EUROPE...AS WELL AS SOUTH CENTRAL, APPARENTLY.
SHARKS IN A POOL...

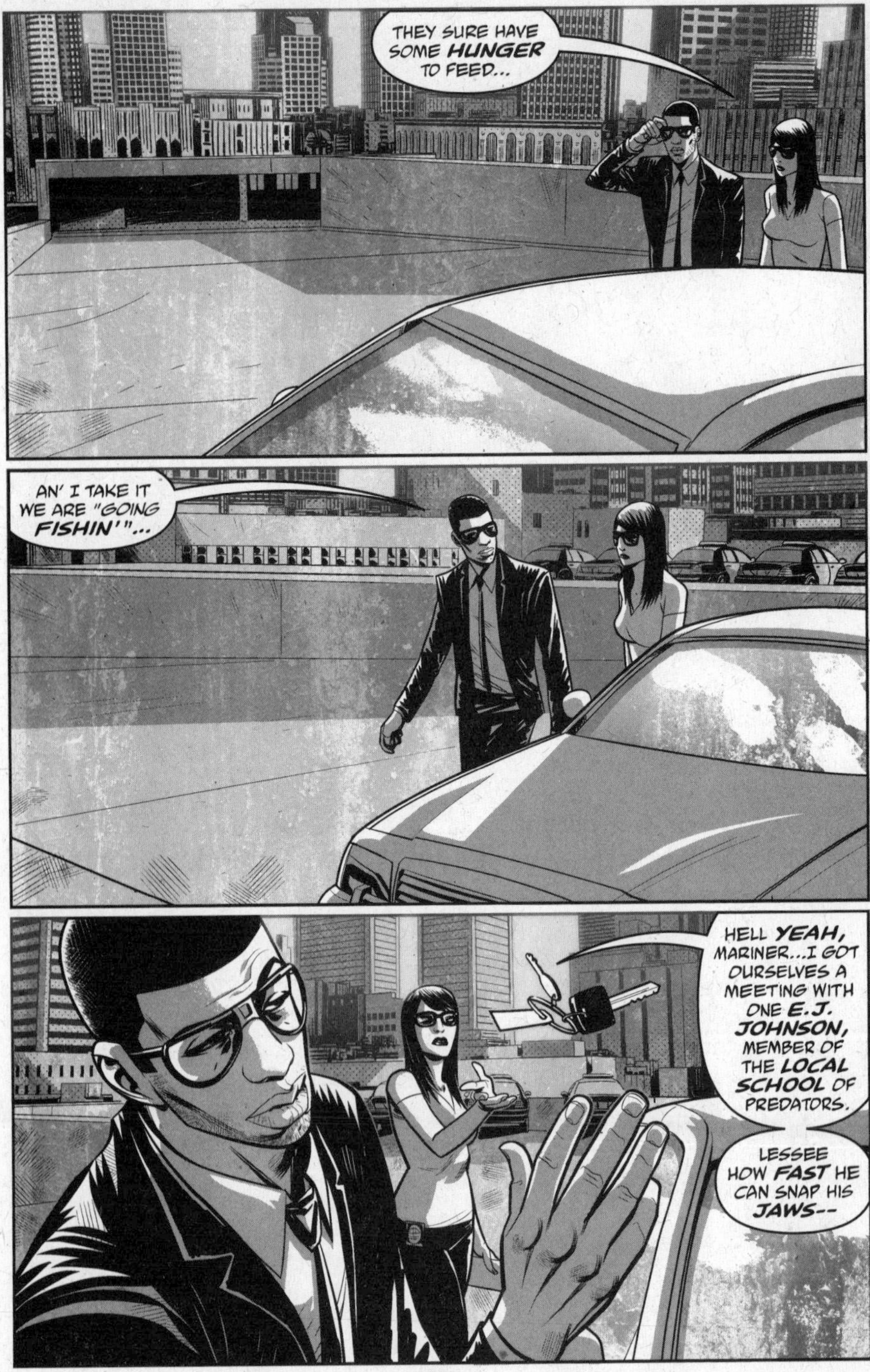
THEY SURE HAVE SOME HUNGER TO FEED...
AN' I TAKE IT WE ARE "GOING FISHIN'"...
HELL YEAH, MARINER...I GOT OURSELVES A MEETING WITH ONE E.J. JOHNSON, MEMBER OF THE LOCAL SCHOOL OF PREDATORS.
LESSEE HOW FAST HE CAN SNAP HIS JAWS--

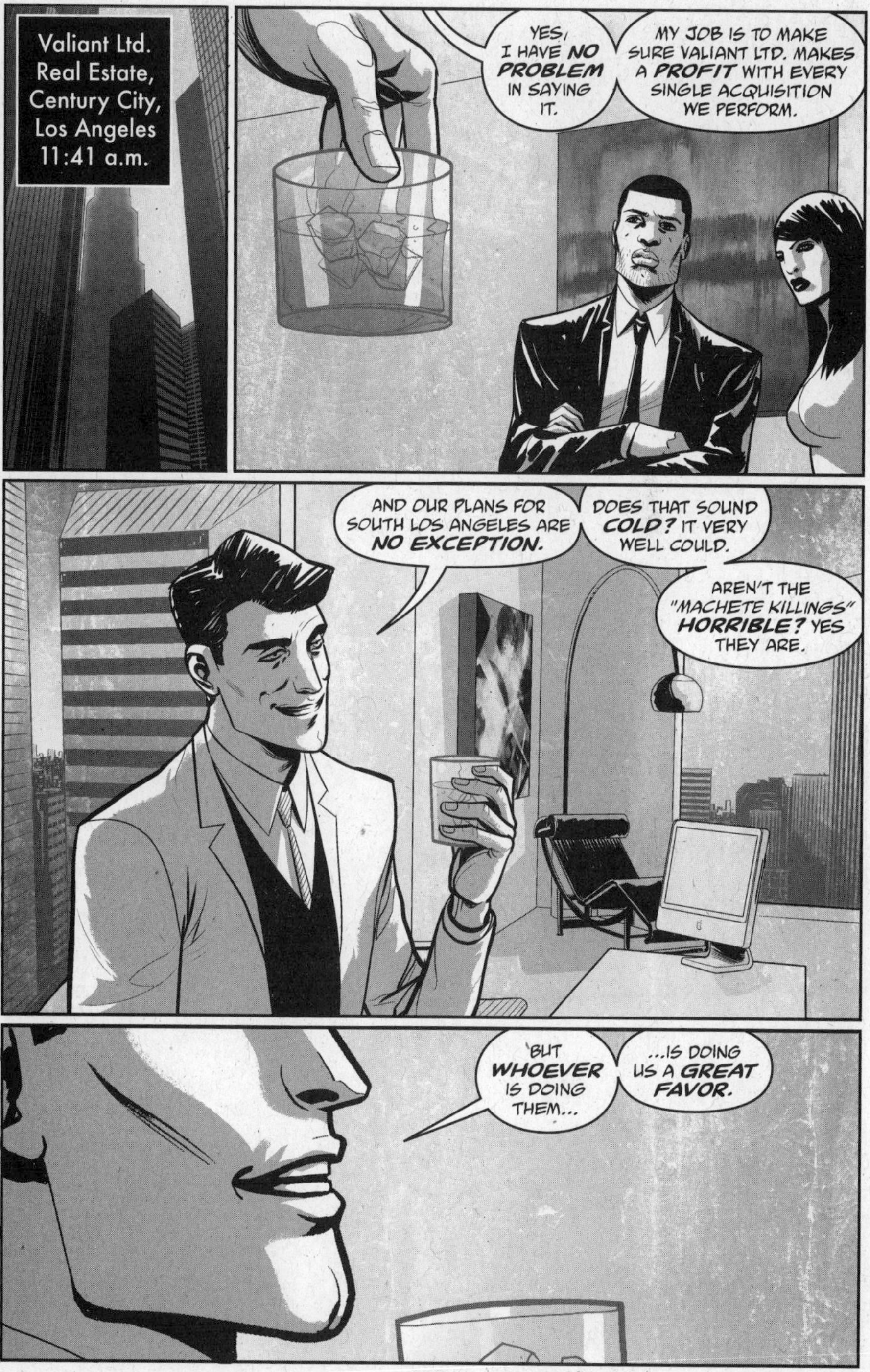
Valiant Ltd. Real Estate, Century City, Los Angeles 11:41 a.m.
YES, I HAVE NO PROBLEM IN SAYING IT.
MY JOB IS TO MAKE SURE VALIANT LTD. MAKES A PROFIT WITH EVERY SINGLE ACQUISITION WE PERFORM.
AND OUR PLANS FOR SOUTH LOS ANGELES ARE NO EXCEPTION.
DOES THAT SOUND COLD? IT VERY WELL COULD.
AREN'T THE "MACHETE KILLINGS" HORRIBLE? YES THEY ARE.
BUT WHOEVER IS DOING THEM...
...IS DOING US A GREAT FAVOR.

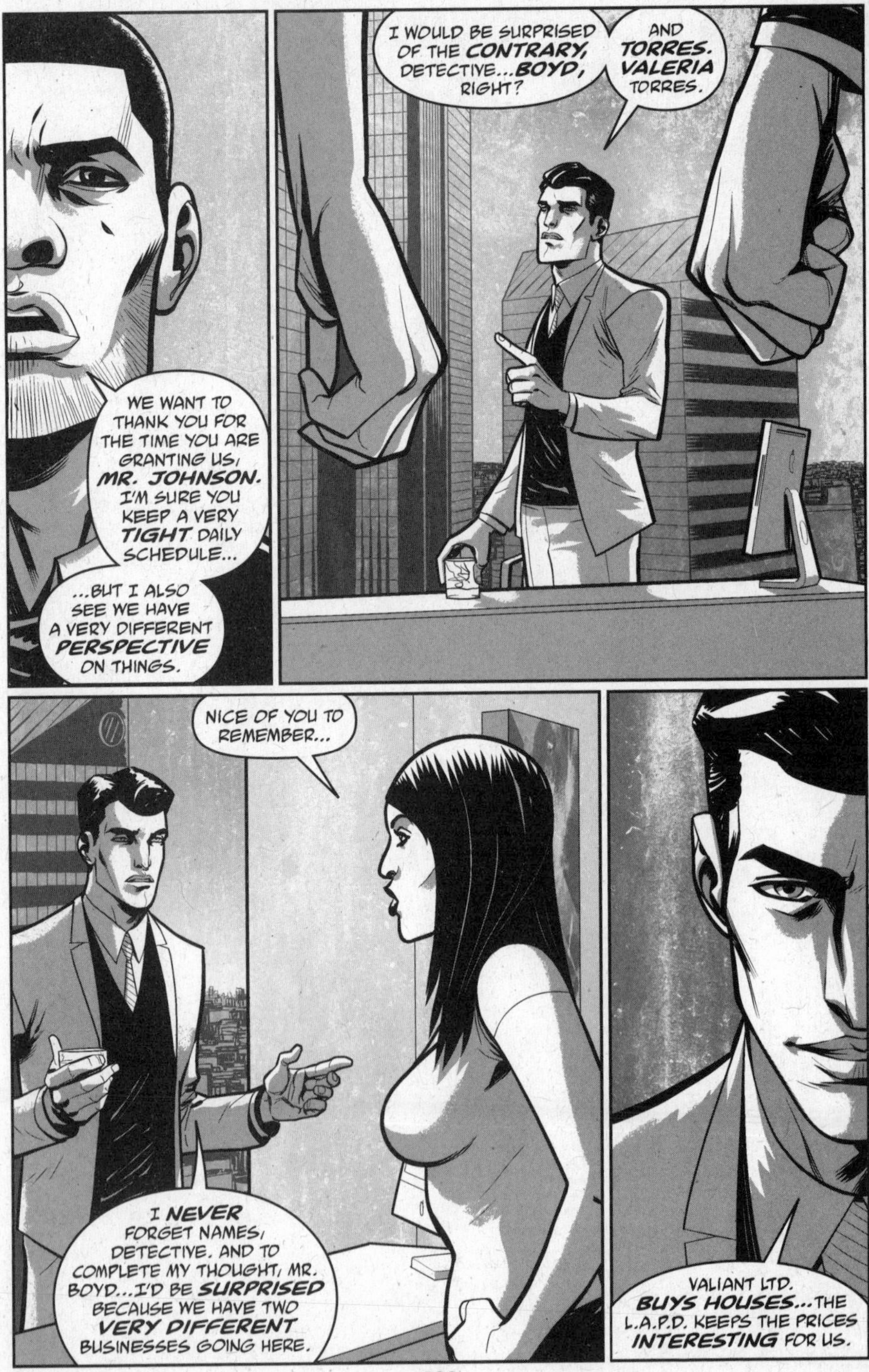
WE WANT TO THANK YOU FOR THE TIME YOU ARE GRANTING US, MR. JOHNSON. I'M SURE YOU KEEP A VERY TIGHT DAILY SCHEDULE...
...BUT I ALSO SEE WE HAVE A VERY DIFFERENT PERSPECTIVE ON THINGS.
I WOULD BE SURPRISED OF THE CONTRARY, DETECTIVE...BOYD, RIGHT?
AND TORRES. VALERIA TORRES.
NICE OF YOU TO REMEMBER...
I NEVER FORGET NAMES, DETECTIVE. AND TO COMPLETE MY THOUGHT, MR. BOYD...I'D BE SURPRISED BECAUSE WE HAVE TWO VERY DIFFERENT BUSINESSES GOING HERE.
VALIANT LTD. BUYS HOUSES...THE L.A.P.D. KEEPS THE PRICES INTERESTING FOR US.

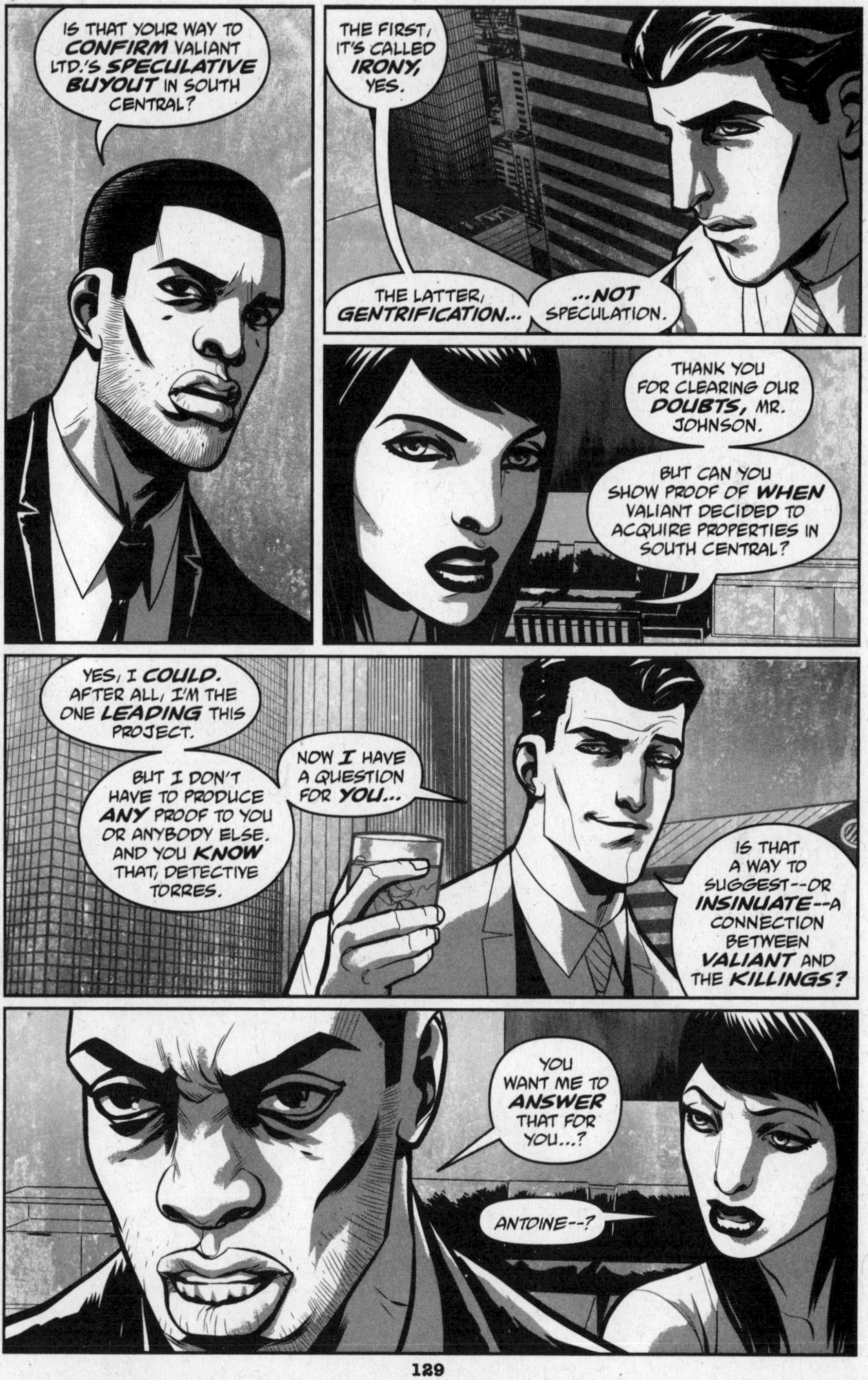
IS THAT YOUR WAY TO CONFIRM VALIANT LTD.'S SPECULATIVE BUYOUT IN SOUTH CENTRAL?
THE FIRST, IT'S CALLED IRONY, YES.
THE LATTER, GENTRIFICATION...
...NOT SPECULATION.
THANK YOU FOR CLEARING OUR DOUBTS, MR. JOHNSON.
BUT CAN YOU SHOW PROOF OF WHEN VALIANT DECIDED TO ACQUIRE PROPERTIES IN SOUTH CENTRAL?
YES, I COULD. AFTER ALL, I'M THE ONE LEADING THIS PROJECT.
BUT I DON'T HAVE TO PRODUCE ANY PROOF TO YOU OR ANYBODY ELSE. AND YOU KNOW THAT, DETECTIVE TORRES.
NOW I HAVE A QUESTION FOR YOU...
IS THAT A WAY TO SUGGEST--OR INSINUATE--A CONNECTION BETWEEN VALIANT AND THE KILLINGS?
YOU WANT ME TO ANSWER THAT FOR YOU...?
ANTOINE--?

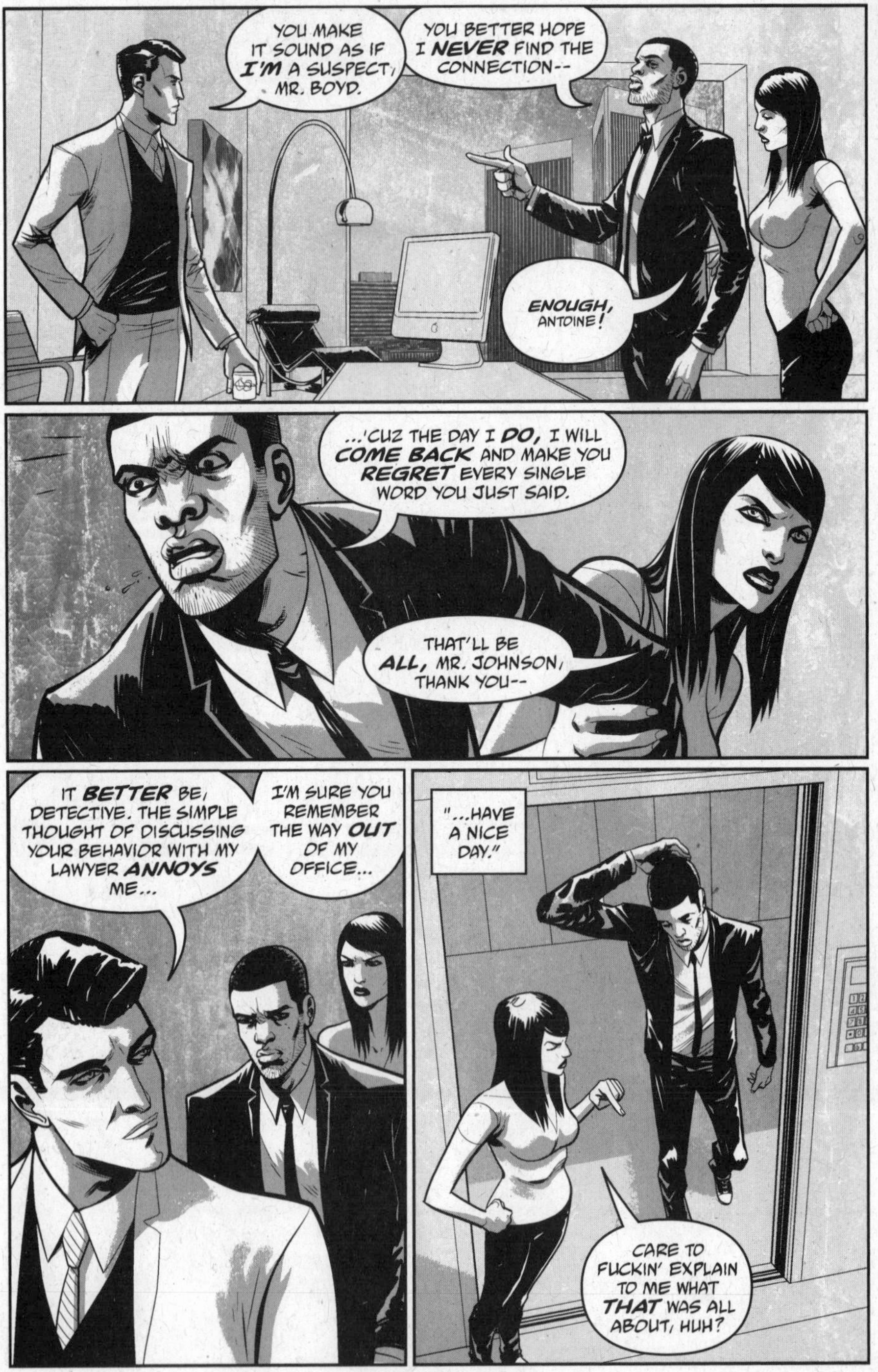
YOU MAKE IT SOUND AS IF I'M A SUSPECT, MR. BOYD.
YOU BETTER HOPE I NEVER FIND THE CONNECTION--
ENOUGH, ANTOINE!
...'CUZ THE DAY I DO, I WILL COME BACK AND MAKE YOU REGRET EVERY SINGLE WORD YOU JUST SAID.
THAT'LL BE ALL, MR. JOHNSON, THANK YOU--
IT BETTER BE, DETECTIVE. THE SIMPLE THOUGHT OF DISCUSSING YOUR BEHAVIOR WITH MY LAWYER ANNOYS ME...
I'M SURE YOU REMEMBER THE WAY OUT OF MY OFFICE...
"...HAVE A NICE DAY."
CARE TO FUCKIN' EXPLAIN TO ME WHAT THAT WAS ALL ABOUT, HUH?

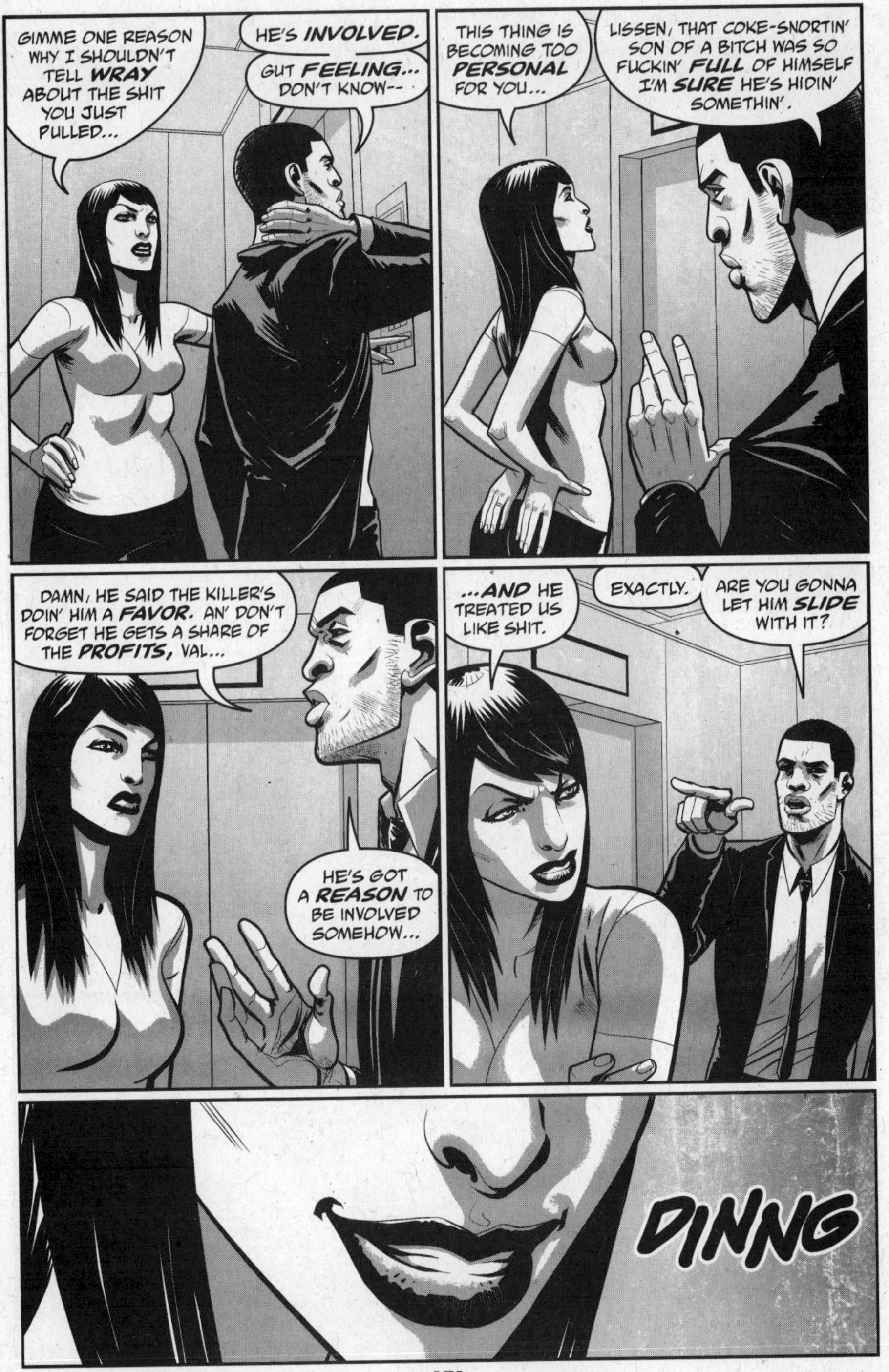
GIMME ONE REASON WHY I SHOULDN'T TELL WRAY ABOUT THE SHIT YOU JUST PULLED...
HE'S INVOLVED.
GUT FEELING... DON'T KNOW--
THIS THING IS BECOMING TOO PERSONAL FOR YOU...
LISSEN, THAT COKE-SNORTIN' SON OF A BITCH WAS SO FUCKIN' FULL OF HIMSELF I'M SURE HE'S HIDIN' SOMETHIN'.
DAMN, HE SAID THE KILLER'S DOIN' HIM A FAVOR. AN' DON'T FORGET HE GETS A SHARE OF THE PROFITS, VAL...
HE'S GOT A REASON TO BE INVOLVED SOMEHOW...
...AND HE TREATED US LIKE SHIT.
EXACTLY.
ARE YOU GONNA LET HIM SLIDE WITH IT?
DINNG

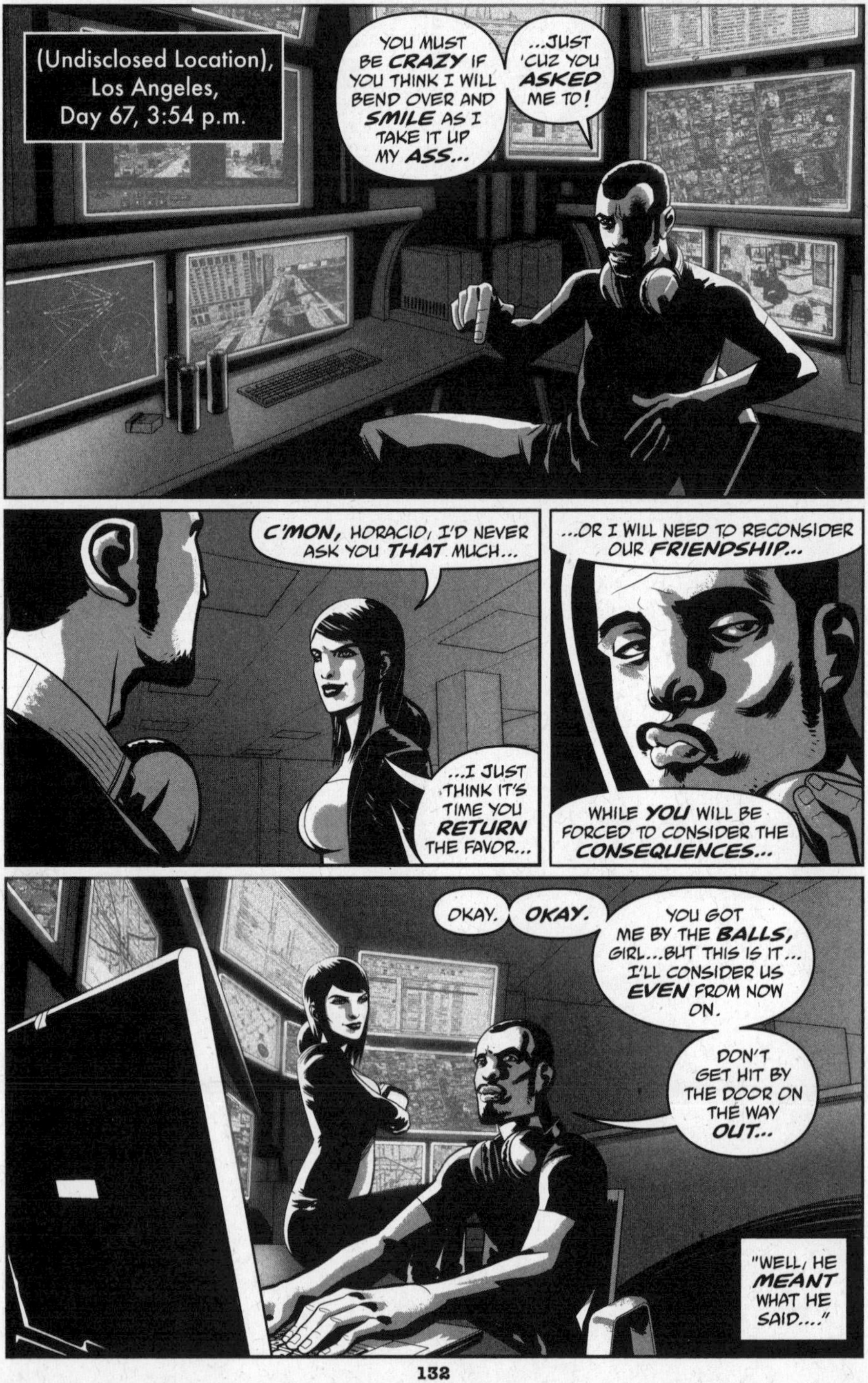
(Undisclosed Location), Los Angeles, Day 67, 3:54 p.m.
YOU MUST BE CRAZY IF YOU THINK I WILL BEND OVER AND SMILE AS I TAKE IT UP MY ASS...
...JUST 'CUZ YOU ASKED ME TO!
C'MON, HORACIO, I'D NEVER ASK YOU THAT MUCH...
...I JUST THINK IT'S TIME YOU RETURN THE FAVOR...
...OR I WILL NEED TO RECONSIDER OUR FRIENDSHIP...
WHILE YOU WILL BE FORCED TO CONSIDER THE CONSEQUENCES...
OKAY.
OKAY.
YOU GOT ME BY THE BALLS, GIRL...BUT THIS IS IT... I'LL CONSIDER US EVEN FROM NOW ON.
DON'T GET HIT BY THE DOOR ON THE WAY OUT...
"WELL, HE MEANT WHAT HE SAID...."

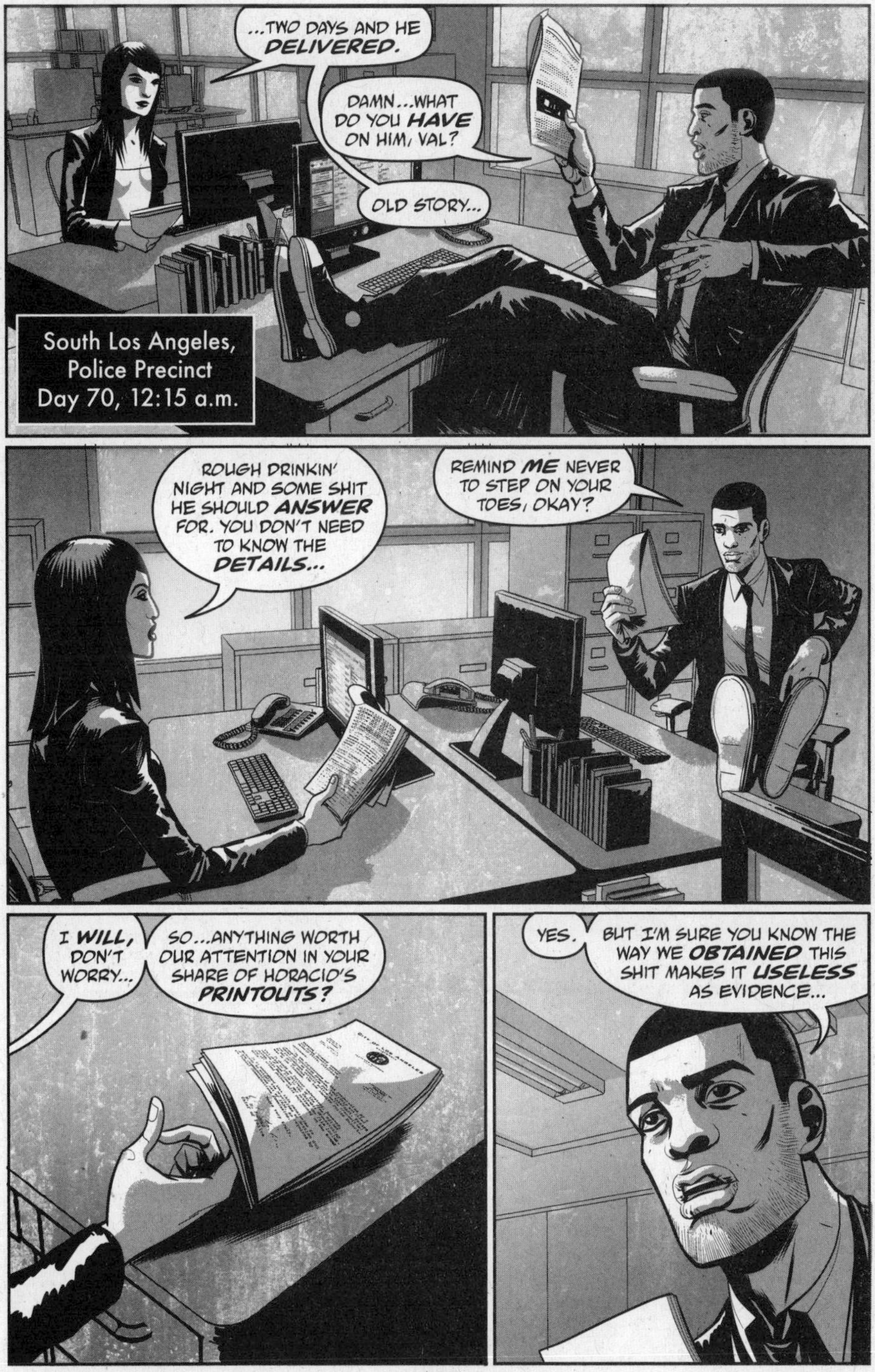
...TWO DAYS AND HE DELIVERED.
DAMN...WHAT DO YOU HAVE ON HIM, VAL?
OLD STORY...
South Los Angeles, Police Precinct Day 70, 12:15 a.m.
ROUGH DRINKIN' NIGHT AND SOME SHIT HE SHOULD ANSWER FOR. YOU DON'T NEED TO KNOW THE DETAILS...
REMIND ME NEVER TO STEP ON YOUR TOES, OKAY?
I WILL, DON'T WORRY...
SO...ANYTHING WORTH OUR ATTENTION IN YOUR SHARE OF HORACIO'S PRINTOUTS?
YES.
BUT I'M SURE YOU KNOW THE WAY WE OBTAINED THIS SHIT MAKES IT USELESS AS EVIDENCE...

NOW YOU'RE STEPPIN' ON MY TOES...

OKAY. MY THOUGHT EXACTLY.

CROSSCHECKING E.J. JOHNSON'S CELL PHONE CALLS, THERE'S A COUPLE OF NAMES THAT STICK OUT.

A COUPLE OF THEM ARE *PUSHERS* WHO SELL COCAINE AND CRACK TO THE *HIGHER-UPS*...

AND OUR *PRINCE CHARMING* FITS THE PART...

...JUST RIGHT. BUT THERE'S *MORE*...

MANY CALLS TO AND FROM *ONE* "KNOWN OFFENDER" WHO'S NOT ONLY A *CRACKHEAD*...

...BUT ALSO HAS A TRACK RECORD OF FELONIES THAT INCLUDES AGGRESSION, DOMESTIC VIOLENCE AND OTHERS.

YOU THINK WE'RE *ONTO* SOMETHING?

UNIVERSAL SVC CHG
UC USER
XES,   FEES
TOTA   of

BER:

09	9:25 AM	E	LOS ANGELES	CA
09	1:30 PM	D	LOS ANGELES	CA
09	11:36 PM	D	LOS ANGELES	CA
09	11:57 PM	D	LOS ANGELES	CA
09	12:15 AM	N	NEW YORK	NY
9	2:33 AM	N	LOS ANGELES	CA
9	10:30 AM	N	LOS ANGELES	CA
9	11:13 AM	N	WASHINGTON	DC
9	12:52 PM	N	LOS ANGELES	CA
	1:32 PM	E	LOS ANGELES	CA
	2:56 PM	D	BALTIMORE	MD
	4:30 PM	D	NEW YORK	NY
	9:30 PM	D	LOS ANGELES	CA
	11:34 PM	D	LOS ANGELES	CA

I THINK WE'D BETTER PAY HIM A *VISIT*...

...AND PRAY IT WON'T BE *TOO LATE*--

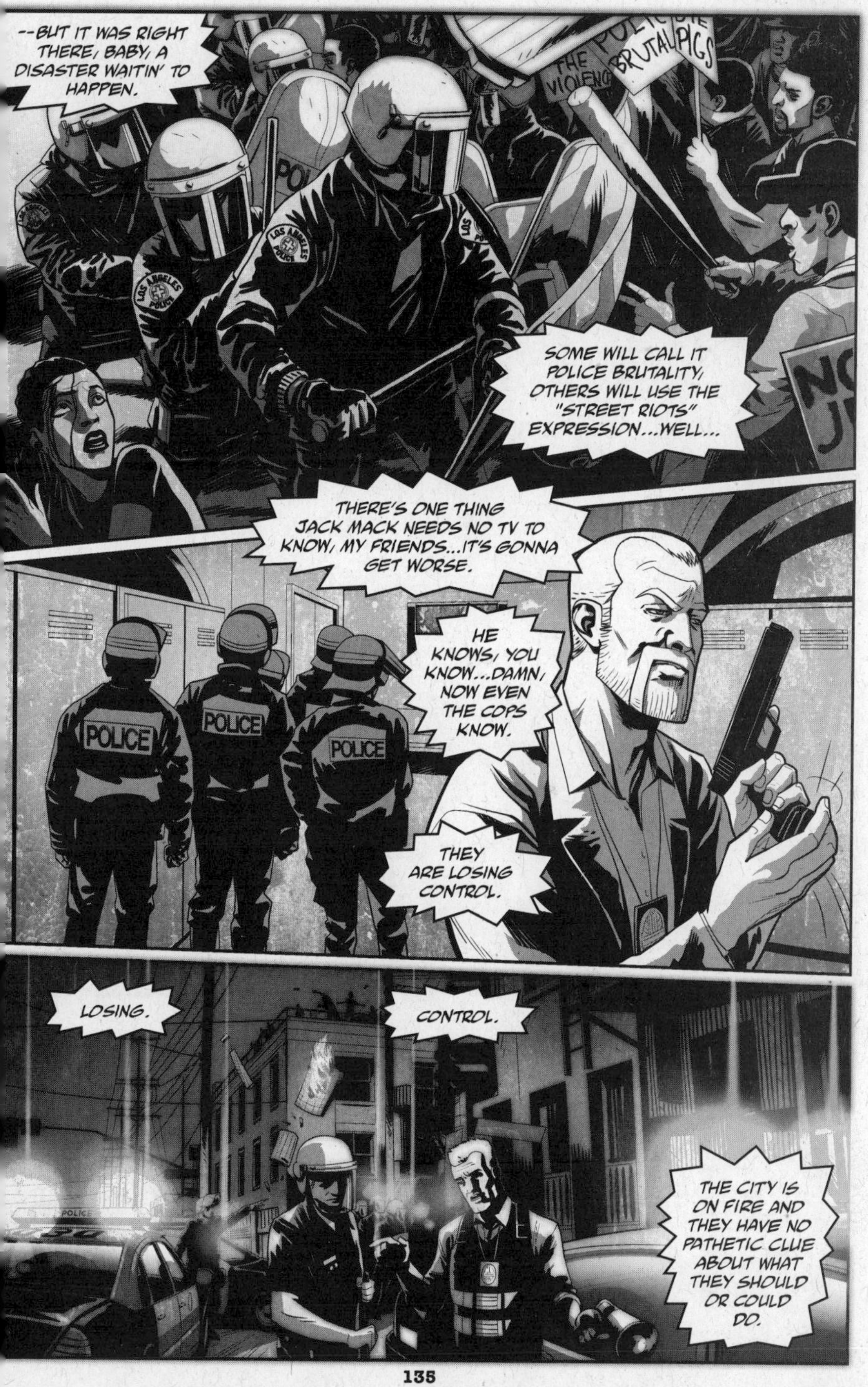
--BUT IT WAS RIGHT THERE, BABY, A DISASTER WAITIN' TO HAPPEN.
THE VIOLENCE
POLICE BRUTALITY
PIGS
POLICE
LOS ANGELES POLICE
SOME WILL CALL IT POLICE BRUTALITY, OTHERS WILL USE THE "STREET RIOTS" EXPRESSION...WELL...
THERE'S ONE THING JACK MACK NEEDS NO TV TO KNOW, MY FRIENDS...IT'S GONNA GET WORSE.
POLICE
POLICE
POLICE
HE KNOWS, YOU KNOW...DAMN, NOW EVEN THE COPS KNOW.
THEY ARE LOSING CONTROL.
LOSING.
CONTROL.
POLICE
THE CITY IS ON FIRE AND THEY HAVE NO PATHETIC CLUE ABOUT WHAT THEY SHOULD OR COULD DO.

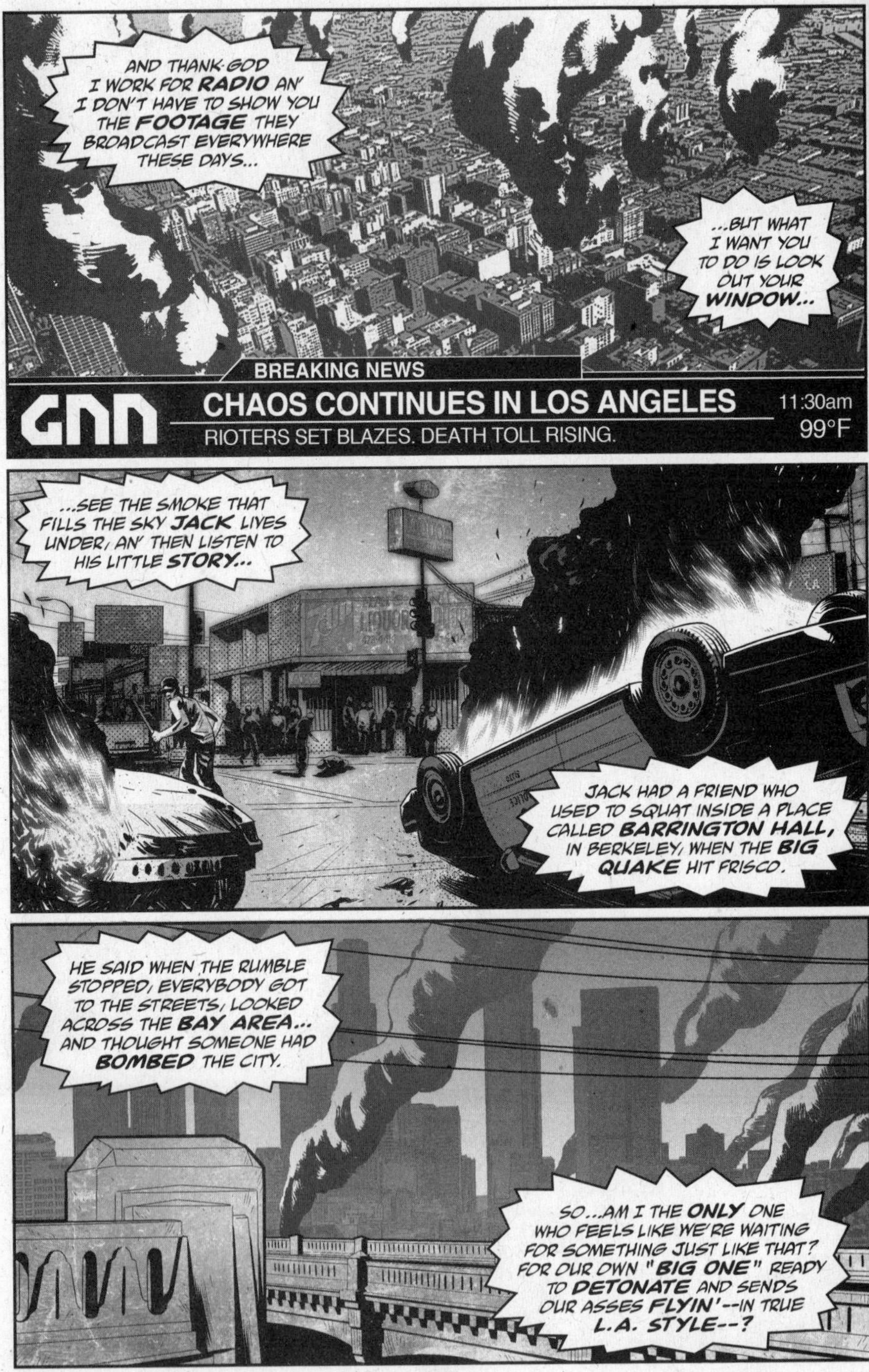
AND THANK·GOD I WORK FOR RADIO AN' I DON'T HAVE TO SHOW YOU THE FOOTAGE THEY BROADCAST EVERYWHERE THESE DAYS...
...BUT WHAT I WANT YOU TO DO IS LOOK OUT YOUR WINDOW...
BREAKING NEWS
GNN
CHAOS CONTINUES IN LOS ANGELES
RIOTERS SET BLAZES. DEATH TOLL RISING.
11:30am
99°F
...SEE THE SMOKE THAT FILLS THE SKY JACK LIVES UNDER, AN' THEN LISTEN TO HIS LITTLE STORY...
JACK HAD A FRIEND WHO USED TO SQUAT INSIDE A PLACE CALLED BARRINGTON HALL, IN BERKELEY, WHEN THE BIG QUAKE HIT FRISCO.
HE SAID WHEN THE RUMBLE STOPPED, EVERYBODY GOT TO THE STREETS, LOOKED ACROSS THE BAY AREA... AND THOUGHT SOMEONE HAD BOMBED THE CITY.
SO...AM I THE ONLY ONE WHO FEELS LIKE WE'RE WAITING FOR SOMETHING JUST LIKE THAT? FOR OUR OWN "BIG ONE" READY TO DETONATE AND SENDS OUR ASSES FLYIN'--IN TRUE L.A. STYLE--?

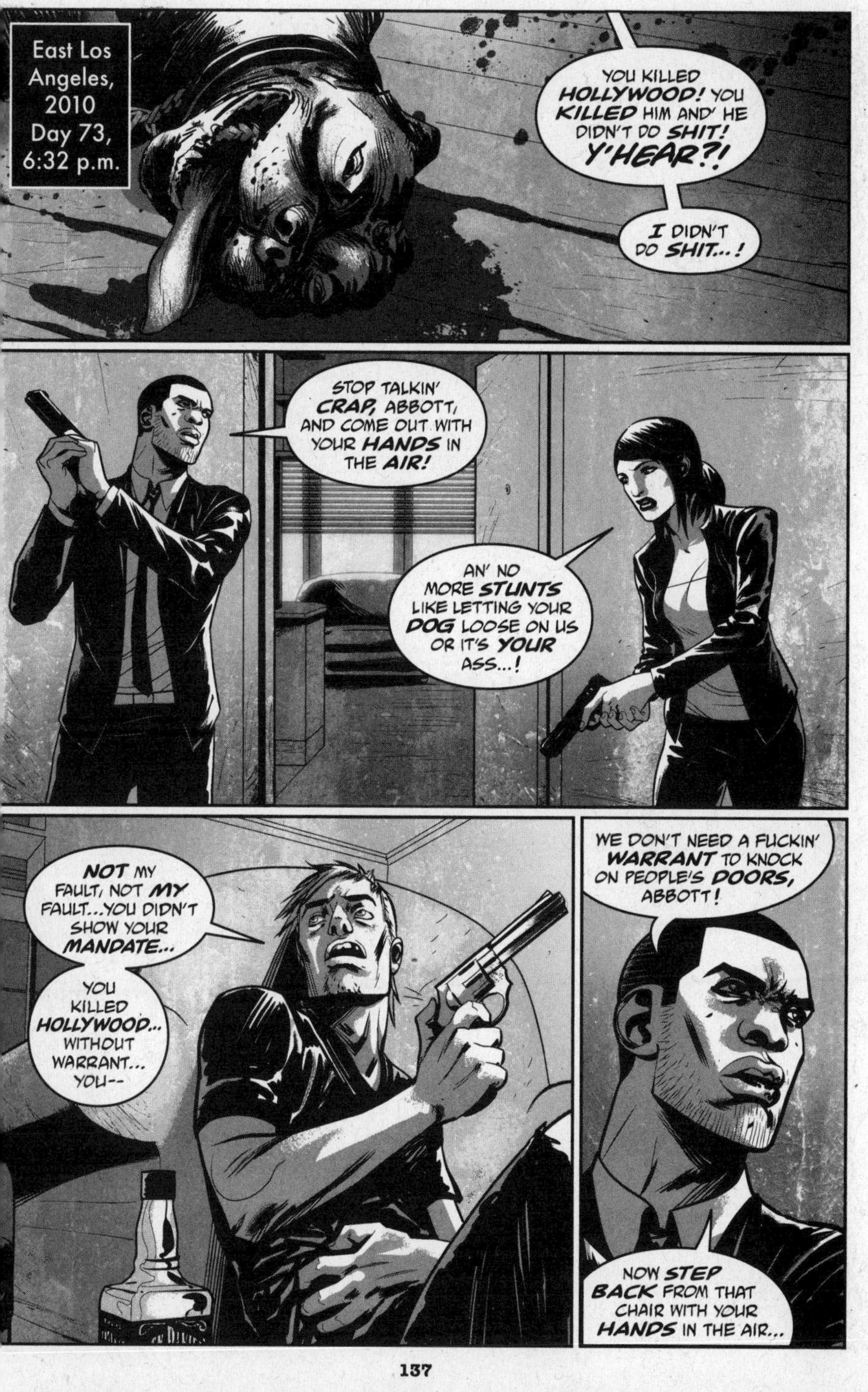
East Los Angeles, 2010 Day 73, 6:32 p.m.
YOU KILLED HOLLYWOOD! YOU KILLED HIM AND' HE DIDN'T DO SHIT! Y'HEAR?!
I DIDN'T DO SHIT...!
STOP TALKIN' CRAP, ABBOTT, AND COME OUT WITH YOUR HANDS IN THE AIR!
AN' NO MORE STUNTS LIKE LETTING YOUR DOG LOOSE ON US OR IT'S YOUR ASS...!
NOT MY FAULT, NOT MY FAULT...YOU DIDN'T SHOW YOUR MANDATE...
YOU KILLED HOLLYWOOD... WITHOUT WARRANT... YOU--
WE DON'T NEED A FUCKIN' WARRANT TO KNOCK ON PEOPLE'S DOORS, ABBOTT!
NOW STEP BACK FROM THAT CHAIR WITH YOUR HANDS IN THE AIR...

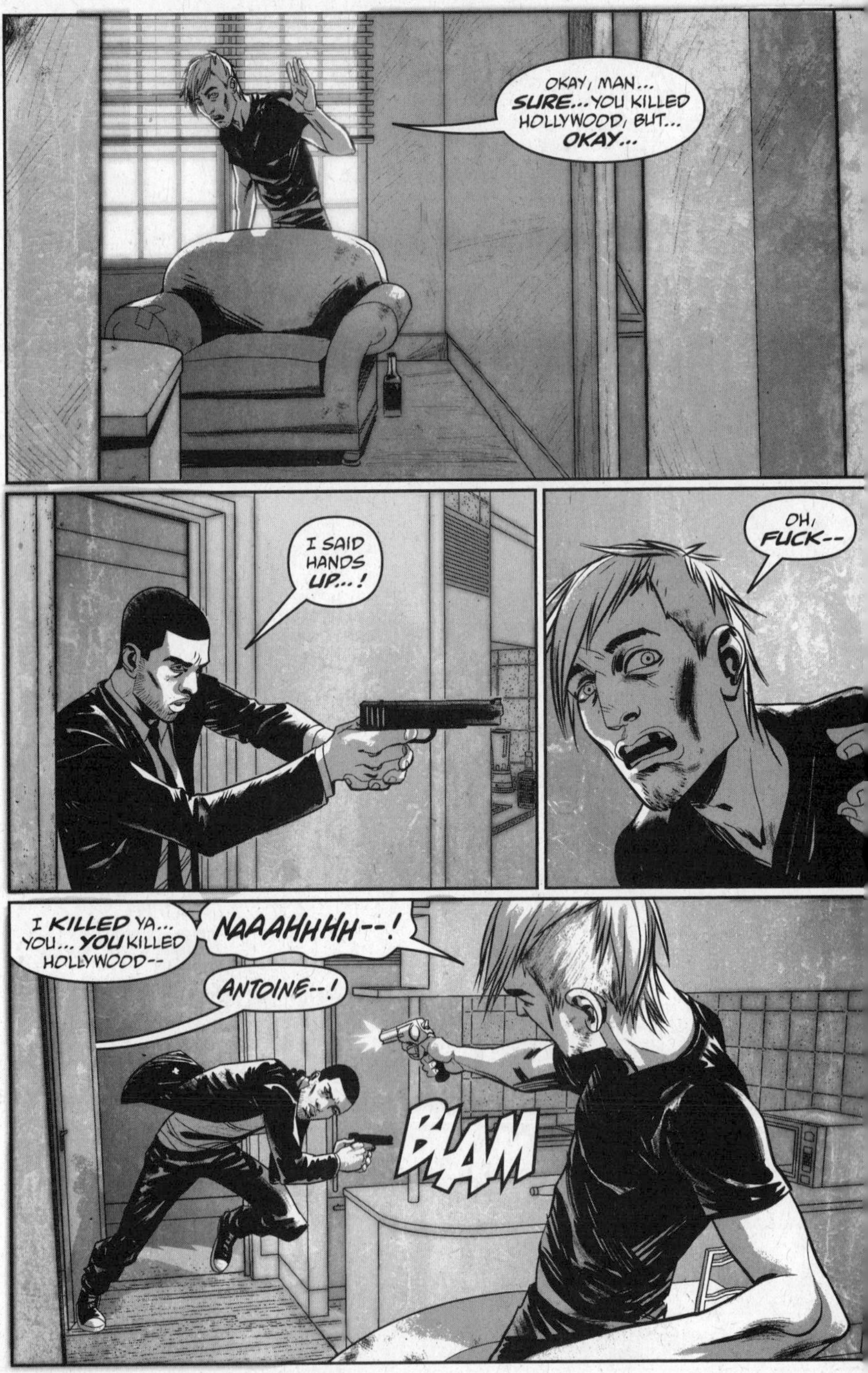
OKAY, MAN... SURE...YOU KILLED HOLLYWOOD, BUT... OKAY...
I SAID HANDS UP...!
OH, FUCK--
I KILLED YA... YOU... YOU KILLED HOLLYWOOD--
NAAAHHHH--!
ANTOINE--!
BLAM

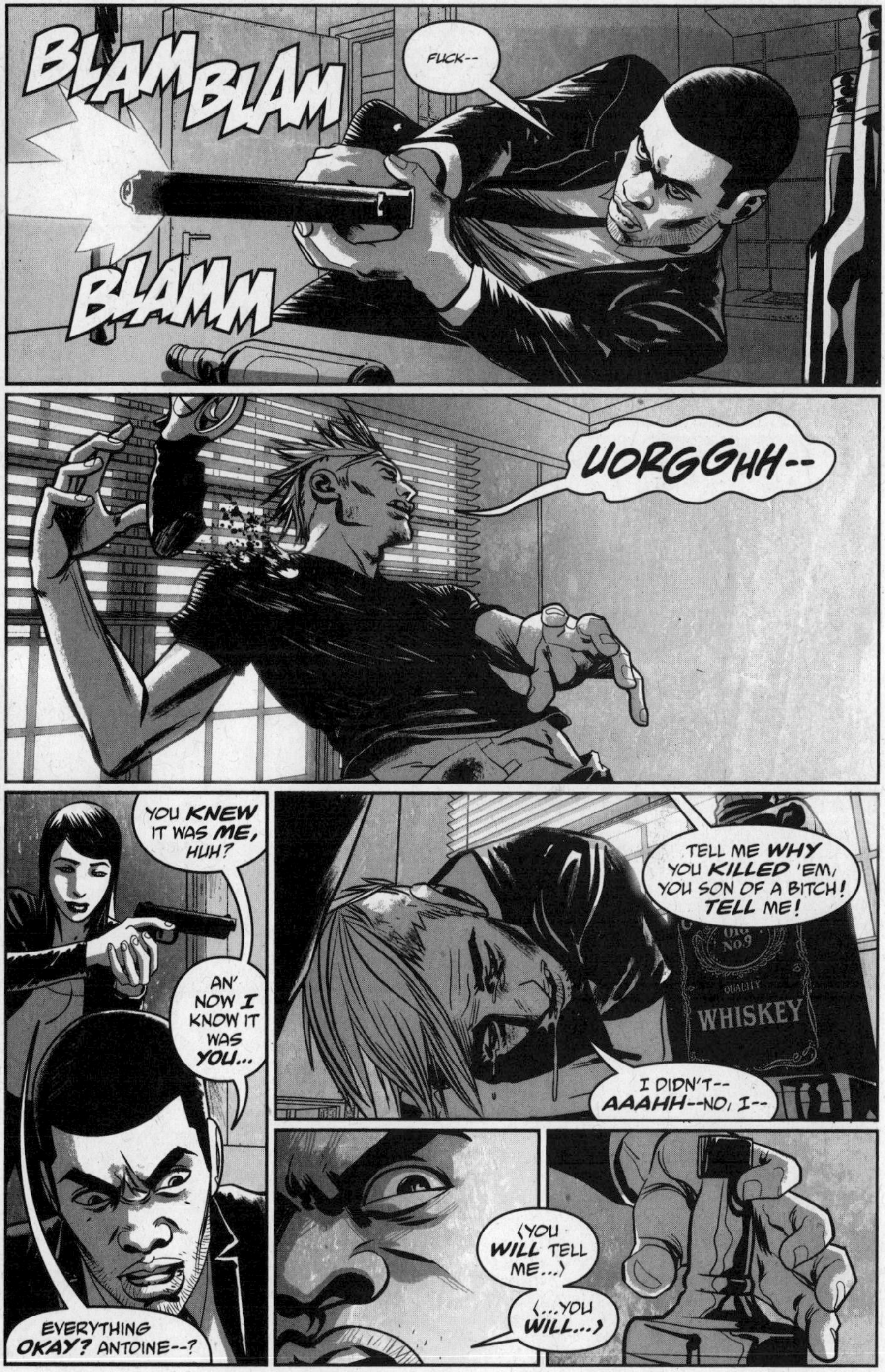
BLAM BLAM
FUCK--
BLAMM
UORGGHH--
YOU KNEW IT WAS ME, HUH?
AN' NOW I KNOW IT WAS YOU...
TELL ME WHY YOU KILLED 'EM, YOU SON OF A BITCH! TELL ME!
No.9
QUALITY
WHISKEY
I DIDN'T-- AAAHH--NO, I--
EVERYTHING OKAY? ANTOINE--?
‹YOU WILL TELL ME...›
‹...YOU WILL...›

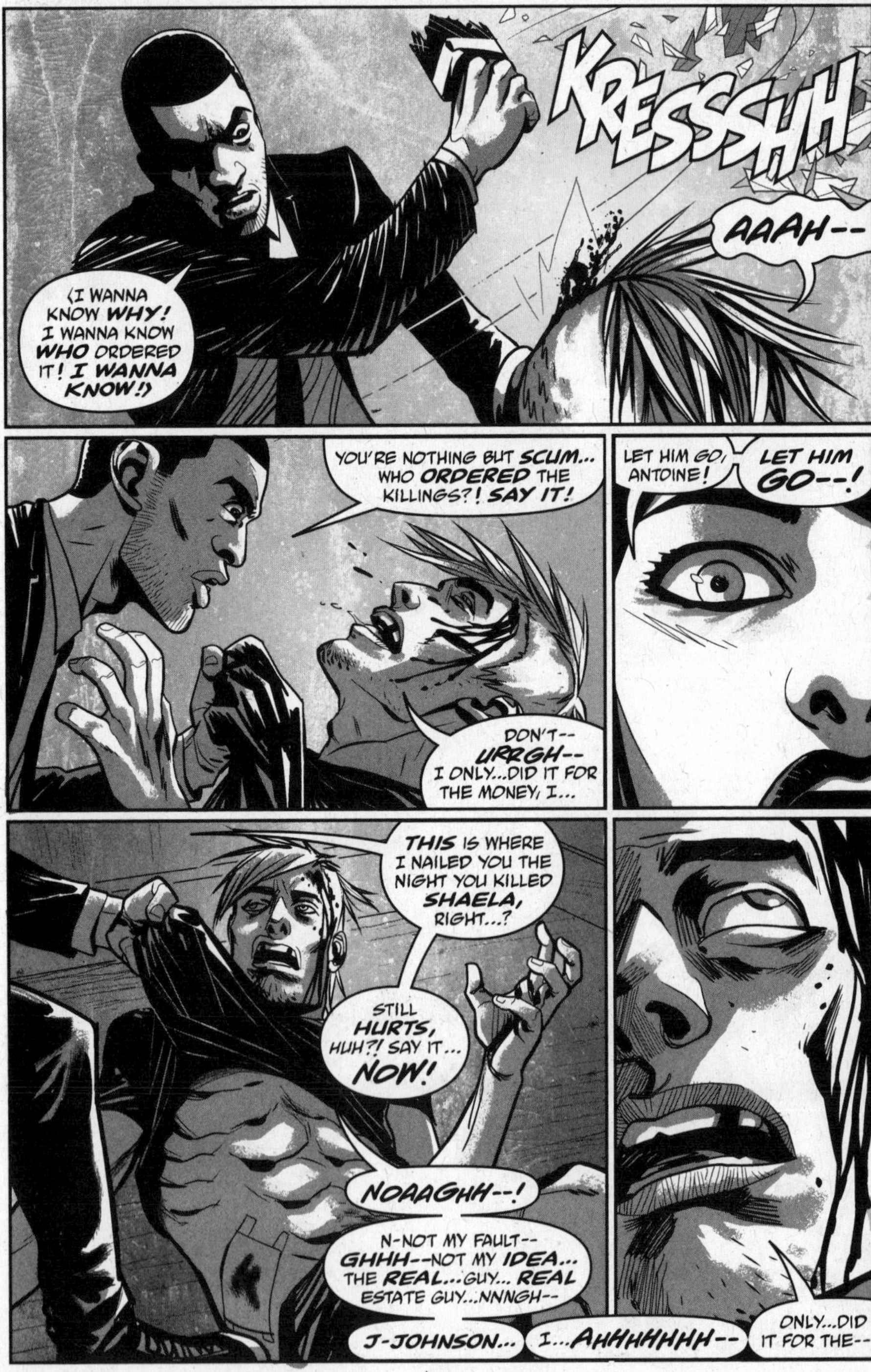
KRESSSHH
AAAH--
‹I WANNA KNOW WHY! I WANNA KNOW WHO ORDERED IT! I WANNA KNOW!›
YOU'RE NOTHING BUT SCUM... WHO ORDERED THE KILLINGS?! SAY IT!
LET HIM GO, ANTOINE!
LET HIM GO--!
DON'T-- URRGH-- I ONLY...DID IT FOR THE MONEY, I...
THIS IS WHERE I NAILED YOU THE NIGHT YOU KILLED SHAELA, RIGHT...?
STILL HURTS, HUH?! SAY IT... NOW!
NOAAGHH--!
N-NOT MY FAULT-- GHHH--NOT MY IDEA... THE REAL...GUY... REAL ESTATE GUY...NNNGH--
J-JOHNSON...
I...AHHHHHHH--
ONLY...DID IT FOR THE--

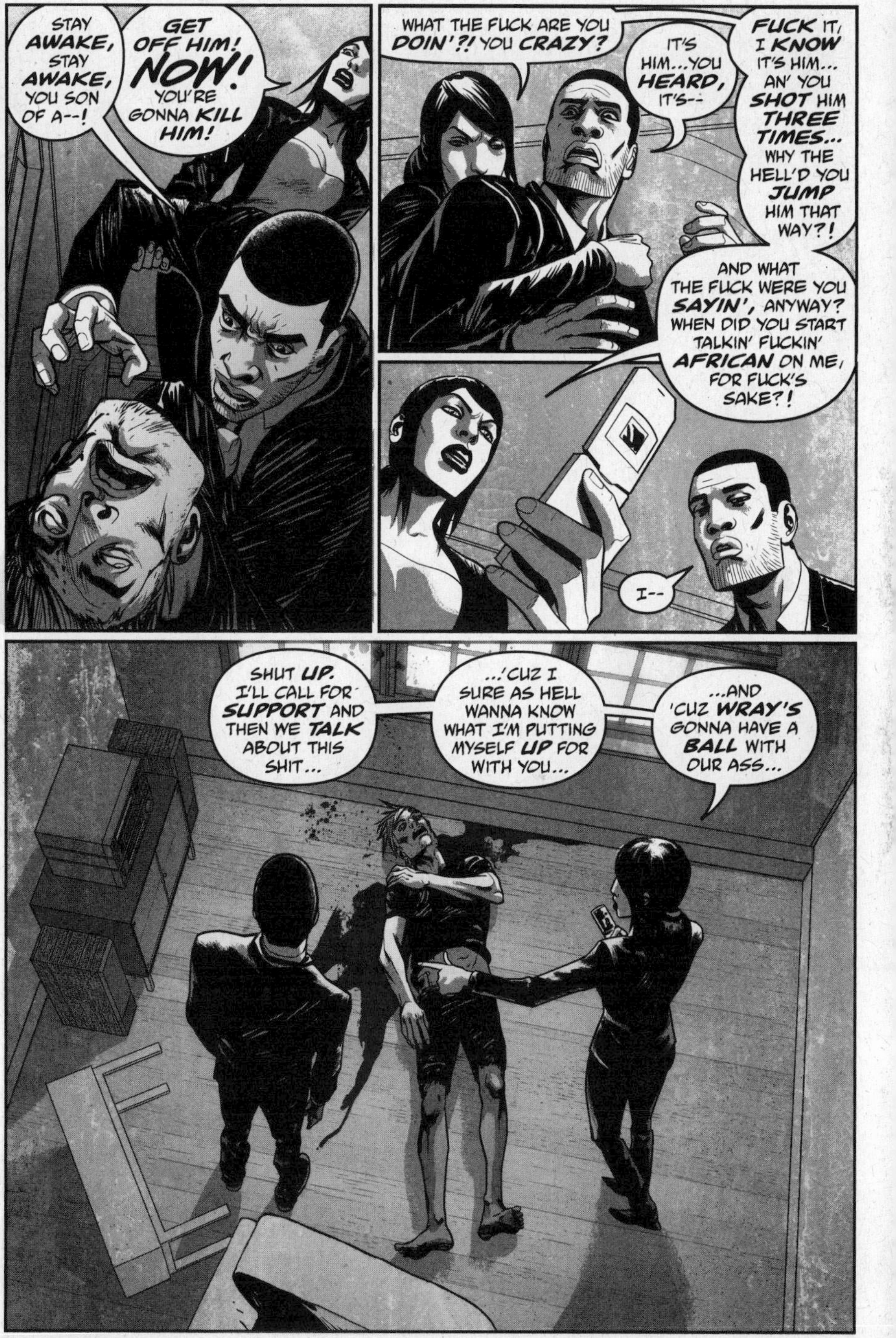
STAY AWAKE, STAY AWAKE, YOU SON OF A--!
GET OFF HIM! NOW! YOU'RE GONNA KILL HIM!
WHAT THE FUCK ARE YOU DOIN'?! YOU CRAZY?
IT'S HIM...YOU HEARD, IT'S--
FUCK IT, I KNOW IT'S HIM... AN' YOU SHOT HIM THREE TIMES... WHY THE HELL'D YOU JUMP HIM THAT WAY?!
AND WHAT THE FUCK WERE YOU SAYIN', ANYWAY? WHEN DID YOU START TALKIN' FUCKIN' AFRICAN ON ME, FOR FUCK'S SAKE?!
I--
SHUT UP. I'LL CALL FOR SUPPORT AND THEN WE TALK ABOUT THIS SHIT...
...'CUZ I SURE AS HELL WANNA KNOW WHAT I'M PUTTING MYSELF UP FOR WITH YOU...
...AND 'CUZ WRAY'S GONNA HAVE A BALL WITH OUR ASS...

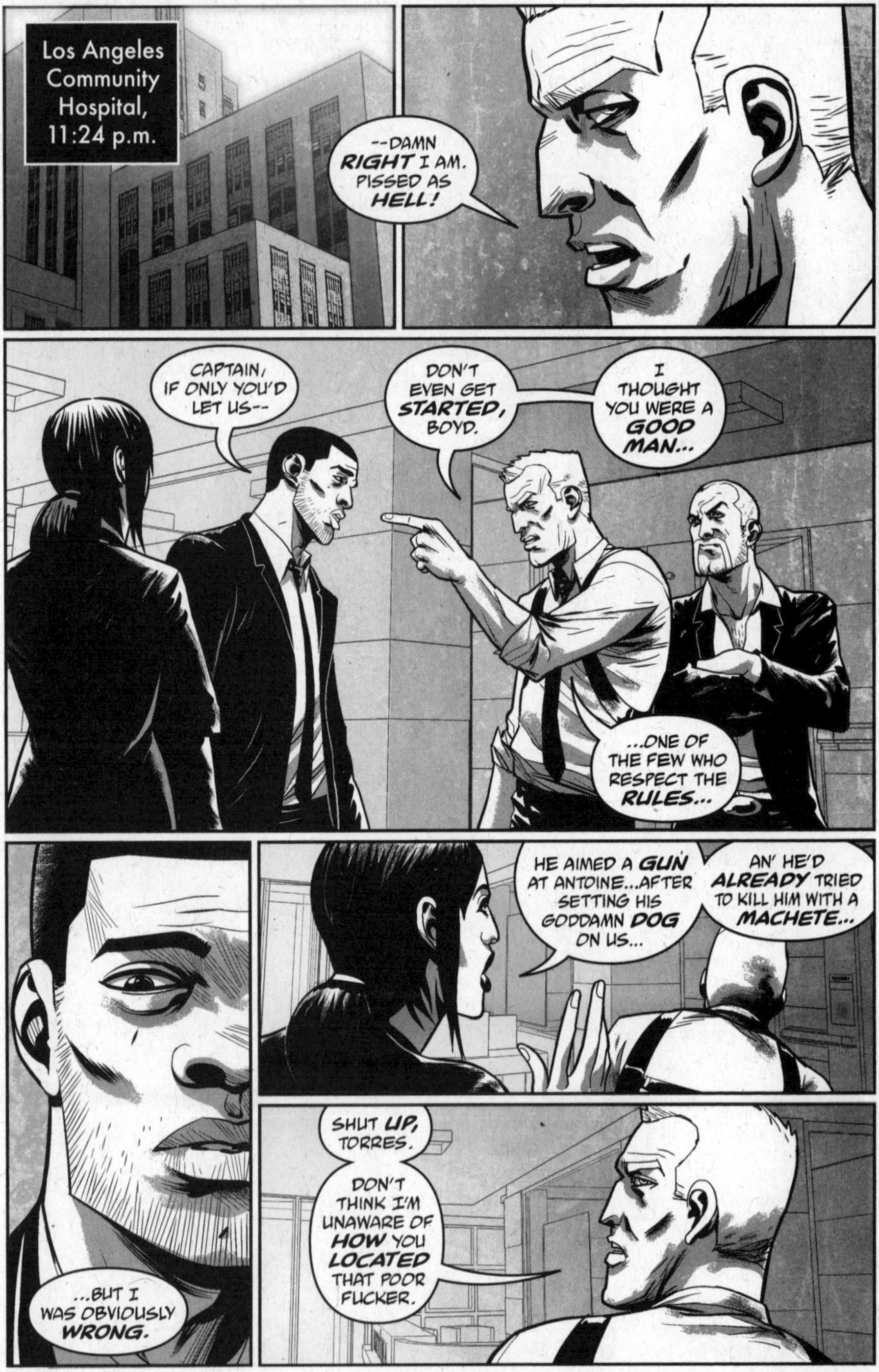

Los Angeles Community Hospital, 11:24 p.m.
--DAMN RIGHT I AM. PISSED AS HELL!
CAPTAIN, IF ONLY YOU'D LET US--
DON'T EVEN GET STARTED, BOYD.
I THOUGHT YOU WERE A GOOD MAN...
...ONE OF THE FEW WHO RESPECT THE RULES...
...BUT I WAS OBVIOUSLY WRONG.
HE AIMED A GUN AT ANTOINE...AFTER SETTING HIS GODDAMN DOG ON US...
AN' HE'D ALREADY TRIED TO KILL HIM WITH A MACHETE...
SHUT UP, TORRES.
DON'T THINK I'M UNAWARE OF HOW YOU LOCATED THAT POOR FUCKER.

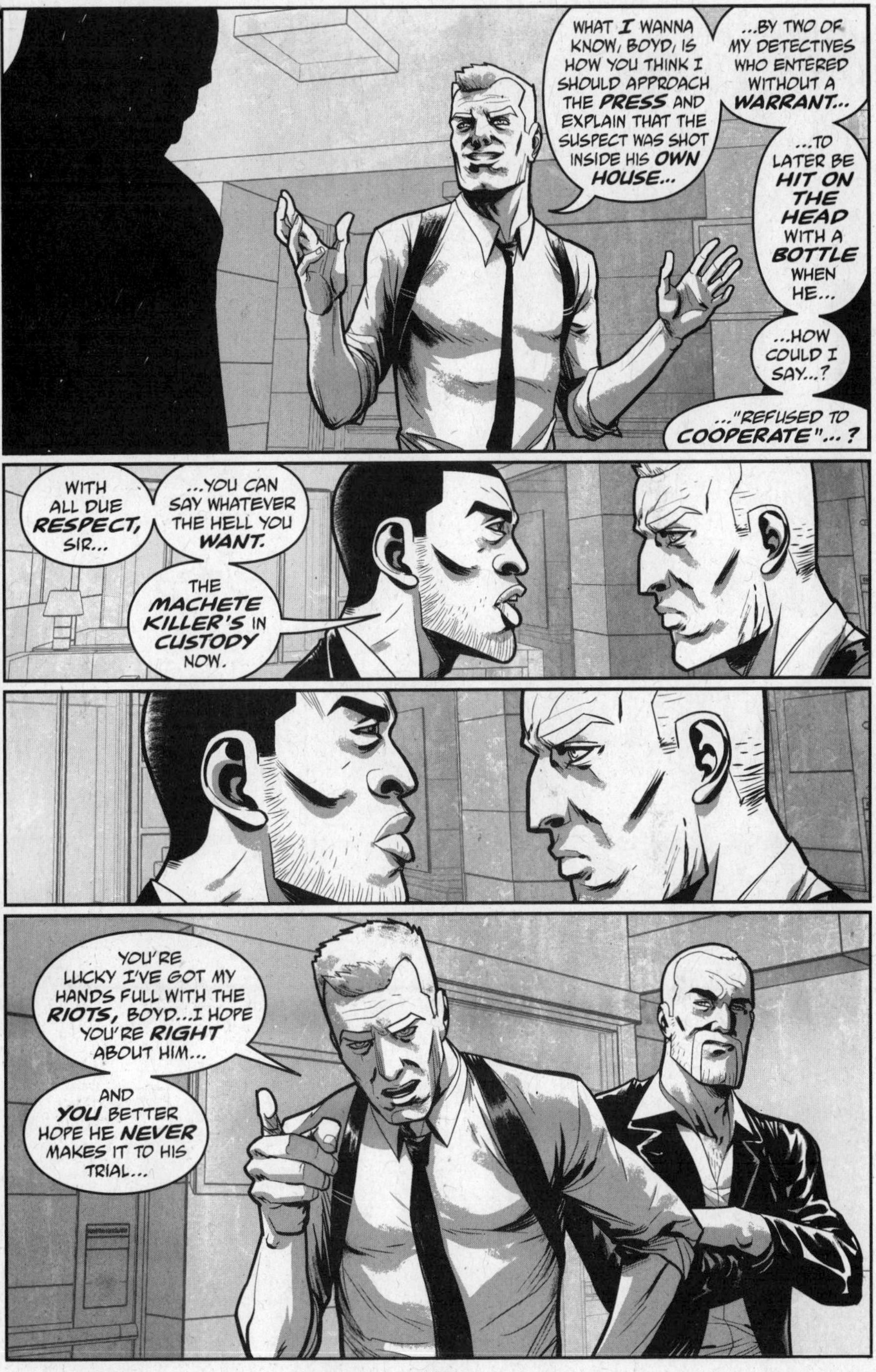
WHAT I WANNA KNOW, BOYD, IS HOW YOU THINK I SHOULD APPROACH THE PRESS AND EXPLAIN THAT THE SUSPECT WAS SHOT INSIDE HIS OWN HOUSE...
...BY TWO OF MY DETECTIVES WHO ENTERED WITHOUT A WARRANT...
...TO LATER BE HIT ON THE HEAD WITH A BOTTLE WHEN HE...
...HOW COULD I SAY...?
..."REFUSED TO COOPERATE"...?
WITH ALL DUE RESPECT, SIR...
...YOU CAN SAY WHATEVER THE HELL YOU WANT.
THE MACHETE KILLER'S IN CUSTODY NOW.
YOU'RE LUCKY I'VE GOT MY HANDS FULL WITH THE RIOTS, BOYD...I HOPE YOU'RE RIGHT ABOUT HIM...
AND YOU BETTER HOPE HE NEVER MAKES IT TO HIS TRIAL...

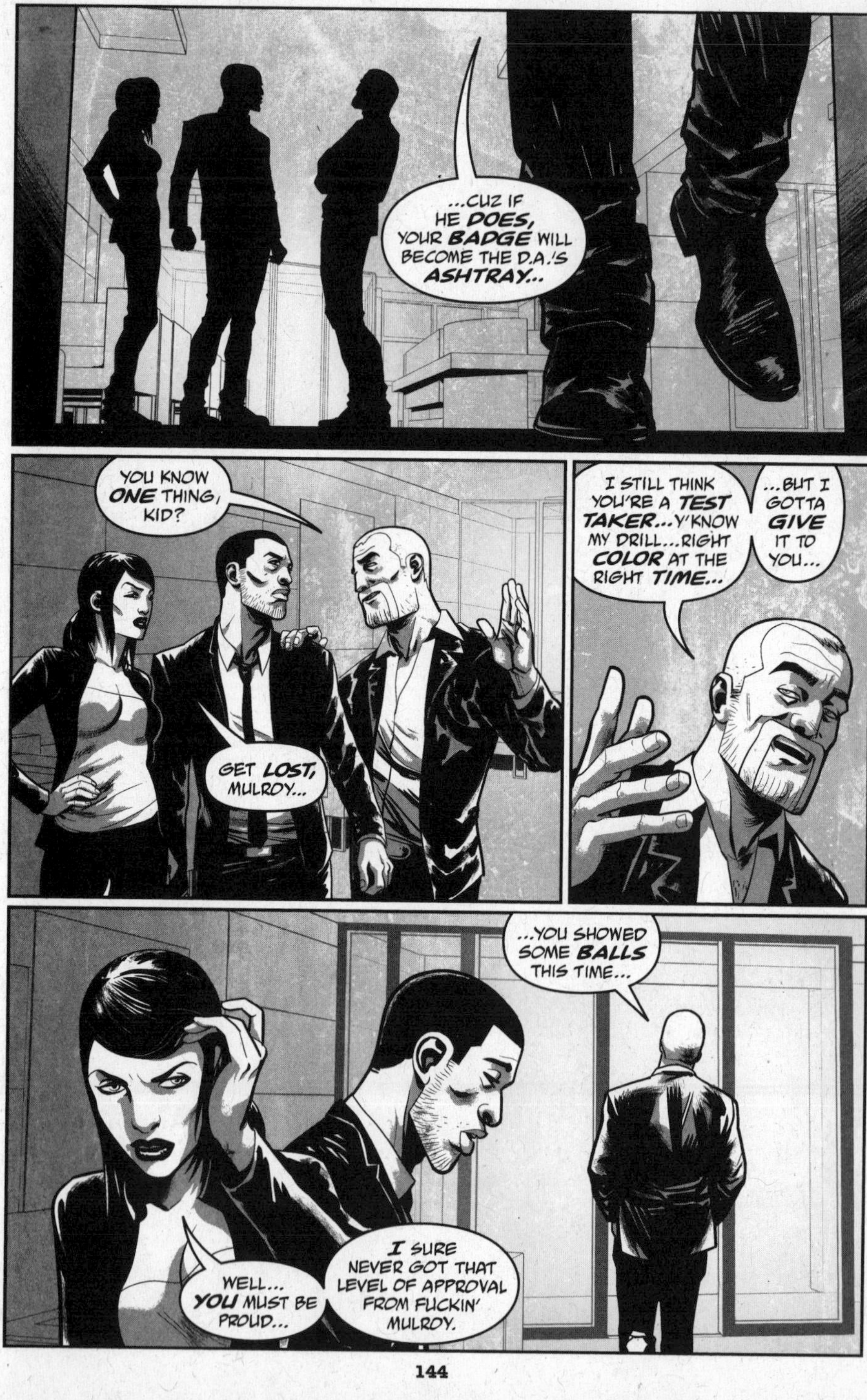
...CUZ IF HE DOES, YOUR BADGE WILL BECOME THE D.A.'S ASHTRAY...
YOU KNOW ONE THING, KID?
GET LOST, MULROY...
I STILL THINK YOU'RE A TEST TAKER...Y'KNOW MY DRILL...RIGHT COLOR AT THE RIGHT TIME...
...BUT I GOTTA GIVE IT TO YOU...
...YOU SHOWED SOME BALLS THIS TIME...
WELL... YOU MUST BE PROUD...
I SURE NEVER GOT THAT LEVEL OF APPROVAL FROM FUCKIN' MULROY.

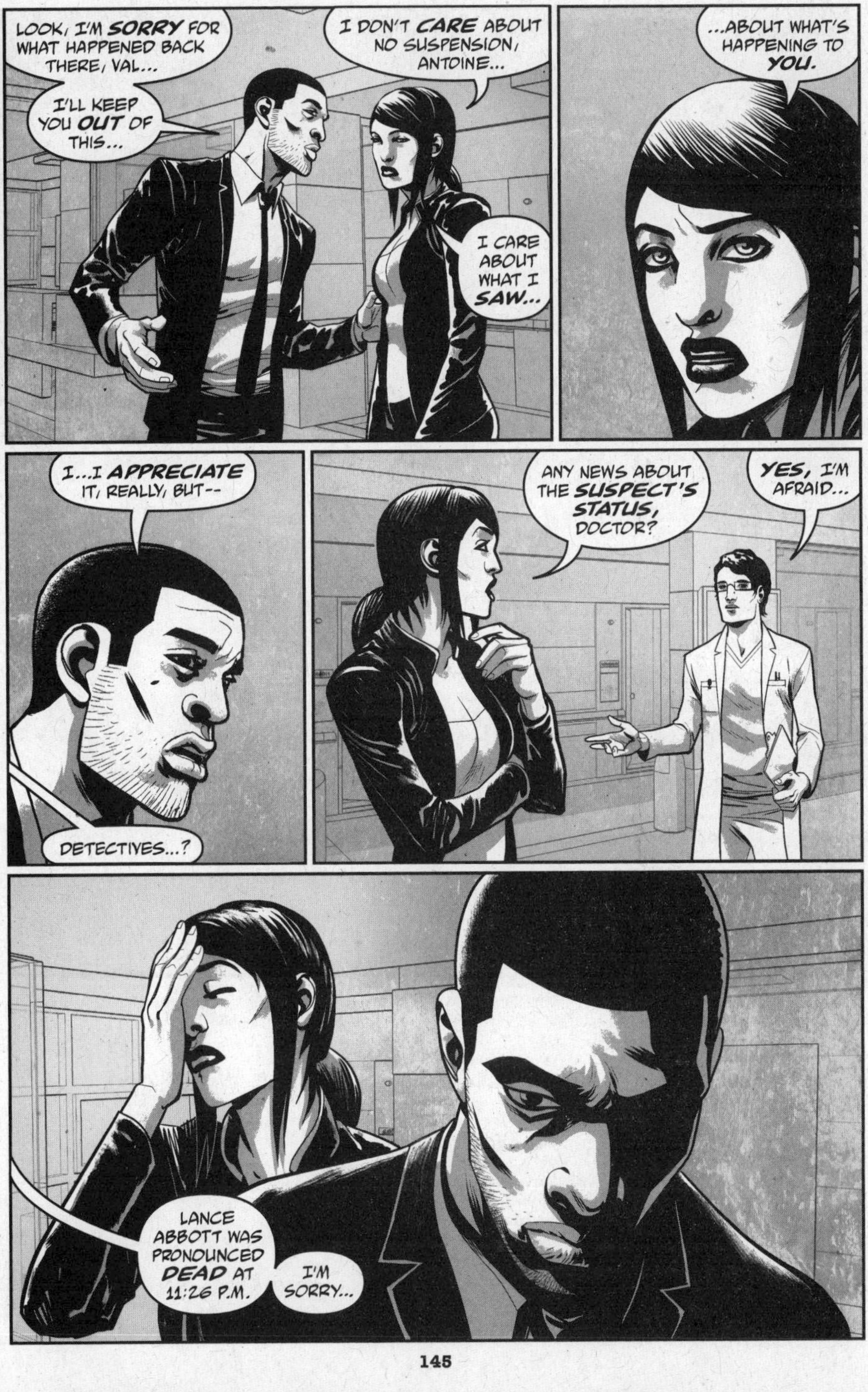
LOOK, I'M SORRY FOR WHAT HAPPENED BACK THERE, VAL...
I'LL KEEP YOU OUT OF THIS...
I DON'T CARE ABOUT NO SUSPENSION, ANTOINE...
I CARE ABOUT WHAT I SAW...
...ABOUT WHAT'S HAPPENING TO YOU.
I...I APPRECIATE IT, REALLY, BUT--
DETECTIVES...?
ANY NEWS ABOUT THE SUSPECT'S STATUS, DOCTOR?
YES, I'M AFRAID...
LANCE ABBOTT WAS PRONOUNCED DEAD AT 11:26 P.M.
I'M SORRY...

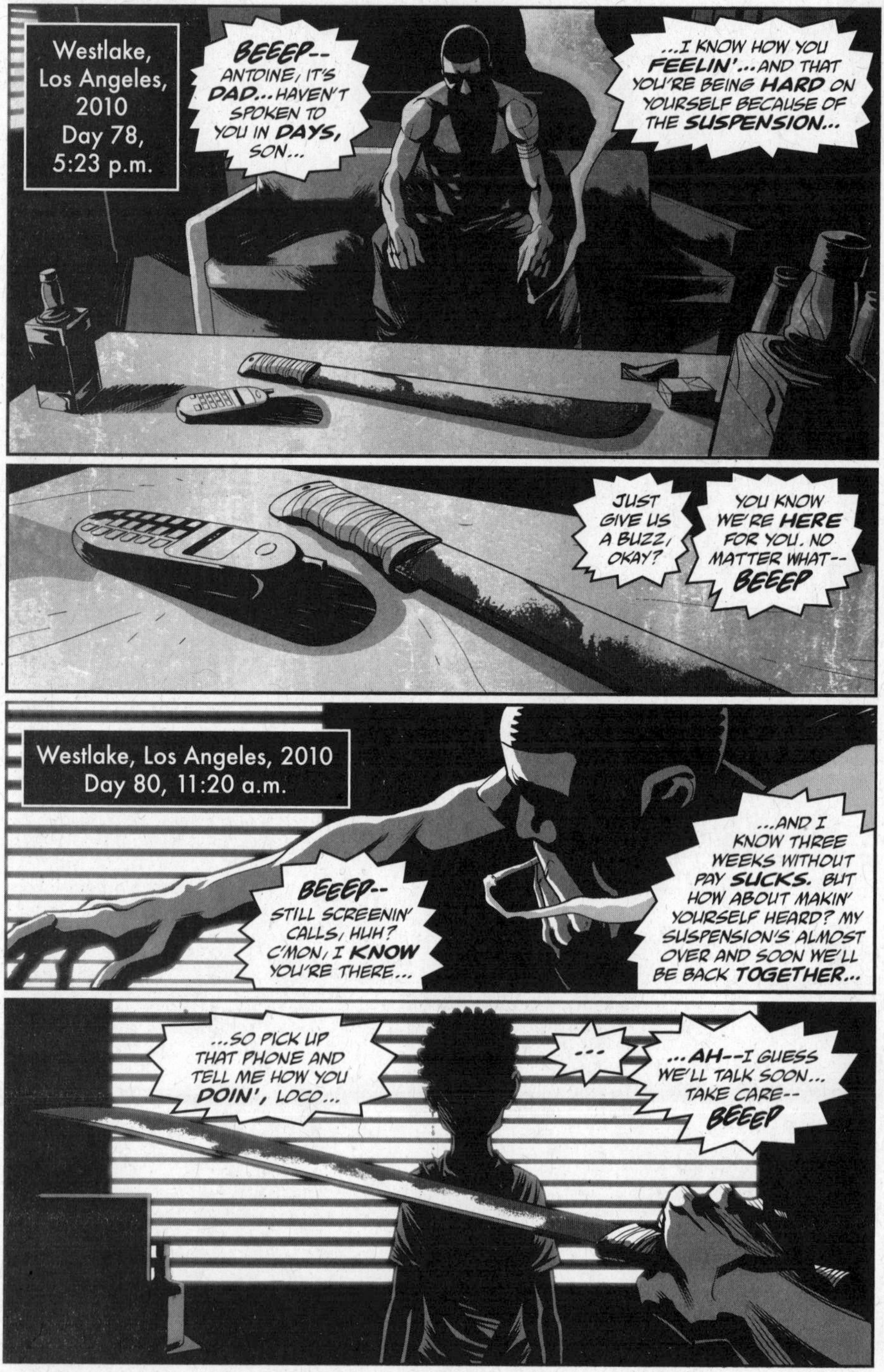
Westlake, Los Angeles, 2010 Day 78, 5:23 p.m.
BEEEP-- ANTOINE, IT'S DAD... HAVEN'T SPOKEN TO YOU IN DAYS, SON...
...I KNOW HOW YOU FEELIN'... AND THAT YOU'RE BEING HARD ON YOURSELF BECAUSE OF THE SUSPENSION...
JUST GIVE US A BUZZ, OKAY?
YOU KNOW WE'RE HERE FOR YOU. NO MATTER WHAT-- BEEEP
Westlake, Los Angeles, 2010 Day 80, 11:20 a.m.
BEEEP-- STILL SCREENIN' CALLS, HUH? C'MON, I KNOW YOU'RE THERE...
...AND I KNOW THREE WEEKS WITHOUT PAY SUCKS. BUT HOW ABOUT MAKIN' YOURSELF HEARD? MY SUSPENSION'S ALMOST OVER AND SOON WE'LL BE BACK TOGETHER...
...SO PICK UP THAT PHONE AND TELL ME HOW YOU DOIN', LOCO...
...
...AH--I GUESS WE'LL TALK SOON... TAKE CARE-- BEEEP

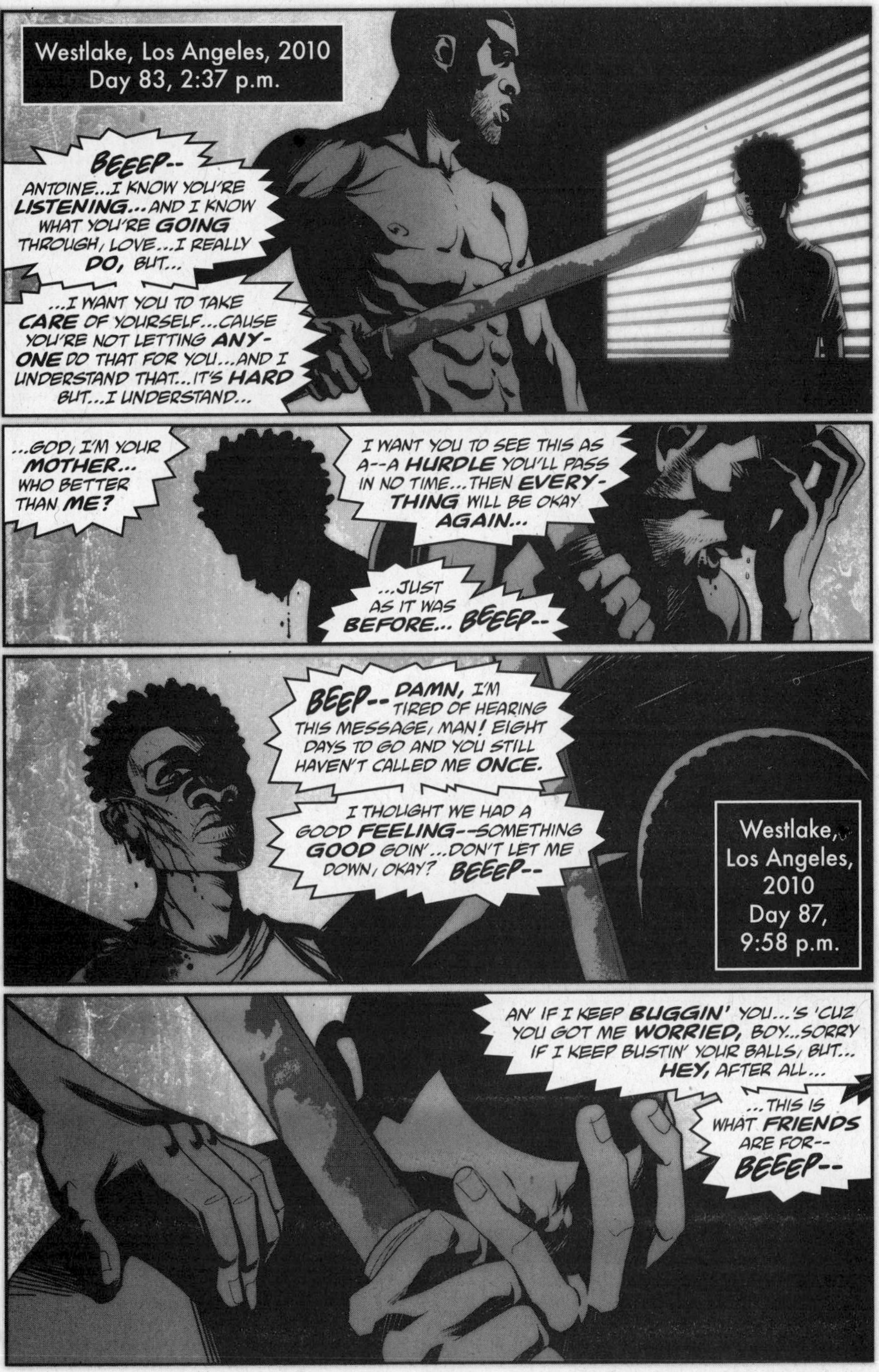
Westlake, Los Angeles, 2010
Day 83, 2:37 p.m.
BEEEP-- ANTOINE...I KNOW YOU'RE LISTENING...AND I KNOW WHAT YOU'RE GOING THROUGH, LOVE...I REALLY DO, BUT...
...I WANT YOU TO TAKE CARE OF YOURSELF...CAUSE YOU'RE NOT LETTING ANY-ONE DO THAT FOR YOU...AND I UNDERSTAND THAT...IT'S HARD BUT...I UNDERSTAND...
...GOD, I'M YOUR MOTHER... WHO BETTER THAN ME?
I WANT YOU TO SEE THIS AS A--A HURDLE YOU'LL PASS IN NO TIME...THEN EVERY-THING WILL BE OKAY AGAIN...
...JUST AS IT WAS BEFORE... BEEEP--
BEEP-- DAMN, I'M TIRED OF HEARING THIS MESSAGE, MAN! EIGHT DAYS TO GO AND YOU STILL HAVEN'T CALLED ME ONCE.
I THOUGHT WE HAD A GOOD FEELING--SOMETHING GOOD GOIN'...DON'T LET ME DOWN, OKAY? BEEEP--
Westlake, Los Angeles, 2010 Day 87, 9:58 p.m.
AN' IF I KEEP BUGGIN' YOU...'S 'CUZ YOU GOT ME WORRIED, BOY...SORRY IF I KEEP BUSTIN' YOUR BALLS, BUT... HEY, AFTER ALL...
...THIS IS WHAT FRIENDS ARE FOR-- BEEEP--

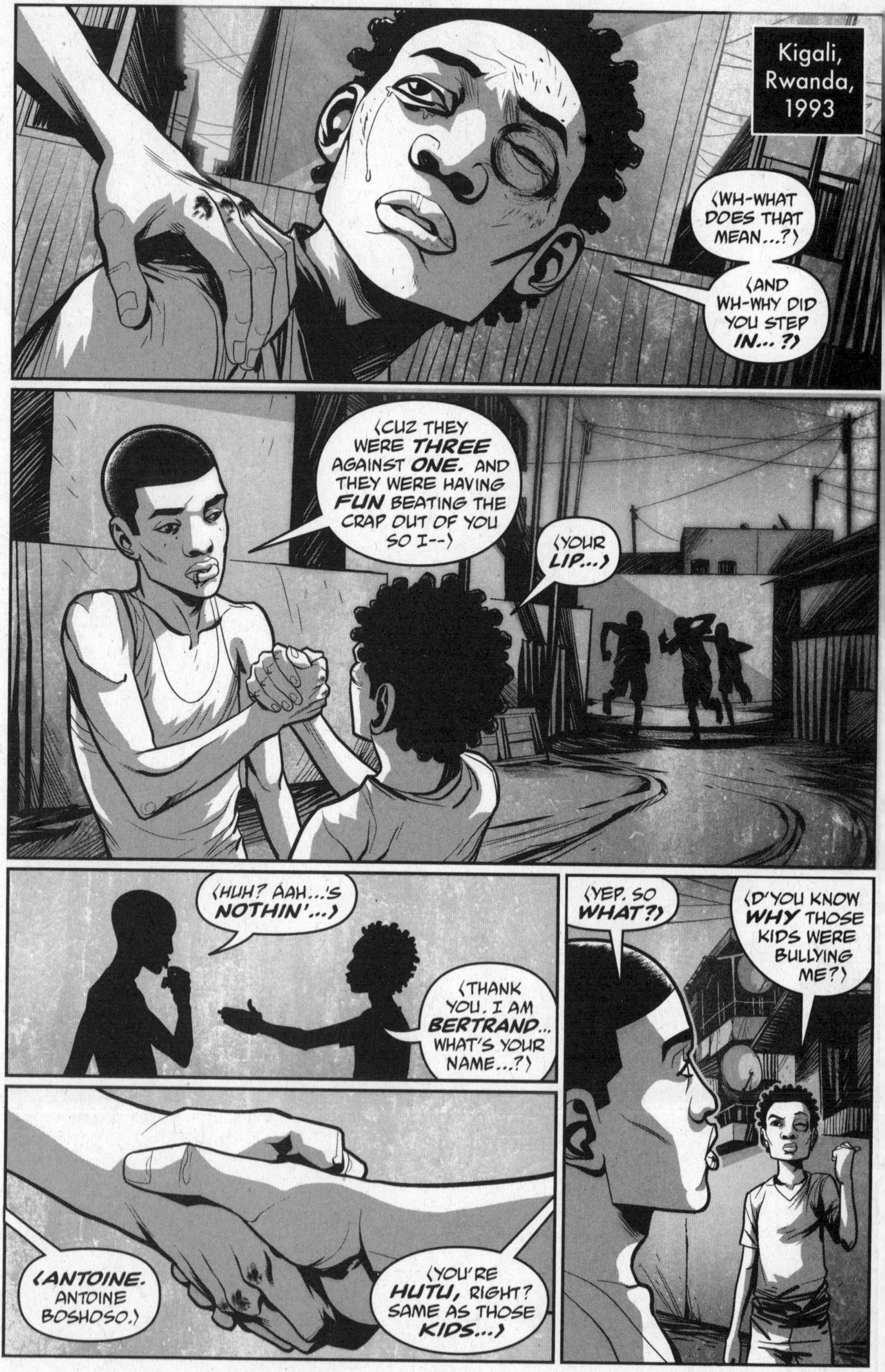
Kigali, Rwanda, 1993
‹WH-WHAT DOES THAT MEAN...?›
‹AND WH-WHY DID YOU STEP IN...?›
‹CUZ THEY WERE THREE AGAINST ONE. AND THEY WERE HAVING FUN BEATING THE CRAP OUT OF YOU SO I--›
‹YOUR LIP...›
‹HUH? AAH...'S NOTHIN'...›
‹THANK YOU. I AM BERTRAND... WHAT'S YOUR NAME...?›
‹ANTOINE. ANTOINE BOSHOSO.›
‹YOU'RE HUTU, RIGHT? SAME AS THOSE KIDS...›
‹YEP. SO WHAT?›
‹D'YOU KNOW WHY THOSE KIDS WERE BULLYING ME?›

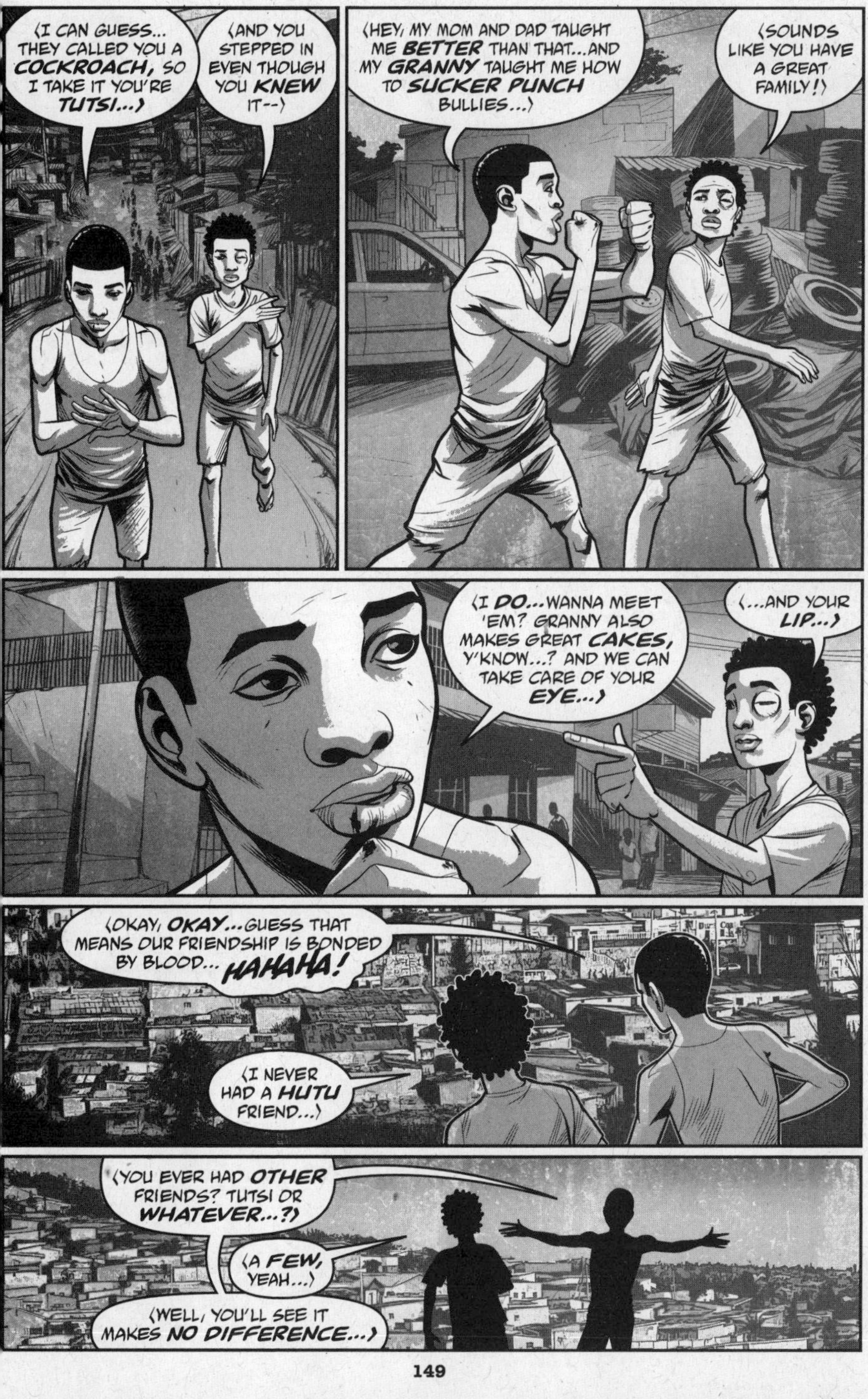
⟨I CAN GUESS... THEY CALLED YOU A COCKROACH, SO I TAKE IT YOU'RE TUTSI...⟩
⟨AND YOU STEPPED IN EVEN THOUGH YOU KNEW IT--⟩
⟨HEY, MY MOM AND DAD TAUGHT ME BETTER THAN THAT...AND MY GRANNY TAUGHT ME HOW TO SUCKER PUNCH BULLIES...⟩
⟨SOUNDS LIKE YOU HAVE A GREAT FAMILY!⟩
⟨I DO...WANNA MEET 'EM? GRANNY ALSO MAKES GREAT CAKES, Y'KNOW...? AND WE CAN TAKE CARE OF YOUR EYE...⟩
⟨...AND YOUR LIP...⟩
⟨OKAY, OKAY...GUESS THAT MEANS OUR FRIENDSHIP IS BONDED BY BLOOD... HAHAHA!
⟨I NEVER HAD A HUTU FRIEND...⟩
⟨YOU EVER HAD OTHER FRIENDS? TUTSI OR WHATEVER...?⟩
⟨A FEW, YEAH...⟩
⟨WELL, YOU'LL SEE IT MAKES NO DIFFERENCE...⟩

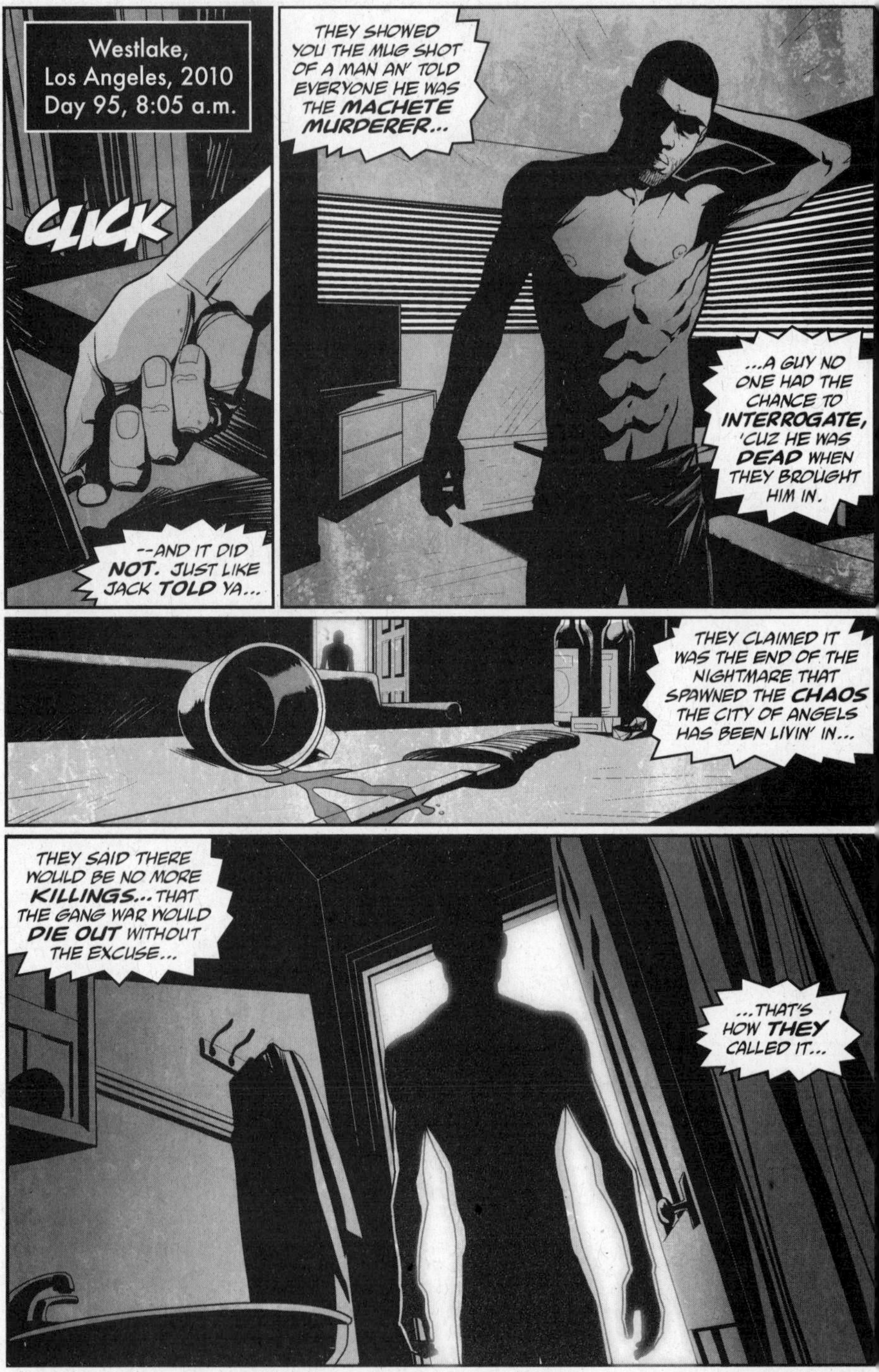
Westlake,
Los Angeles, 2010
Day 95, 8:05 a.m.
CLICK
--AND IT DID NOT. JUST LIKE JACK TOLD YA...
THEY SHOWED YOU THE MUG SHOT OF A MAN AN' TOLD EVERYONE HE WAS THE MACHETE MURDERER...
...A GUY NO ONE HAD THE CHANCE TO INTERROGATE, 'CUZ HE WAS DEAD WHEN THEY BROUGHT HIM IN.
THEY CLAIMED IT WAS THE END OF THE NIGHTMARE THAT SPAWNED THE CHAOS THE CITY OF ANGELS HAS BEEN LIVIN' IN...
THEY SAID THERE WOULD BE NO MORE KILLINGS...THAT THE GANG WAR WOULD DIE OUT WITHOUT THE EXCUSE...
...THAT'S HOW THEY CALLED IT...

...OF *BROTHAS* AN' *SISTAHS* BEIN' CUT TO *PIECES* LIKE THAT. AN' YOU *BELIEVED* IT. IT WAS THE RIGHT THING TO DO...BUT *JACK* DIDN'T, *NOSSIR.*

AN' NOW EVERYBODY KNOWS JACK WAS *RIGHT.* 'CAUSE *ANOTHER* WOMAN WAS HACKED UP LAST NIGHT...

SO, UNLESS *LANCE ABBOT,* CRACKHEAD AND OUR ALLEGED MACHETE MURDERER GOT BACK FROM THE *GRAVE...*

...JACK SAYS THE L.A.P.D. HAS TOLD US ALL *ANOTHER* TALL TALE. AN' NOW THEY'LL NEED TO FIND *ANOTHER* WAY TO SWIPE THEIR OWN SHIT UNDER THE CARPET...

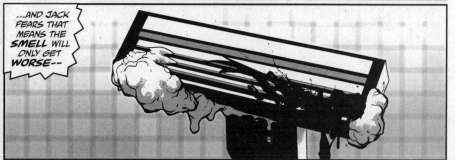

...AND JACK FEARS THAT MEANS THE *SMELL* WILL ONLY GET *WORSE--*

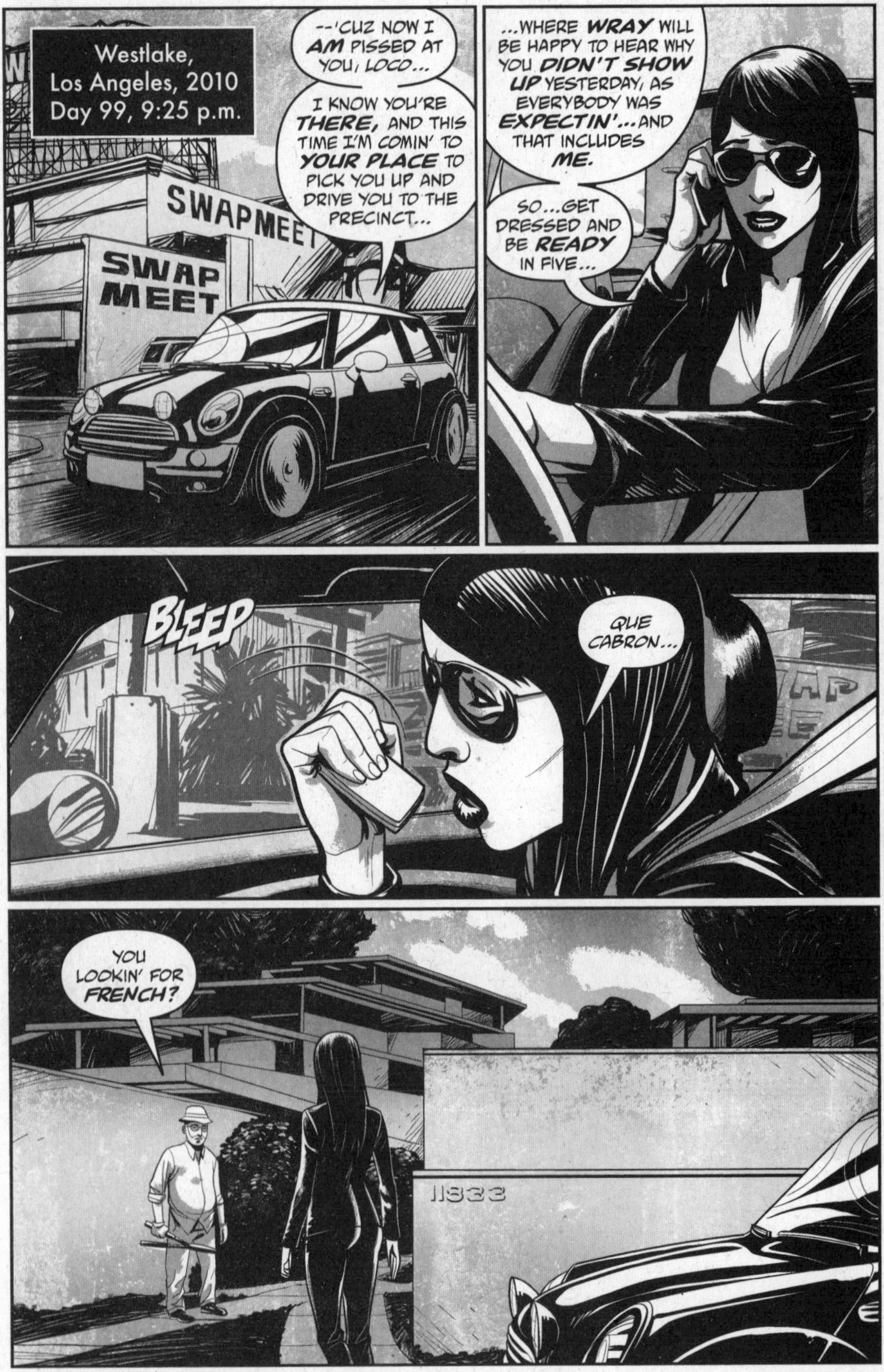

Westlake, Los Angeles, 2010 Day 99, 9:25 p.m.
--'CUZ NOW I AM PISSED AT YOU, LOCO...
I KNOW YOU'RE THERE, AND THIS TIME I'M COMIN' TO YOUR PLACE TO PICK YOU UP AND DRIVE YOU TO THE PRECINCT...
SWAPMEET
SWAP MEET
...WHERE WRAY WILL BE HAPPY TO HEAR WHY YOU DIDN'T SHOW UP YESTERDAY, AS EVERYBODY WAS EXPECTIN'...AND THAT INCLUDES ME.
SO...GET DRESSED AND BE READY IN FIVE...
BLEEP
QUE CABRON...
YOU LOOKIN' FOR FRENCH?
11833

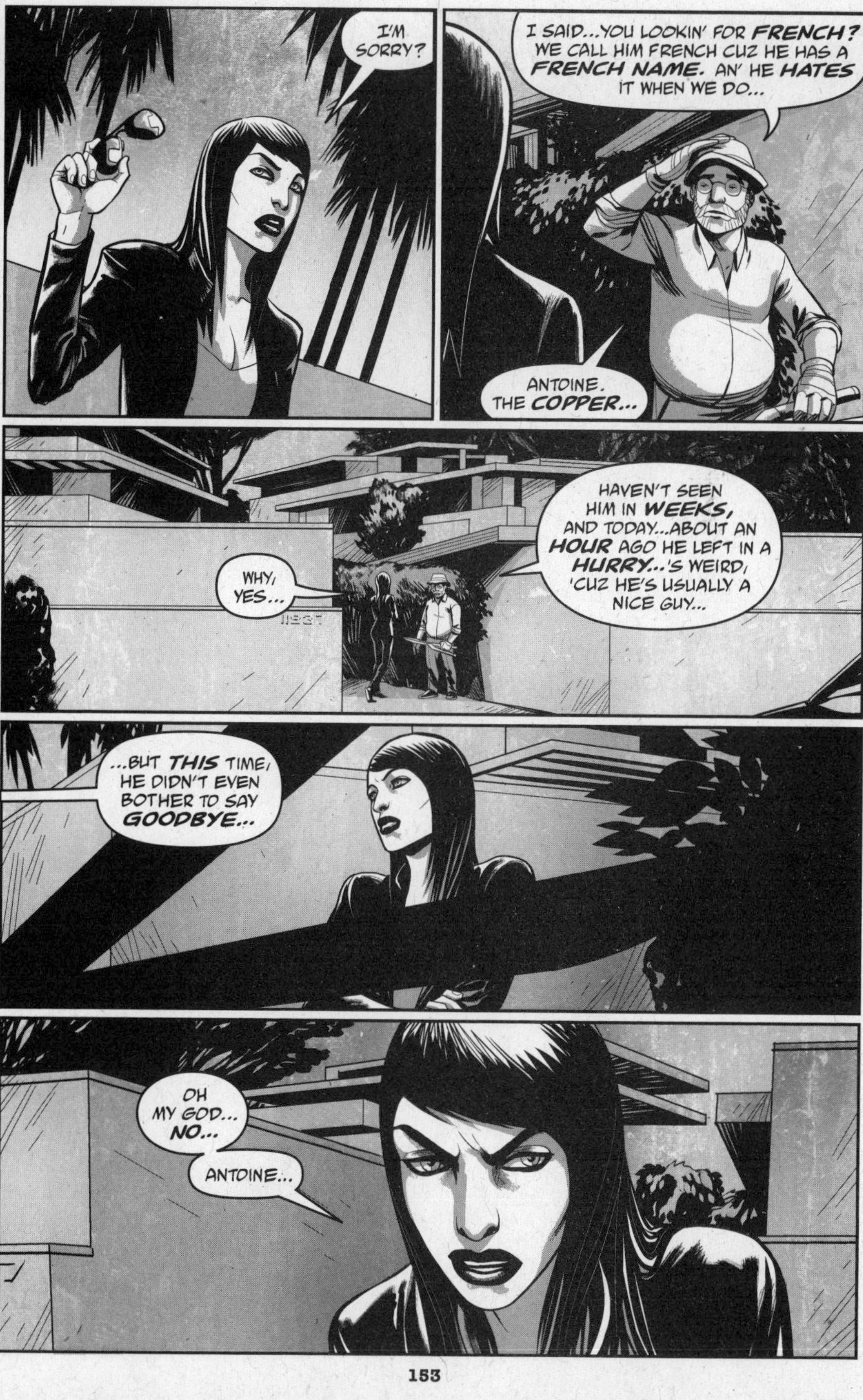
I'M SORRY?
I SAID...YOU LOOKIN' FOR FRENCH? WE CALL HIM FRENCH CUZ HE HAS A FRENCH NAME. AN' HE HATES IT WHEN WE DO...
ANTOINE. THE COPPER...
WHY, YES...
HAVEN'T SEEN HIM IN WEEKS, AND TODAY...ABOUT AN HOUR AGO HE LEFT IN A HURRY...'S WEIRD, 'CUZ HE'S USUALLY A NICE GUY...
...BUT THIS TIME, HE DIDN'T EVEN BOTHER TO SAY GOODBYE...
OH MY GOD... NO...
ANTOINE...

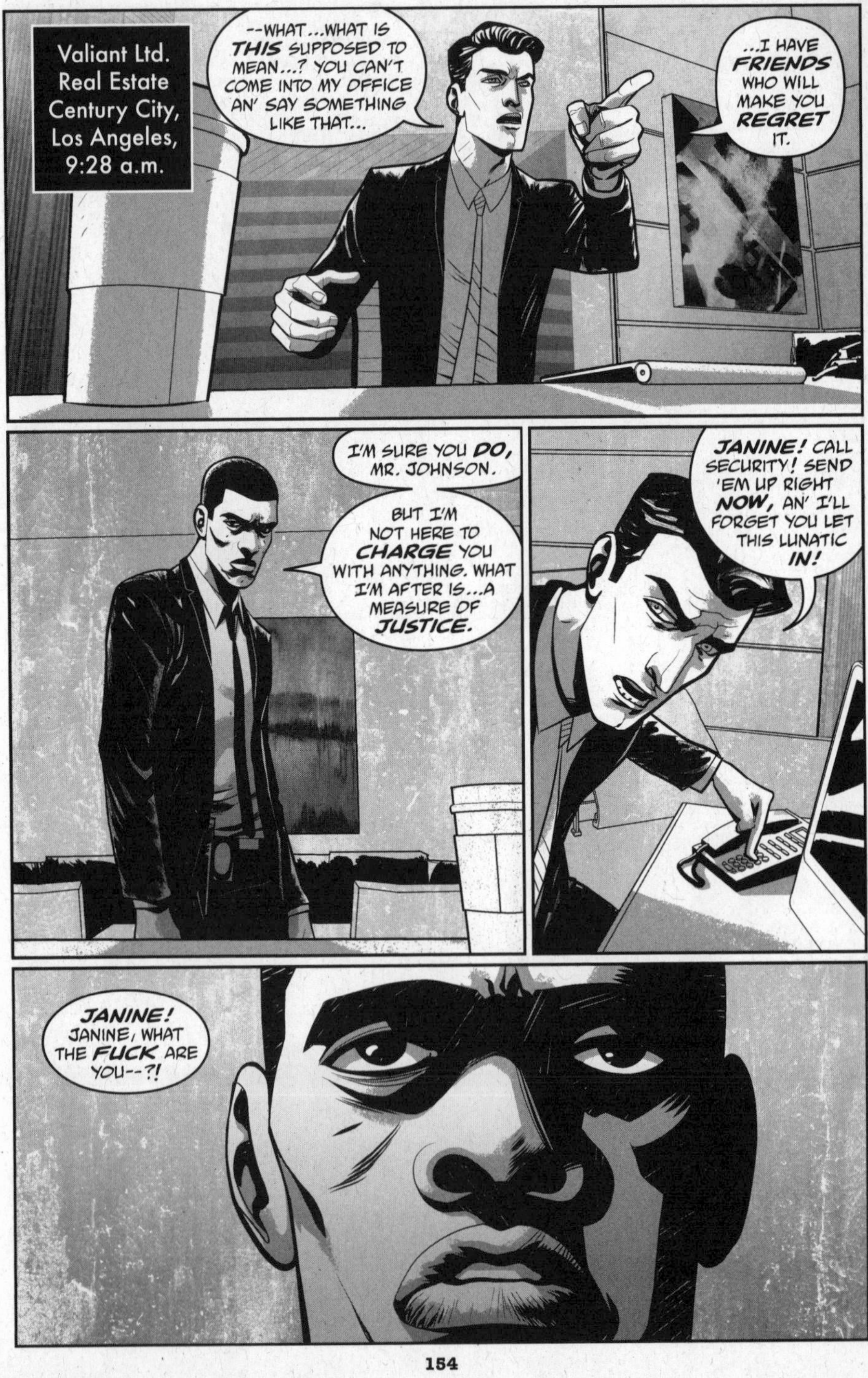
Valiant Ltd. Real Estate Century City, Los Angeles, 9:28 a.m.
--WHAT...WHAT IS THIS SUPPOSED TO MEAN...? YOU CAN'T COME INTO MY OFFICE AN' SAY SOMETHING LIKE THAT...
...I HAVE FRIENDS WHO WILL MAKE YOU REGRET IT.
I'M SURE YOU DO, MR. JOHNSON.
BUT I'M NOT HERE TO CHARGE YOU WITH ANYTHING. WHAT I'M AFTER IS...A MEASURE OF JUSTICE.
JANINE! CALL SECURITY! SEND 'EM UP RIGHT NOW, AN' I'LL FORGET YOU LET THIS LUNATIC IN!
JANINE! JANINE, WHAT THE FUCK ARE YOU--?!

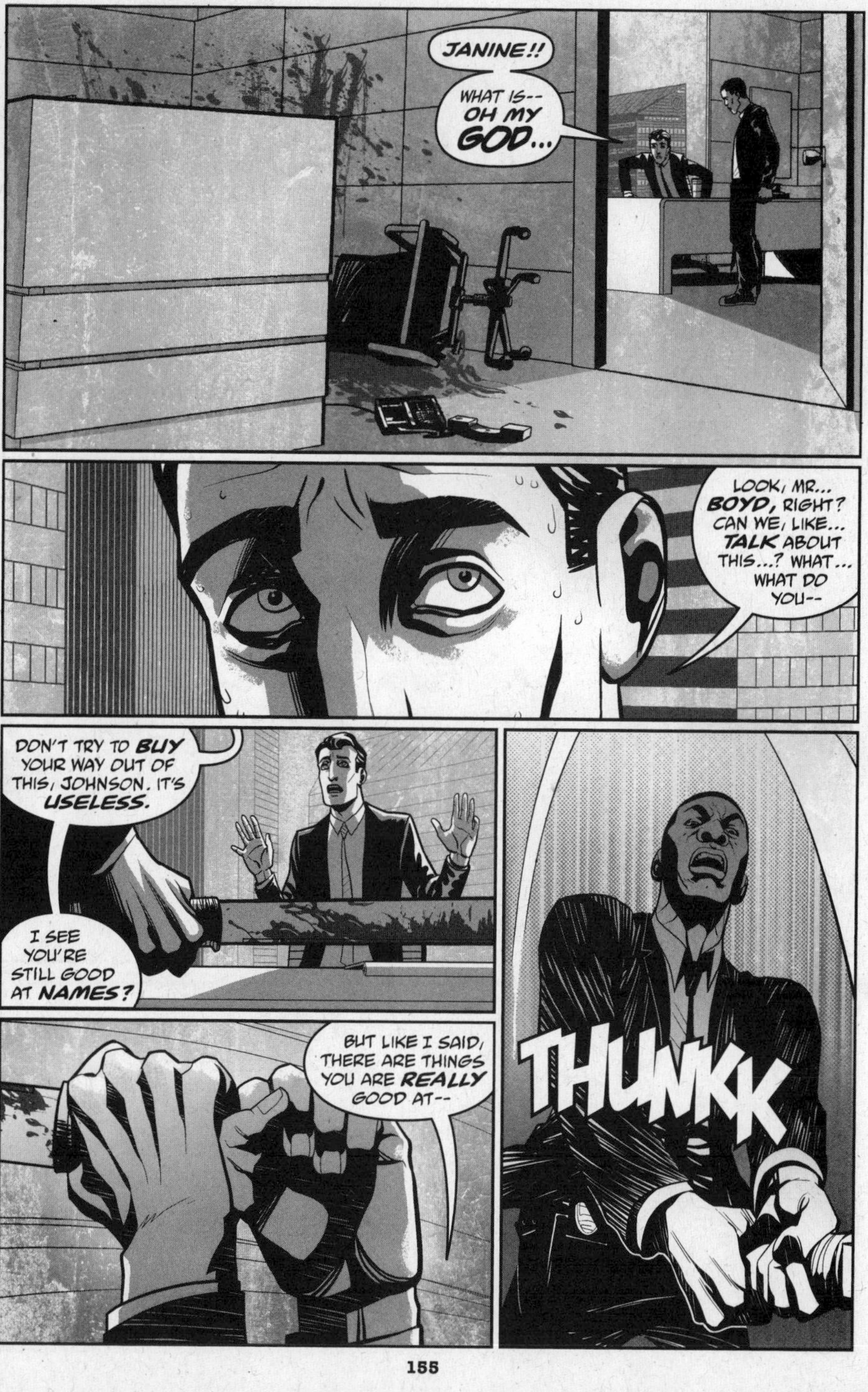
JANINE!!
WHAT IS-- OH MY GOD...
LOOK, MR... BOYD, RIGHT? CAN WE, LIKE... TALK ABOUT THIS...? WHAT... WHAT DO YOU--
DON'T TRY TO BUY YOUR WAY OUT OF THIS, JOHNSON. IT'S USELESS.
I SEE YOU'RE STILL GOOD AT NAMES?
BUT LIKE I SAID, THERE ARE THINGS YOU ARE REALLY GOOD AT--
THUNKK

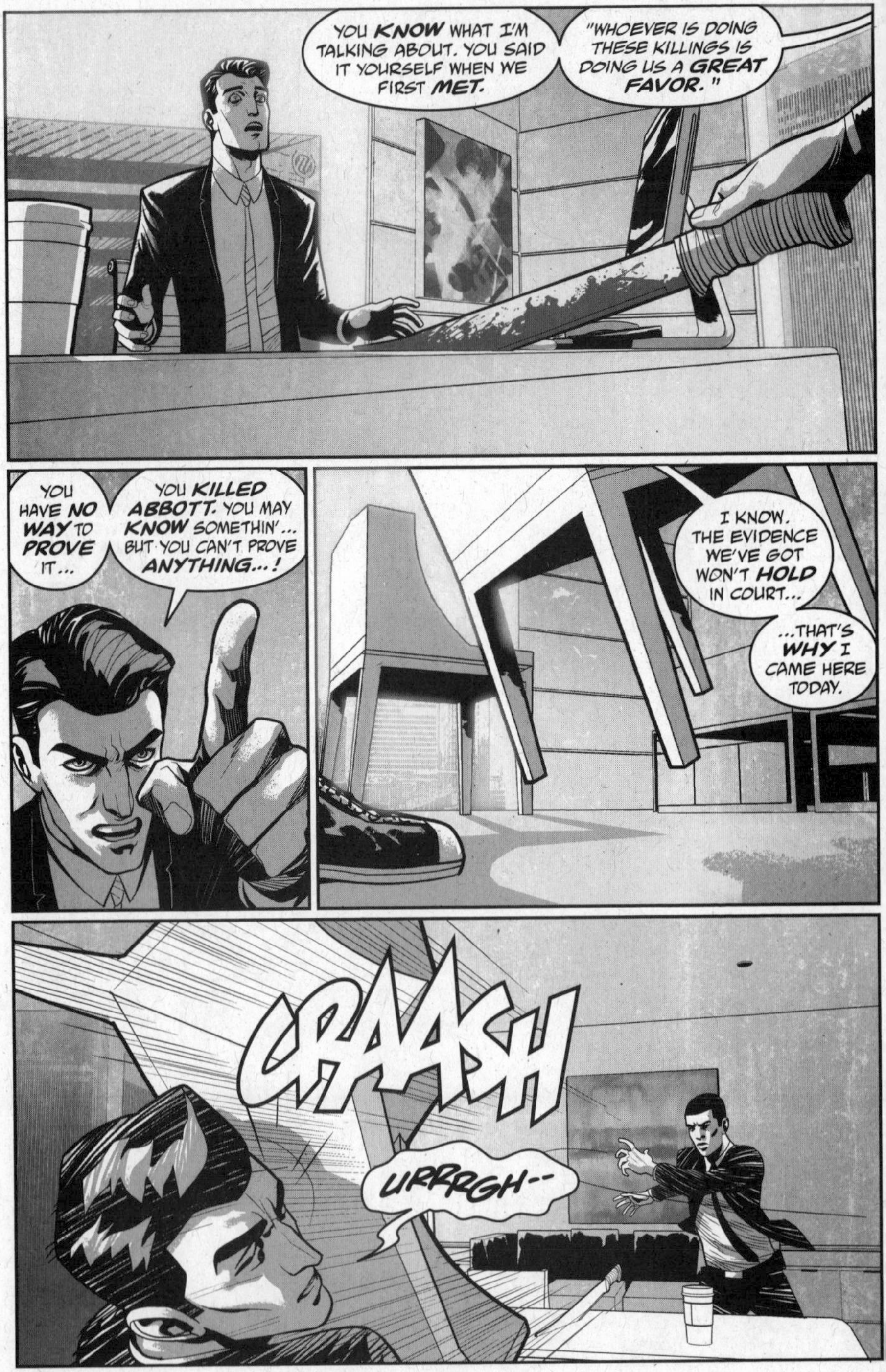
YOU KNOW WHAT I'M TALKING ABOUT. YOU SAID IT YOURSELF WHEN WE FIRST MET.
"WHOEVER IS DOING THESE KILLINGS IS DOING US A GREAT FAVOR."
YOU HAVE NO WAY TO PROVE IT...
YOU KILLED ABBOTT. YOU MAY KNOW SOMETHIN'... BUT YOU CAN'T PROVE ANYTHING...!
I KNOW. THE EVIDENCE WE'VE GOT WON'T HOLD IN COURT...
...THAT'S WHY I CAME HERE TODAY.
CRAASH
URRRGH--

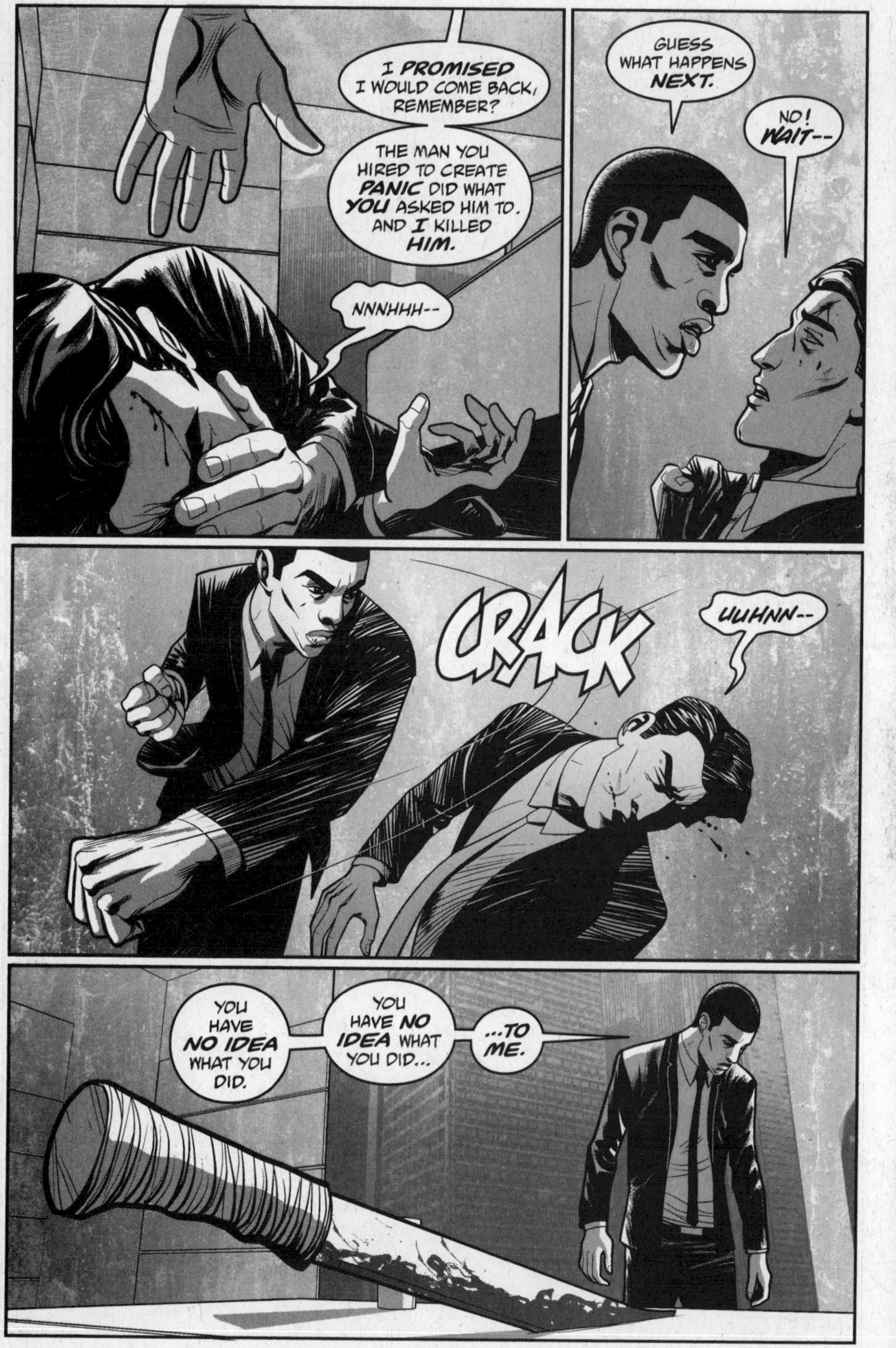
I PROMISED I WOULD COME BACK, REMEMBER?
THE MAN YOU HIRED TO CREATE PANIC DID WHAT YOU ASKED HIM TO. AND I KILLED HIM.
NNNHHH--
GUESS WHAT HAPPENS NEXT.
NO! WAIT--
CRACK
UUHNN--
YOU HAVE NO IDEA WHAT YOU DID.
YOU HAVE NO IDEA WHAT YOU DID...
...TO ME.

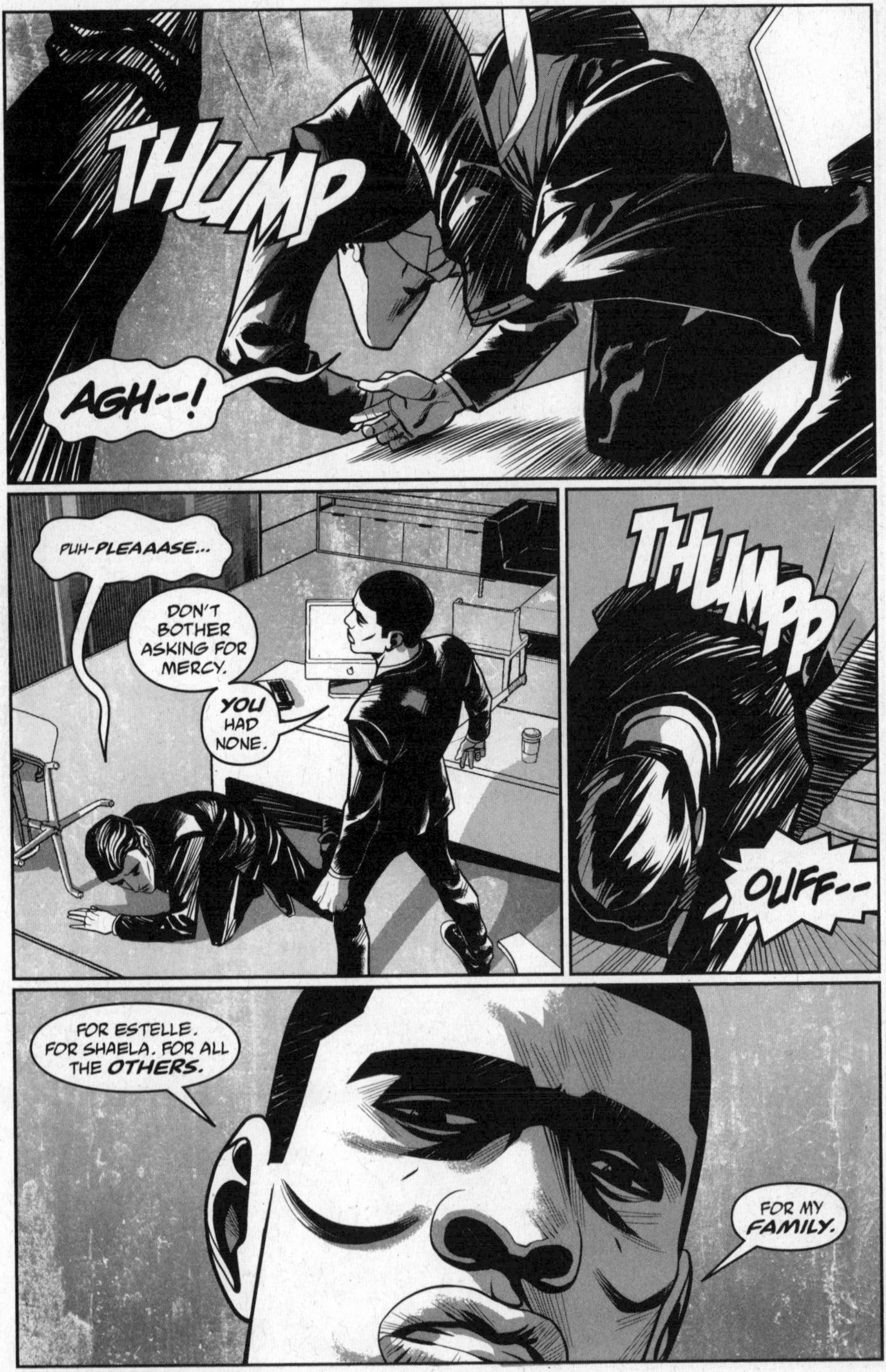
THUMP
AGH--!
PUH-PLEAAASE...
DON'T BOTHER ASKING FOR MERCY.
YOU HAD NONE.
THUMPP
OUFF--
FOR ESTELLE. FOR SHAELA. FOR ALL THE OTHERS.
FOR MY FAMILY.

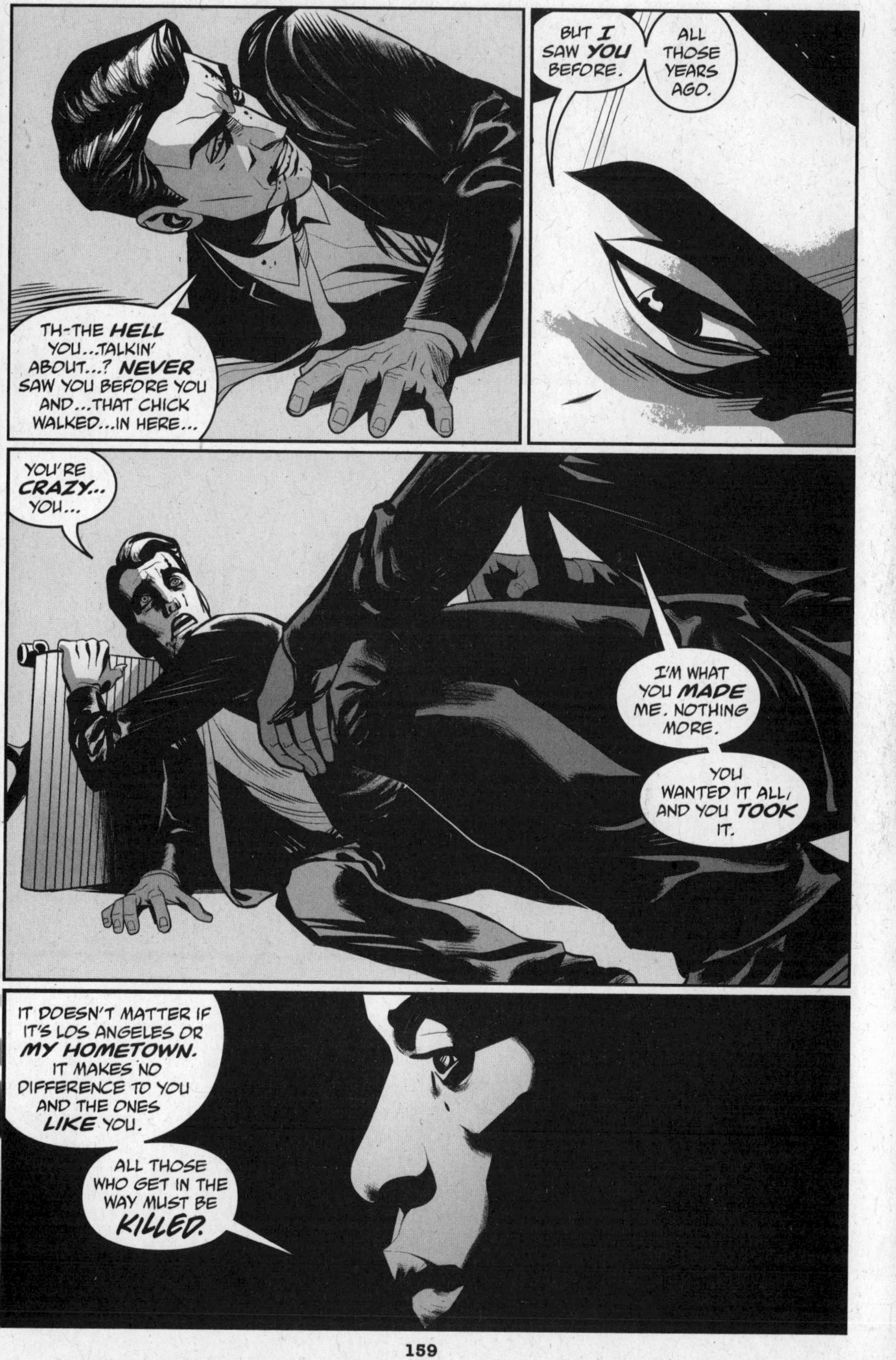
TH-THE HELL YOU...TALKIN' ABOUT...? NEVER SAW YOU BEFORE YOU AND...THAT CHICK WALKED...IN HERE...
BUT I SAW YOU BEFORE.
ALL THOSE YEARS AGO.
YOU'RE CRAZY... YOU...
I'M WHAT YOU MADE ME. NOTHING MORE.
YOU WANTED IT ALL, AND YOU TOOK IT.
IT DOESN'T MATTER IF IT'S LOS ANGELES OR MY HOMETOWN. IT MAKES NO DIFFERENCE TO YOU AND THE ONES LIKE YOU.
ALL THOSE WHO GET IN THE WAY MUST BE KILLED.

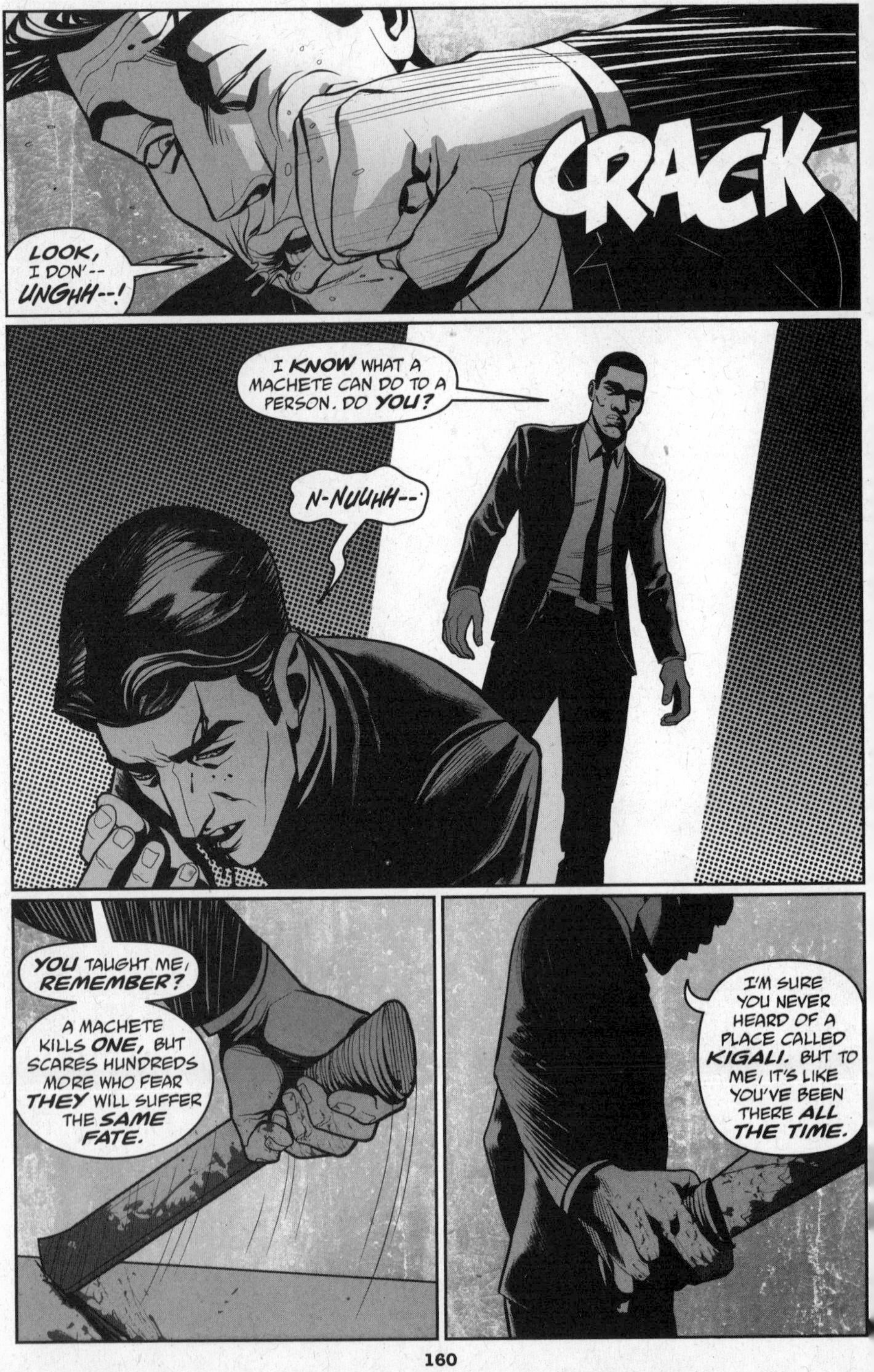
CRACK
LOOK, I DON'-- UNGHH--!
I KNOW WHAT A MACHETE CAN DO TO A PERSON. DO YOU?
N-NUUHH--
YOU TAUGHT ME, REMEMBER?
A MACHETE KILLS ONE, BUT SCARES HUNDREDS MORE WHO FEAR THEY WILL SUFFER THE SAME FATE.
I'M SURE YOU NEVER HEARD OF A PLACE CALLED KIGALI. BUT TO ME, IT'S LIKE YOU'VE BEEN THERE ALL THE TIME.

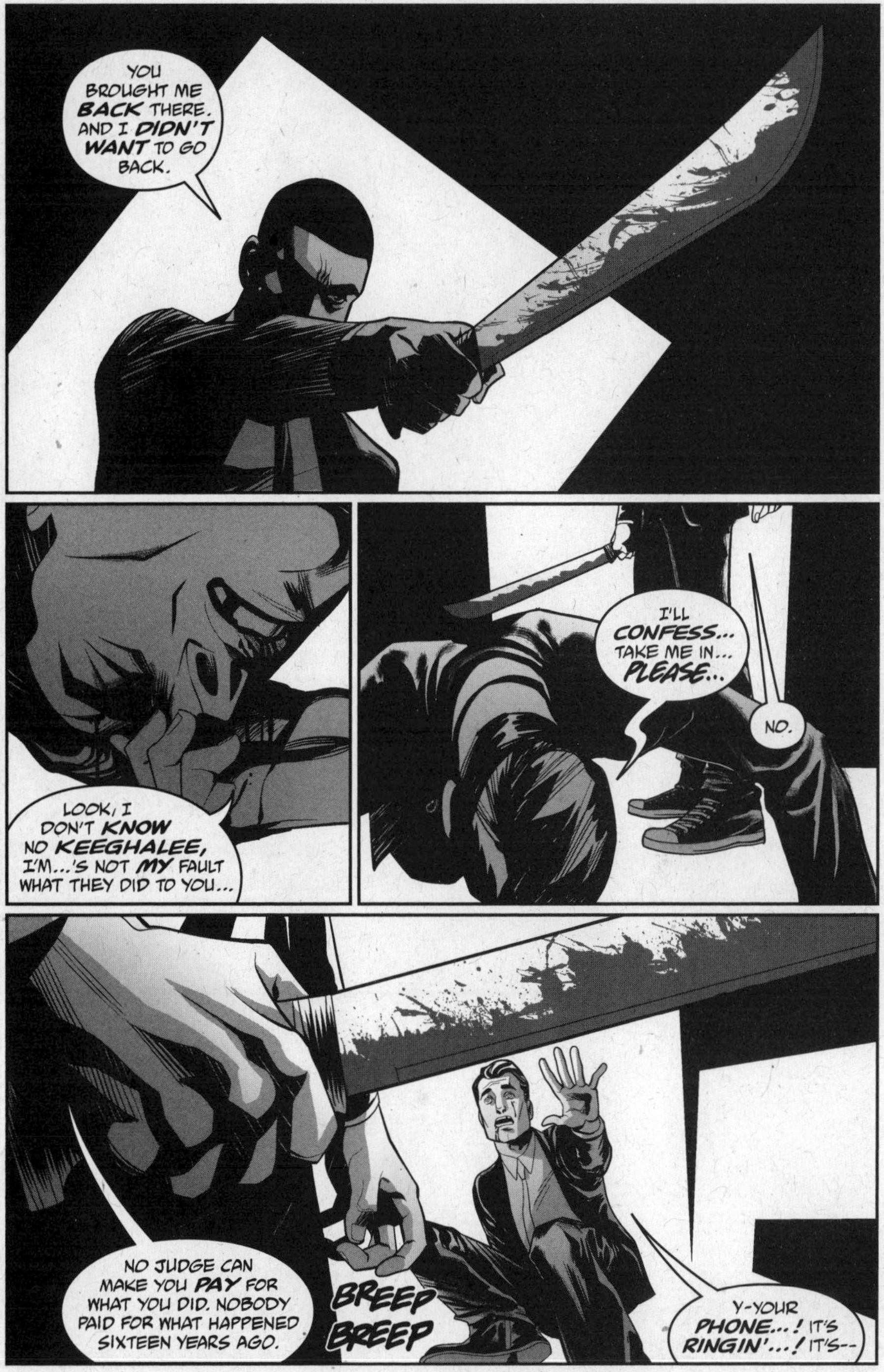
YOU BROUGHT ME BACK THERE. AND I DIDN'T WANT TO GO BACK.
LOOK, I DON'T KNOW NO KEEGHALEE, I'M...'S NOT MY FAULT WHAT THEY DID TO YOU...
I'LL CONFESS... TAKE ME IN... PLEASE...
NO.
NO JUDGE CAN MAKE YOU PAY FOR WHAT YOU DID. NOBODY PAID FOR WHAT HAPPENED SIXTEEN YEARS AGO.
BREEP BREEP
Y-YOUR PHONE...! IT'S RINGIN'...! IT'S--

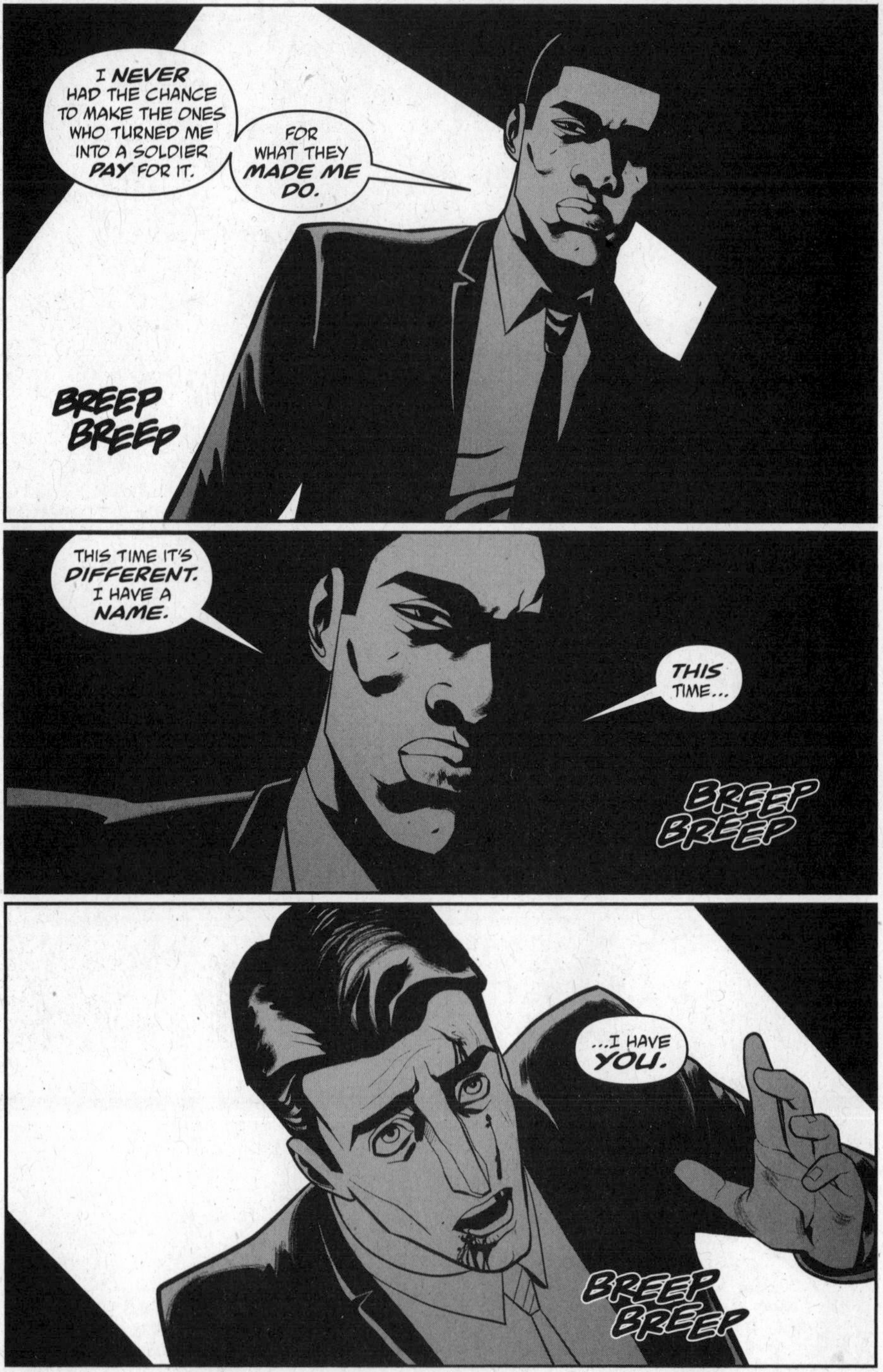
I NEVER HAD THE CHANCE TO MAKE THE ONES WHO TURNED ME INTO A SOLDIER PAY FOR IT.
FOR WHAT THEY MADE ME DO.
BREEP BREEP
THIS TIME IT'S DIFFERENT. I HAVE A NAME.
THIS TIME...
BREEP BREEP
...I HAVE YOU.
BREEP BREEP

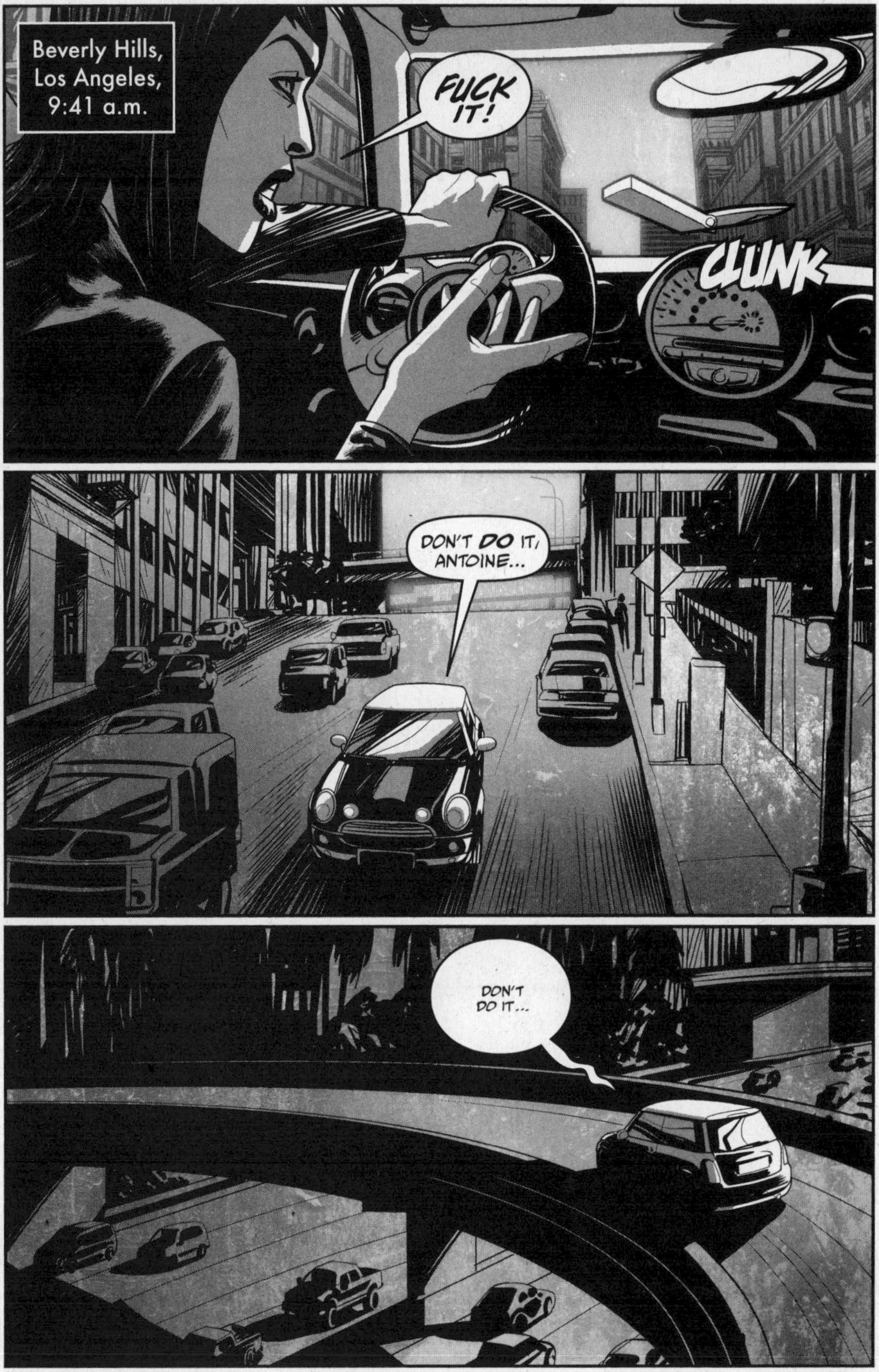
Beverly Hills, Los Angeles, 9:41 a.m.
FUCK IT!
CLUNK
DON'T DO IT, ANTOINE...
DON'T DO IT...

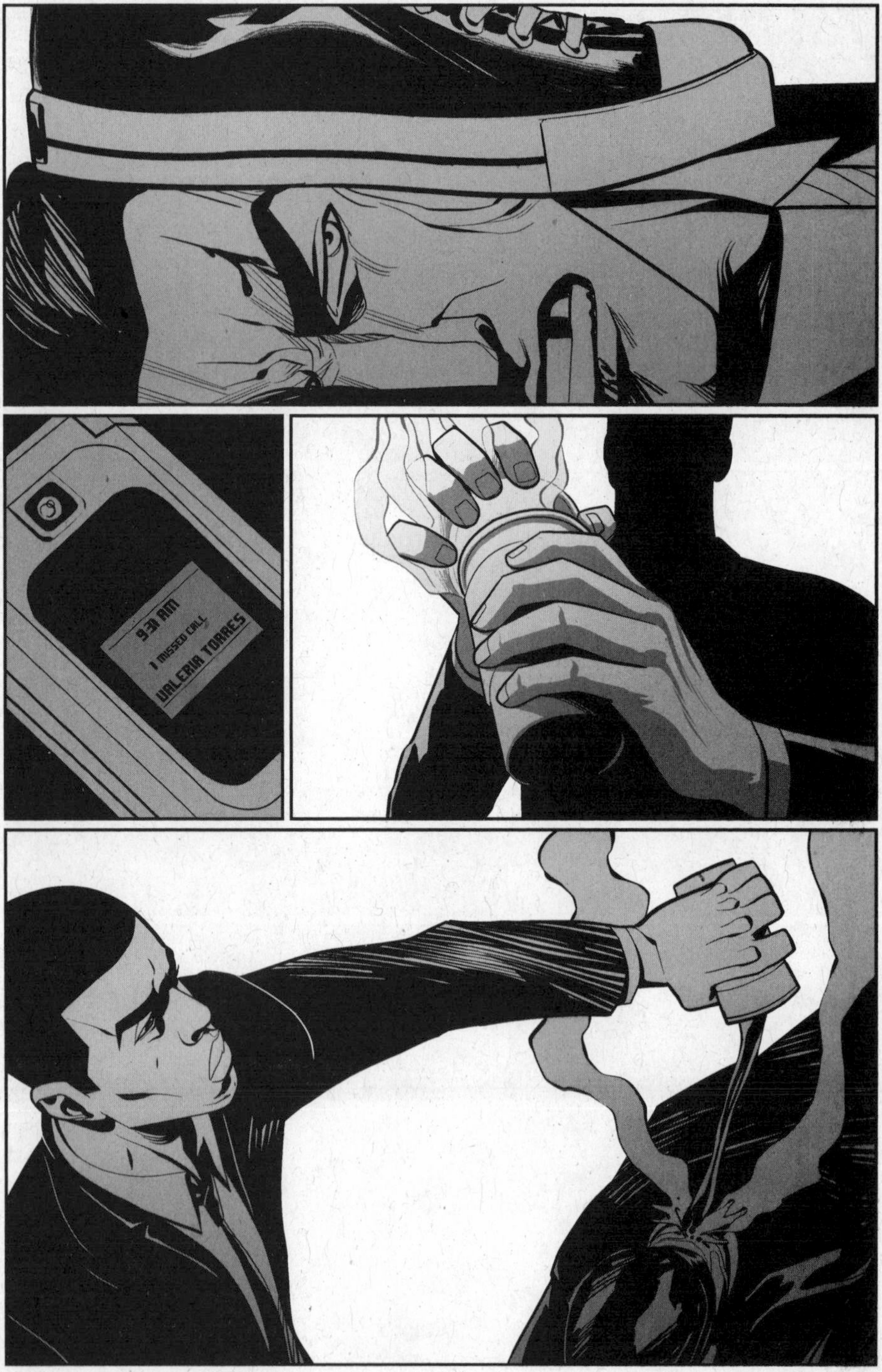
9:31 AM
1 MISSED CALL
VALERIA TORRES

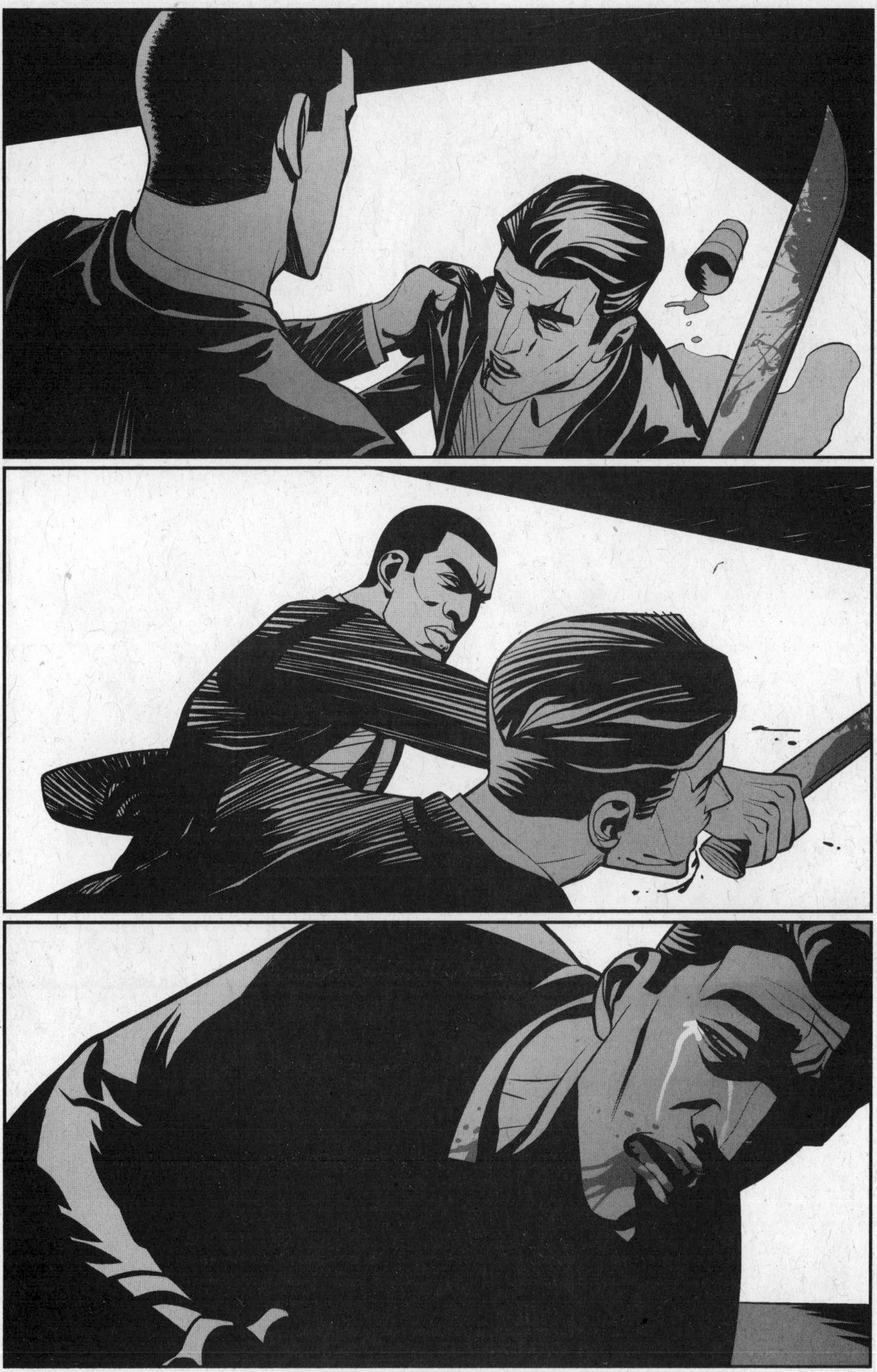

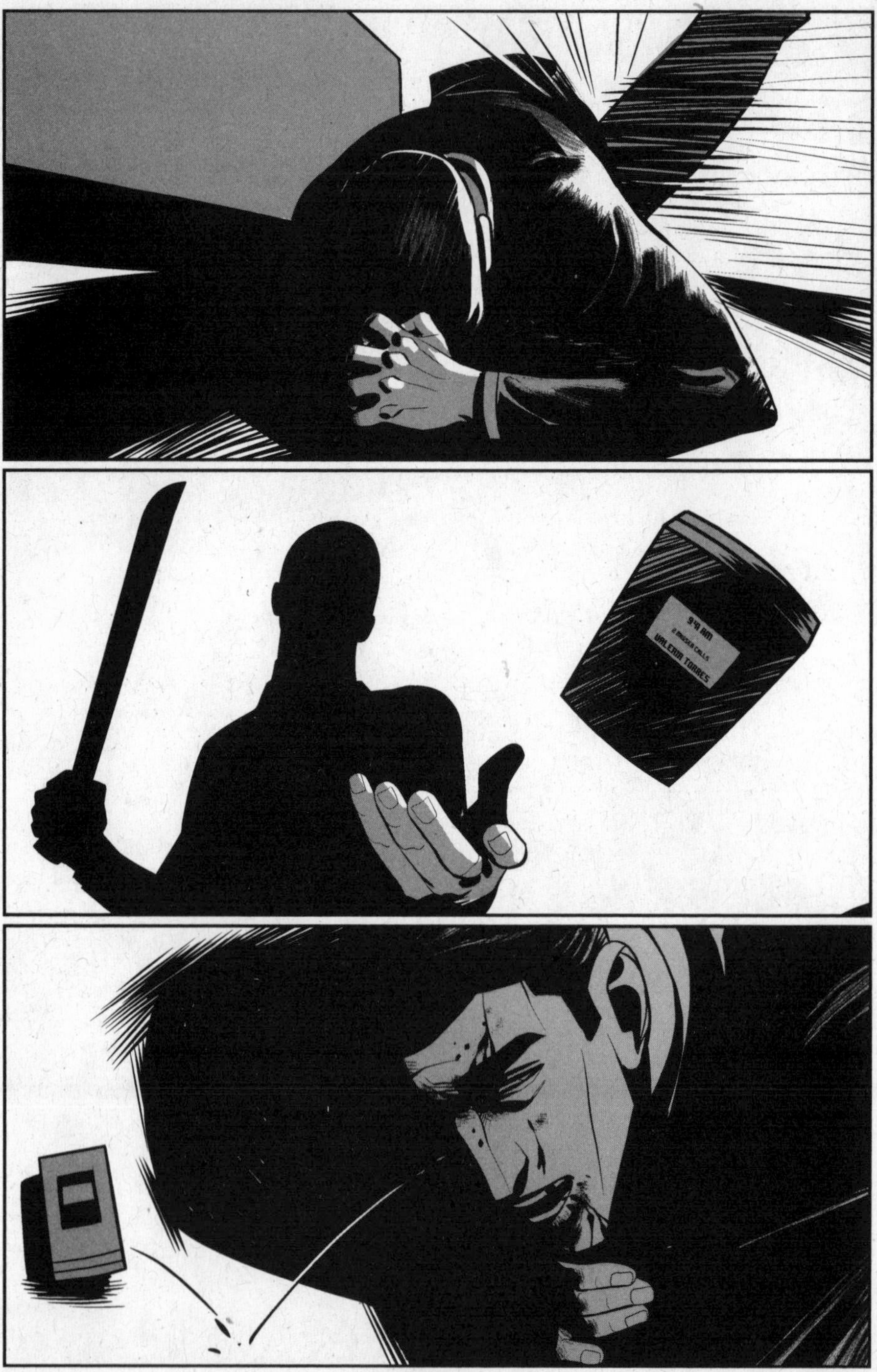
9:41 AM
2 MISSED CALLS
VALERIA TORRES

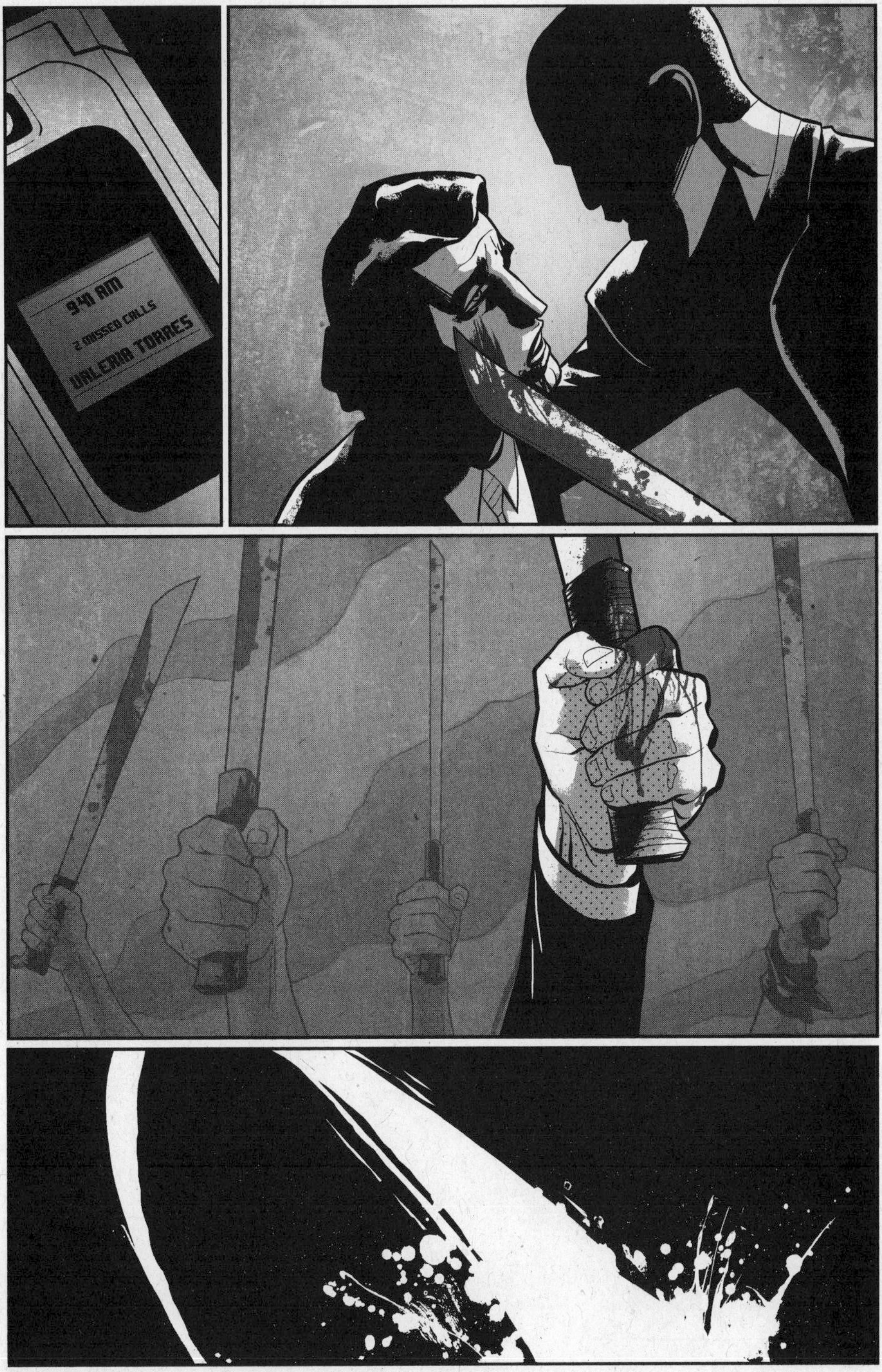
9:41 AM
2 MISSED CALLS
VALERIA TORRES

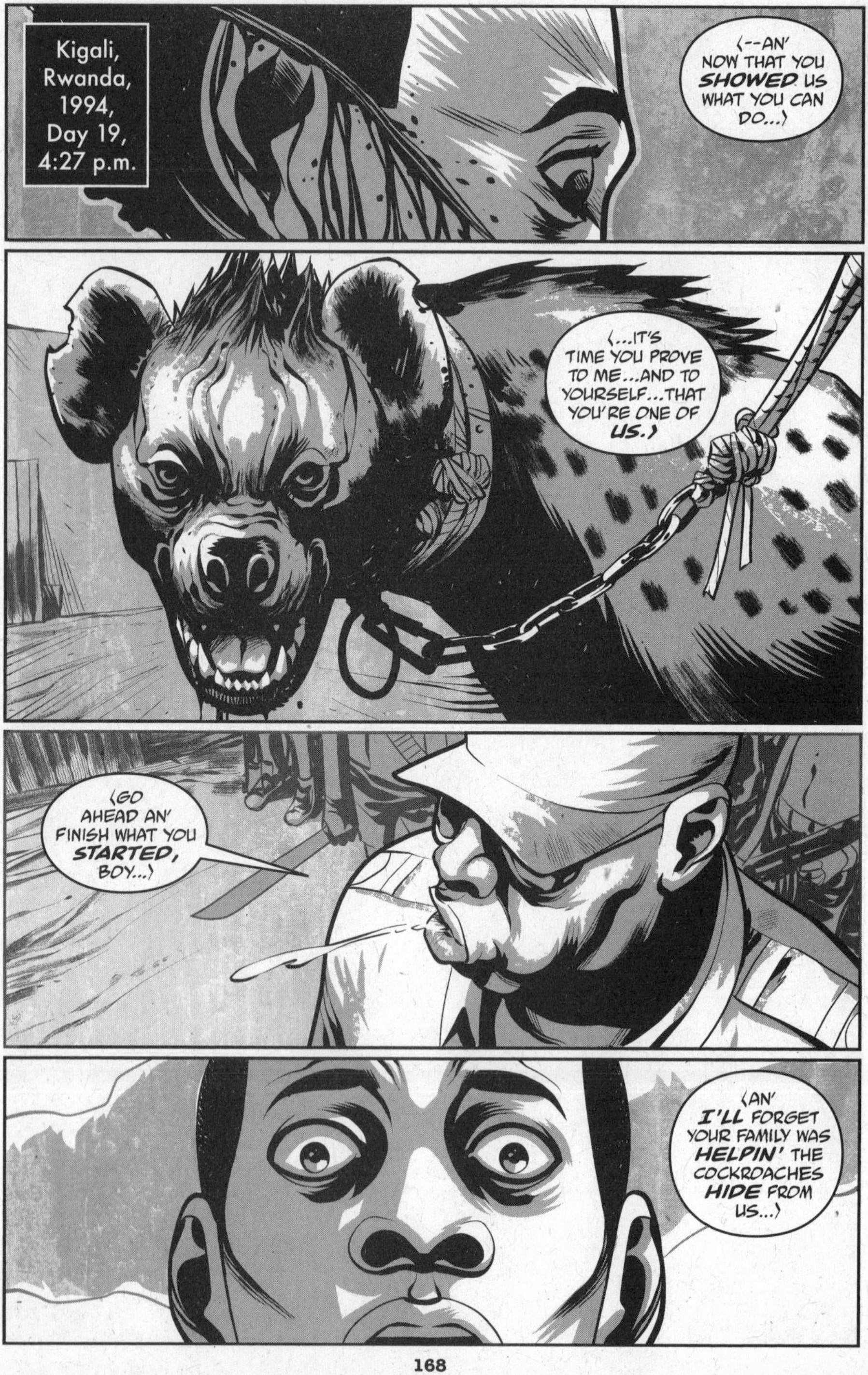
Kigali, Rwanda, 1994, Day 19, 4:27 p.m.
⟨--AN' NOW THAT YOU SHOWED US WHAT YOU CAN DO...⟩
⟨...IT'S TIME YOU PROVE TO ME...AND TO YOURSELF...THAT YOU'RE ONE OF US.⟩
⟨GO AHEAD AN' FINISH WHAT YOU STARTED, BOY...⟩
⟨AN' I'LL FORGET YOUR FAMILY WAS HELPIN' THE COCKROACHES HIDE FROM US...⟩

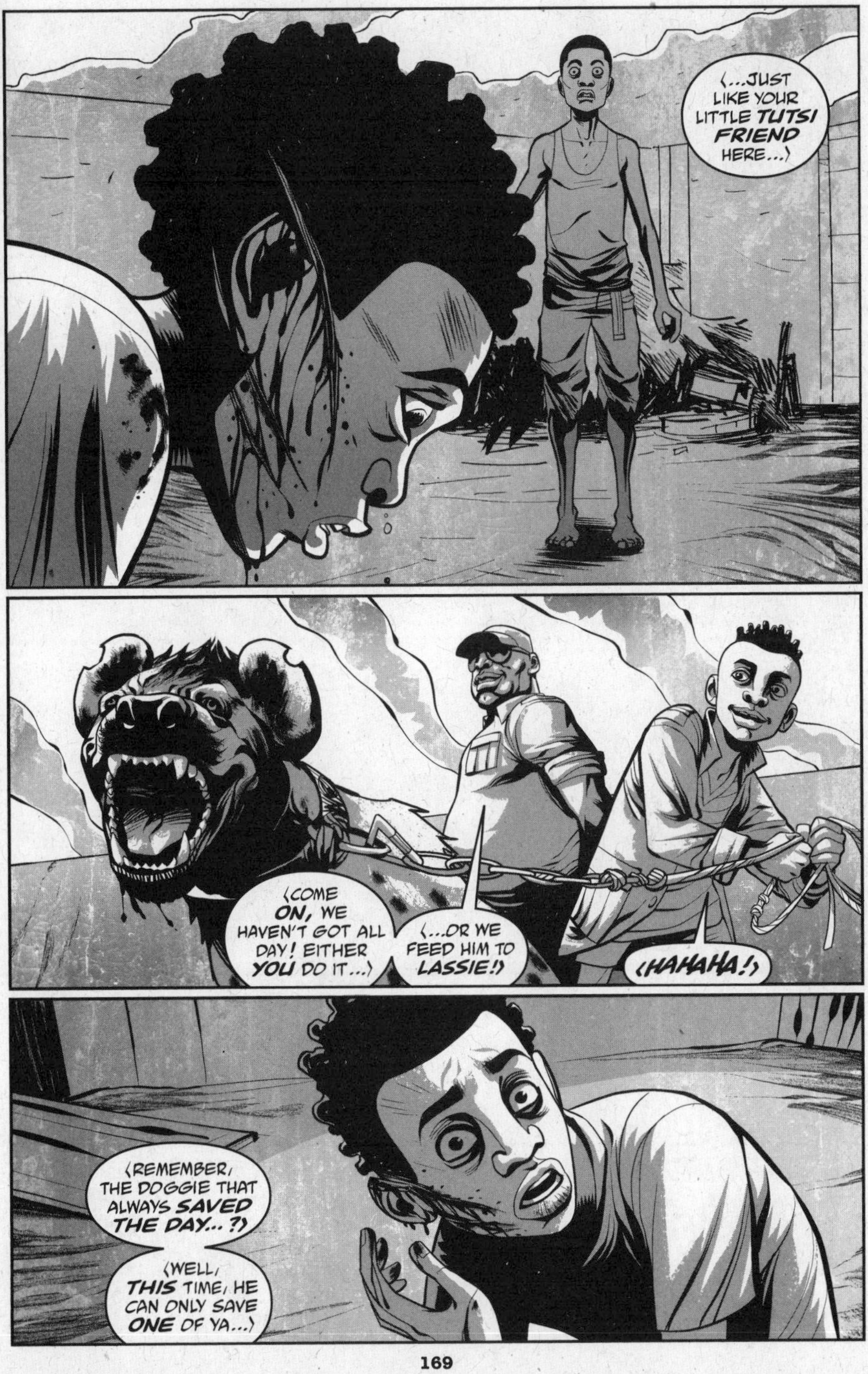
‹...JUST LIKE YOUR LITTLE TUTSI FRIEND HERE...›
‹COME ON, WE HAVEN'T GOT ALL DAY! EITHER YOU DO IT...›
‹...OR WE FEED HIM TO LASSIE!›
‹HAHAHA!›
‹REMEMBER, THE DOGGIE THAT ALWAYS SAVED THE DAY...?›
‹WELL, THIS TIME, HE CAN ONLY SAVE ONE OF YA...›

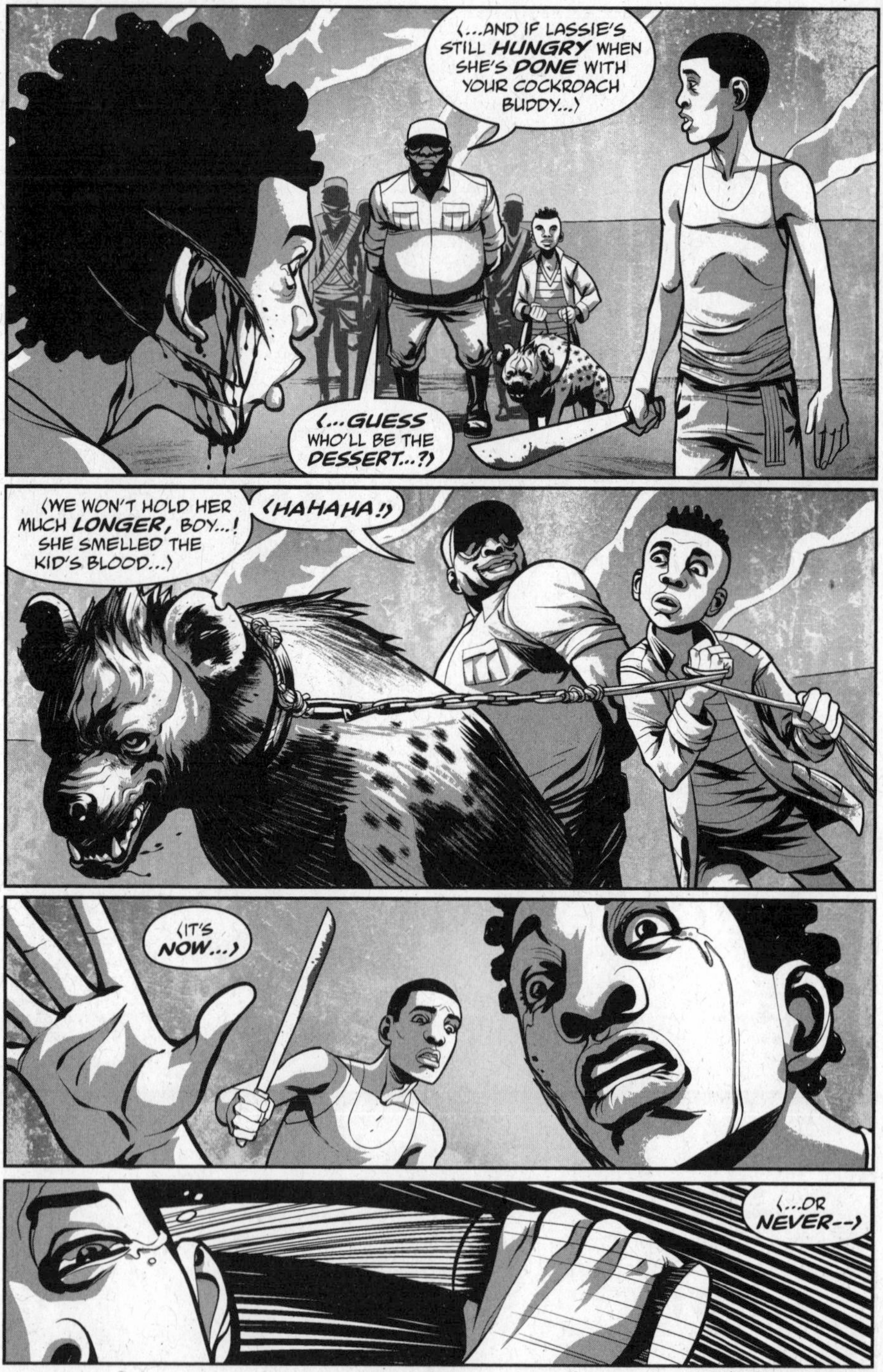
‹...AND IF LASSIE'S STILL HUNGRY WHEN SHE'S DONE WITH YOUR COCKROACH BUDDY...›
‹...GUESS WHO'LL BE THE DESSERT...?›
‹WE WON'T HOLD HER MUCH LONGER, BOY...! SHE SMELLED THE KID'S BLOOD...›
‹HAHAHA!›
‹IT'S NOW...›
‹...OR NEVER--›

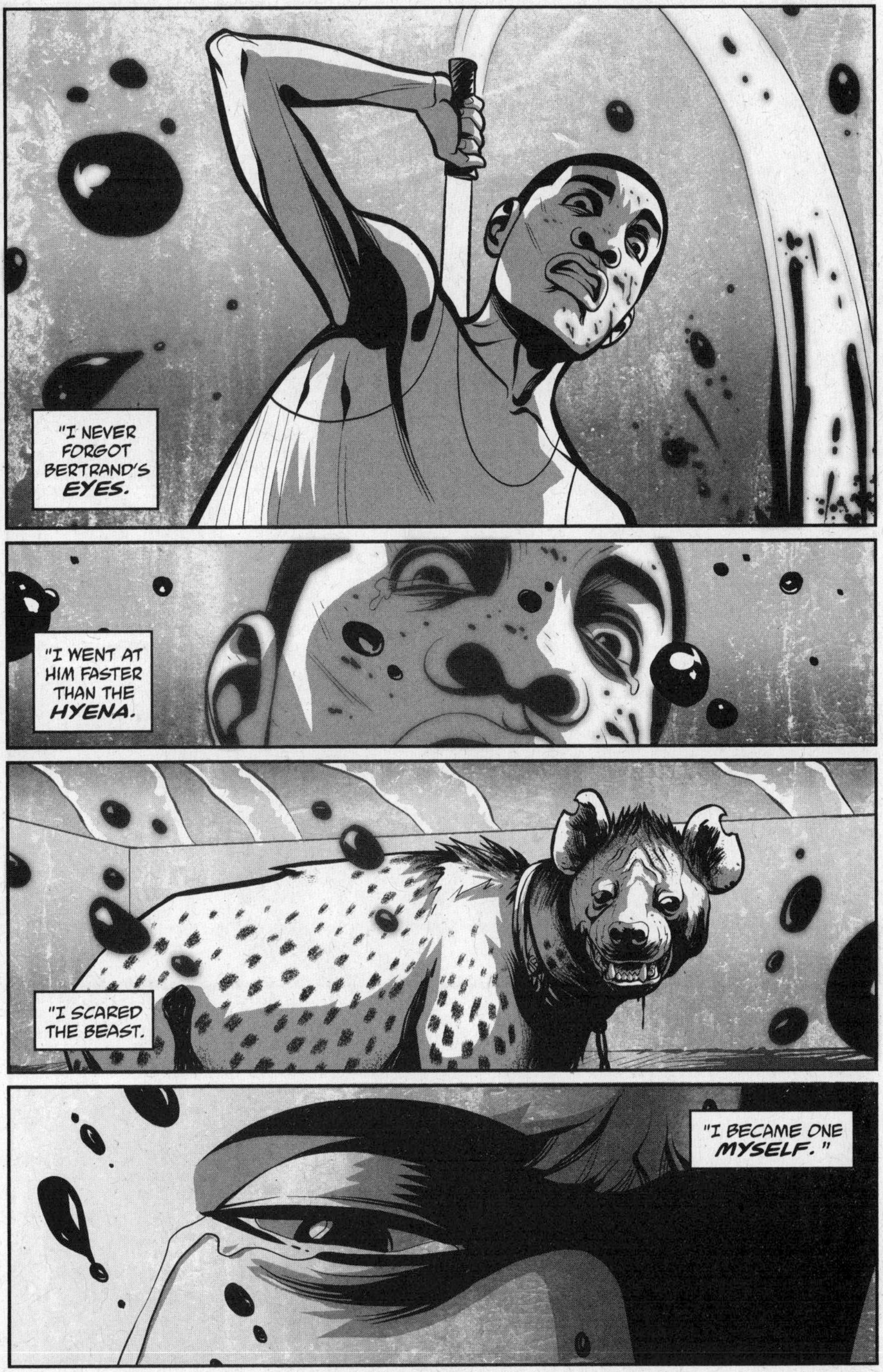
"I NEVER FORGOT BERTRAND'S *EYES*.
"I WENT AT HIM FASTER THAN THE *HYENA*.
"I SCARED THE BEAST.
"I BECAME ONE *MYSELF*."

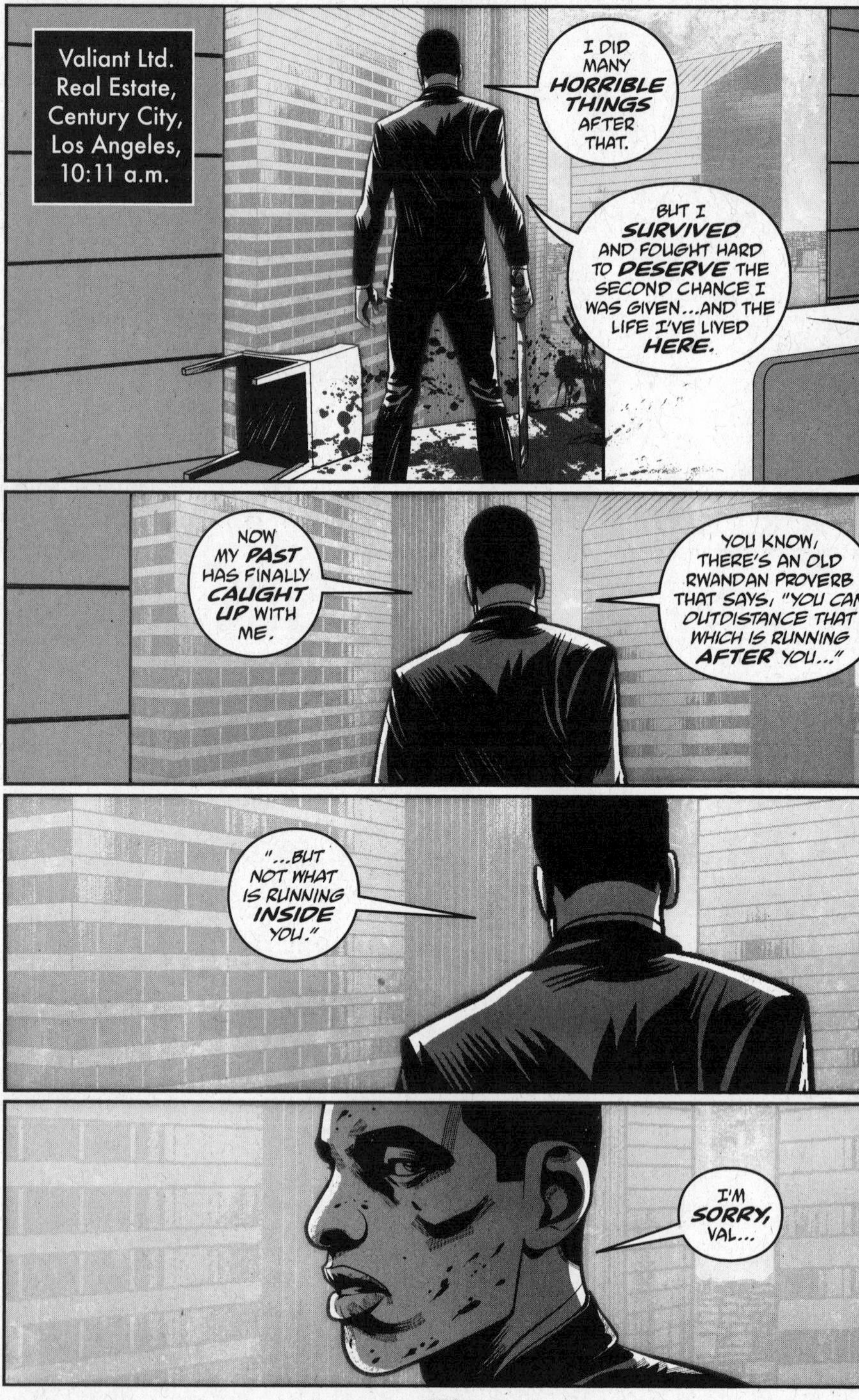

Valiant Ltd. Real Estate, Century City, Los Angeles, 10:11 a.m.
I DID MANY HORRIBLE THINGS AFTER THAT.
BUT I SURVIVED AND FOUGHT HARD TO DESERVE THE SECOND CHANCE I WAS GIVEN...AND THE LIFE I'VE LIVED HERE.
NOW MY PAST HAS FINALLY CAUGHT UP WITH ME.
YOU KNOW, THERE'S AN OLD RWANDAN PROVERB THAT SAYS, "YOU CAN OUTDISTANCE THAT WHICH IS RUNNING AFTER YOU..."
"...BUT NOT WHAT IS RUNNING INSIDE YOU."
I'M SORRY, VAL...

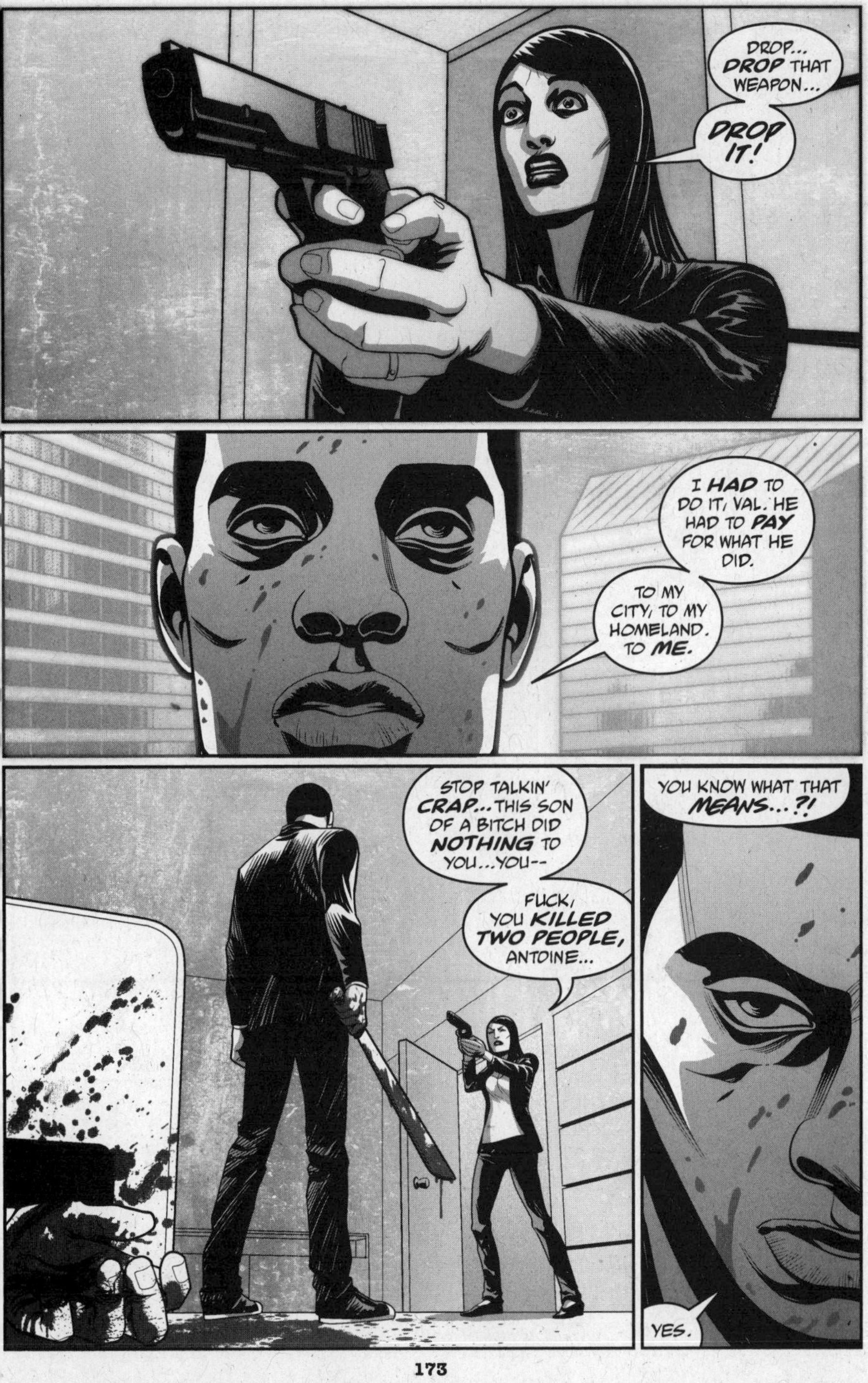
DROP... DROP THAT WEAPON...
DROP IT!
I HAD TO DO IT, VAL. HE HAD TO PAY FOR WHAT HE DID.
TO MY CITY, TO MY HOMELAND. TO ME.
STOP TALKIN' CRAP... THIS SON OF A BITCH DID NOTHING TO YOU... YOU--
FUCK, YOU KILLED TWO PEOPLE, ANTOINE...
YOU KNOW WHAT THAT MEANS...?!
YES.

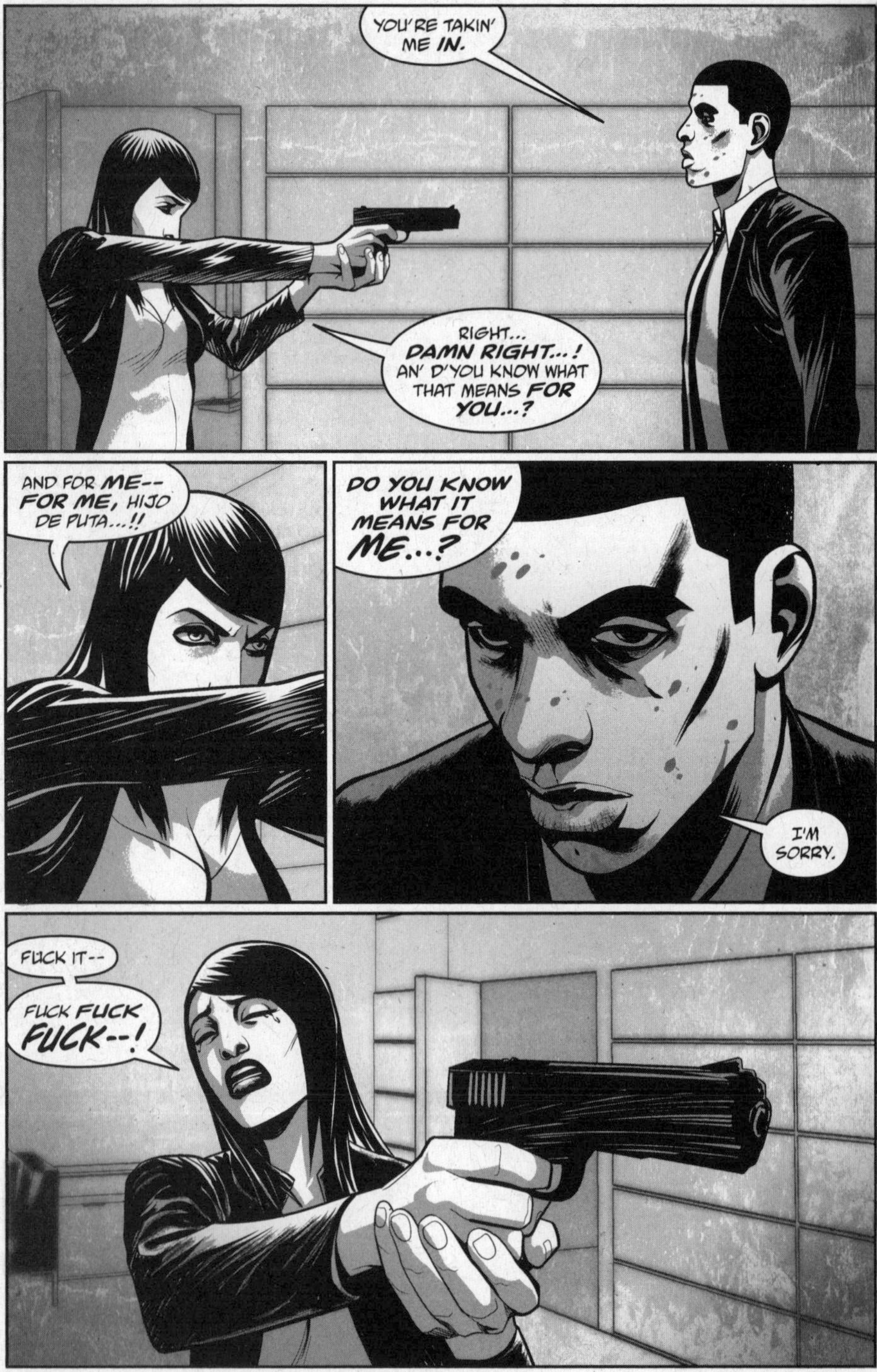
YOU'RE TAKIN' ME IN.
RIGHT... DAMN RIGHT...! AN' D'YOU KNOW WHAT THAT MEANS FOR YOU...?
AND FOR ME-- FOR ME, HIJO DE PUTA...!!
DO YOU KNOW WHAT IT MEANS FOR ME...?
I'M SORRY.
FUCK IT--
FUCK FUCK FUCK--!

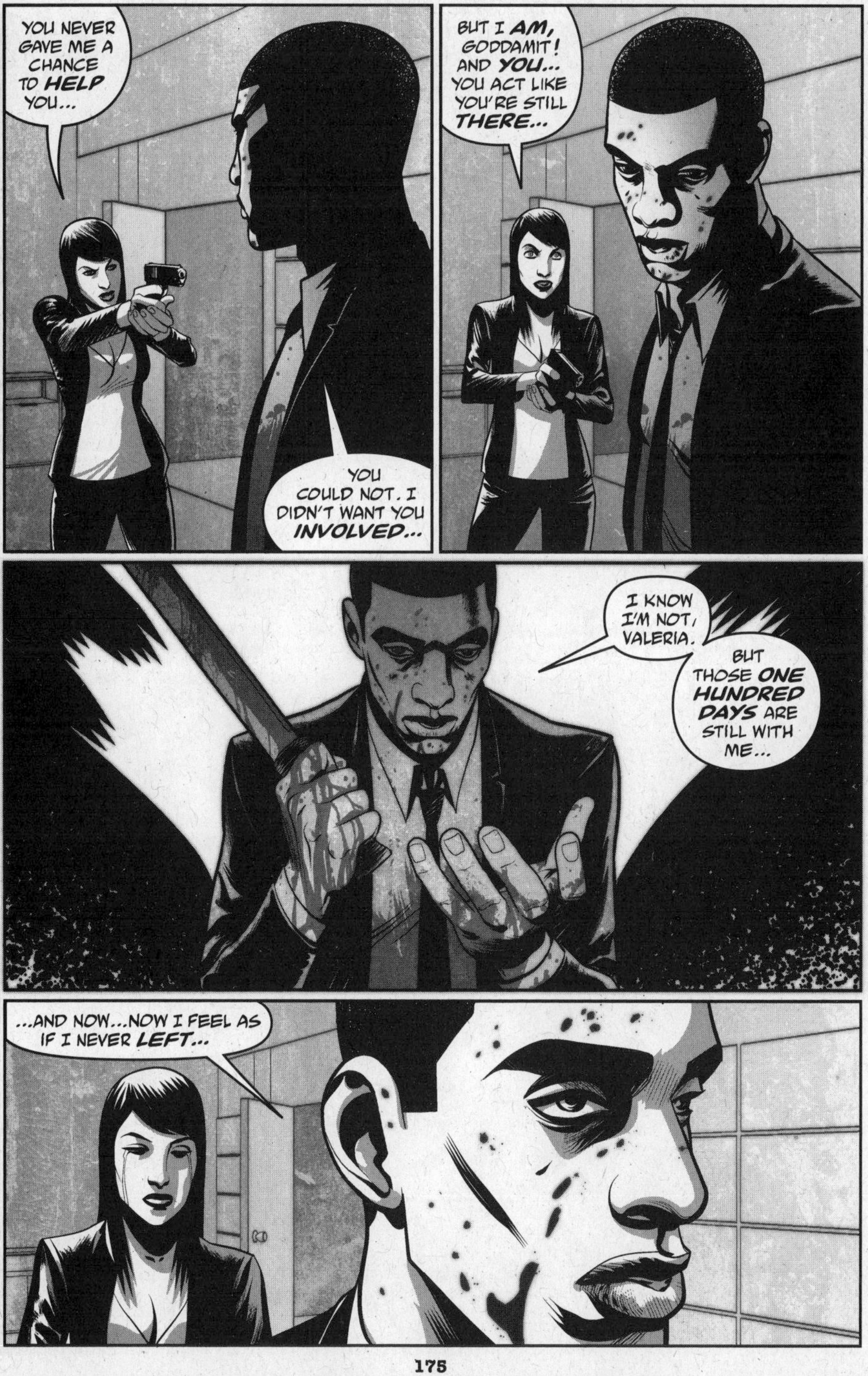

YOU NEVER GAVE ME A CHANCE TO HELP YOU...
YOU COULD NOT. I DIDN'T WANT YOU INVOLVED...
BUT I AM, GODDAMIT! AND YOU... YOU ACT LIKE YOU'RE STILL THERE...
I KNOW I'M NOT, VALERIA.
BUT THOSE ONE HUNDRED DAYS ARE STILL WITH ME...
...AND NOW...NOW I FEEL AS IF I NEVER LEFT...

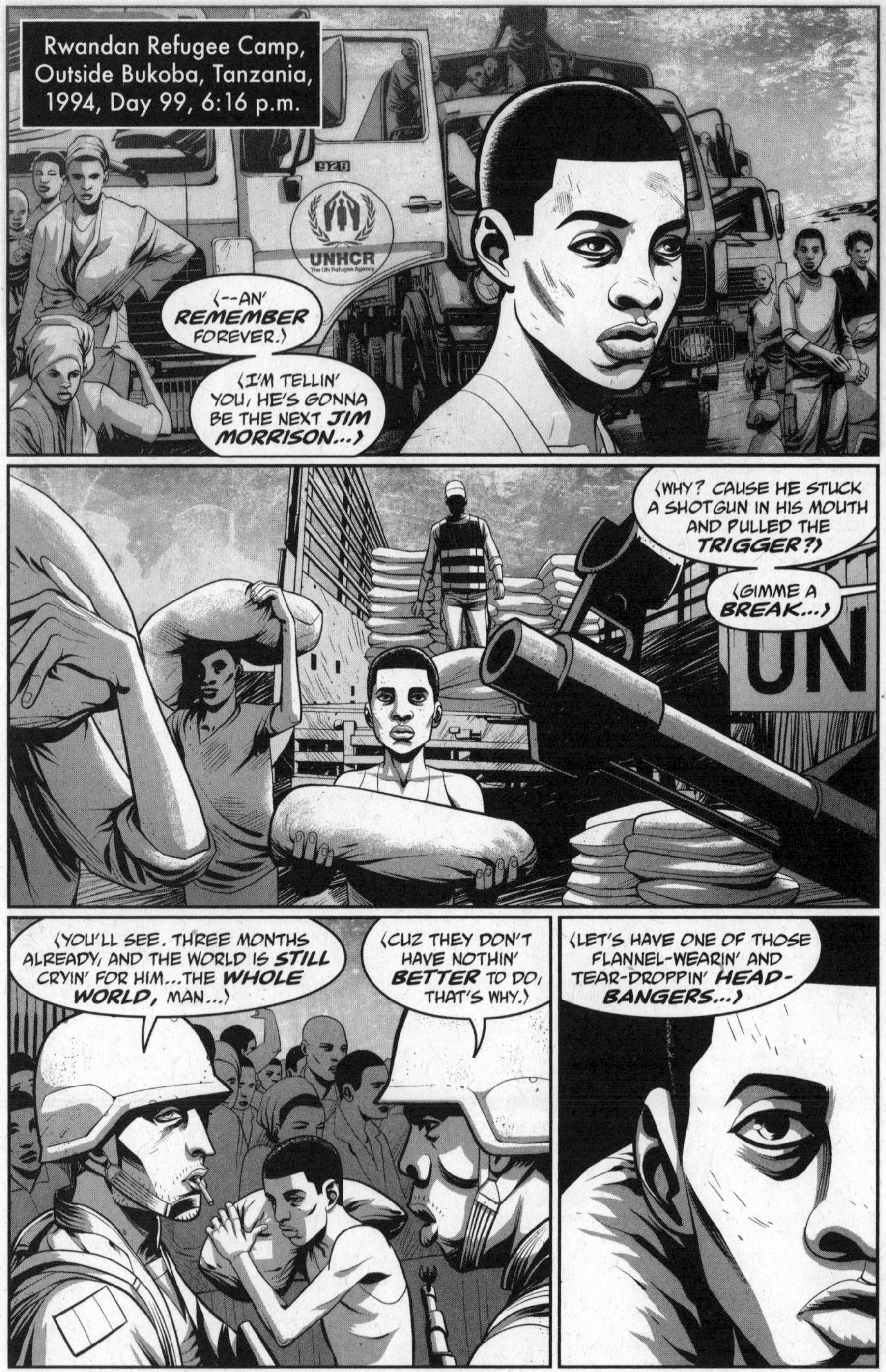
Rwandan Refugee Camp, Outside Bukoba, Tanzania, 1994, Day 99, 6:16 p.m.
928
UNHCR
The UN Refugee Agency
⟨--AN' REMEMBER FOREVER.⟩
⟨I'M TELLIN' YOU, HE'S GONNA BE THE NEXT JIM MORRISON...⟩
⟨WHY? CAUSE HE STUCK A SHOTGUN IN HIS MOUTH AND PULLED THE TRIGGER?⟩
⟨GIMME A BREAK...⟩
UN
⟨YOU'LL SEE. THREE MONTHS ALREADY, AND THE WORLD IS STILL CRYIN' FOR HIM...THE WHOLE WORLD, MAN...⟩
⟨CUZ THEY DON'T HAVE NOTHIN' BETTER TO DO, THAT'S WHY.⟩
⟨LET'S HAVE ONE OF THOSE FLANNEL-WEARIN' AND TEAR-DROPPIN' HEAD-BANGERS...⟩

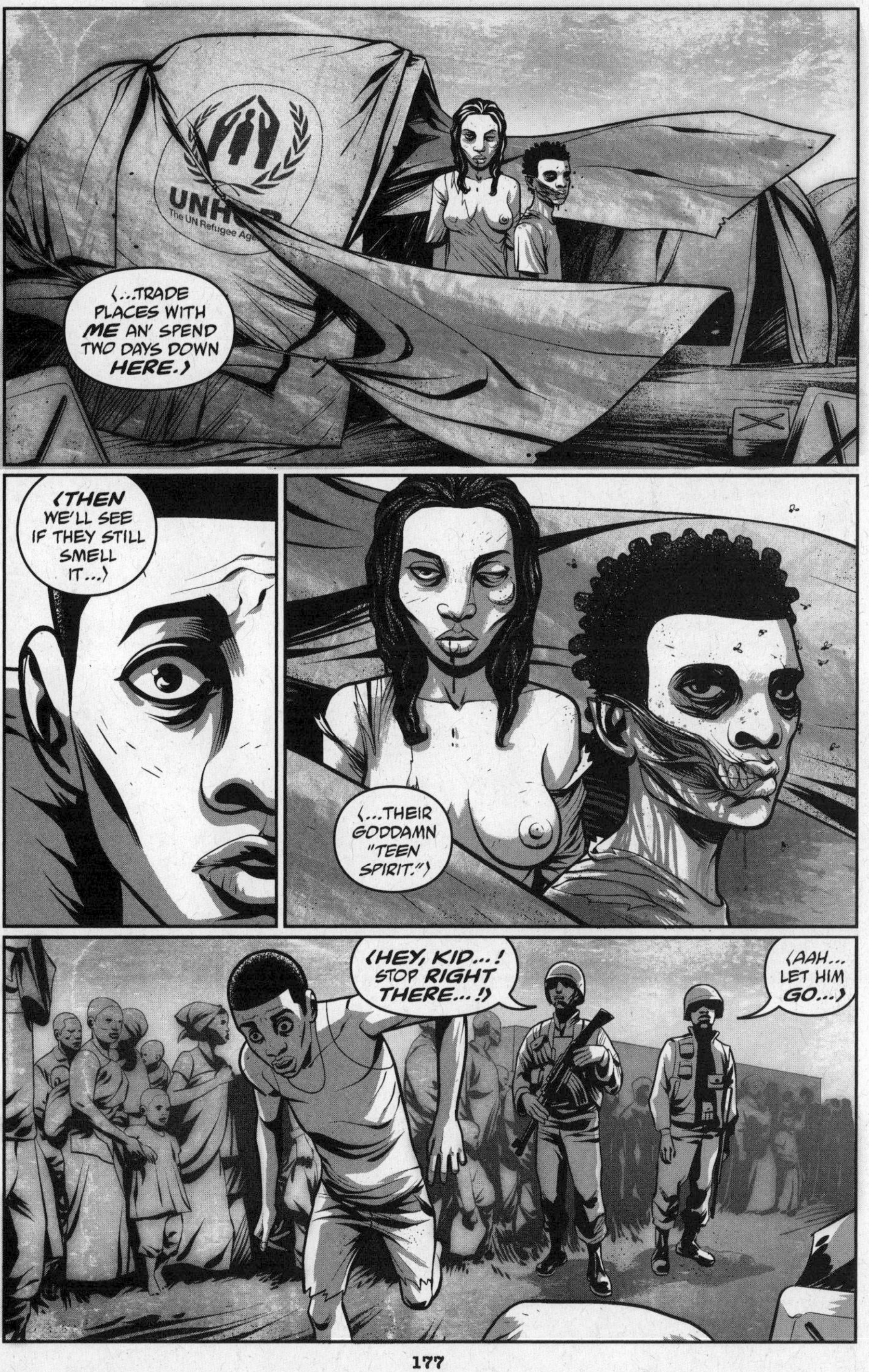

‹...TRADE PLACES WITH ME AN' SPEND TWO DAYS DOWN HERE.›
‹THEN WE'LL SEE IF THEY STILL SMELL IT...›
‹...THEIR GODDAMN "TEEN SPIRIT."›
‹HEY, KID...! STOP RIGHT THERE...!›
‹AAH... LET HIM GO...›

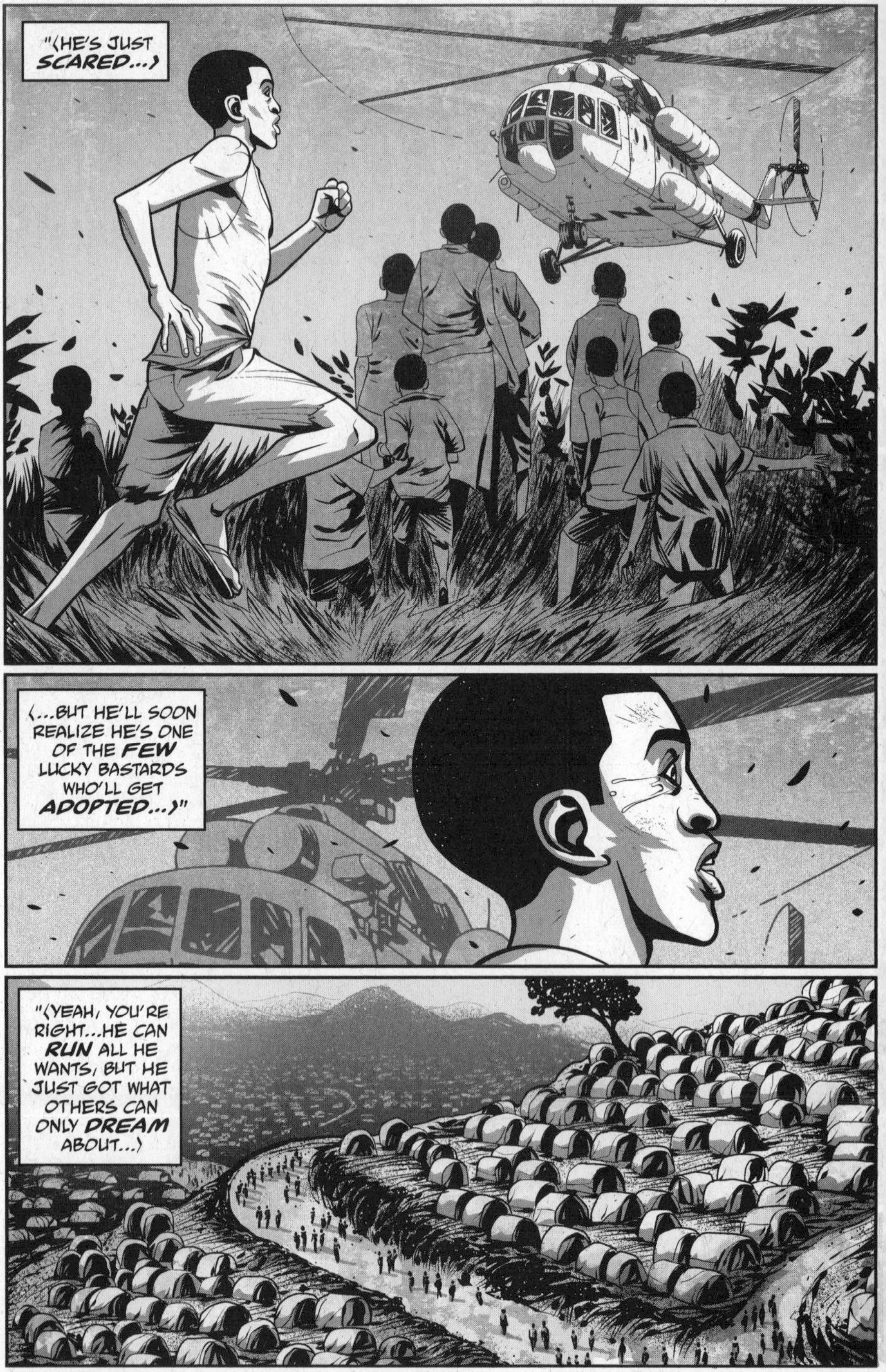
"‹HE'S JUST SCARED...›
‹...BUT HE'LL SOON REALIZE HE'S ONE OF THE FEW LUCKY BASTARDS WHO'LL GET ADOPTED...›"
"‹YEAH, YOU'RE RIGHT...HE CAN RUN ALL HE WANTS, BUT HE JUST GOT WHAT OTHERS CAN ONLY DREAM ABOUT...›

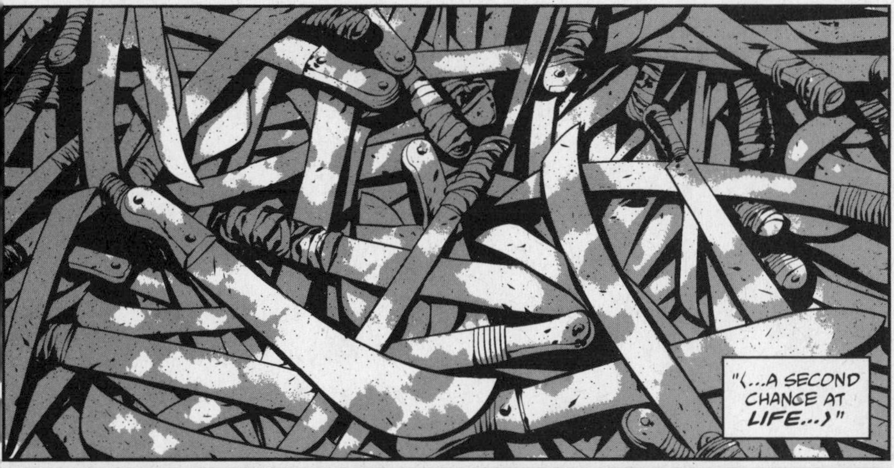
"‹...A SECOND CHANCE AT LIFE...›"

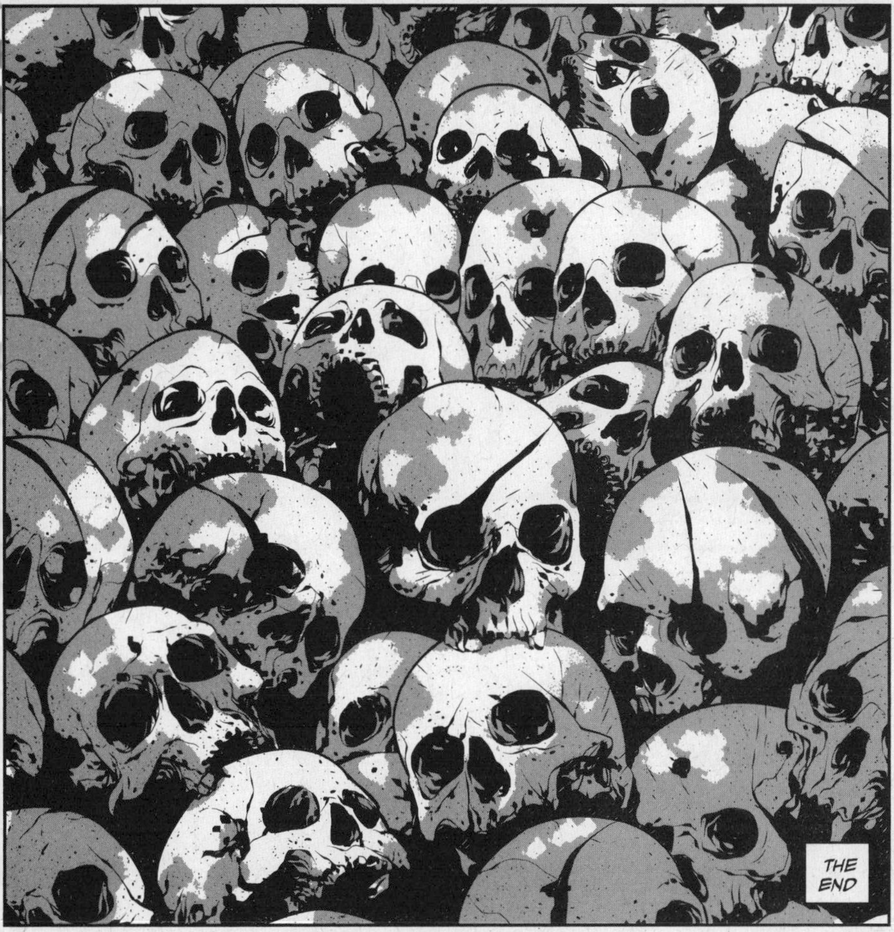
THE END

NOCHE ROJA
SIMON OLIVER
ART BY JASON LATOUR
VERTIGO CRIME

DON'T MISS THESE OTHER VERTIGO CRIME BOOKS

NOCHE ROJA

Written by **SIMON OLIVER**
Art by **JASON LATOUR**

At the border, life is cheap. But death costs nothing at all.

"Deftly merges noir with a torn-from-the-headlines story. Noir is timeless, and this book proves it!"
– **Christos Gage** (AREA 10)

RAT CATCHER

Written by **ANDY DIGGLE**
(THE LOSERS)
Art by **VICTOR IBAÑEZ**

A washed-up FBI agent on a desperate hunt for a notorious mob hit man finds out the hard way that he's the assassin's latest target!

"Compelling graphic storytelling, full of twists, turns and vivid characters."
– **Dave Gibbons** (WATCHMEN)

ANDY DIGGLE
ART BY VICTOR IBAÑEZ
RAT CATCHER
VERTIGO CRIME

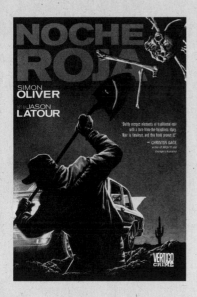

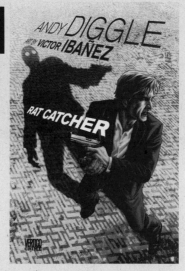

MORE FROM VERTIGO CRIME

AVAILABLE NOW

THE CHILL

Written by JASON STARR
(Best-selling author of *Panic Attack* and *The Follower*)

Art by MICK BERTILORENZI

A modern thriller steeped in Celtic mythology —
a broken-down cop tracks a seductive killer who
possesses the supernatural power known as "the
chill." Can he stop her before her next victim
dies horribly... but with a smile on his face?

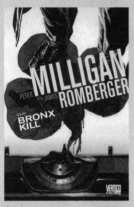

THE BRONX KILL

Written by PETER MILLIGAN
(GREEK STREET)

Art by JAMES ROMBERGER

A struggling writer is investigating his Irish cop
roots for his next novel. When he returns home
from a research trip, his wife is missing and finding
her will lead him to a dark secret buried deep in his
family's past.

AREA 10

Written by CHRISTOS N. GAGE
(*Law & Order: SVU*)

Art by CHRIS SAMNEE

When a detective — tracking a serial killer who
decapitates his victims — receives a bizarre head
injury himself, he suspects a connection between
his own fate and the killer's fascination with
Trepanation — the ancient art of skull drilling.